THE CONSTITUTION

AND THE

AMERICAN PRESIDENCY

SUNY Series in The Presidency: Contemporary Issues

John Kenneth White, Editor

THE CONSTITUTION

AND THE

AMERICAN PRESIDENCY

edited by

Martin L. Fausold
and
Alan Shank

State University of New York Press

Published by
State University of New York Press, Albany

For information, address the State University of New York Press,
State University Plaza, Albany, NY 12246

Production by Christine M. Lynch
Marketing by Dana E. Yanulavich

Library of Congress Cataloging-in-Publication Data

The Constitution and the American presidency / edited by Martin
   Fausold and Alan Shank.
       p.   cm. — (SUNY series in the presidency. Contemporary
   issues)
     Includes bibliographical references.
     ISBN 0-7914-0467-6. — ISBN 0-7914-0468-4 (pbk.)
     1. Presidents—United States—History.   2. Executive power—United
   States—History.   3. United States—Constitutional history.
   I. Fausold, Martin L., 1921-   .   II. Shank, Alan, 1936-   .
   III. Series.
   JK511.C66   1991
   353.03'13—dc20   90-9460
                                                                        CIP

10 9 8 7 6 5 4 3 2

To
Donald R. McCoy
"...gentleman an' scholar."
R. Burns

CONTENTS

Foreword
Forrest McDonald ix

Preface xiii

Acknowledgments xv

Introduction: The Presidency and
Constitutional Development xvii

Part I.   Constitutional Development of the Presidency:
           Historical Perspectives

           Introduction to Part I 3

           1. The Jefferson Presidency and Constitutional
              Beginnings
              Ralph Ketcham 5

           2. The Constitution and the Presidencies:
              The Jackson Era
              Robert V. Remini 29

           3. The Constitution of the Lincoln Presidency
              and the Republican Era
              Michael Les Benedict 45

           4. The Constitution of the Theodore Roosevelt
              Presidency and the Progressive Era
              William H. Harbaugh 63

           5. The Constitution of the Hoover and
              F. Roosevelt Presidency and the
              Depression Era
              Ellis W. Hawley 83

           6. The Constitution of the Truman Presidency
              and the Post-World War II Era
              Donald R. McCoy 107

Part II.   The Constitution and the Modern Presidency:
                Political Science Perspectives

                Introduction to Part II 131

        7. The Constitutional Presidency in American
            Political Development
            Jeffrey K. Tulis 133

        8. The Constitution and Presidential Budget
            Powers: The Modern Era
            Louis K. Fisher 147

        9. The Modern Presidency and the Constitution:
            Foreign Policy
            Louis W. Koenig 171

       10. Presidential War Powers, the War Powers
            Resolution, and the Persian Gulf
            Richard M. Pious 195

       11. The Presidency and the Future of
            Constitutional Government
            Donald L. Robinson 211

Afterword   Presidential Power and the
            Ideological Struggle Over Its Interpretation
            Theodore J. Lowi 227

An Historian's Last Word
    Martin L. Fausold 245

A Political Science Perspective
    Alan Shank... 247

Contributors... 251

Notes 257

Subject Index.. 303

Name Index 317

FOREWORD

————————————————— *Forrest McDonald*

For the better part of two decades, Martin Fausold and Alan Shank have been conducting a more or less ongoing symposium of scholars of the American presidency, making SUNY-Geneseo a most exciting center of study on the subject. At one time or another they have drawn as participants almost every major student in the field, both from the ranks of historians and political scientists. The symposia came to a climax — but, one hopes, not an end — during the 1987–88 academic year, when eleven distinguished scholars of various persuasions went, one after another, to Geneseo to deliver public lectures and take part in discussions. All eleven reconvened in the spring of 1988, when, with Ted Lowi and myself acting as "master critics," a rousing two-day thrashing-out of the whole subject took place. The book you are about to read is the result.

Several themes run through the various essays, but the most persistent is the tension between the exercise of presidential power on what Professor Lowi calls the Fast Track ("the track of secrecy, unilateral action, energy, commitment, decisiveness") and on the Slow Track (the "Separation of Powers Track"). In part, as several authors point out, that tension derives from the language and structure of the Constitution. Article II vests "the executive power" in the president, but only after Article I has given most of the traditional royal prerogatives, or at least a share in them, to one or both houses of Congress.

Now, though we are accustomed to praising the Framers for their statecraft and wisdom, that fateful ambiguity was the result not of design but of slipshod craftsmanship. Throughout the grand convention of 1787 there was at least a vague consensus that an executive must be created, but no one could think of a way of electing one that would be safe from corruption and foreign intrigue. Accordingly, no one was comfortable with the idea of entrusting the office with significant powers. Thus when the Committee of Detail prepared the first draft of a constitution in early August, a president was provided for, but

ix

most of the executive powers (including the powers to make treaties, name ambassadors, and appoint Supreme Court justices) were lodged exclusively in the Congress, especially the Senate. Not until the adoption of the electoral college system on September 6 — two working days before the main labor of the convention was finished and turned over to a Committee on Style for the final drafting of the Constitution — was a safe way of electing the president hit upon. Properly, the delegates should then have thoroughly reconsidered presidential power, but they were tired, irritable, and anxious to go home; and besides, ambiguity of phrasing did not seem particularly dangerous since George Washington, whom everyone knew would be the first president, could be trusted to fill in the details of the office in a suitable manner. As a result, the Framers made only slight adjustments, thereby institutionalizing the problem of a two-track executive.

But the problem is not attributable solely to dereliction of duty on the part of the Framers: it is inherent in the very idea of a limited executive. It had been delineated as early as the thirteenth century by Henry Bracton in *De Legibus et Consuetudinibus Angliae* and the fifteenth by Sir John Fortescue in *De Laudibus Legum Angliae*, both of which works all American lawyers had studied. Bracton described the two "tracts" of royal power as *gubernaculum* (governing) and *jurisdictio* (speaking the law). Fortescue called the kingdom a *dominium politicum et regale:* in one, the king's power was exercised according to the law and in consultation with the magnates (or parliament); in the other the king's power was absolute and unbounded.

This duality is inseparable from any effort to have a government of laws, because laws by nature are general and cannot cover every contingency: in myriad circumstances somebody — the executive — must act swiftly, decisively, and unilaterally. In a popular government this need is most pronounced, and it reaches its fullest expression in urgent circumstances. As Thomas Jefferson said, "In times of peace the people look most to their representatives; but in war, to the executive solely."

Our authors all treat the problem of tension between the branches of government and the distribution of powers, but they are not in agreement as to the implications. The historians among them, dealing with individual presidents, tend to look upon Congress and the courts as unfortunate obstacles which hindered the efforts of their protagonists to do what was good for the country. Professor Tulis, from a different perspective, shares that attitude. The other political scientists are most skeptical of presidential power and tend to seek its curtailment or at least want to check its excesses. Professor Robinson is the only one, however, to propose specific constitutional changes — namely, a variation of the practice in parliamentary systems of calling special elections on occasions of "no confidence" in the president — to rectify executive abuses.

As a limited-government conservative, I view the matter somewhat differently from any of our authors. I prefer to have the powers of all branches strictly limited and balanced by counterweight powers in the states and in private non-governmental institutions. Accordingly, I applaud the constitutional structure, regard the tensions as a positive good, and wish merely for a return to the Constitution as written.

And perhaps in its actual functioning, the government is, for non-structural reasons, severely limited. The presidency is often described as the most powerful office in the world. That is stuff and nonsense. Power is the capacity to do things, to cause one's will to be transformed into action, and by that criterion the president has precious little power. I would indeed go so far as to assert that the government of the United States as a whole has all but lost the capacity to govern: the ongoing budgetary chaos is but one symptom of a chronically paralytic condition. Professor Robinson's proposals — or for the matter of that, adoption of the British system *in toto* — might end the paralysis in government. But when I consider the calibre of those who have populated the offices in Washington during my lifetime, I wonder whether that would be a blessing or a curse. As the wag said, Thank God we don't get nearly as much government as we pay for.

I do not expect many readers to share my sentiments. I only urge that you read on. When you finish this book you will be able to think about its subject in a more enlightened way than you can just now.

PREFACE

In the summer of 1986 we conceived of the idea of celebrating the bicentennial of the Constitution by having eleven scholars (six historians and five political scientists) address the relationship, over time, of Article II to the development of the American presidency. The National Endowment for the Humanities funded the program, and the scholars came singly to Geneseo, New York, in the fall of 1987 to offer their scholarly views—the historians examining in sequence the presidencies of Jefferson, Jackson, Lincoln, T. Roosevelt, F. Roosevelt, and Truman; the political scientists assessing the contemporary presidency, respectively, in terms of its 1787 constitutional convention roots and the constitutional aspects of its congressional relations and its domestic, war, and foreign affairs conduct. The same scholars returned, en masse, in the spring of 1988 to test their ideas with each other and with two master critics, historian Forrest McDonald and political scientist Theodore J. Lowi.

Our single suggestion to the participants was that five guidelines regarding the relationship of the Constitution and presidential development be considered: Executive power and prerogative, separation of powers, national welfare, ceremonial and administrative powers, and foreign and war powers. These considerations, largely drawn from Article II of the Constitution, were intended to give a sharper focus to the papers and to the ensuing dialogue. The guidelines purposely excluded mention of political ideology and party for fear that such considerations might range the papers and dialogue far afield from the "constitutional" development of the presidency. The scholars, of course, were given discretion to emphasize variously the guidelines and to examine other influences on the constitutional development of the presidency. Although, by and large, the assessments did center on the guidelines, exceptions, such as party and ideology, permeated some of the papers and the dialogue. In fact, one interesting exception to the guidelines suggested that the Constitution's congressional segment, Article I, has as much bearing on the presidency as does Article II.

Not unexpectedly, historians and political scientists in the Geneseo program, true to their disciplines and by the nature of their respective assignments, revealed varying views of constitutional development of the presidency. Although a frequent meshing occurred, historians addressed more the facts of presidential behavior and seemed to exude more optimism than pessimism for their particular presidents as heroic and positive figures important to the development of the presidency. Political scientists, in their examination of the recent presidencies, tended to relate constitutional provisions and problems to domestic and foreign policy issues of the past fifty years (from FDR to Reagan). Their approach to constitutional development of the presidency was quite expectedly more sweeping, "critical," and more committed to solutions, offering a range of reforms—modest to radical—including fundamental alterations in the balance of power between the presidency and the Congress.

Political scientists seemed particularly troubled by the escalation of the War Model presidency of recent decades and of its seeming constitutional obtrusiveness and deadlock. Still, historians and political scientists complemented and taught each other at Geneseo, although frequently feigning dismay at their colleagues in the other discipline. In the end, the historian among the two of us who directed the program came to see that constitutional crises have afflicted and tested the presidency past and present, and, therefore, is less inclined to perceive as rare the present constitutional plight. The political scientist, on the other hand, stresses more the peculiar severity of the constitutional quandary of today's presidency.

As codirectors of the program we have learned mightily over the past year the constitutional predicaments of the American presidency past and present. Surely the readers of this book will likewise learn. Aside from the towering quality of papers which, with little question, marked the high point of the nation's Bicentennial attention to the subject, we are fortunate to have critics Forrest McDonald and Theodore Lowi construct, respectively, a Foreword and an Afterword, which add considerably to the book.

Martin L. Fausold
Department of History
SUNY–Geneseo

Alan Shank
Department of Political Science
SUNY–Geneseo

ACKNOWLEDGMENTS

As codirectors of this project we wish to thank the members of our respective departments for assisting us in many large and small ways over the course of the year, most noteworthy secretaries Joan Orton and Liz Ancker. We appreciate the clerical help of Dan Spiess. Of course, we express particular gratitude to the National Endowment for the Humanities for providing scholars and citizens an opportunity to design celebrating programs which educate the public about the American Constitution and for awarding this particular project. Donald Robinson and Ted Lowi were particularly helpful as early reviewers of this project. It goes without saying that the Research Foundation, both of State University of New York and of SUNY–Geneseo, aided us enormously in constructing the project and helping to implement it. In that regard, particularly, we thank Geneseo's Dean of Graduate Education and Research, Douglas Harke, and his superb staff secretaries, Nancy Baker-Mann and Julie Nevin. Numerous other people from Geneseo helped at various stages of carrying out the project, not the least Mrs. Alice W. Strong for frequently opening her fine historic homestead, Hartford House, to our guests and participants.

Our faculty colleagues at Geneseo, particularly William Derby, Kenneth Deutsch, Robert Goeckel, Val Rabe, and Jim Somerville, were most helpful at various stages of this project and participated in the Fall 1987 seminars with the NEH history and political science scholars. These seminars included participation by Geneseo faculty, students enrolled in our experimental course, and scholars from various colleges and university centers of the State University of New York. They included Lynn Parsons, Richard Ellis, William Graebner, Arthur Ekirch, William Andrews, Sarah Liebschutz, Stephen Pendleton, Ray Duncan, and Henry Steck.

Of course, we thank the scholars who reworked their papers for this publication. It goes without saying that any errors in the book are ours, not theirs.

Over the years this institution has been engaged in important scholarly and public projects and conferences, many of them interdisciplinary. Their impact on the scholars and the public has been described as what a university should be about. Frequently hovering over these projects in a helpful way beyond any call of duty has been a midwestern friend, Donald R. McCoy, University Distinguished Professor at the University of Kansas. We proudly dedicate this book to him.

Martin L. Fausold
Alan Shank

INTRODUCTION:
THE PRESIDENCY AND
CONSTITUTIONAL DEVELOPMENT

The presidency occupies a central constitutional role in American government. The chief executive is the focus of leadership, authority, and policy direction. Presidential power expands in response to demands that neither Congress nor the courts can fulfull. The modern presidents, beginning with Franklin Roosevelt, have been the principal leaders in responding to world war, economic crisis, budget deficits, and various international tensions. These foreign and domestic challenges require presidential leadership to protect, defend, and define the national interest.

When the Founding Fathers wrote the Constitution, they were reacting, in part, to the excesses and abuses of executive power imposed by the British Crown during the colonial and revolutionary war experiences. They were also trying to develop an independent executive branch that was not included in the Articles of the Confederation. The Framers focused major attention on the specifics of legislative power and authority as a check on executive power. They designed a tripartite system of separation of powers and checks and balances to achieve an equilibrium between the executive and legislative branches.

According to James Madison, the principal architect of the federal government's structure at the Constitutional Convention, the system of separated powers and checks and balances was necessary to control political power.[1] In *Federalist Paper,* Number 51, Madison argued that too much governmental power causes abuses that endanger personal liberty and security. Uncontrolled power can lead to tyranny. If the executive gains power at the expense of the legislature, the consitutional system could be threatened. To prevent any of the three branches—executive, legislative, judicial—from dominating the other two, each must be relatively independent. This is achieved by separation of powers. Also, the three branches would have checks and balances over each other to counteract power concentration and domination of any one branch over the other two.

The Madisonian model is one of limited government. Neither the executive nor the legislative are dominant. However, the Madisonian emphasis on balance and equilibrium between the executive and legislative has two principal liabilities: It is an inherently adversarial structure and it frequently produces stalemate or inaction. Forrest McDonald[2] argues that the Founding Fathers distrusted executive power so much that they created a constitutional design which made it difficult for the two branches to cooperate. Separation of powers was favored over the British choice in the 1720s of a ministerial system which merged the executive and legislative branches and reduced the Crown to a ceremonial role. The constitutional conflicts between the two branches make policy initiatives and innovations difficult to achieve without extraordinary presidential or legislative leadership and executive-legislative cooperation. McDonald argues that this has been infrequent except for wartime and economic crises.

In contrast to the Madisonian model of checking potential executive abuses, Alexander Hamilton, in *Federalist Paper*, Number 70, struck a particularly modern note by arguing for "energy" in the executive, "as a leading character in the definition of good government." Hamilton believed that vigorous executive leadership was "essential to the protection of the community against foreign attacks; it is not less essential to the administration of the laws."

Hamilton's essay identified several important characteristics of a strong presidency. First, the president should be vigorous in carrying out constitutional roles and responsibilities by demonstrating "energy." If he does this, then "good" or "effective" government will result. Second, the president's authority in international and domestic policy is equally important. He is responsible for protecting the nation and administering the laws. Third, the constitution provides the president with four sources of authority to meet his responsibilities. These are unity (a single executive), duration in office (a four-year term with unlimited reeligibility until enactment of the Twenty-second Amendment), adequate compensation, and competent powers (found in Article II of the Constitution).

The formal constitutional powers of the president enable the chief executive to be both independent and interdependent in policy-making responsibilities. Congress cannot control the president. The chief executive is protected by the Madisonian concept of separation of powers. The president also shares power with Congress. This makes the executive both an independent and coterminous branch of the national government. Second, the executive participates in the policy-making process as an equal partner with Congress. Through "competent powers," the executive checks and balances the legislative branch.

The Hamiltonian chief executive is a strong leader who protects the nation against foreign attacks, administers the laws, and secures liberty against the dangers of ambition, faction, and anarchy. Nearly all of the strong presidents of the nineteenth and twentieth centuries defended their constitutional authority in Hamiltonian terms. When abuses of presidential power occurred, Congress usually asserted the Madisonian model of equilibrium and checks and balances.

Most presidents prefer the Hamiltonian view of executive power. They exercise active and positive leadership rather than defer to Congress in negative or passive ways. The six presidents discussed by the historians in Part I of this book—Thomas Jefferson, Andrew Jackson, Abraham Lincoln, Theodore Roosevelt, Franklin Roosevelt, and Harry Truman—were all vigorous leaders. Together with the presidents serving from 1952 to the present, they promoted executive policy initiatives in Congress, exercised a ceremonial role as leader of the entire nation, rose above party politics and became national leaders, and, since John Kennedy, established a plebiscitary relationship with the public through direct communication in televised speeches and messages from the Oval Office.

The Hamiltonian model of vigorous executive leadership is more applicable to presidential foreign policy leadership and crisis management than it is to the domestic policy arena.

Presidents have had much more flexibility in foreign policy initiatives than in domestic policy proposals. Unless some kind of economic catastrophe (e.g., the Great Depression of the 1930s) occurs requiring the exercise of extraordinary executive powers, presidents must acknowledge a sharing of domestic policy initiatives with an active and involved Congress.

Constitutional checks and balances, fortified by Madison's warning in *Federalist Paper*, Number 51, that "ambition must be made to counteract ambition" usually have modified or delayed executive domestic policy initiatives. We can see this in the proposals by Truman for civil rights; in Eisenhower's initiatives to return various federal programs to the states; in the delays to enact Kennedy's New Frontier initiatives in civil rights, aid to education, and health insurance for the elderly; in the resistance to Nixon's decentralization efforts and welfare reform proposals under New Federalism initiatives; in Carter's energy and urban policy proposals; and in the inability of Reagan to go as far as he wanted in cutting federal spending for the poor and the needy and to return programs to the states and the private sector. Exceptions to this usual pattern include FDR's First New Deal, Johnson's Civil Rights and War on Poverty initiatives, and Reagan's early budget and tax cuts and increases in military spending.

The reasons for executive inability to act quickly on domestic policy initiatives are not difficult to identify. After the president announces proposals in the State of the Union address, his initiatives must gain support from interest groups, state and local governments, and Congress. Each of these competitors can counteract the "ambition" of a "vigorous executive" (to use the notions of Hamilton and Madison).

Interest groups, which are not mentioned in the Constitution, are referred to by Madison as "factions" in *Federalist Paper*, Number 10. These are the non-governmental associations which influence domestic policy by promoting benefits for their members and preventing government action harmful to their members. Interest groups provide campaign funds to members of Congress and get support for their views. The president must convince interest groups to support his initiatives or find ways to counteract them. Frequently, he is unsuccessful or stalemated.

The federal system of fifty state and thousands of local governments presents a situation of considerable complexity and fragmentation of power for an ambitious domestic policy president. The president is required to build coalitions and gain support from many governors and mayors. There is a sharing of responsibility between national policy goals and the actual provision of services by state and local governments.

Congress sees itself as a partner with the president on domestic policy, both from the standpoint of its seventeen clauses of power in Article I, Section 8, of the Constitution and from the constituency-based nature of Congress in serving the people back home. Congress expects the president to lead the House and Senate in domestic initiatives, but Congress also expects to deal with the president in the final determination of policy results. Consequently, Congress expects the president to persuade, bargain, negotiate, and compromise. It expects the president to give and take. This takes time and effort from an ambitous president. The president needs to expend enormous political resources and capital to achieve major domestic policy intitiatives.

The three principal limits to domestic policy—interest groups, the intergovernmental system, and Congress—can be overcome by a vigorous Hamiltonian-type president. This has occurred on at least two occasions since 1945: Johnson's initiatives on civil rights, voting rights, and the Great Society antipoverty and aid to education program in 1964–65; and Reagan's $35 billion budget cuts, $225 billion tax cuts, and huge increases in defense spending in 1981. The ingredients for their achievements were clear: enormous landslide election victories, partisan support in Congress, quick response by Congress in the early months of the new administration, public support for the new president resulting from assassination—in the case of Johnson, sympathy for Kennedy; for Reagan, an unsuccessful assassination attempt— favorable media publicity and enough interest group support to overcome strong opposition. Both presidents benefited from a combination of effective leadership and a perceived need for change which mobilized huge voting support in Congress early in their presidencies. Without these ingredients, most presidents faced the normal obstacle course on domestic policy. James MacGregor Burns has characterized this obstacle course as a "deadlock of democracy,"[3] which means protracted battles with Congress and interest groups on major domestic policy initiatives of any president.

According to Forrest McDonald,[4] contemporary examples of executive-legislative policy deadlock or stalemate include electoral politics and the Twenty-second Amendment. The Republican party has an electoral advantage over the Democrats in presidential contests, while the Democrats dominate the House of Representatives. Control of the Senate has become more competitive. Consequently, the presidency and at least one house of Congress are usually in partisan disagreement over domestic policy. The Twenty-second Amendment, limiting the president to two terms, produces a lame-duck syndrome in the president's second term. The president and Congress do not need each other, and an adversarial relationship occurs. By the third year of the second term, the president usually shifts attention away from domestic initiatives to foreign policy.

The president is much less interdependent with Congress in foreign policy initiatives. In *Federalist Paper*, Number 69, Hamilton carefully distinguished between the sharing of powers and independence of the American executive in foreign policy, particularly as commander in chief and in making treaties. The sharing of presidential authority was in sharp contrast to the British King who had nearly absolute powers in these two areas. The King had "the entire command of all the militia" while "the president will only have command of such part of the militia of the nation as by legislative provision may be called into the actual service of the Union... The President is to have power, with the advice and consent of the Senate, to make treaties... The King of Great Britain is the sole and absolute representative of the nation in all foreign transactions."

The strong presidents of the past two centuries dominated U.S. foreign policy. They shared power with Congress in treaty-making and appointments and needed appropriations for military and other foreign actions. At the same time, the presidency, beginning with FDR, became nearly autonomous in two important areas: the national security state and warmaking powers. The absence of effective constitutional constraints created a potential for enormous abuses of executive power. Arthur Schlesinger, Jr., characterized this problem as the danger of an "imperial presidency."[5]

World War II, Cold War, Soviet aggression, the nuclear age, the worldwide responsibilities of the United States, international crises and emergencies—all of these factors have resulted in a demand for strong presidential leadership in the last fifty years. Presidents have sufficient constitutional and legislative authority to meet these challenges. The president is the commander in chief of the armed forces, the principal negotiator of treaties and executive agreements, the chief diplomatic representative of the nation, and has congressional authority to appoint certain officials, such as the NSC adviser, without senatorial approval. The principal legislative enactment which guarantees strong foreign policy leadership is the 1947 National Security Act. This law established the Central Intelligence Agency, the National Security Council, the Defense Department, and the Joint Chiefs of Staff. The president was provided an enormous institutional apparatus and bureaucracy to conduct intelligence-gathering, to coordinate information from the State and Defense Departments, to unify the armed services and their military commanders, and to engage in covert activities. This institutional structure is essential to a strong foreign presidency.

The problem of the foreign policy presidency, as stated earlier, is unchecked authority and the potential for abuse. This has occurred on at least three occasions since 1945: the Vietnam War, Watergate, and the Iran-Contra Affair.

The Vietnam War showed that the president (Lyndon Johnson) can initiate and conduct war which has no resolution, which has misguided objectives, and which lacks the necessary support from Congress and the American people. President Nixon's extension of the Vietnam War into Cambodia was as questionable as Johnson's earlier escalation. The abuse of power was obvious: The conduct of a full-scale war in a distant part of the world requires the support of more than a group of executive "cold warriors" making policy in the White House. An isolated executive became unaccountable to Congress and the public and caused great damage to the country.

The same holds true for Watergate and the Iran-Contra Affair. When President Nixon used the CIA to prevent the FBI from investigating Watergate and established "plumbers" and enemies lists, he showed contempt for constitutional procedures and the rights of individuals. The "third-rate" burglary of the Democratic Party Headquarters became a political fiasco for Nixon, leading to calls for his impeachment and resulting in his eventual resignation from office. The point is that Nixon used the national security apparatus to develop the coverups in Watergate.

The Iran-Contra Affair of the Reagan presidency also shows the dangers of isolation when the executive develops a foreign policy without consulting with Congress or informing the American public. Here the issue was gaining the release of American hostages in Lebanon by trading arms to Iran and then using the profits from these arms sales to aid the rebel forces in Nicaragua. Reagan's problem was that Iran was a State Department–designated "terrorist" country which had held American hostages since 1979 during the Carter presidency. The Ayatollah Khomeini was one of the most hostile anti-American demagogues in the world. Further, Congress had specifically prohibited arms shipments to the Nicaraguan Contras at the very time that Lt. Col. Oliver North, General Richard Secord, and Albert Hakim were involved in establishing secret Swiss bank accounts and overseas offshore companies to channel funds to the Contras. The point is that the national security apparatus was used for these covert and illegal activities. The National Security Council staff assumed operational functions, when in fact the 1947 law confined them to staff functions. Further, according to the Tower Board report, President Reagan was unaware of the Contra diversion and mismanaged this entire affair.

The last point to be made about the unilateral nature of presidential actions concerns the war power. Since 1945, the United States has been involved in two full-scale wars in Korea and Vietnam, along with military engagements in Lebanon, Grenada, Libya, Panama, and elsewhere without having a single declaration of war by Congress. The constitutional requirement of having Congress initiate war by declaring it, has been superseded by presidents who are both the intitiators of war and its conductors.

Congress enacted the War Powers Resolution in 1973 over President Nixon's veto in an effort to regain constitutional participation in the war power. The resolution requires that the president inform Congress within forty-eight hours after U.S. troops are committed to combat, and that the president must consult with Congress. Combat must end within sixty days unless Congress extends the deadline for return of U.S. troops. Four observations can be made about the War Powers Resolution. First, every president from Nixon to Bush has claimed that the law is an unconstitutional limitation on the executive's powers as commander in chief. Second, no president has consulted with Congress prior to committing U.S. troops. Third, the power of Congress to force the withdrawal of troops within sixty or ninety days may constitute a legislative veto. Such legislative vetoes were declared unconstitutional by the Supreme Court in 1983.[6] Finally, the Supreme Court has refused to rule on the enforcement provisions of the War Powers Resolution.

Constitutional Authority and The President

Three kinds of presidential powers are found in the Constitution—in Article II and in the lawmaking process section of Article I: powers exercised by the president alone, powers that are shared with the Senate or both houses of Congress, and negative powers to prevent action by Congress. Exclusive presidential authority found in Article II includes commander in chief of the armed forces, granting of pardons and reprieves for federal crimes, receiving ambassadors, faithfully executing the laws, and appointing officials to lesser offices. Presidential powers shared with the Senate include the treaty-making process (requiring two-thirds approval) and the appointment of ambassadors, judges, and other high cabinet and executive officials.

The president also shares powers with both houses of Congress in the legislative process. A bill becomes a law either with the president's approval or by a two-thirds vote overriding a veto. Negative powers include presidential vetoes of legislation, executive privilege or the power to withhold information from Congress, and impoundment of appropriated funds. Neither executive privilege nor impoundment are found in the Constitution. These powers are the result of Supreme Court decisions (executive privilege) or legislative authorization (impoundment). Another type of negative executive power is the president's authority to order sequestration (across-the-board budget cuts) under the Gramm-Rudman-Hollings law when the president and congress cannot agree on a budget deficit-reduction plan.

The following eleven essays—six by historians and five by political scientists—are divided into two parts: historical perspectives on the presidency and constitutional development from Thomas Jefferson to Harry Truman, and the modern presidency and various policy and leadership issues in the constitutional context from 1945 to the present. The essays address several aspects of the Constitution, particularly Articles I and II as they affect the presidency, including:

1. *Executive Power:* Do the words "executive power" in Article II mean a grant of discretionary power, or did the constitutional Framers intend it as a general power within the context of

subsequent enumerated powers (''faithfully execute the office,'' ''Commander in Chief,'' ''require...opinions,'' ''make treaties,'' ''appoint ambassadors...judges...and other officers,'' etc.)? Does the Constitution, during times of crisis, suggest an executive prerogative power than can supersede constitutional constraints? What is the constitutional meaning of ''executive privilege''?

2. *Dual Administrative and Ceremonial Roles of Presidents:* In addition to the president's administrative responsibilities, does the Constitution include a ceremonial role? If so, were the constitutional Framers aware that England was separating the chief of government and ceremonial roles as the United States joined them? How does the ceremonial role compare in significance to the president's chief administrative role?

3. *Separation of Powers:* Does the Constitution suggest that any one of the three branches of government is superior to the other? Is it constitutionally permissible for each branch to interpret the Constitution on its own? To what extent did the constitutional Framers permit a sharing of power between the Congress and the president?

4. *National Welfare:* How have Americans used their constitutional authority to promote federal government involvement in economic affairs and domestic social welfare policies and programs? Does the ''General Welfare'' clause in the Preamble enable the president to assume ''executive power'' through positive action? Are there any other constitutional provisions in Articles I or II that facilitate the growth and expansion of executive power in domestic policy?

5. *Foreign Relations and the War Power:* Is the president generally preeminent in making foreign policy, or is policy shared with Congress? Is the treaty-making power a principal basis for presidential foreign policy? What are executive agreements? Does presidential control of foreign policy enhance the possibility of an ''imperial presidency?''

How extensive is presidential authority under the commander-in-chief clause? Does the presidential oath imply the use of ''emergency powers'' and ''executive prerogative'' in national emergency and foreign military engagements?

Does the United States have two constitutions—a ''War Constitution'' that grants extraordinary executive powers in times of domestic and international crisis, and a ''Peace Constitution'' where the chief executive is constrained by Articles

I, II, and III provisions dealing with the separation of powers and checks and balances?

PART I

Constitutional Development of the Presidency: Historical Perspectives

Introduction to Part I

The six essays in Part I emphasize the historical continuity of expanded constitutional authority in the presidencies of Thomas Jefferson, Andrew Jackson, Abraham Lincoln, Theodore Roosevelt, Franklin Roosevelt, and Harry Truman. The Hamiltonian view of presidential authority is clearly evident in these essays. Whenever power sharing with the Congress or the courts was necessary, these strong presidents took the initiative and set the policy agenda for the other two branches. Consequently, all six presidents established significant domestic, foreign, and military constitutional precedents for their successors.

Ralph Ketcham shows that Jefferson supported the Hamiltonian concept of active, initiative-taking executive leadership even though the two men were strong rivals when serving George Washington. Jefferson's activist leadership was particularly demonstrated in territorial expansion—the Louisiana Purchase (1803)—and in the Embargo Act of 1807 which Ketcham argues prevented international aggression and was an example of peaceful economic coercion which resulted in resistance to militarism at home.

Andrew Jackson, according to Robert Remini, established the modern presidency by asserting himself as the head of government and not merely an equal partner in a tripartite system. Jackson elevated both the ceremonial and chief executive roles through his enormous public esteem as war hero and by creative use of the veto power in forcing Congress to abolish the U.S. Bank. Jackson also exercised absolute power over the entire executive branch when he discharged the Treasury Secretary after the Secretary refused to remove government deposits from the U.S. Bank.

Abraham Lincoln acted on the proposition that the language of Article II of the Constitution delegated broad executive powers, particularly in the commander-in-chief clause and the presidential oath, which enjoined him "to preserve, protect and defend the Constitution of the United States." Michael Les Benedict argues that Lincoln was not a "constitutional dictator" during the Civil War since he never asserted inherent or prerogative powers in defiance of Congress. Lincoln always conceded that Congress could overrule and control his actions.

According to William Harbaugh, the growth of executive power under Theodore Roosevelt reflected changes in the economy wrought by the industrial revolution. However, expanded executive power was accompanied by the growth of congressional, judicial, and business power. The expansion of regulatory agencies embodied a conscious effort to create an administrative state. The growth of executive power was most pronounced in foreign affairs.

Ellis Hawley focuses upon the executive response to economic crisis during the Depression era of the 1930s. He describes how early efforts by Herbert Hoover to promote cooperation between business and government failed, thereby leading to FDR's more expansive efforts. Roosevelt, in the First New Deal, became national legislative leader, securing statutory grants of power that were delegated to new administrative agencies. Hawley describes the period from 1935–37 as one of constitutional crisis between the executive and the Supreme Court. From 1937–39, the president and Congress battled over executive reorganization. Beginning in 1939, the focus shifted to war preparation, the new national security state and future constitutional implications of an "imperial presidency."

Donald McCoy shows that Harry Truman was fully prepared to interpret the Constitution dynamically in order to meet the challenges confronting his administration. The postwar period brought the United States into a position of superpower on the world scene. Truman expanded the president's powers as chief diplomat and commander in chief in supporting and promoting the United Nations Charter (1945), NATO (1949), and the Marshall Plan (1948). He had less success in policies involving civil rights, protecting internal security, and use of emergency powers in the Steel Seizure case.

Chapter 1

The Jefferson Presidency and Constitutional Beginnings

————————————————————— *Ralph Ketcham*

Here Ralph Ketcham freshly notes that Jefferson believed in and implemented a symbiotic relationship between an active unitary executive leadership and a republican government of virtue. In his first inaugural address Jefferson asserted that the American government under the Constitution would be "the strongest on earth," largely because of the Founders' Aristotelean argument that good government was essential to society's good life. Both the Louisiana Purchase (1803) and the Embargo (1807) were manifestations of powerful leadership and republican virtue—the former by extending the sphere of republican government, the latter by preventing international aggression and resisting militarism at home. Master Critic Forrest McDonald at Geneseo disagreed with Ketcham, noting that he overlooked the Herbert Croly syndrome, by which McDonald meant that Jeffferson (and Jackson) had converted faith in the people not into strong government, but into the people's distrust of national power. Critic Theodore Lowi thought that Ketcham (and other scholars) were running "the presidency backward," that this paper, like other presidential studies, was manifesting a new 1980s theology of conservative justification of a strong communal presidency, such as that of Ronald Reagan. Needless to say, Ketcham, in his retort at Geneseo, disagreed with McDonald's view that Jefferson's distrust of government left the presidency in ruins. Also, Ketcham saw little of Lowi's analogy of the Jefferson and Reagan presidencies both being conservative. "I don't know what he is talking about," said Ketcham.

One of Thomas Jefferson's most puzzling comments, at least most often remarked on as somehow mystifiying in the overall pattern of his thought, is the statement in his first inaugural address that he intended to preside over a government that was "the strongest...on earth." This assertion seems the more odd because later in the same address he speaks of the need for "a wise and frugal government" leaving citizens largely "free to regulate their own pursuits of industry and

5

improvement." The "essential principles of our government," he said further, are reduced to a few republican precepts: international peace, vigorous state governments, "mild and safe corrective of abuses," majority rule, civil supremacy over the military, and low taxes linked to low government expenses. These principles seem to evoke the familiar Jefferson who sounded the alarm during the 1790s against Hamiltonian plans for exalted national power, retrenched the federal bureaucracy after 1801, and all together believed "that government is best which governs least." He is thus seen as the authentic American spokesman for the Lockean, radical Whig, "oppositionist" view, often regarded as the dominant ideology of the American Revolution, trumpeting the virtures of limited, "checked-and-balanced" government responsive to the "convenience" of the governed.

So, what can we make of his insistence that, under the new Constitution, Americans had created "the strongest government on earth?" He gave one clue in the famous preceding remark that "we are all republicans—we are all federalists." He meant that Americans were united in devotion to the "republican form" and to the federal union of the states. Thus, instead of divisive quarrels over basic ideology, Americans were agreed on fundamentals—and this despite the bitter election battle just concluded. In fact, the contending politicians had, finally, accepted a peaceful change in the presidency and would, Jefferson believed, for the most part cooperate with the new administration. This agreement on basic principles and the acceptance by opposition leaders and parties of the new government gave it a strong foundation.

Even more important, though, was the attitude of the citizens toward their government. It was "the only one" in the world, the new president avowed, "where every man, at the call of the laws, would fly to the standard of the law, and would meet invasions of the public order as his own personal concern."[1] Jefferson had in mind both the strength the government derived from the *willing* support of its consenting citizens and the authority it would thus have to act on their behalf for the public good. Though Jefferson had a poignant awareness of the cruel and unjust burdens imposed by most governments, and had an abiding faith in the capacity of unfettered individuals to lead happy and prosperous lives, he had as well a deep sense of the enduring, indispensable uses of government—uses more properly and effectively carried out by governments willingly supported by the people than by those depending on force, fraud, and conscription. Strong government, then, meant to Jefferson firmness of support by the people and capacity to act in the public interest.

In the same address Jefferson also expressed an interesting and important conviction about the "sacred principle" of majority rule. "To be rightful," he said, it "must be reasonable," meaning that it not violate the rights of the minority; such would be oppression of the sort the American Revolution had acted against. Instead of continued dissension and domineering majority rule, then, Jefferson called for a restoration of a "harmony and affection" in society, under law, that would allow all "to unite in common efforts for the common good." The president saw his victory at the polls not as a partisan triumph that would allow his (now majority) following to impose its will, but rather as a chance for rule according to reason, that is, according to principles of right and justice conducive to the general welfare. This linkage of majority rule to ideas of reason and justice reveals Jefferson's life-long attention to the *quality* of citizenship necessary if rule by the people was to result in *good* government. He believed that only a citizenry of "informed discretion" would likely elect wise and able leaders who in turn would nourish and encourage improved understanding among the people. Thus, in extolling majority rule, strong government, reason, and right principle, Jefferson articulated a concept of republican leadership of high importance—and which in his opinion was essential to the constitutional frame of government so recently and hearteningly used in his victory at the polls. He believed that his election reflected the preponderance of right reason in the electorate, that he thus had received a mandate to lead in accord with that right reason, and that the result should and would be active pursuit by the government of the public interest. This view, moreover, is both consistent with the intent of the framers of the Constitution and in accord with Jefferson's own conduct as president.

Jefferson offered a key to both his own and his founding colleagues' source of this philosophy, linking leadership, citizenship, and good government, when he attested in 1825 that the Revolutionary generation had been of "one opinion," of "harmonized sentiments," in naming Aristotle and Cicero along with Locke and Sidney as authors of "the elementary books of public right."[2] Aristotle is mentioned first, doubtless from Jefferson's methodical, chronological habits, but he was also first in the basicity of his *Politics* to the political understanding of the founding era. Most of the Framers learned Latin and Greek (twenty-five of the members 39 of the Constitutional Convention had formal, classical educations) as part of their preparatory and college studies. Princeton, for example, at the time of James Madison's entrance, required applicants to "render Virgil and Tully's orations into English and turn English into true and grammatical Latin, and to be so well acquainted with the Greek, as to render any part of the Four Evangelists in that language into Latin or English."[3]

As students learning Latin and Greek, they absorbed the rich ideals of leadership and public life implicit in the writings of Homer, Cicero, Virgil, Livy, Plutarch, and others. Then, their first systematic study of politics was very likely cast in the then conventional, Aristotelian framework: Governments were by one, the few, or the many, and in each category there were good and bad forms. Kings could be tyrants or, in the eighteenth century designation, "benevolent despots," the few could be oligarchs or aristocrats, while rule by the many could be turbulent and corrupt mob rule (what Aristotle termed "democracy"), or good government under a constitutional polity. The key in any case was not the number who ruled, but the quality of government that resulted; whether, in Aristotle's terms, governments are good, ruling "with a view to the common interest," or "perversions," ruling "with a view to the private interest."[4]

The American founders, of course, were also well aware of more modern currents of political and social thought learned from Francis Bacon, Hobbes, Locke, the English "Cato," Bolingbroke, Adam Smith, Montesquieu, Hume, and others, but two factors controlled, or even subordinated the impact of "modernity" on the founders. First, the "moderns" themselves, though preoccupied with new learning, were nonetheless Enlightenment figures stimulated by the revival of classical ideas. Thus, even the forward-looking thinkers so impressive to Americans—Jefferson's "trinity of immortals," Bacon, Newton, and Locke, for examples—were learned classicists living within a world view deeply responsive to the wisdom of Greece and Rome. David Hume, increasingly recognized as a major influence on the American founders, wrote that "a man, who is only susceptible of friendship, without public spirit or a regard to the community, is deficient in the most material part of virtue."[5] This publicly cognizant understanding of virtue, plus the implication of human "deficiency" if "public spirit" is missing, reveal the loud echoes of antiquity in the neoclassical world of the eighteenth century. Like Aristotle and Cicero, it was simply impossible for a Jefferson or a Hamilton to depreciate the political, to devalue the uses of good government, as a Thoreau, or a William Graham Sumner, or a Ronald Reagan would do in later centuries.

Secondly, the classical outlook was "second nature" to educated people of the eighteenth century because it was learned first, as pupils studied Latin and Greek, usually before extensive contact with important modern writers. As students learned to read Cicero's eloquent Latin they also learned of the dangers posed by military control of politics, and as they read Livy's idealized history of the Roman republic they absorbed lessons in leadership and in the requirements of responsible citizenship. The widsom of Greece and Rome, experienced as schoolboys, furnished, so to speak, the folklore, the "morality plays," and the basic concepts of human nature and society for the founding generation. Though they would later respond to Locke's insistence on the natural right of self-government, or to the English "Cato's" stirring defense of free speech, these concepts were an overlay only on their already deeply ingrained, classical understanding of the political and its importance in human affairs.

This understanding of the political has an important and often overlooked or misconstrued influence on the ideas of leadership—and citizenship—of those who drafted, supported, and opposed the Constitution of 1787 in the United States. The debates both during and after the Federal Convention reveal the essentially qualitative emphasis of all concerned. That is, those drafting the Constitution expected their work to be judged according to the *quality* of government it would provide: Would it "establish Justice, insure domestic Tranquility, provide for the common defence, promote the general Welfare.... secure the Blessings of Liberty" and altogether "form a more perfect Union"? Note the capitalized nouns emphasizing the essentials: Justice, Tranquility, Welfare, Blessings of Liberty, Union—all qualities of the society, vital to the people, and to be sustained by government—as Aristotle had taught and as Jefferson believed all his life. With these agreed-upon goals, or "goods," the problem then becomes one of framing a government—processes, institutions, and so on—that will be effectual to these ends.

As the debates of 1787–88 indicate clearly, all were aware that government by one, or the few, *might*, theoretically, best sustain the goals sought. Thus Hamilton countenanced an executive in office for life, and John Adams upheld the uses of a candidly aristocratic senate. Oppositely, some antifederalists supposed a division of the union or a much-heightened emphasis on local town-meeting-type government would be best. These ideas, though, fell outside the also-agreed-upon "American genius" for a republican union; that is, a government deriving all its power, finally, from the people (the majority principle), some form of representation rather than "pure" democracy, and a federation that would retain the states as important parts of the system—the republican and federal principles Jefferson had in mind in 1801. These were the procedural, or institutional "givens" in 1787–88, but they were accepted only because the revolutionary ideology and experience had validated them as peculiarly suited to the achievement of Justice, Tranquility, Welfare, and Liberty. Thus, what Americans were agreed on in 1787–88 was *both* the Aristotelian emphasis that government should be an active agent for pursuit of the public good (Justice, etc.) *and* the Lockean emphasis that government should derive from the consent of the governed. But it was just as much agreed that to retain its validity, the procedure of majority rule would have to be so organized as to retain the *substantial* good of nourishing the public good. Put oppositely, the democratic process would deserve repudiation if it proved hostile to that good. The constant awareness of the revolutionary generation of their responsibility in "trying" government by consent, whether they would enhance or diminish its standing in the world, meant that they would have to "make it work," cause it to result in "the good life," reflect what Hume called "public spirit." Otherwise it would not merit praise or even survival.

By 1787, the revolutionary generation was much more aware than it had been in 1776 of the complexities of good self-government—of the difficulty of being *wise democrats*. Then, as during the long dispute with Britain leading up to independence, attention had focused on the legislature. Drawing on the ancient English practice of the people's voice in government being confined to one branch of the legislature (the House of Commons), and on the colonial experience of the lower house being the place of effective assertion of local interests against imperial power, Americans in 1776 tended to think government by consent consisted largely of a fully empowered, responsive legislature. Somehow the "superior" and "inferior" offices—the executives who administer the law and the citizens who elect the legislators—are less attended to. Thoughtful people realized, of course, that the character and qualifications of the electors are of ultimate importance. It was also clear freedom and well-being in society depended critically on good or bad execution of the laws—Pope's oft-quoted couplet was

> For forms of government let fools contest—
> That which is best administered is best.[6]

But, initially at least, confidence reposed in the capacity of the legislature to embody the public good.

Soon, though, difficulties appeared on all sides. Efforts by the Continental Congress to draft Articles of Confederation stalled first in Congress, then in the state legislatures, and resulted (after five years of bickering) in a document widely regarded as inferior to the ad hoc procedures it replaced. Among its obvious deficiencies were the lack of provision for executive power and a marked distancing of its officers from "the people." The states debated, drafted, and redrafted constitutions that increasingly reflected disenchantment with the assumption of legislative supremacy. Governors proved impotent to cope with problems of either war or peace, and, whatever the voter qualifications or frequency of elections, the performance of the state legislatures was widely disapproved. The acts of the Maryland legislature "uniformly tended to disgust its citizens" (1784), North Carolina laws were "the vilest collection of trash" (1780), and the New York legislature "daily committed the most flagrant acts of injustice" (1787), according to not necessarily unbiased observers.[7] Jefferson's frustrating experience as governor of Virigina (1779–81), and his growing disdain for the state's constitution, focused on what he considered the excessive power given to the legislature.

Though these concerns, even fears, drove some critics back toward such antidemocratic devices as hereditary office-holding and more stringent limitations on suffrage, a much more creative, and in the end more influential, reaction turned to "republican solutions": how could executive energy be both derived from the people and enlisted on behalf of good (as opposed to tyrannical) government, and how could the "discretion of the people" be improved so they would choose better (more able, wiser) officials? The two directions were linked, moreover, because in order for the executive power to be both a substantial check on and a qualitative supplement to the flawed legislature, and remain within the republican principle, it too would require derivation from and dependence on a *qualified* electorate. This equation was apparent to Jefferson in the 1780s, and it grew in prominence throughout the rest of his life.

Debate in the Federal Convention revealed the close connection between the construction of the executive power and assumptions about the capacity of the people for self-government. The Convention began with its members puzzled and uncertain about both problems. Madison had confessed to Washington a month before it opened that, while he was convinced there must be a national executive, he had "scarcely ventured as yet to form my own opinion" about its selection or powers.[8] When the Convention first considered executive power, for the only time Madison recorded that "a considerable pause ensued"—the members had no urgent or decided opinions on the subject. James Wilson, however, who had the clearest ideas about executive power, and had eventually the greatest influence on its construction, early asserted two vital propositions: that "the executive consist of a single person," and that he be elected by the people. To Wilson the executive could be as thoroughly republican an officer as a legislator. "Prejudices against the Executive," he told the Federal

Convention, "resulted from a misapplication of the adage that the parliament was the palladium of liberty." That may have been true "where the Executive was really formidable" and was independent of the people as in Great Britain, Wilson explained, but in a republic where the executive power was both limited and derived from the people, the situation was entirely different.[9] In fact, under such a government the legislature was more likely to threaten liberty, because, as Madison put it, "wherever the real power in a Government lies, there is the danger of oppression." In the United States, where "the real power lies in the majority of the Community," oppression (laws neglectful "both of public Good and private rights") would most likely come "from acts in which the Government is the mere instrument of the major number of the constituents." This tendency, so apparent, Madison wrote Jefferson, in the performance of state legislatures during the 1780s, was deeply troubling because it called "into question the fundamental principle of republican Government...according [to which] Right and power, being both invested in the majority, are held to be synonymous."[10] This, of course, laid bare the root, nagging difficulty taken most seriously by theorists of self-government in the founding era: "If majorities are often wrong, on what grounds, or with the aid of what devices, can it be proper for them to rule?"

Gouverneur Morris helped the convention of 1787 move away from legislative preoccupations by pointing out that since "the Legislature will continually seek to aggrandize and perpetuate themselves....one great object of the Executive is to controll the Legislature." Harking back to Roman and Tudor examples, Morris pointed out that "the Executive Magistrate should be the guardian of the people, even of the lower classes, against Legislative tyranny, against the Great and the wealthy who in the course of things will necessarily compose the Legislative body." Proceeding to the question before the Convention, how to properly construct the executive department, Morris asserted that it "ought to be so constituted as to be the great protector of the Mass of the people." After examining the arguments many delegates had made about the vices attendant on legislative election of the executive, Morris explained what he thought was the obvious answer to the troublesome problem of selection: "If [the executive] is to be the Guardian of the people let him be appointed by the people." They would, moreover, be the "best Judges" of the quality of the judicial appointments and the military duties of the president. Since the people would "feel the effects" of these important exercises of power, it was fitting that they have the authority to retain or remove those responsible for them. Morris thus favored a broadly empowered executive elected by the people and eligible for reelection to make him sensible while in office of the need to administer the laws in the public interest.[11]

James Wilson anticipated Jefferson's view when he tied Morris' argument closely to the republican character of the new Constitution. Wilson insisted repeatedly that the stability and justice of republican government required that it rest, like a pyramid, on the broad base of the people themselves. At the Pennsylvania Constitutional Convention of 1790 he observed that good government had to be both "efficient and free.... But... to render government efficient, power must be given liberally; to render it free as well as efficient, those powers must be drawn from the people, as directly and as immediately as possible." This proposition was a commonplace among American Whigs of the revolutionary era in discussing *legislative* power, but Wilson moved boldly to apply it as well to the executive: "He who is to execute the laws will be as much the choice, as much the servant and, therefore, as much the friend of the people as he who makes them." In fact, Wilson found the grant of power to the executive necessary for "efficient" government safe and justifiable *only* if the executive was held in direct responsibility to the people. This "chain of connection," as he put it, would keep the executive attuned to "the interests of the whole," generally less susceptible to the blandishments of special interests than notoriously faction-ridden legislatures.[12]

In Wilson's argument, the ancient idea accepted by Morris of the executive (monarch) being the protector and friend of the people received its legitimate foundation. Far more than a heredity, an absolute monarch might in some mystical way be sensitive to the rights and needs of "his people," a popularly elected executive would have immediate, practical attentiveness to those rights and needs. At least as much as the legislature, an elected executive would conform to the republican ideal of a responsible, public (spirited) official acting in the interest of the community as a whole—exactly the posture Jefferson took at his inauguration as president.

Even the device of the electoral college was viewed by Wilson and others as an acceptable, relatively minor departure from the idea of executive dependence on the people. The bugaboo of corrupt, intriguing election by the legislature, nonetheless advocated by many delegates and even implanted in the first draft constitution of August 6, 1787, had been avoided. Wilson supposed that the presidential electors would be in substantial accord with the will of the people. The president, then, would indeed be their "friend" and advocate, giving voice and effect to the public will in a way that would not only prevent invasion of private rights but also allow and encourage the pursuit of programs for the good of the nation as a whole—precisely the guiding idea of republican government—and of traditional conceptions of patriot leadership.

The opposition to popular election of the president revealed how the question of executive leadership was tied to that of the competence of the electorate. In opposing direct election, George Mason "conceived it would be as unnatural to refer the choice of a proper character for Chief Magistrate to the people, as it would to refer a trial of colours to a blind man." The size of the country, he thought, would make it impossible for the people to properly "judge of the respective pretensions of the Candidates." Charles Pinckney feared that in popular elections the people would be misled by "a few active and designing men," while Elbridge Gerry thought such a mode of election "would certainly be the worst of all" because the people were "uninformed" and gullible. He believed, for example, that good governors of Massachusetts and New Hampshire, who had done their "duty" by insisting on necessary but unpopular fiscal restraints, had been "turned out for it" by the people in direct elections.[13] In fact, though a few delegates at the Convention argued that direct election was theoretically attractive, most believed that in practice the incapacities of the voters would result in the choice of unqualified leaders. Thus the convention faced again the basic question of the ability of the people to fulfill wisely *their office* of self-governing citizen.

Members of the Federal Convention generally accepted the idea that citizenship, active participation, in a self-governing society required *qualification*, that is, some grounds for supposing that the voting (and even more, office-holding) would be exercised with responsibility to the public good and with reason and a sense of justice. To some members this meant a version of the restriction, familiar in ancient Greece, modern Britain, and some of the new states, of suffrage to freeholders, on the hallowed principle that those with "a stake in society," those who owned part of it (land), could be expected to vote responsibly and fairly. On the other hand, those without such a stake would be indifferent to the public good and unjust to those with property. John Dickinson stated the traditional argument that freeholders were "the best guardians of liberty. . . . The restriction of the right [to vote] to them [was] a necessary defence against the dangerous influence of those multitudes without property and without principle, with which our Country, like all others, will in time abound."[14]

Though the Convention rejected all explicit property qualifications for either voting or office-holding and the severe restrictions on office-holding for non-native citizens, the more liberal arguments objected not to the *idea* of voter qualification, but to the foolishness or injustice of the restrictions proposed. As was often the case during the Convention, George Mason stated the republican ideal most forthrightly:

"The true idea...was that every man having evidence of attachment to and permanent common interest with the Society ought to share in all its rights and privileges." This qualification, he thought, was not restricted to freeholders. Merchants, artisans, and financiers who owned no land, and parents of children destined to live in the country, might also feel the requisite "permanent attachment." Madison added that "the right of suffrage is certainly one of the fundamental articles of republican Government." Though he agreed with Dickinson that "the freeholders of the country would be the safest repositories of Republican liberty," Madison was, like Mason, moving toward a broadened understanding of freehold suffrage: possession of land was surely not the only circumstance or quality that would make a person a responsible citizen. In fact, as some members pointed out, several states already permitted taxpayers, merchants, heads of families, and adult sons of "substantial farmers" as well as landowners to vote in some elections. Other members asked whether service in the armed forces during the Revolution was not sufficient evidence of attachment to the country.[15] Clearly, members of the Convention did not regard the traditional freehold restriction as entirely consistent with the emerging republican ideology of the new nation—but how could *responsible*, rather than selfish, manipulated, mindless, or factional participation be accentuated? Members were equally united in taking that question seriously.

In three short speeches, Benjamin Franklin discerned most profoundly the issues underlying the debate on suffrage and citizenship. He rejected outright the supposed connection between wealth (possession of property, landed or otherwise) and public virtue: "Some of the greatest rogues he was ever acquainted with, were the richest rogues." Though the poor were perhaps tempted to dishonesty to overcome poverty, Franklin thought the rich at least as much tempted because "the possession of property increased the desire of more property." The Scripture required, Franklin noted, that "Rulers...should be men hating covetousness." The author of *Poor Richard's Almanac* was well aware that the industrious tradesman and the yeoman farmer were at least as likely to develop in their occupations the essential moral qualities of citizenship as was the rich merchant or large landholder—to say nothing of the slaveowner. If this were so, on what just grounds could suffrage and office-holding be conferred on some and denied to others?

Franklin then alluded to the high reputation American governments had in Europe, and the value of this in attracting ambitious and talented immigrants. Should the constitution "betray a great partiality to the rich," he observed, it would hurt the United States in "the esteem of the most liberal and enlightened men.... [and] discourage the common people from removing to this country." In urging quick qualification of new citizens for office-holding, Franklin thought their preference for the United States, evidenced by their choice and by their exertion in crossing the Atlantic, "is a proof of attachment [to America] which ought to excite our confidence and affection."[16] It was not wealth, then, that was the essential mark of the good American citizen, but rather attachment to the nation because of its freedom and justice and opportunity. Franklin had enlarged on the same point five years earlier in his advice on who should emigrate to the United States. A "mere Man of Quality," one without talent or virtue who merely prided himself on pedigree, wealth, or courtly sophistication, Franklin said, would be "despised and disregarded," while the farmer and artisan were "in honor [in America] because their employments are useful." The only encouragements offered to immigrants were "what are derived from good Laws and liberty." With such "advantages" poor but hard-working persons could soon own farms, or "establish themselves in Business, marry, raise families," and, speaking of Pennsylvania, after "one or two years residence [be given] all the Rights of a Citizen."[17] To Franklin, the qualifications for citizenship were clearly moral ones.

He even pointed out a critical linkage between granting rights of participation and encouraging the proper exercise of them. Great attention, he said, should be paid to "the virtue and public spirit of our common people." Those qualities were evident, he thought, among American seamen captured by the British during the Revolution who refused to purchase release from prison by "entering on board the Ships of the Enemies to their country." British prisoners, on the other hand, readily enlisted on board American ships. This "contrasting... patriotism," Franklin believed, "proceeded...from the different manner in which the common people were treated in America and Great Britain." To deny people the rights of citizenship, the right to vote and participate in government, would "depress" and "debase" their patriotism and sense of public responsibility. Thus, the extension of suffrage to the people (which in any case, under republican ideals, those already in office had no right to limit) would be a positive encouragement to their proper exercise of that right.[18] Franklin was formulating, and urging implantation in the new Constitution, a theory of citizenship linked to good leadership and good government: If ambitious, industrious people, grateful for the freedom and opportunity afforded by good laws and encouraged in virtue by the nature of their occupations, were given the rights of citizenship, the very exercise of those rights would help insure that the people would be able to choose good leaders. Franklin, like Jefferson, made the critical "wager" required at some stage in every effort to join self-government and good government: that the people were capable of attaining the skill and judgment needed to make wise and public-spirited choices. As Jefferson explained late in life, if citizens acted foolishly, the remedy was not to limit their participation but to "inform their discretion."[19]

Where, then, were members of the Convention headed in considering suffrage, the right to hold office, and the need for good leadership in a republic? Under the urging of Franklin, Mason, Wilson, and others, and with at least the hesitant support of all but a few delegates, the Convention refused to tie the new government to schemes of land or wealth-restricted suffrage or office-holding. It did this in part for reasons of practical disagreements among the delegates, but more fundamentally because the old rationale for property-based, stake-in-society suffrage was revealed as deeply flawed. At the same time, the members were equally unwilling to assert on the face of it that everyone (even all white, adult males) in a republic were qualified to vote. They continued to accept the ancient equation between good government (results not process) and properly qualified exercisers of power—as Aristotle had taught. This meant, as Jefferson's thought and career would attest most profoundly, that the achievement of *good self-government* was complex and problematic, yet not impossible in a democratic society. Part of the hesitancy on the part of the Convention arose, moreover, from its realization that the new United States was perhaps the first nation to address the question of good government in its new form: could the people, ultimately all of them in the internal logic of human equality, be so nurtured and organized politically, so that self-rule might aspire to long-recognized standards of good government for a good society—for example, "establish justice, insure domestic tranquillity, provide for the common defense, promote the general welfare, and secure the Blessings of Liberty?"

Two partially understood, perhaps problematic, yet portentous ideas, then, lurked in the "considerable pause" that ensued when the Federal Convention first took up the design of the executive department. First was a time-honored conviction that purposeful government led by a powerful, active executive might be, as it always had been, the essential means to a beckoning national prosperity, freedom, and greatness. Second was the dawning awareness that this sort of executive might, in a republic, be not a threat to liberty and the public good but instead be the very instrument of that liberty and good. The principle of government empowered by consent, that is, could transform the often tyrannical executive into, in Wilson's words, "the servant and friend of the people"—exactly Jefferson's intent in 1801.

The linkage of the ideas, moreover, apparent to and accepted by all members of the Convention (though some doubted or denied the premises of one or more of the propositions), was both simple and crucial: Only a properly qualified citizenry would likely elect a properly qualified executive fit to execise the broad powers of leadership good government itself required. Though many other forces helped shape the office of president, it is also clear that the provisions for the executive in the Constitution emerged in part from this linkage of ideas. The framers in devising the Constitution *did* have in mind positive, Aristotelian ideas of active government, as well as ideas of consent (e.g., Locke), separation of powers (e.g., Montesquieu), refinement of representation (e.g., Hume), and distrust of power (e.g., English Whigs). The president *was* vested with "the executive Power" in its full eighteenth-century connotations, and his wide grant of specific powers were such that they became a major target of opponents of the Constitution—but the authority had been conferred, was ratified, and remained in the document for presidents to use.

And the president *was* to be elected, indirectly but unconditionally, by the people. The electoral college idea, as the Convention debates show clearly, rested not on hostility to government by consent but on earnest intention to protect that principle from two corruptions equally damaging to good government: mindless, demogogic, circus-like campaigns among the people at large, and cabalistic, faction-ridden executive elections in Congress or in state legislatures. The Convention *did* accept the essence of the argument of Morris and Wilson that the president could be depended upon to be the vigorous friend of the people if they were given the power to choose him. Finally, in refusing to limit suffrage in the Constitution itself, and in allowing liberal provision for immigrants to become citizens, the Convention attested at least a guarded confidence in the idea that the people—common people, from anywhere in the world—might possess, or come to possess, the "virtue and public spirit" to elect similarly qualified officials, especially in the amply empowered presidency.

When Jefferson saw the new Constitution he responded favorably at once, objecting only to the omission of a bill of rights and to the eligibility of the president for reelection. He wrote in 1789 (from France) that "I approved from the first moment, of the great mass of what is in the new constitution, the consolidation of the government, the organization into Executive, legislative and judiciary," and the veto power (though he wanted it exercised in conjunction with the judiciary). Following Washington's election as the first president, Jefferson even withdrew his opposition to reeligibility in that case because, he asserted, Washington's "executive talents are superior to those...of any man in the world," and "the confidence reposed in his perfect integrity" was vital to overcome opposition to the new government.[20] In other words, *if* the executive power was exercised by an exceptionally talented person, and also one of "perfect integrity" (that is, unselfishly devoted to the public good) then there would be no objection to his remaining in office—the essential was the *quality* of the leadership. Washington epitomized the aristocrat of "talent and virtue" Jefferson always idealized and which, in some degree at least, he hoped might characterize all participants in government, citizens as well as officials.

Hence, Jefferson entered Washington's cabinet in 1790, determined to make the administration efficient, stable, and effective in its leadership of the nation. Though Jefferson came to be deeply troubled by Hamilton's manipulation of executive power, Hamilton himself testified that while they "were in the administration together, [Jefferson] was generally for a large construction of the Executive authority."[21] Then, in his own administrations, despite lingering Whig biases for legislative supremacy, executive limitation, and "mild" government, all heightened by a decade of opposition to Federalists-in-power, Jefferson himself provided vigorous leadership that has earned him a place on everyone's list of the half dozen most able American presidents. He understood, advocated, and practiced the art of active leadership.

The grounds of this executive vigor was Jefferson's own acceptance of an Aristotelian sense of both the uses of good government and the possibility of conducting it according to an objective idea of the public good. (His aphorism that government is best which governs least applied especially to the federal government, and to the excesses in it engineered during twelve years of Federalist rule.) Jefferson believed that regimes could ruin or uplift a state or a nation. When his granddaughter wrote glowingly of the prosperity, beauty, and happiness of western Massachusetts in 1825, he replied, remembering his own earlier journey (1791) through what "was then mostly desert....that it was now what thirty-four years of free and good government have made it."[22] It simply would not have occurred to Jefferson to suppose that government was relatively unimportant in human affairs, or that it was a largely negative agency best subordinated to economic or other private interests or energies. Though he believed earnestly in the beneficent potential of free individuals, he did not see this as in any way diminishing the need for pursuit of the public good through acts of government.

This general faith in the need for and the value of publicly exercised power was also a key part of his concept of citizenship. A rather casual, largely defensive citizenship, tuned to the protection of individual rights and interests and vigilant against malfeasance in office, now often seen as the essence of public participation, had little appeal to Jefferson. It would to him have been grossly inadequate and a betrayal of the rich, positive connotations of an Aristotelian citizenship. In fact, like Aristotle, Jefferson believed an indispensable dimension of freedom was public liberty, the responsible participation in the affairs of the polity. His constant attention to the *quality* of citizenship—grounded in possession of land, education for all, and participation in local government—rested squarely on the need for the poeple to possess knowledge and virtue if they were to govern well. Even his conduct as president, sometimes regarded as retaining the age-old aristocratic bias, had vital overtones of educating and setting a moral tone for citizens as well as office-holders. Thus he introduced informality and "pell-mell" into presidential etiquette and social life. He worked with, even as he led, the people's representatives in Congress, and through letters and addresses he conducted a continuous campaign of public education.

Jefferson summarized his views in letters written at the beginning and at the end of his presidency. He would seek, he wrote in 1801, as the foundation of his administration, to move the "whole people. . . . the great machine of society," toward notions of "ideal right." Then, a year after leaving office, he wrote of the obligation of the president to "unite in himself the confidence of the whole people," thus to mobilize "the energy of the nation" in pursuit of the common good— echoing what he had thought were the marks of Washington's high qualifications for the office. These letters reveal often-misunderstood aspects of Jefferson's thought that led John Randolph of Roanoke, Henry Adams, and a whole school of modern historians to regard Jefferson as contradictory and even hypocritical. These letters, that is, seem not to conform evenly to his assertion before the election of 1801 that he was "for a government rigorously frugal and simple" that did not aggrandize either federal power over the states or executive power over legislative.[23] In office, in conformity to what Randolph and others thought were Jefferson's republican principles, he reduced the federal judiciary, the armed forces, the national debt, the bureaucracy, and taxes. But he also established the military academy, called for a national university and a national road, and dispatched the Lewis and Clark expedition, all measures of active leadership, national purpose, and enlargement of government. His call for a constitutional amendment to authorize these "great objects of public education, roads, rivers, canals, and such other objects of public improvement as may be thought proper," because he believed powers to do these things "are not among those enumerated in the Constitution," reveal *both* his fidelity to constitutional government *and* his virtually unlimited willingness to use government, when appropriate, for public purposes. He meant to govern responsibly under a constitution ratified by the people, but he sought also to use the active agency of government, and his leadership of it, in the public interest. He intended, he said in the midst of delicate negotiations with Congress in 1806, to preside over a government of "design," and not of "chance."[24]

Two major episodes of Jefferson's presidency, the Louisiana Purchase and the Embargo, reveal his earnest willingness to use the powers of government on behalf of the public good. Though the lull in the war between France and Great Britain eased international tensions generally during his first term, the news of the retrocession of Louisiana by Spain to France in 1802, and the abrupt closing of the port of New Orleans to American shipping and produce, alarmed Jefferson. Napoleon seemed intent on making New Orleans and the huge territory west of the Mississippi part of a French Caribbean empire. This prospect at once transformed France, Jefferson wrote, from America's traditional ally into "our natural and habitual enemy," the inevitable status of any vigorous foreign power possessing New Orleans, "through which the produce of three-eighths of our territory must pass to market, and from its fertility it will ere long yield more than half our whole produce and contain more than half our inhabitants." With typical hyperbole, Jefferson declared from "the day that France takes possession of New Orleans...we must marry ourselves to the British fleet and nation." With a powerful, aggressive France, rather than "feeble, pacific" Spain, in possession of New Orleans and the Louisiana territory, Jefferson foresaw years of "irritability," if not outright war.[25] With the nation shorn of its fortunate geographic isolation from European quarrels, and compelled to arm and fight and intrigue, the president feared for the very survival of the republican experiment. The crisis was grave, and the need for the government to act urgent.

Jefferson and his cabinet, largely overcoming scruples about the constitutionality of acquiring new territory for the nation, sent envoys to Paris to purchase New Orleans and West Florida from the impulsive Napoleon. Through both luck and good management the envoys were offered, and purchased, not only New Orleans but the entire Louisiana territory, lands west of the Mississippi more than doubling the area of the United States. This fabulous news reached Jefferson in Washington on the Fourth of July 1803. Though he still had serious reservations about the constitutionality of the purchase—"the Constitution has made no provision for our holding foreign territory, still less for incorporating foreign nations into our union"[26]—he was determined to take advantage of Napoleon's sudden decision to sell. He called a special session of Congress and took the lead in urging ratification of the purchase treaty, trusting that the "evil of [loose] construction" of the Constitution would in this case be more than balanced by the good achieved and the solid support, indeed enthusiasm, among the people for the purchase.[27] Since in Jefferson's mind securing a constitutional amendment was a formal sign the people approved of the explicitly unsanctioned purchase, he viewed the wide public support as an informal substitute for the amendment.

As the chief executive of the republic, however, Jefferson believed constitutional scruples and diplomatic technicalities paled beside the multiple public advantages that ensued. First and foremost, the purchase removed permanently the threat of constant quarrel and war over use of the land and waters of the Mississippi. Since war and preparation for war were antithetical to all of Jefferson's republican ideals, to act to avoid them was of transcending importance. Second, the purchase allowed the nation to stand clear of dependent alliance, dangerous to liberty, on either of the great warring powers of Europe. Third, the purchase, arranged without armed attack, set a precedent for peaceful settlement of disputes between nations—a propitious extension, in Jefferson's view, of republican ideals to the lawless and violent international arena. Fourth, the acquisition of a territory inhabited by French- and Spanish-speaking aliens afforded an opportunity to extend the union, equitably and rationally, to a previously unrepublican culture—a challenge Jefferson and his colleagues accepted eagerly and capably as they planned for the government of the new territories. Finally, turning to the vast, unexplored, and largely vacant lands of the upper Missouri and Mississippi Valleys, Jefferson saw a beckoning vision: "We may lay off a range of States on the western bank [of the Mississippi] from the head to the Mouth, and so, range after range, advancing compactly as we multiply."[28] That this settlement seemed sure to be largely fertile yeoman farms gathered into equal, self-governing states, of course, was uniquely pleasing to a ceaseless advocate of circumstances likely to nourish responsible citizens.

Thus, the Louisiana Purchase was a model act for a wise and vigorous republican executive. Jefferson's preoccupation, throughout his presidency, with the acquisition, exploration, government, and settlement of the territory is entirely in keeping with his deepest-held maxims of public life. Shortly after retiring from the presidency, reflecting on the rapid progress in the west from settlement to territorial status and finally to full statehood, Jefferson wrote his successor that "I am persuaded no constitution was ever before so well calculated as ours for extensive empire and self-government."[29] His successor, the principal architect of the Constitution, understood Jefferson's meaning exactly and profoundly: the Constitution was meant to encompass an "empire for liberty," that is, provide for the addition to the Union, under the guidance of the Congress and the executive branch, of equal, self-governing states that would validate the idea of the extended republic Madison had himself articulated in the *Federalist Papers*. The conception also both exemplified the model of republican leadership implicit in the Constitution (recall the 1787 explications of James Wilson), and nourished the style of citizenship essential to the election and support of such leaders.

The Embargo of 1807 was just as bold, active, and idealistic in conception as the Louisiana Purchase, but much more problematic, complex, and ill-fated in its implementation. Jefferson and Madison had been advocates of commercial retaliation since the pre-revolutionary trade restraints to resist British measures in the colonies; these measures, they thought, demonstrated the effectiveness of measures short of war in international relations. During the 1790s both men had been persistent advocates of "reciprocity," that is, insistence on American retaliation against unfair British regulation of the trans-Atlantic and West Indian trade so important to the economies of both nations. Such measures continued to occupy their minds as renewed, life-and-death warfare drove England and France to wholesale depredations on American sea-going commerce in 1806 and 1807. Though war with either or both nations was in one sense justified, the unpreparedness of the United States for war, the desire to protect American ships from attack, and Jefferson's desire for one final effort at commercial coercion led to the Embargo Act of December 22, 1807: American ships were forbidden to leave harbors for foreign ports, and foreign ships, although allowed to bring cargo to the United States, were required to leave in ballast. Three months later Congress passed parallel regulations that governed trade along the land frontiers with the Spanish and British colonies.

Jefferson knew the choices facing the nation were grim: "What is *good* in this case cannot be effected," he wrote Secretary of the

Treasury Albert Gallatin on the eve of the Embargo. "We have, therefore, only to find out what will be *least bad*."[30] Worst would be to suffer the assault and humiliation of the warring powers without response. Such a course would forfeit national independence, encourage international arrogance and lawlessness, and degrade republican principles. Almost as harmful in its effects, the unmilitary president thought, would be entrance into the world war then raging. The inevitable accompaniments of war—taxes, conscription of men and resources, contract profiteering, diversion from domestic needs, foreign intrigue, executive aggrandizement, and military glorification—were deeply antithetical to republican precepts such as "mild" government, honesty, reason, and attention to the needs of the people. This was especially so, both Jefferson and Madison believed, in the early days of the republic when attitudes were unsettled and institutions untested. During his presidency, as the Napoleonic wars raged, Jefferson saw himself "trusted with the destinies of this solitary republic of the world, the only monument of human rights, and the sole depository of the sacred fire of freedom and self-government."[31] Thus he was determined, boldly and forthrightly, to try a policy hopefully both faithful to republican principles and effective in the dangerous international arena—the Embargo.

Things went wrong almost from the beginning. Many American vessels hastily departed, fully laden, before the Embargo became effective, and others were able to depart even later under loopholes in the legislation. International trade, moreover, proved far more flexible than Jefferson and Madison had envisioned. Both warring nations managed somehow to secure vital supplies. Britain, especially, increasingly received from Canada (either directly or by transhipment) the goods supposedly obtainable only from the United States. Thus she felt no effective pressure from the Embargo and instead stepped up her depredations and arrogance. Napoleon was even less affected.

Worse, from the standpoint of Jefferson's republican principles, the policy had increasingly calamitous domestic effects. The greater-than-expected injuries to the nation's economy, especially to New England commerce, heightened both general discontent and a sense of regional unfairness and animosity. Furthermore, Americans seemed less inclined to discipline themselves for the general good than the policy required. Smuggling and evasion of the law were rife from the Canadian border to the Mississippi bayous. Though many law-abiding traders bore patiently the inroads on their commerce and profits, many others evaded or defied the law, thus creating the politically unhealthful scene of honest sufferers forced to watch criminal profiteers become rich.

The administration was thrust into a double bind. Its policy failed to produce the intended international result, while it did undermine basic republican precepts at home. Nonetheless, Jefferson and his supporters perservered, pushing through Congress in April 1808 an Enforcement Act that empowered Secretary Gallatin's border and port officials to exercise complete control over shipping in dozens of ports and trade across hundreds of miles of frontier. Federalists renewed charges of dictatorship. "The colossal power of a majority had put down the still small voice of reason, and had declared that strength alone should reign," Massachusetts Congressman Livermore declared.[32] With Jefferson urging Gallatin to "crush every example of forcible opposition to the law," instructions went out for port collectors to man armed patrol vessels with volunteers, for marshalls to form posses to apprehend smugglers, and even for governors to call out the militia, if necessary, to enforce the law. The president explained further that "the great leading object of the Legislation was, and ours in execution of it ought to be, to give complete effect to the embargo laws. They have bidden agriculture, commerce, navigation to bow before that object, to be nothing in competition with that." When Gallatin reported continuing widespread lawbreaking, Jefferson replied in puzzled alarm: "This embargo law is certainly the most embarassing one we have ever had to execute. I did not expect a crop of so sudden and rank growth of fraud and open opposition by force could have grown up in the U.S."[33]

An excruciating crisis was at hand. A policy requiring, so it seemed, not only the minute control of all the coastal commerce of the United States, but also the dispatch of regular troops and the calling out of the militia against American citizens, had been put in place by republican advocates of "mild" government. Though Jefferson and his colleagues were quite willing to act vigorously to impose a policy they believed to be in the public interest, they were also appalled at the implications. Upset, it seemed, were all the republican pieties about deference to the will of the poeple and insistence on shunning the age-old tendency of government to ride "booted and spurred" on the backs of the people. "I felt the foundations of the government shaken under my feet," Jefferson wrote, when the petitions of protest poured in from New England.[34]

Even as orders went out for army and navy commanders to enforce the law, though, Jefferson and the cabinet decided *not* to pursue the policy any further. It had failed as a diplomatic weapon and at home it was doing immense damage to the body politic: it entailed measures of force against the people and provoked in them mass disaffection to the government, both circumstances fatal to a republican polity.

Jefferson's idea of presidential leadership, then, involved *both* a willingness, an obligation, to act in the public interest even in ways pervasively regulating life in the nation, *and* a clear sense of priorities that forbade him to impose a virtual military dictatorship merely to prove a point about law enforcement. It simply was not worth it, it was not justifiable under republican precepts, for the president to turn the nation into an armed camp virtually in occupation of some parts of the country. Earnest both to be faithful to the Constitution and to retain the essentially benign relationship between the people and their government, Jefferson nonetheless had a keen sense of the public good toward which he had a serious responsibility to lead and a large sense of the power of government to be effective toward that end.

The most creative, even radical aspect of Jefferson's thought, though, resting on his rather traditional (Aristotelian) ideas of the uses of government and of leadership in the public interest, was his determination to at the same time maintain the "inviolable republican principle": government according to the consent of the governed registered through representative processes. He saw more clearly than the other Founders the need for, and worked more persistently to achieve, improvement in the quality of citizenship essential to good, democratic government. Jefferson's equivocation on freedom of the press reveals his twin concerns. While president he complained bitterly of lying, slanderous newspapers as "polluted vehicles" that made a farce of reasoned public debate. He even approved "selected prosecution" of violently partisan newspapers, all part of his concern to improve and guide the people's understanding. But he also often expressed faith that the people could withstand "abuses of the press," and ultimately "discern between truth and falsehood."[35]

He had a responsibility, that is, as a leader, to attend to the *quality* of public debate in order to help create the informed citizenry essential to good government in a republic—a citizenry that, to complete the circle, would then be likely to elect wise and able leaders. By thus uniting in his own outlook and practice incessant attention both to providing active, purposeful leadership and to the development of an informed, public-spirited citizenry, he sought to combat charges that democracy would lack effective leadership and that it would be ruined by the ignorance and selfishness of the people. He knew that the solution of both problems was necessary—and the genius of his thought and of his presidency was to see that the two problems had to be solved *together* if they were to be solved at all. Jefferson sought to shape a presidential office empowered to lead actively on behalf of good government, and devoted to the improvement of and respect for the voice of the people. In this way, he accepted the ancient wisdom of Aristotle on the nature and benefits of good government, but added to it the dawning idealism of the Enlightenment that the people themselves (ultimately *all* the people), properly improved in their discretion as Jefferson put it, could provide wisely for the conduct of their common concerns.

The American presidency, then, had its origin in a climate of political thought still steeped in the classical, civic republican, convictions that a good society required good government, that good government required active leadership, and that active leaders required the support of public-spirited citizens. Though emphasis in characterizing the American Constitution and American government under it has often been on "checks and balances" and on the Bill of Rights, all designed to restrain government and protect individual rights (fair enough up to a point), an additional emphasis on the uses of active government is also imbedded in the Constitution. In fact, its very ambiguity can be seen more properly as a creative opportunity than as a flaw or limitation. It arose because American government was founded in the flux that existed as the Western World moved into the modern age. Ideas of free trade, capitalist enterprise, industrial revolution, diversifying interests, individualism, and democratic politics burgeoned all around the Atlantic world of the founders. Yet, more traditional ideas of community, moral purpose, political obligation, and patriot leadership remained strong.

The founders were thus well aware not only of the debate over the moral dangers of commerce and self-seeking, but also of the probably demeaning effect of them on the public virtue essential to social accord in a richly textured human community. The notion of citizenship they accepted, then, was *both* "modern" in its insistence on individual and increasingly universal participation, and "classical" in its concern for political obligation and public virtue. And their conception of leadership, resting on the consent of the people but also positioned for active pursuit of "ideal right," was consistent with and dependent on such citizenship. The leader would, on the model of the Duke of Chou, Nehemiah, Pericles, and other fabled leaders, have to rule actively, wisely, and selflessly for the public good, but, in a new requirement, he would also have to be chosen by the people and thus be responsible to them. These conceptions were evident in the debates of the Convention of 1787 and also characterized the presidency of Thomas Jefferson.

Chapter 2

The Constitution and the Presidencies: The Jackson Era

_____ *Robert V. Remini*

Robert Remini in this paper argues that Andrew Jackson was the first "modern president," claiming constitutional primacy for the office of the chief executive. As president, Jackson unprecedentedly imposed control upon the legislative and executive branches—over, for example, the former by a creative use of the veto; and over the latter by the removal of his secretaries of the treasury. Remini describes eloquently Jackson's remarkable hold upon the affections of the American people. The president believed absolutely in democracy. A novel emphasis, however, is seen with Remini's view of a Jacksonian cautiousness regarding many of his relationships with other branches of government and with the states. Thus, today, Jackson appeals to both the conservative and liberal sides of the political spectrum. Conservatives are drawn to Jackson's commitment to limited government, strict economy, and support of states rights, while liberals find irresistible his populistic notions about liberty, egalitarianism, and democracy. In his response to Remini's paper, Theodore Lowi agreed that Jackson was a president who left a constitutional legacy of a strong presidency, although he thought Remini was almost as ideological as Arthur Schlesinger, Jr., in viewing Jackson as a predecessor to Franklin Roosevelt's presidency. Lowi thought Congress set more of the national agenda than did Jackson, as, for example, by the "annual sessions laws." Remini's disagreement with Lowi on this score was total. He insisted that Jackson, in fact, was the first president to set the national agenda.

From the very beginning of my serious investigation into the presidency of Andrew Jackson, it became obvious to me that this extraordinary personality influenced and reshaped the executive office to an unparalleled degree. I suppose I should have realized it at the very outset of my research, knowing as I did that I was working with a very dynamic, charismatic, forceful, and intimidating personality. Andrew

Jackson was bigger than life, as were many of the other political figures of the Jacksonian age, including Henry Clay, Daniel Webster, and John C. Calhoun, among others. But Old Hickory is quite special. His personality, shaped to some extent by his military command for over a decade and by his victories over the Indians, the British, and the Spanish, had a force and thrust that could terrorize opponents with a glance. He simply dominated everyone around him. It was his nature. And he expected to be obeyed when he gave an order. James Parton, his first biographer, said that Jackson was like a fighting cock all his life: very kind to the hens who clucked around him, giving them many a nice kernel of corn, but savage with all who challenged him, using beak and spur to bloody and defeat them.[1]

A man of such compelling personality was bound to place his mark on everyone and every institution that seriously interested him. He would not be Andrew Jackson if he had failed to leave the presidency radically altered from what it was when he first assumed the office. He even restructured the White House mansion itself. And I'm not referring to the repair of the house occasioned by the mayhem committed in and on that stately mansion during his inauguration. I mean the fact that the White House was an unprepossessing-looking pile until Jackson added the north portico. The colonnade at the entrance gave the mansion a distinctive, attractive, and commanding look. Without it the White House would be just another nondescript government building.

Thus, as I pursued my research into Jackson's presidency, I found it less and less surprising that, in the course of his eight years in office, he had radically expanded and enhanced the powers of the chief executive. Indeed, he so reconstituted his office that in my little book on the Bank War I declared him to be the "first modern President" in our history.[2] In fact, I subtitled that volume, "A Study in the Growth of Presidential Power."

In much of my writing in the past decade or so I confess that I have placed great emphasis on the "revolutionary" aspects of the changes wrought during the Jacksonian years. Moreover, I have insisted on their modernity. But I would also like to point out, particularly now that I have finished my three volume biography of Jackson, that in all the changes he initiated or attempted to initiate, what he did remained deeply rooted in tradition. In other words, one must keep in mind Jackson's sense of the past and its value. Historical continuity isn't easily broken, and Jackson was more respectful of it than is generally appreciated. Of course, he could be exceedingly contradictory. He is remembered as a passionate advocate of states rights and yet also as an intense nationalist who substantially advanced the power of the central government. He denied the authority of the federal court in the Bank War and yet condemned the South Carolina nullifiers for not submitting their grievances to the court—all of which should remind us that Jackson could respond in different ways to different conditions. He was not the kind of ideologue who was stuck in a fixed position. And it was this very flexibility that assisted him in remaking the office of the president.

There are other factors to be kept in mind as well. For one thing, he was extraordinarily popular with the electorate, more popular than Washington, Jefferson, Franklin, or Madison had ever been. And he knew it. Which meant that he could invoke popular support—or claim that he had it, which was usually the case—to force compliance from those who resisted his will. Michael Chevalier, the French traveler, claimed—and I think he's correct—that Jackson's tactics in politics were not so much to respond to popular opinion as it was to "throw himself forward with the cry of, 'Comrades, follow me!' "[3] I think Jackson's presidential power was enhanced to a considerable extent by his enormous popularity with the electorate, which Congress appreciated, and the fact that the people believed him to be their champion and representative in Washington who was forever fighting for their interests against corrupt aristocrats.

It can easily be understood, therefore, that when you have a determined, commanding, willful, and extremely popular politician in the White House, something is going to happen, something that may very well make a lasting impression.

The most obvious example of Jackson's tremendous impact on the presidential office, as well as his unique understanding of the separation of powers among the three branches, occurred during the Bank War. As you know, the Congress, urged on by Clay and Webster, acted upon Nicholas Biddle's request for a recharter of the Second National Bank and overwhelmingly passed the necessary legislation extending the life of the Bank for another twenty years. Jackson returned the bill with a ringing veto message; in that veto he not only cited constitutional arguments against recharter but he also cited political, social, economic, and nationalistic reasons as well. With respect to the constitutional question, Jackson noted that the Supreme Court in the case *McCulloch v. Maryland* had declared the Bank constitutional. "To this conclusion," he declared, "I cannot assent." Both Houses of Congress and the executive must decide for themselves what is or is not constitutional, he said, and act accordingly. "It is as much the duty of the House of Representatives, of the Senate, and of the President to decide upon the constitutionality of any bill or resolution which may be presented to them for passage or approval as it is of the supreme judges when it may be brought before them for judicial decision." Jackson would not deny the right of the court to pass on the constitutionality of a bill, but he would deny that the court is the final or the exclusive interpreter of the Constitution. What he argued was the equality and independence of each branch of government. "The authority of the Supreme Court," he went on, "must not, therefore, be permitted to control the Congress, or the Executive when acting in their legislative capacities, but to have only such influence as the force of their reasoning may deserve."[4] Jackson rejected the notion that four men (five persons today) could dictate what 15 million people (250 million today) may or may not do under their constitutional form. That was not democracy, as he saw it. That was oligarchy. That was aristocracy. And he rejected it.

He has a point. Indeed, he is right. It is *not* democratic when five individuals can decide upon every conceivable issue for hundreds of millions of people.[5] That's oligarchy, as he said; that's aristocracy. But that is precisely what the Founding Fathers wanted in the Constitution: a balanced mix of democratic, oligarchic, and monarchical forms. Jackson broke with the Founding Fathers on this point. The only form he approved was the democratic form, even though he himself was constantly accused of exercising monarchical powers as president.

I noticed in the *American Heritage* magazine of a few months ago that a number of scholars were asked to make suggestions about amending the Constitution in order to improve it. Two distinguished constitutional scholars, Don Fehrenbacher of Stanford University, and Herman Belz of the University of Maryland, argued for limiting the powers of the court. "In their exercise of power the courts have far exceeded the limited political role intended by the Framers of the Constitution," said Belz.[6] Both scholars argued that this limiting of judicial power could be effected by congressional legislation, not formal amendment.

But Jackson's veto is remembered more for other reasons than its argument about the constitutional power of the Supreme Court. It is the way he expanded his veto power that is so important. The first six presidents vetoed a total of nine times, and in every instance they cited constitutional grounds for the veto. Presumably a bill's unconstitutionality was the *only* ground upon which a president could void legislation. Indeed, men like Henry Clay insisted that the executive veto might only be used in those instances involving a question of constitutionality. Jackson thought otherwise. In his veto he cited many reasons for his action and thereby claimed for the president the right to participate in the legislative process. By vetoing for reasons other than constitutional, he notified the Congress that they must consider his views on all bills *before* passing them or run the risk of a veto. It meant he was assuming legislative powers. And everyone knew it. Jackson's position essentially altered the relationship between the legislative and executive branches of government. The president was becoming the head of the government, the first among equals, not simply an equal partner with the other two branches.

It had always been argued that the legislature was the centerpiece of government, the branch closest to the people and the most representative of their will. Again, Jackson thought otherwise. Not only did he claim to serve as chief of state, but he soon declared that he, as president, represented all the people. His enemies immediately denounced his position and his argument. The Washington *National Intelligencer* claimed that the veto power "enabled the President...to usurp the legislative power." The question henceforth, said the editors, "is not what Congress will do, but what the President will permit."[7] Daniel Webster agreed: "According to the doctrines put forth by the President," he declared in a speech to the Senate immediately following the veto, "although Congress may have passed a law, and although the Supreme Court may have pronounced it constitutional, yet it is, nevertheless, no law at all, if he, in his good pleasure, sees fit to deny its effect; in other words, to repeal or annul it."[8] Jackson, he continued, "claims for the President, not the power of approval, but the primary power of originating laws."[9]

As the Bank War intensified, Jackson further strengthened his office when he decided, against the advice of his secretary of the treasury (and several other members of his cabinet, let it be said), to remove the federal deposits from the Second National Bank. Treasury Secretary William Duane refused Jackson's direct order to remove the deposits, and he also refused to resign his cabinet post even though he had earlier promised to do so if he and the president could not agree upon a common course of action. So Jackson summarily dismissed him. But that created a problem that earlier presidents had deftly avoided, namely the right of the chief executive to dismiss anyone whose appointment had been confirmed by the Senate. Put another way, since all cabinet posts were created by the Congress and each office filled through appointment and the confirmation of the Senate, did that not suggest that dismissal also required legislative concurrence? This seemed particularly true of the treasury secretary because he handled public funds. But no one knew the answer to this question. No previous president had ever dismissed a cabinet officer. Previous presidents nudged objectionable persons into resigning. In that way the constitutional problem was sidestepped. Moreover, wasn't the secretary of the treasury accountable to the Congress, rather than the president, in the disbursement of public funds? The law creating the Treasury Department, it should be remembered, never called it an "executive" department. Also, the secretary was required to make his reports to Congress, not the president. And since the Congress had already expressed its satisfaction with the Bank and its care of federal funds, wasn't the secretary obliged to follow its command rather than the command of the president?

A difficult problem to resolve, one that had no precedents whatsoever. But the tough-minded general had little trouble with it. He believed that all officials of the executive office fell totally and completely under the president's authority—and that included the secretary of the treasury, whether his department was called an executive department or not. They were *his* appointees, not the Congress'. They were to obey *him*. No one else. They were to follow *his* orders, not those of the Congress. With respect to the United States treasury and the dispersal of government funds, his attitude and action placed public funds, to a considerable extent, in the hands of the president and, therefore, gave him additional and important authority. Here again Jackson established a new dimension of presidential power. Thus, by his action, he had assumed total authority to remove all cabinet officers without notifying Congress, much less asking its consent, and, to a very considerable degree, he had seized control of the treasury. And that can be a very dangerous source of power, as recent presidents have demonstrated. Senator John C. Calhoun, on the Senate floor, called Jackson's action the "robbery of the treasury." The plundering of the Roman treasury by Julius Caesar was an act of virtue compared to Andrew Jackson's recent conduct, he said. "With money and corrupt partisans...[the voice of American liberty will be stifled], the revolution be completed, and all the powers of our republic, in like manner, be consolidated in the president, and perpetuated by his dictation."[10]

In tilting power more toward the executive and undermining the separate but equal doctrine of the Founding Fathers, Jackson was asserting more and more his role as the direct representative of all the people. He had become the spokesman and symbol of the electorate. And I think he intuitively understood his symbolic and ceremonial role because of the tour of the Middle and New England states he took to calm public fears immediately after the Nullification Crisis.[11] The people genuinely saw him as the head of the government, as their representative and their spokesman. And he conducted himself in office quite in accordance with that perception.

Critics at the time saw what was happening. I'm sure you've all seen the cartoon of 1832 showing Jackson represented as King Andrew the First, clad in robes befitting an emperor and wearing a crown and holding a scepter in one hand and a scroll in the other on which is written the word, "veto." Opposition newspapers tried to warn the electorate about the dangers inherent in Jackson's presidential conduct. "The true power of this government," preached one editorial, "*ought* to be to lie in the Congress of the United States. . . . It was never contemplated that its deliberately expressed opinions should be lightly disregarded—its well considered acts repeatedly rejected—and its legal authority overtopped by another and differently constituted power." But that was exactly what Jackson was doing, said this newspaper, and he claimed to be doing it in the name of the people. "Congress is the *democratic* branch of the government," this journal continued, not the executive. "If power is safe anywhere in a Republic it is safe with the representatives."[12]

Congress tried repeatedly to discourage Jackson from removing the deposits from the National Bank, but he went right ahead dispersing public funds as he, not Congress, directed. At length the Senate censured him in a formal vote; whereupon Jackson responded in a "Protest" message wherein he said that the "president is the direct representative of the American people." And not only was the chief executive "elected by the people," he was "responsible to them." No previous president had ever made such a claim. It was a modern idea in keeping with the democratic spirit of the times, but it was certainly not one the Whigs in Congress could approve. Said Senator Webster on the floor of the upper house: "This is not the language of the Constitution. The Constitution no where calls him the representative of the American people; still less their direct representative. . . . Where, then, is the authority for saying that the President is *the direct representative of the People?* . . . I hold this, Sir, to be a mere assumption, and dangerous assumption."[13]

Senator Henry Clay agreed. Jackson claims to be "the sole Executive," said Clay, "all other officers are his agents, and their duties are his duties. . . . I deny it absolutely. There exists no such responsibility to the President. All are responsible to the law . . ."[14]

Senator Benjamin W. Leigh of Virginia went further. "Until the President developed the faculties of the Executive power, all men thought it inferior to the legislature—he manifestly thinks it superior; and in his hands the monarchical part of Government . . . has proved far stronger than the representatives of the States. . . ."[15]

Even Jackson's enemies, such as Leigh, realized he had expanded the powers of the presidency. He did more, I think. He liberated the executive office from the position of prime minister, responsible only to the Congress. He was no longer the head of a coordinate branch of government. As far as he was concerned, the president was the chief of state accountable to the people. He set the national agenda. He set the priorities. He set the future goals for the entire nation. He widened his responsibility to include all the people, and if the people disagreed with him or his policies and goals, they could replace him.

"To a degree quite unforeseen by the Framers of the Constitution," wrote Anthony Lewis in *The New York Times* recently, "the President has the initiative in our system. He acts; Congress reacts. Power is centered in the White House."[16] Andrew Jackson had a great deal to do with the president seizing the initiative and with centering power in the White House.

In restructuring the role of the president, Jackson was no doubt unconsciously taking advantage of a number of important changes that had occurred and were occurring in American society—an expanding economy, for one thing, that had produced a rising democracy with an electorate that demanded a greater say in the operation of their government. Over the last forty or more years the nation had been slowly evolving from a republic, which is what the Founding Fathers thought they had created by their document, into a democracy. The government had always been based on consent, but consent was indirectly given through the legislature. Now, under Jackson, it was being expressed through the executive and supposedly in a very direct manner by national election. For, in his Protest message, Jackson insisted that he had destroyed the Bank not only because it was corrupt and a danger to the liberty of the electorate, but in accordance with "a solemn decision of the American people" expressed in the presidential election of 1832 when they reelected him over Henry Clay in a contest based on the issue of "Bank or no Bank."[17] The people, had expressed their will, and their representative in Washington, namely the president, had carried it into effect.

For Jackson did believe in democracy—participatory democracy. He believed in it with a passion. And by democracy he meant majoritarian rule. "The people are the government," he said, "administering it by their agents; they are the Government, the sovereign power."[18] "*The majority is to govern,*" he announced in his first message to Congress in December, 1829; and he repeated that commitment at every opportunity.[19] He brushed aside what he called "intermediary" agencies that stood between the people and their government—even those deliberately placed there by the Founding Fathers. To the people, he declared, belonged the right "of electing their Chief Magistrate." Not an electoral college which could alter their choice; and certainly not the House of Representatives who, as everyone knew, had altered it when they elected John Quincy Adams in the House election of 1825 because Henry Clay had directed that it should be altered, despite the results of the general election held the previous fall. The people wanted Andrew Jackson for President in that fall election, and had given him a plurality of popular and electoral votes, but the House disregarded their obvious choice and jammed John Quincy Adams down their throats. Such "corruption" could never happen, in Jackson's view, if *popular* election, and no other, determined the selection of the president. "The people are sovereign," he reiterated, "their will is absolute."[20]

Since the people rule and have a right to select their chief magistrate, "let us, then," said Jackson in his first message to Congress, "amend our system" to allow "the fair expression of the will of the majority" to determine who will serve as president. He therefore recommended the passage of a constitutional amendment that would not only eliminate the electoral college, but also reduce the President's tenure to a single term of four or six years. This latter recommendation was intended to place the chief executive "beyond the reach of any improper influences...and that the securities for this independence may be rendered as strong as the nature of power and the weakness of its possessor will admit."[21] Imagine the agony of Watergate that could have been avoided had this proposal been engrafted onto the Constitution. Too often presidents spend much of their first term in office "plotting" (and I use the word advisedly) to win reelection. A single term, such as Jackson advocated, would obviate the need for such activities.

Jackson also advocated the election of federal judges—although he did not propose it formally to Congress. In an interview with George Bancroft, the historian and politician, Jackson explained his position. "He thinks," wrote Bancroft, "*every* officer should in his turn pass before the people, for their approval or rejection. In England the judges should have independence to protect the people against the crown." Not in America, however. "Here the judges should not be independent of the people, but be appointed for not more than seven years. The people would always re-elect the good judges," he said.[22]

It's not that Jackson had such a jaundiced view of judges—after all he was a justice of the Tennessee superior court at one time—as it was his optimistic opinion of the ability of the American people and their capacity for self-rule. He believed them virtuous and politically intelligent. Surely in selecting judges of the Supreme Court, for example, they couldn't do much worse than several of our former presidents have done in the past—for example, the two judges that President Nixon unsuccessfully tried to foist upon the American people.

But in the matter of the right of the Supreme Court to interpret the Constitution, Jackson had very strong and positive views. As I have already stated, he would accept the right of the Court to interpret the Constitution, but not the contention that the Court was the *final* authority on the meaning of that document. He had no problem in recognizing the right of the Court to interpret the *law*, but he insisted that all three branches of government had the right to decide matters of constitutionality, leaving to the people, acting through the ballot box, the final decision as to ultimate meaning. What he was arguing in this matter was the equality of each branch—which is ironic in view of his success in expanding the powers of the chief executive—and the ultimate authority of the electorate. But Jackson could be inconsistent if not contradictory. As Kermit Hall has pointed out in his book *The Politics of Justice*, Jackson "recognized the responsibility of the federal judiciary to settle a host of constitutional issues." For example, he would not sanction the demand of some Democrats to "reform" the lower courts by restricting their jurisdiciton, nor would he allow the repeal of the Judiciary Act of 1789.[23]

But he refused to go to the courts himself regarding the character of abolitionist literature and got promptly entangled in a series of constitutional questions over the freedom of the mails. He believed that abolitionist literature was revolutionary and wicked because it fomented "servile insurrection"—that is, slave against master. Should such literature be allowed to circulate freely through the mails? Jackson asked Congress to address the matter and enact legislation prohibiting the circulation of such material. But Congress refused. Instead, the Post Office Act of 1836 forbade postmasters from detaining the delivery of mail and, as a result, southern postmasters regularly disregarded this legislation and refused to deliver the tracts in the belief that federal authority over the mail ceased at the point of reception. Not until 1857 did the attorney general, Caleb Cushing, decide that a postmaster may refuse to deliver mail of an incendiary character but that it was up to the courts to decide what was and what was not incendiary.[24]

Although Jackson would not go to the courts for a ruling on abolitionist tracts and would not concede the right of the Supreme Court to have the last word on interpreting the Constitution, still he never defied the court—even in the Cherokee cases. As you no doubt remember, Chief Justice John Marshall ruled in the case *Cherokee Nation v. Georgia* that the Indians were "domestic dependent nations," subject to the United States as a ward to a guardian. They were not subject to individual states or state law, as Jackson contended. I might point out here that the Constitution gives no specific authority to the federal government for treating with the Indians, but by the treaty clause it was assumed to have such right. In spite of Marshall's decision that they were "domestic dependent nations in a state of pupilage," the United States until 1871 maintained the legal fiction that the tribes were independent nations. From its first treaty in 1778 to the last in 1871, all 370 treaties signed by the United States, with one exception, maintained the policy that Indian titles to their lands could be extinguished only through treaty with the tribes who were recognized as having a legal claim to the land.[25] As a consequence, the Cherokee Nation refused to submit to Georgia law. Georgia had boycotted these proceedings, refusing to acknowledge the right of the court to direct its actions. Shortly thereafter the Georgia legislature, in late December 1830, prohibited white men from entering Indian territory after March 1, 1831, without a license from the state. This law was aimed at keeping troublesome missionaries from stirring up Indian unrest, and in short order a dozen or so missionaries were rounded up for violating the law. Most of them accepted pardons from the governor in exchange for a promise that they would cease violating Georgia law. But Samuel A. Worcester and Dr. Elizur Butler refused the pardon and were thrown in jail. They sued for their freedom, and in the case *Worcester v. Georgia* the Supreme Court on March 3, 1832, declared that the Georgia law was unconstitutional and issued a formal mandate ordering the Georgia superior court to reverse its decision. The Supreme Court then adjourned.

Since the Supreme Court had adjourned without doing anything but declare Georgia law invalid and ordering the superior court to reverse its decision, there was nothing further for the federal government to do to implement the decision. Not until the Supreme Court either summoned state officials before it for contempt for refusing to obey its order or issued a writ of habeas corpus for the release of the two missionaries could anything more be done. According to the Judiciary Act of 1789, the Supreme Court could issue an order of compliance only when a case had already been remanded without response; and since the court had adjourned and would not reconvene until January 1833 (practically an entire year later), action in the case ceased. Not only was the president under no obligation to act, but there is some question as to whether the Court could itself do anything since the existing habeas corpus law did not apply in this case because the missionaries were being detained by state authorities, not federal authorities. That is one reason why I do not believe that Jackson said: "Well: John Marshall has made his decision: *now let him enforce it!*"[26] It certainly sounds like Jackson. And he was perfectly capable of defying the court. But had he actually used these words, it would have implied that the decision of the Supreme Court was binding on all, including the president of the United States, and Jackson would never have acknowledged such a power. The quotation may indeed convey Jackson's feelings about the Court and its decision in the *Worcester* case, but surely he would never have said anything to suggest the Court's primacy in deciding what was essentially a political question. Rather, Jackson realized that Marshall's decision hung suspended in time, that is, until the superior court of Georgia responded to Marshall's mandate. That's why Jackson wrote to his friend John Coffee: "The decision of the supreme court has fell still born, and they find that it cannot coerce Georgia to yield to its mandate."[27] Actually, no one expected Jackson to do anything because there was nothing for him to do. What needs to be remembered, of course, was that at this very time the crisis with South Carolina over nullification was gathering momentum, and any false move on Jackson's part could trigger a confrontation with Georgia, something the president was desperate to avoid. So he had to act with extreme caution—which he did. Prudence, not defiance, best characterizes Jackson's reaction to the *Worcester* case. As one scholar has observed, Jackson deserves credit for his caution in dealing with a potentially explosive issue and should not be criticized for his supposed inaction.[28]

Eventually the situation was resolved. Jackson convinced the legal counsel for the missionaries and the friends of the Cherokees in Congress that he would not interfere in the operation of Georgia laws. He convinced them that the only solution to the problem was the removal of the Cherokee Nation west of the Mississippi River. Even Justice John McLean, who wrote a concurring opinion in the *Worcester* case, advised the Cherokee delegation in Washington to sign a removal treaty.[29] At the same time, Governor Lumpkin of Georgia was cajoled into pardoning the missionaries. When William Wirt, the legal counsel for the Nation, agreed to make no further motion before the Supreme Court, the governor yielded to the appeals of the administration and on January 14, 1833, ordered the release of Worcester and Butler from prison.[30] The danger of a confrontation with Georgia dissolved and the tragic removal of the Cherokee Nation began in earnest.

Because Jackson was such a unique individual, it is difficult to arrive at hard-and-fast conclusions regarding his performance and contributions as president. He did increase executive power in a variety of ways, and he converted the chief executive into a head of state. He did so with the conviction that he was simply executing the popular will. He had a great knack for labeling *his* will as the popular will. I suppose this is inevitable when you're dealing with strong presidents. He always took charge; because he had a fierce sense of duty, he always insisted that the responsibility was his for whatever action was taken. Indeed, he seemed to revel in this sense of responsibility, and many cartoons at the time invariably had Jackson saying in an overhead balloon, ''I take the responsibility.''

In foreign affairs he scored a number of successes—such as the treaty with Great Britain reopening the West Indian trade, the signing of a number of most-favored-nation treaties with foreign powers, and the payment of spoliation claims by several European nations. Of course, the controversy with France over spoliation was unnecessarily aggressive and combative.

Jackson outlined his general foreign policy at the outset of his administration. In his first annual message to Congress he said that he would ''ask nothing that is not clearly right, and to submit to nothing that is wrong.''[31] But what is interesting and significant, I think, is the attention Jackson paid to the prerogatives of the Congress in foreign affairs. In terminating the difficulties with Great Britain over the West Indian trade, he sought to demonstrate American goodwill in ending restrictions against British ships coming to the United States from the West Indian islands by going to Congress in the spring of 1830 and asking their cooperation. On May 26, 1830, he sent a message to both houses of Congress, explaining to the members that if England agreed to cooperate after Congress had adjourned, he wanted permission to act independently and remove United States restrictions on the basis of a reciprocal agreement. He suggested to Congress the propriety of allowing him to act by proclamation once Britain consented to permit American ships into the West Indies. Congress agreed, Britain consented to reciprocity, and the West Indian trade dispute, going back to the start of the nation as an independent republic, ended.

This is one example of Jackson's respect for the prerogatives of Congress in foreign affairs. Indeed, he sometimes looked to Congress for guidance and direction in pursuing his foreign policy. The Texas matter is a case in point. He desperately wanted to recognize Texas' independence following the Battle of San Jacinto, but he would not do it until Congress took the lead. He realized the risks involved in plunging headlong toward recognition. He appreciated the necessity of acting with the support and approval of the Congress.

In pursuing a policy of demanding nothing not clearly right and tolerating nothing that was wrong, Jackson aimed at winning global recognition of the sovereignty and rights of the United States. "I have no desire to impair the rights or interest of others," he told the foreign ministers in Washington only a month after his inauguration. But by the same token he expected the rights of the United States to be respected. Where differences existed, he said, "I would desire to settle them on the most fair & honorable terms, in that spirit of frankness so congenial with my nature, and the spirit of our government."[32] Which was why he was so hell-bent on demanding payment by foreign countries for the legitimate debts they owed. And, except for the French spoliation controversy that triggered the worst passions in Jackson, he was brilliantly successful in cajoling foreign nations—after years of stalling and hemming and hawing—into acknowledging our claims and paying what they owed. He obtained $12 million in indemnity. And it should be remembered that Europe was very reluctant to acknowledge American rights. This was a republican country, and its successes at home and abroad were seen as destructive to the very foundations of the monarchical governments in Europe.

But perhaps what is most noteworthy about Jackson's importance and impact upon the Constitution was his unique reading of the *nature* of the Union. During the nullification controversy with South Carolina, he issued a proclamation on December 10, 1832, in which he said: "I consider, then, the power to annul a law of the United States, assumed by one State, *incompatible with the existence of the Union, contradicted expressly by the letter of the Constitution, unauthorized by its spirit, inconsistent with every principle on which it was founded, and destructive of the great object for which it was formed.*"[33] This proclamation comes close, contends one modern historian, "to being the definitive statement of the case for perpetuity" of the Union.[34] The United States, Jackson said, existed under the Confederation and was rendered more perfect by the Federal Constitution. The Constitution, he continued, "forms a *government*, not a league," a government in which all the people are represented and which operates directly on the people themselves. A "single nation" having been formed, citizens of the states became American citizens and owe obedience to the Constitution and its laws.[35] Jackson was the first American statesman to offer publicly the doctrine of the Union as a perpetual entity. He was the first statesman to publicly deny the states the right of secession. Abraham Lincoln later extracted from this proclamation the basic argument he needed to explain and justify his intended course of action to meet the secession crisis in 1861.[36]

Jackson's proclamation, written with the assistance of his secretary of state, Edward Livingston, is a major statement in constitutional law. It came about because Andrew Jackson loved the Union fervently, and in his own unique and inimitable way tried to preserve it from those who would deliberately or unwittingly destroy it.

In summation I would submit that the presidential office ballooned to new dimensions under Jackson. The so-called "imperial presidency" begins with him—which is why I have presumed to argue that he is the first modern president. He was an aggressive chief executive, jealous of his rights, who had a vision of where he wanted to take this country. Because of his popularity and control of the Democratic party, he succeeded in accomplishing many of his goals: removal of the Indians, destruction of the national bank, revision of the tariff, elimination of the national debt, and payment of foreign debts owed to this country or its citizens. And, of course, he preserved the Union against the threat of secession and civil war.

His relations with Congress varied with the issues. He had trouble with the Senate until the very end of his administration; and considering the presence of men like Clay, Calhoun, and Webster in the upper chamber, any President was certain to experience a good deal of trouble. On such matters as the Bank and internal improvements, Jackson would not give way to the judgement of Congress or the views of some of his closest advisers, including those in his so-called Kitchen Cabinet; and he used his veto power in a new and creative way to implement his intentions; but in foreign affairs he frequently deferred to the legislature and waited for it to indicate the appropriate direction. As you can see, there were no hard and fixed rules guiding his behavior as President. He was a pragmatic, determined, clever, resourceful, and extremely popular politician who understood and respected the tradition of the past but who also knew when to step outside that tradition and act on his own. As one historian has noted: "Andrew Jackson was simultaneously a harbinger of change and a representative of tradition."[37]

Chapter 3

The Constitution of the Lincoln Presidency and the Republican Era

─────────────────────── *Michael Les Benedict*

Michael Les Benedict's paper makes clear that during the Civil War Abraham Lincoln interpreted Article II of the Constitution as delegating broad powers to conduct the war—commander in chief, executive power, and a presidential oath to "preserve, protect and defend the Constitution of the United States." While some scholars maintain that Lincoln's view resulted in a "constitutional dictatorship," this author calls such claims gross exaggerations. On the contrary, with stimulating clarification, Benedict shows that Lincoln's use of inherent power did not interfere with his conceding to Congress the power to override or control his executive actions. Forrest McDonald at Geneseo praised Benedict's view of Lincoln's moderate and lawful presidency. So did we, except to differ with Benedict on Lincoln's contribution to the presidential legacy. Lowi described Lincoln's contribution to presidential development as a "legacy of mythology." "By 1875," said Lowi, "you would not know there had been a war or a Lincoln." "He was a great, great president," answered Benedict, "by his goals, his achievements of those goals, and by his Constitutional behavior."

In the winter of 1837–38 young Abraham Lincoln was asked to deliver a lecture before the Young Men's Lyceum, the vibrant cultural center of his hometown, Springfield, Illinois. Lincoln was then only 27, an aspiring lawyer only recently admitted to the bar, but—like many ambitious young lawyers—already active in local politics. He chose for his topic "The Perpetuation of Our Political Institutions." Lincoln was worried about a pervasive impatience with the formalities of law, which had been manifested in vigilante and lynch law from one end of the country to the other in 1836 and 1837. There was, he lamented, a "growing disposition to substitute the wild and furious passions in lieu of the sober judgements of courts, and the worse than savage mobs for the executive ministers of justice." Were that spirit to continue,

45

he warned, American constitutional insitutions would be in jeopardy. Lincoln had already seen how the hero-worshiping masses had sustained Andrew Jackson's abuse of presidential powers in pursuit of his wrong-headed policies. Out of continued disorder some worse demagogue could arise, some despot who would promise security to those who feared disorder but who at the same time would appeal to the pride and the passion of the mob. Such a demagogic genius would scorn to accept governmental offices as framed and limited by the founders. "Think you these places would satisfy an Alexander, a Caesar, or a Napoleon? Never! Towering genius. . . scorns to tread in the footsteps of any predecessor, however illustrious. It thirsts and burns for distinction; and if possible, it will have it." To resist the appeal of such a giant, Americans had to reconfirm their commitment to law. "Let every American, every lover of liberty. . . swear by the blood of the Revolution, never to violate in the least particular the laws of the country; and never to tolerate their violation by others. . . . Let reverence for the laws. . . become the *political religion* of the nation. . . ."[1]

In his gloomy peroration, Lincoln articulated the fear of executive power that characterized American Whigs, who, as they saw it, had organized politically to resist the presidential tyranny of "King Andrew" Jackson, just as English Whigs had opposed tyrannical use of monarchical power. American Whigs inherited republican suspicion of executive power, perceiving it always to be the greatest threat to liberty.[2] Lincoln, like other Whigs, saw his suspicions confirmed as Democratic President James K. Polk maneuvered the United States into an unjust war and whipped congressional Democrats into line behind his domestic and foreign policies. As Democratic presidents claimed to represent the American people more directly than members of Congress—"represent[ing]. . . the whole people of the United States, as each member of Congress represents a portion of them," as Polk put it—Whigs complained, "This is not the language of the Constitution," and worried about the "latitude of construction" of presidential powers that have "of late prevailed."[3]

A good Whig president "should desire the legislation of the country to rest with Congress, uninfluenced by the executive in its origin or progress," Lincoln urged his favorite candidate for the Whig presidential nomination, Zachary Taylor. After Taylor received the nomination, he declined to state his position on a variety of controversial issues, insisting they would be decided by Congress. That was the right attitude, Lincoln answered critical Democrats. A president ought to leave policy-making to the people through Congress. That each of the Democratic presidents had combined what ought to be a rarely used veto power "with platforms, and other appliances, as to enable him...to take the whole legislation into his own hands, is what we object to, and is what constitutes the broad difference between you and us," he argued. Democrats "transfer legislation...from those who understand, with minuteness, the interests of the people, and give it to the one who does not, and can not so well understand it."[4]

What an irony it is that historians and political scientists would recognize this young Whig's subsequent presidency as creating broad new doctrines of presidential authority, as establishing "the high-water mark of the exercise of executive power in the United States" up to 1937, that Lincoln has been perceived even to have created a "constitutional dictatorship," acting "in desregard of law and Constitution" in order to save the Union.[5]

Still accepted in the political science literature, the notion that Lincon exercised dictatorial powers is no longer accepted by historians.[6] Contrary to a widely held view, Lincoln did not ascend to a palsied presidency. Democrats had held the office for sixteen of the twenty-four years since the great Jackson had retired, and a strong, independent presidency was a cardinal article of the Democratic faith. It was, as an historian of the presidency titled his chapter on the period, the time of "The Presidency Consolidated."[7] The power of the Jacksonian presidents rested both on their instutitional and political positions. Institutionally, presidents could set the legislative agenda through their annual messages and through the annual reports of their department heads, in which they requested appropriations and legislation to deal with particular problems. Even more important was the position of the president as a party leader. Despite the state-by-state organization of the political parties, presidential elections were what energized ordinary voters and bound them to their parties. Rarely would a local party candidate run far ahead or behind the head of his ticket in presidential elections. Thus their political fortunes were intimately tied to his, providing powerful incentive for local organizations to sustain his programs.[8] Presidential distribution of patronage was crucial to party organization.[9] Most important, mid-nineteenth-century government was party government. As Polk said, "The Democratic party were in a majority in Congress and would be held responsible for whatever was done" with regard to his legislative program as a Democratic president.[10] When a president was able to maintain the unity of his Cabinet, controlling its members' official relations with Congress and their distribution of the patronage, he could exercise immense authority. That was the secret of Polk's success. His administration "succeeded because he insisted on being its center and in overruling and guiding all his secretaries to act so as to produce unity and harmony," one of them remembered. Twenty years later, radical Republican critics would cite the same factors as the basis of Lincoln's powerful influence in Congress. "Congress is a mob—the Admt. a *unit*," Wendell Phillips complained. "Hence its success" in frustrating radical legislative initiatives.[11] Even James Buchanan, remembered for his paralysis in the secession crisis, had been able to force an unpopular pro-slavery program through a recalcitrant Congress and to isolate the most popular Democratic politician in the North—Stephen A. Douglas— through his control of the patronage. His apparent deference to the Supreme Court in the pro-slavery Dred Scott case and his disclaimer of power to resist secession should be understood in light of his general pro-slavery and pro-southern policies. Presidential refusals to act, especially to enforce law, can be among the most devastatingly effective exercises of presidential authority.[12]

Overall, our efforts to understand the mid-nineteenth-century presidency suffer from our lack of information on key points. There has been no general study of the operation of Congress during this period. Therefore, we do not know the degree to which department heads and congressional committees cooperated in devising legislation and whether or not a significant amount of legislation actually emanated from the executive branch.[13] We have had no general study of the patronage system, which was a key element in the relations between president and Congress, as well as the president and his party.[14] We have paid little attention to the degree to which Congress delegated powers to the executive branch, except for the legislation of the Civil War years.[15] Studies of these questions very well might put our understanding of the nineteenth-century presidency in a different light. Nonetheless, Lincoln, facing the greatest crisis in our national history, unquestionably established presidential powers beyond those his predecessors had ever found occasion to claim, and he exercised those powers with a vigor that would not be equalled by any nineteenth-century successor.

From the beginning of the secession crisis, Lincoln perceived a source of power in the simple fact that Article II, Section 3 of the constitution obligates the president to "take Care that the Laws be faithfully executed." He found power, too, in the oath required of the president—its words specified in the Constitution itself—enjoining him "to preserve, protect, and defend the Constitution of the United States." These obligations implied an executive power to take the actions necessary to fulfill them, he argued. He was artfully diffident when he explicated on that obligation in his inaugural address.

Fulfilling these obligations was, in fact, "only a simple duty on my part," that "the Constitution itself expressly enjoins upon me," Lincoln shrugged. The fulfillment of these simple, inescapable obligations could hardly be regarded as a menace.[16] Lincoln's immediate predecessor, James Buchanan, had insisted that he could not counteract secession no matter how much he wished to; Lincoln averred that he could not avoid executing the laws of the United States where he had the power, no matter how reluctant he was to do so. In both cases immense consequences followed from apparently simple statements of duty. Buchanan in effect gave the southerners permission to usurp the authority and property of the national government and to repudiate their obligation to obey its authority; Lincoln promised to enforce national law in the South wherever local residents could be found to fill national offices and where federal authority still ran—meaning Charleston harbor, squarely in the center of which sat Fort Sumter.

When South Carolinians fired on Sumter, Lincoln called a special session of Congress to meet July 4, 1861, ten weeks in the future. As president, authorized and bound by the Constitution and his oath to enforce the laws of the United States, he intended to initiate measures to overcome resistance to their execution himself. What power did he have to undertake the task? First, there was the law for the suppression of domestic violence passed by Congress in 1795 and amended in 1807. Under that law, Lincoln issued a proclamation commanding insurrectionists to disband and calling forth the state militias to suppress resistance to the laws.[17] At the same time Lincoln proclaimed a blockade of southern ports, evidently relying on the fact that the 1807 amendment authorized him to utilize national armed forces, as well as the state militias, to subdue insurrections.[18] But even this was hardly enough to deal with the crisis. As the Massachusetts state militia traveled through Maryland to reinforce federal forces at Washington, they encountered open and guerilla resistance. There was similar resistance in the Florida Keys, still occupied by federal forces. Disloyal men had to be jailed or deported beyond Union lines until the danger was past. Therefore, Lincoln authorized military commanders to suspend the operation of writs of habeas corpus, the process through which people wrongfully imprisoned secure their release, in the northeast corridor between New York and Washington, in the South and contested areas along the border states, and ultimately throughout the nation.[18] Military officers began to imprison active traitors and in some cases those merely suspected of treasonous sympathies. Because there was no necessity to justify these incarcerations to judges, analysts have referred to them as "arbitrary arrests."[20] Finally, Lincoln issued a proclamation expanding the various branches of the army and navy and calling for volunteers to fill the new positions.[21]

While existing congressional laws authorized the president to call up the militia and use national forces to suppress insurrection, it was rather clear that the expansion of the army and navy and the suspension of the writ of habeas corpus went beyond what Congress had contemplated. Many have argued that the proclamation of the blockade also exceeded the power Congress had delegated the president. Did the president have constitutional authority to take such actions in the absence of congressional legislation? The Constitution bars the suspension of the writ of habeas corpus except in cases of rebellion or invasion. That injunction appears in Section 9 of Article I—the article of the Constitution that delineates the powers of Congress. The natural conclusion was that the Constitution authorized Congress and not the president to suspend the operation of the writ. Critics quickly challenged presidential authority, and a petition for the writ was filed with Chief Justice Roger Taney, acting in his capacity as circuit court judge in Maryland, on behalf of one of the state's leading southern sympathizers, John Merryman. Taney, who harbored southern sympathies bordering on disloyalty, issued the writ in the most dramatic way possible, holding that the power to suspend the privilege of the writ of habeas corpus lay with Congress alone. In an astonishing opinion, he went even further, denying that the president had any general authority to suppress resistance to United States laws on his own— ignoring the congressional laws specifically authorizing him to do so. All a president could do was to wait until recalcitrant citizens resisted some specific legal process—a writ, an order, an arrest warrant—issued through the courts. Then, if the courts were unable to enforce their process themselves, they could call on the president for help. "But in exercising this power," the president would be acting "in subordination to judicial authority, assisting it to execute its process and enforce its judgments."[22] Lincoln refused to obey the writ or credit the opinion.

The controversy raised two important constitutional issues. The first was, did the president have the power to suspend the privilege of the writ of habeas corpus without congressional authorization? Second, if the courts ruled that he did not, was he bound to obey their decision? As to the question of the power to suspend the privilege of the writ, Lincoln insisted that he had it. Although the limits on suspension of the writ were placed in the first, largely congressional, article of the Constitution, the language did not specifically state where the authority lay. "As the provision was plainly made for a dangerous emergency, it can not be believed the framers of the instrument intended that in every case the danger should run its course until Congress could be called together, the very assembling of which might be prevented...by the rebellion," Lincoln insisted in justifying his conduct.[23]

Recognizing that Congress might also legislate on the subject,[24] Lincoln in effect claimed a concurrent power. It arose, Lincoln's attorney general Edward Bates made clear, out of the President's constitutional obligation to execute the laws and the oath quoted above. All this, Bates insisted, made the president "in a peculiar manner, and above all other officers, the guardian of the Constitution—its *preserver, protector,* and *defender.*"[25] To carry out those obligations, the Constitution vested in the President "all the *executive power* of the nation."[26] Thus, the clause of Artice I vesting the executive power of the United States in the president was not a mere definition of duties, it was a delegation of positive powers. Moreover, even though there was no "necessary and proper" clause in Article II, as there was in the article that enumerated congressional powers, the power to do whatever necessary to carry out the president's executive functions was implied by the obligations imposed on him. "The end...is required of him; the means and instruments...are lawfully in his hands; but the manner in which he shall use them is not prescribed, and could not be prescribed, without a foreknowledge of all the future changes and contingencies of the rebellion," Bates wrote. "He is...thrown upon his discretion, as to the manner in which he will use his means to meet the varying exigencies as they arise."[27] Although the administration presented this argument to sustain its suspension of the privilege of the writ of habeas corpus, it obviously had a more general application and justified the blockade and the expansion of the army and navy as well.

Despite these constitutional arguments, in his message to the special session of Congress, Lincoln also claimed that these measures were justified by "public necessity," "whether strictly legal or not."[28] That language suggests that Lincoln claimed a presidential power to act beyond the law in response to grave necessities—an "emergency power" in times of crisis. Occasionally Lincoln suggested that the Civil War in general precipitated such a grave emergency that the president could transgress particular constitutional limitations. In defending his refusal to honor Taney's writ of habeas corpus for Merryman, he asked, "Are all the laws *but one* to go unexecuted, and the Government itself go to pieces lest that one be violated?"[29] One could not save the Constitution if the nation itself were destroyed, he insisted. Thus, his oath to preserve the Constitution imposed a primary obligation to save the nation. That oath justified him in doing whatever was necessary to fulfill it. "I felt that measures, otherwise constitutional, might become lawful, by becoming indispensable to the preservation of the constitution, through the preservation of the nation," he explained in a public letter to one Albert G. Hodges.[30] Such language seems to approach the position of those who, like Thaddeus Stevens, argued that the war posed a challenge beyond the ability of constitutional power to meet, that the Constitution served a preexisting nation and could not be permitted to obstruct its preservation.[31] But in fact, Lincoln never took such a position, as will be made clear below.

Lincoln argued this way primarily in political contexts, urging Americans to sustain him even if unconvinced by his constitutional arguments. Thus, after arguing that the emergency could justify suspension of the writ of habeas corpus even in the absence of clear legal authority, he insisted, "But it was not believed that this question was presented. It was not believed that any law was violated," because the Constitution *did* authorize the president to suspend the privilege of the writ.[32] The Hodges letter, too, was prepared for publication and was designed primarily as a political defense of distasteful measures. When the administration was called upon to defend the legality of the blockade in the courts, its counsel made no argument from necessity. Rather, they combined the executive power argument—that the Constitution implied executive power to enforce laws—with a broad interpretation of the laws of 1795 and 1807, arguing that they left the president with discretion, as chief executive and defender of the Constitution, over how to use the forces Congress authorized him to call upon.[33]

Nonetheless, when one combines Lincoln's claim of inherent executive powers and a special obligation to defend the Constitution, his argument that emergencies can justify presidential action beyond what might be "strictly legal," and the Jacksonian position that the president represents the people more directly than does the Congress, one approaches the "presidential stewardship" theory of government espoused most forcefully by Theodore Roosevelt. Like Lincoln, Roosevelt rejected "the view that what was imperatively necessary for the Nation could not be done by the President unless he could find some specific authorization to do it. My belief was that it was not only his right but his duty to do anything that the needs of the Nation demanded unless such action was forbidden by the Constitution or by the laws."[34] The difference was that, by necessity, Lincoln meant something more urgent than Roosevelt, who believed that *necessary* meant little more than useful.[35]

Lincoln's defiance of Taney raises the question of presidential power to refuse obedience to court decisions. Lincoln offered an essentially political, rather than legal, defense in his message to the special, July session of Congress. This was when he asked whether the government had to go to pieces rather than one law be violated. In court, Attorney General Bates justified Lincoln's course with the argument that since "the President and the judiciary are co-ordinate departments of the government, I do not understand how it can be legally possible for a judge to issue a command to the President. . . . " Suppression of insurrection is a political duty, he added. As a political question, it lay beyond the cognizance of the courts. For breach of that political trust, the president was liable "before the high court of impeachment, and before no other human tribunal."[36]

It is not clear how far Lincoln had traveled from the days when he had held obedience to law as articulated by the courts essential to liberty. After the Supreme Court's pro-slavery decisions of the 1850s, his views had become ambiguous, and he had expended a great deal of effort trying to resolve that ambiguity in his debates with Stephen A. Douglas in 1858, without much success.[37] Rather than issuing an order to the president, Taney was content to remit the Merryman case to the political arena, ostentatiously submitting to superior force in declining to order officers of the court to take further steps to execute his process. His Merryman opinion became a staple of the opposition political attacks on Lincoln.[38]

There is no way to know whether Lincoln would have relied on Bates's questionable argument to defy Supreme Court decisions adverse to his interpretation of presidential power. In the *Prize Cases*, in which his authority to proclaim the blockade of the South was challenged, the majority of the justices affirmed that Lincoln did have the requisite authority, although the vague language of the opinion did not specify whether it had been conferred by the laws of 1795 and 1807 or was inherent in what the justices called "the whole Executive power," conferred upon the president "to take care that the laws be faithfully executed."[39] It was up to the president to determine "what degree of force" was required and, the justices affirmed in a direct repudiation of Taney's Merryman opinion, this "is a question to be decided *by him*, and this Court must be governed by the decisions and acts of the political department of the Government to which this power was entrusted."[40]

Naturally, Taney was one of the four justices who dissented from the Court's decision. The warmaking power of the United States resided solely in Congress, the dissenters insisted. All the president's power to suppress the insurrection arose out of the laws of 1795 and 1807, and neither these laws nor any inherent executive power conferred a general war power upon him. In language that applied as much to suspension of the privilege of the writ of habeas corpus as to confiscation of ships running a blockade, the dissenters avowed, "Congress alone can determine whether war exists or should be declared; and until they have acted, no citizen of the States can be punished in his person or property, unless he has committed some offence against a law of Congress . . . which made it a crime, and defined the punishment."[41]

In 1863 the potential for conflict between the Supreme Court and the president arose again, as the great Peace Democrat Clement L. Vallandigham challenged the right of a military commission to try him for inciting opposition to the government. The judge advocate general of the army argued that the Constitution and laws governing the Court's appeals and habeas corpus jurisdiction did not confer power to decide the case. Since the Court agreed, the question of obeying its writ never arose.[42] Not until 1866, after Lincoln had died, did the Supreme Court discover an instance in which the president had exceeded his constitutional authority. In *Ex parte Milligan* the justices unanimously decided that the president had no inherent power to authorize military trials of civilians, even where and when the privilege to secure a writ of habeas corpus was suspended; a bare majority held that even Congress lacked power to authorize such proceedings, except where the ordinary courts were closed by war or rebellion.[43] But since the decision coincided with the political interests of the new president, Andrew Johnson, there was no danger he would defy it.

However, Johnson made clear that he would not concede authority to the courts directly to control his actions, even when they coincided with his political preferences. When southern state officials asked the court to enjoin the president from enforcing the Reconstruction laws, which he himself opposed, Johnson's administration denied the Court's power to control the political action of a coordinate branch of government, in much the same language that Bates had used on Lincoln's behalf: "The President of the United States is above the process of any court or the jurisdiction of any court to bring him to account as President. There is only one court or *quasi* court that he can be called upon to answer for any dereliction . . ., and that is not this tribunal but one that sits in another chamber of the Capitol"—that is, the Senate acting as a court of impeachment.[44] Making this argument in *Mississippi v. Johnson,* the president's counsel hinted forcefully that Johnson would refuse to obey any such injunction,[45] but the majority of the justices avoided the potential confrontation. Refusing to concede that the president was beyond any Court process, especially one involving a purely ministerial duty, the justices agreed that it would be inappropriate to enjoin presidential enforcement of a law upon an allegation of unconsitutionality, and they seemed to indicate that the courts could not formally restrain presidential action through an injunction in any case.[48]

The result of Lincoln's defiance of Taney, the Supreme Court's reluctance to challenge him during the war, and its decision in *Mississippi v. Johnson* was to suggest broad power in the president to act on his own conception of presidential duty and authority, free from formal judicial constraints. They provide welcome precedents for modern presidents who for reasons of state, politics, or personal interest, have also considered whether to resist court decisions.[47]

Separate in theory from Lincoln's inherent executive power to assure enforcement of national law, but inevitably confused in superficial analysis, was his authority as commander in chief of the armed forces under Article II, Section 2. Like Washington and Polk before him, Lincoln played an extremely active role in devising military strategy, determining promotions, and controlling the distribution of forces and commands.[48] But he went far beyond this. As commander in chief, Lincoln claimed general authority to make rules governing the military itself, to establish procedures for governing occupied Confederate territory, to promulgate regulations for carrying on trade through southern lines, to suspend the operation of the writ of habeas corpus throughout the United States, to control the process by which state governments would be restored in rebel territory, and even to decree emancipation of all slaves behind rebel lines.[49] Most of these activities were, on their face, legislative. Some, such as the power to make rules governing the armed forces, are explicitly delegated to Congress in the Constitution itself. Others, such as the emancipation of slaves, had been conceded by nearly everyone to have been beyond the authority of any branch of the national government. In exercising such broad authority, Lincoln effected, in the words of Edward S. Corwin's standard study, "a complete transformation in the President's role as Commander-in-Chief."[50]

In his claims to inherent executive authority, powers implied by his obligation to execute the laws and defend the Constitution, and war powers as commander in chief, Lincoln set precedents for presidentail power that remain potent today. His activities and legal justifications are regularly cited in the standard analyses of presidential power.[51] But did he set precedents for the exercise of what the great political scientist Clinton Rossiter called "constitutional dictatorship"? In making that judgment Rossiter adopted the Webster's Dictionary definition of dictator: "one...exercising...absolute authority in government."[52] "Absolute authority," of course, means authority from which there is no appeal and of which there is no control.

Anyone truly familiar with the Lincoln presidency must reject the notion that Lincoln exercised this kind of authority. First, even when making their boldest claims for presidential immunity from judicial process, Lincoln's legal representatives acknowledged his amenability to impeachment for abuse of power. But beyond this, unlike present-day advocates of inherent presidential powers, Lincoln never claimed that they operated to limit powers the Constitution had expressly delegated to Congress.[53] Although the Constitution delegated some powers to the president rather than to Congress, especially the power to supervise military operations as commander in chief, Lincoln's resident expert on the war powers, Solicitor of the War Department William Whiting, made clear, "The power of Congress to pass laws on the subjects expressly placed in its charge by the terms of the constitution cannot be taken away from it, by reason of the fact that the President...also has powers, equally constitutional, to act upon the same subject-matters."[54] Thus, when he addressed the special session of Congress called to deal with the outbreak of the rebellion, Lincoln acknowledged its ultimate authority over the steps he had taken, trusting, he said, that Congress would ratify them, which it did.[55] He left "entirely to the better judgment of Congress" whether to enact legislation controlling the suspension of the privilege of the writ of habeas corpus,[56] and when Congress did so in 1863, he followed the terms of the act. His administration cooperated with the Joint Congressional Committee on the Conduct of the War, which by questioning strategy, tactics, and assignments of commanders trenched most closely upon authority the president could claim for himself alone. Yet Lincoln never once claimed an executive privilege to withhold information from it.[57]

Even in the area of Reconstruction, where Lincoln and the Republican congressional majority differed most radically on policy, he never denied Congress's final authority. He did refuse to sign the Wade-Davis Reconstruction Act, thus preventing it from becoming law through what is known as a "pocket veto." But the Constitution expressly delegates to the president that share in the legislative power. In a proclamation explaining the reasons for withholding his signature on the bill, Lincoln made no suggestion that he considered it beyond congressional authority. Rather, he explained that he did not wish to commit himself to any single plan, and especially that he did not want to set aside the free state constitutions and governments already established under his auspices in Louisiana and Arkansas.[58] Indeed, the latter objection amounted to a clear concession that a congressional law would have superseded his own authority over Reconstruction as commander in chief of the armed forces.

In the maneuvering over Reconstruction that followed, Lincoln did his best to secure the Reconstruction program he wanted from Congress or, alternatively, to forestall congressional agreement on any legislation at all. But he never denied Congress's constitutional power to pass legislation if a majority of its members could arrive at a consensus. It was Lincoln's political success at preventing congressional Republicans from arriving at such a consensus, rather than any claim of exclusive constitutional power over Reconstruction, that led Henry Winter Davis to lament, "Congress has dwindled from a power to dictate law and the policy of the Government to a commission to audit accounts and appropriate moneys to enable the Executive to execute his will and not ours."[59]

Likewise, Lincoln claimed only a concurrent power with Congress to emancipate the slaves of rebels. Congress had acted by prohibiting military officers from returning runaway slaves to their owners and by making slaves liable to confiscation.[60] But owners could still seek to recover runaway slaves through legal process, while, as James G. Randall made clear in his classic study of constitutional issues in the Civil War, the Confiscation Act was fatally defective in its failure to provide any court enforcement procedures.[61] After a delay of more than a year, Lincoln concluded that slavery constituted so powerful a strategic resource for the South that he was justified as commander in chief in proclaiming the emancipation of all slaves behind rebel lines.[62] But this was hardly a denial of congressional authority. In fact, Lincoln drew specific attention to prior congressional legislation in his preliminary emancipation proclamation.[63]

What Lincoln did deny, both to himself and to Congress, was the power to decree abolition of slavery as an institution, as distinguished from the emancipation of the slaves of rebels. As Whiting pointed out, there was a "distinction between emancipating or confiscating slaves, and abolishing the laws which sustain slavery in the Slave States." Whiting illustrated the point as follows: "If all the horses now in Massachusetts were to be confiscated, or appropriated by government to public use, though this proceeding would change the legal title to these horses, it would not alter the laws of Massachusetts as to personal property; nor would it deprive our citizens of the legal right to purchase and use *other* horses."[64]

In Lincoln's view, confiscation and emancipation of the slaves of rebels was a legitimate use of both his war power and that of Congress. But abolition of slavery itself went beyond the war power and thus beyond the powers delegated to the national government by the Constitution. In his Reconstruction program, Lincoln went as far as he believed he could to eliminate slavery permanently. In return for amnesty, he required rebels to take an oath to obey the Emancipation Proclamation, and he vowed to recognize state governments restored under his Reconstruction program only if they "in nowise contraven[ed]" that oath.[65] But he could not simply decree that new state constitutions had to include provisions abolishing slavery, and when Congress included such a provision in the Wade-Davis Reconstruction Act, Lincoln specifically denied its power to do so.[66]

The reason for Lincoln's tortuous distinction between abolition and emancipation was his commitment to the federal system. Lincoln was among our country's greatest nationalists. His articulations of American nationality are among the classics of our political and constitutional literature. Yet, like most mid-nineteenth-century Americans, he had a more rigid idea of a separation between state and national power than we have today. Throughout the war, Lincoln struggled to limit the constitutional implications for federalism of the broad powers both he and Congress were exercising. He constantly drew attention to the difference between the nation's war powers and its authority in peacetime. The very necessity to maintain that distinction limited what he and Congress could do in wartime and how they coud do it. Thus, when General Benjamin F. Butler proposed to have the residents of occupied Norfolk, Virginia, vote on whether to proceed with a program of municipal improvements, Lincoln ordered him to desist. Butler might justify a wide range of municipal improvements on military grounds—"the cleansing of the City necessary to prevent pestilence in your army," for example. "But you should do so on your own avowed judgment of a military necessity, and not seem to admit that there is no such necessity, by taking a vote of the people on the question. Nothing justifies the suspending of the civil by the military authority, but military necessity. . . ."[87] When Secretary of the Treasury Salmon P. Chase complained that Lincoln had applied the Emancipation Proclamation only to slaveowners behind enemy lines, Lincoln responded that to apply it within Union lines, "must I not do so, without the argument of military necessity. . .? Would I not give up all footing upon constitution or law?. . .Could it fail to be perceived that without any further stretch, I might. . .change any law in any state?"[68]

None of this suggests a claim or exercise of dictatorial power. On the contrary, Lincoln was solicitous of constitutional law and congressional prerogative. Not so his successor, Andrew Johnson. Like Lincoln, but to a much greater degree, Johnson pursued policies, centering on Reconstruction, that differed from those desired by a majority of congressmen. Like Lincoln, he claimed inherent presidential power to carry his policies into effect. But *unlike* Lincoln, and *like* more recent presidents, Johnson insisted that the existence of a presidential power served to *limit* congressional power. The president as commander in chief had *exclusive* power to govern the South and reestablish state governments there, Johnson claimed. As an incident to that power, he and not Congress could determine what changes would be instituted in southern law and society. Thus what led to the crisis of Johnson's impeachment was not—as standard political science texts state—a "reaction against the executive,"[69] but rather a new claim of exclusive presidential powers that went far beyond what Lincoln ever proposed. Moreover, to sustain that claim Johnson utilized presidential powers in such a way as to frustrate the enforcement of congressional legislation that had passed over his veto, again something that Lincoln never had attempted. Of course Johnson lost his struggle (although one might attribute the ultimate failure of Republican Reconstruction to his intransigence). He barely escaped removal upon impeachment, and the southern states were restored to the Union on Congress's terms, not his.[70]

Analysts of the presidency have referred to the years that followed as a period of presidential "authority in abeyance," "congressional government," and even "the hegemony of the Senate."[71] But to a large extent what they describe is merely a return to normal after the abnormal years of the Civil War and Reconstruction. During the crisis, both the president and Congress had expanded their reach dramatically.[72] Afterwards, both subsided.

When Ulysses S. Grant became president, he intended to remain above party. At the same time he conceded final authority over policy to Congress. "I shall on all subjects have a policy to recommend, but not to enforce against the will of the people," he explained.[73] At first, Grant provided hardly more leadership to his Cabinet than he did to Congress. Each was expected to take charge of his own department and carry out its responsibilities independently, and even to decide how to fill government positions—that is, whether to honor the traditional patronage system or to reform the civil service by establishing a more neutral system of appointment and removal.[74]

However, it quickly became clear that the government could not operate effectively in the absence of presidential leadership both of government and party. In the absence of such leadership, Republicans divided bitterly over Reconstruction issues, civil service reform, and tariff reform.[75] By 1870 the party began to suffer from the drift, and all sides demanded that Grant unify his Cabinet and exert his influence. Grant finally responded, changing the Cabinet, firming his party's position on most of the issues, and using his power over the patronage to strengthen and regularize state and local Republican political machinery. As a direct consequence, dissident Republicans in 1872 bolted the party to nominate a rival Republican presidential candidate, in a struggle, as one of their leaders described it, of *Republicanism vs. Grantism*.[76] Although Grant's power really was based on a reciprocal alliance between himself and Republican party leaders, opponents attributed it to his power over patronage. "He does not mean to be a despot but he wants to have his will. Such is the character of his personal government," a leading dissident Republican characterized Grant's administration.[77]

Grant's opponents complained about his abuse of presidential power—especially his use of the patronage to sustain Republican political "machines," his effort to force through the Senate a treaty to acquire sovereignty over Santo Domingo (now the Dominican Republic), and his intervention in southern election disputes. His successor, the reformer-backed Republican Rutherford B. Hayes, promised to abandon Grant's practices. But in fact Hayes, too, was a potent president. On his own authority he promulgated a regulation barring federal office-holders from holding party positions—thus undermining the political machines which opposed him.[78] He appointed to key patronage positions enemies of party leaders and forced their confirmations through the Senate over their objections.[79] He ended Republican Reconstruction in the South by withholding the protection of federal troops from beleaguered southern Republicans.[80] Yet Hayes he did send troops to quell violence during labor conflicts, matters traditionally well within state jurisdiction.[81]

Moreover, when the Democratic-controlled Congress sought to remove Hayes's discretion over the use of troops to enforce federal law, he stoutly resisted. In a bitter constitutional and political confrontation, he vetoed the Army Appropriation bill of 1879 rather than acquiesce to an amendment barring use of the army where elections were being held. Hayes insisted that it was essential that he have access to military force to enforce federal laws. Democrats tried to coerce him to sign the measure by refusing to provide funds for the army without it. Hayes stood firm. Coercing a president to approve legislation by threatening to withhold essential appropriations threatened the president's constitutional role in the legislative process, he insisted. With Republican congressmen successfully sustaining Hayes's vetoes, the Democrats had to give up.[82] President Garfield and the Democrat Grover Cleveland won similar confrontations.[83] No post–Civil War president repudiated Lincoln's claims of presidential power; they repudiated Johnson's, which had exceeded Lincoln's.

Observers disagreed about the power of the presidency in the 1870s and 1880s. Woodrow Wilson, frustrated at the inefficiency of American government compared to European models, complained of the inability of American presidents simply to set policy and secure congressional acquiescence.[84] But other analysts saw things differently. Henry Jones Ford, in his *Rise and Growth of American Politics* concluded that "from Jackson's time to the present day...political issues have been decided by executive policy."[85] Some even urged abolition of the office to save American liberty.[86] Most accurate probably were the ambivalent observations of such observers as the great constitutional jurisprudent Judge Thomas McIntyre Cooley and the English political anaylst James Bryce, who recognized both the presidency's potential and the restraints imposed by an equally powerful Congress.[87]

Most of all, the presidency remained the focal point of American politics. Despite the disastrous administration of Andrew Johnson, Congress never did successfully reverse the presidents' claims to represent the American people as a whole. Therefore, the president remained the paramount leader of the American governmental system. Grant, Hayes, Garfield, and Cleveland all harnessed that power at crucial moments of their presidencies. The resources of the office were there. All that was required was a confident and resolute politician to exercise them.

Chapter 4

The Constitution of the Theodore Roosevelt Presidency and the Progressive Era

———————————— William H. Harbaugh

William Harbaugh's paper concentrates on the constitutional expansion of presidential power under Theodore Roosevelt, noting, however, that such growth must be understood in the context of executive branch development of the prior McKinley presidency and the subsequent Taft and Wilson presidencies; and in relationship to the growth of congressional, judicial, and business power. Harbaugh also notes that the increase of executive power was most pronounced in foreign affairs; that indeed Theodore Roosevelt stamped his imprint on foreign policy with a force equalled by few peacetime presidents and was exceeded by only a few wartime presidents. The author describes Roosevelt's attempt to establish a new administrative state—à la antitrust enforcement—as only partially successful. Harbaugh is both critical and understanding of the Roosevelt presidency. McDonald, in his observations of Harbaugh's papers (and those of Hawley and McCoy) suggested that the two Roosevelts and Truman were as often manipulated as well as being manipulators. Critic Lowi agreed with Harbaugh that the growth of the T. Roosevelt presidency must be put in the context of congressional and business growth. In fact, commented Lowi, there was probably a "net shrinkage" of presidential growth during the T. Roosevelt presidency. To both critics Harbaugh reiterated his paper's manifestations of Roosevelt's presidential growth, and charmingly suggested that Forrest McDonald "stay in the eighteenth century."

This paper reviews aspects of the growth of executive power in the Cleveland and McKinley administrations, then focuses on its continued expansion under Theodore Roosevelt. A final section treats developments in the administrations of William Howard Taft and of Woodrow Wilson prior to American entry into World War I. The underlying assumptions are these: the growth of presidential power should not be viewed in isolation from the growth of congressional and judicial power and, especially, private economic power; the expansion of federal regulatory commissions embodied a conscious effort by all three Progressive Era presidents—Roosevelt, Taft and Wilson—to create a new administrative state.[1]

Late Nineteenth Century Developments

The extraordinary growth of federal power outlined in these pages began with the creation of the Interstate Commerce Commission in 1887 and continued for a century thereafter under strong and weak presidents, dominant and submissive congresses, broad and strict constructionist judges. Always, of course, politics, personality, and philosophy affected the particulars. Some presidents inclined more, and some inclined less, to independent action; some congresses and some presidents were more solicitous than others of their own or the states' prerogatives; some Supreme Court cases lent themselves more readily than others to arrogation of power by the judiciary. Nevertheless, the conclusion is inescapable: almost every president, including anticentralists like Cleveland and Taft, pursued a constitutionally expansive course during these years; both Congress and the Supreme Court frequently acquiesced in the chief executive's expansive policies. The action of the Cleveland administration during the Pullman Strike of 1894 and the response of the judiciary to that action are illustrative.

Determined to assure movement of United States mail and interstate commerce generally, President Cleveland dispatched federal troops to the scene of the strike just outside Chicago. He did so over the vehement protest of the governor of Illinois and in spite of the implication in Article IV of the Constitution that federal power should be invoked against domestic violence only on the request of the state legislature or governor. Cleveland believed that he faced a national emergency. He further believed, or at least his attorney general believed, that the Supreme Court's ruling in *Neagle* four years earlier gave the president implied powers to defend the "peace of the United States."[2]

The case which grew out of the Pullman affair, *In re Debs*, resulted in a sweeping affirmation of federal power. In words that failed to mention Article IV even as they acknowledged the dual nature of the American system, Justice David J. Brewer held that, within the limits of its enumerated powers, the federal government possessed "all the attributes of sovereignty, and, in the exercise of those enumerated powers, acts directly upon the citizen, and not through the intermediate agency of the state."[3]

William McKinley, a stronger and more purposeful figure than most historians have recognized, further expanded the power of the presidency. A few observers perceived this at the time. "In the legislative branch of the Government," wrote one, "it is the executive which influences, if it does not control, the action of Congress; while the power originally vested in the executive alone has increased to an extent of which the framers had no prophetic vision." This was notably true of foreign affairs, where McKinley set patterns of conduct that persist to this day.[4]

Expansion began with a clear, though hardly unprecedented, circumvention of the Constitution following the Senate's failure to ratify an annexation treaty with Hawaii: successful exertion of pressure on Congress to annex the islands by joint resolution. Unwilling on the end of the Spanish-American War to turn over colonial matters to Congress and lacking clear precedents in any event, McKinley then used his war powers to formulate as well as to execute colonial policy. This not only gave him what Secretary of War Elihu Root described as "an enormous and arbitrary power over Spanish islands," it effectively reduced Congress's role to that of a ratifying body.[5]

McKinley's dispatch of troops to Peking during the Boxer Rebellion of 1900 to protect the American legation and otherwise advance the United States interests graphically demonstrated the new accretion of executive power and corresponding diminution of congressional power. As Arthur Schlesinger observes in his *Imperial Presidency*, the action more or less marked the beginning of the twentieth-century practice of deploying American troops abroad in peacetime against foreign governments, as distinguished from private groups such as the Barbary Pirates. So expansive, indeed, did the president's role in foreign policy become under McKinley that then Professor Woodrow Wilson substantially modified his theory of congressional supremacy in reaction to it. When foreign affairs become dominant, Wilson wrote in 1900, the "Executive must...utter every initial judgment, take every first step of action, supply the information upon which it is to act, suggest and in large measure control its conduct." McKinley, he asserted, was then "at the front of affairs, as no president, except Lincoln, has been since the first quarter of the nineteenth century."[6] Against this background, Theodore Roosevelt became president of the United States on September 14, 1901.

The Square Deal and Executive Power

Roosevelt's first annual message to Congress testified eloquently to his evolutionary conception of law and society. "When the Constitution was adopted, at the end of the eighteenth century," he wrote, "no human wisdom could foretell the sweeping changes, alike in industrial and political conditions, which were to take place at the beginning of the twentieth century. At that time it was accepted as a matter of course that the several States were the proper authorities to regulate, so far as was then necessary, the comparatively insignificant and strictly localized corporate bodies of the day. The conditions are now wholly different and wholly different action is called for."[7]

By the turn of the century, the revolution in communications had made New York closer to San Francisco in some respects than it had been to Philadelphia when the Constitution was framed. By then, too, the forces of centralization had penetrated all but the most remote reaches of society and had begun to reshape all major institutions: commerce, industry, and labor; the larger religious denominations; rural, urban, and higher education; federal, state, and local government. Centralizing tendencies were strongest in industry and commerce. By 1904, the year Roosevelt won a term in his own right, six business groups controlled 95 percent of the nation's railroad mileage, and in 1909, the year he left office, corporations produced 79 percent of all the country's manufactured goods. As the president later said, "Centralization has already taken place in the world of commerce and industry. All I ask is that the National Government look this fact in the face."[8]

From the beginning of his presidency, Roosevelt comported himself as a kind of national steward. Early in the winter of 1902 he startled the business community by instituting antitrust proceedings against the Northern Securities Company, a huge railroad combine recently organized by the Hill-Morgan and Harriman-Loeb interests. He designed to test the virtually defunct Sherman Anti-Trust Law, signal his independence of Republican congressional leaders, and affirm the power of his office. He further conceived that the threat of dissolution might swing the business community behind his nascent plan for continuous regulation of large corporations. Six months later an industry-wide coal strike prompted Roosevelt to break precedent by intervening on the side of the striking miners. In the process, he came close to expanding the executive power far beyond conventional, and probably constitutional, limits.[9]

Concluding in the summer of 1903 that a bitter, five-month-long strike in the anthracite fields threatened an acute shortage of fuel that winter, and fearful that this would provoke an urban crisis "only less serious than the civil war," Roosevelt devised an ingenious strategy to prevent it. He arranged for the governor of Pennsylvania to request him to send in federal troops, then ordered the commanding general to prepare to have the troops seize the mines. The seizure plan rested upon the same implied or inherent power theory of the Constitution that some of Brewer's bald assertions in *Debs* apparently rested upon. But it also encompassed a wholly different matter: deprivation of private property under the Fifth and Fourteenth Amendments.[10]

Roosevelt himself was unclear of his constitutional ground. He believed that the common-law doctrine which allowed peasants to "take" wood in severe weather gave the public "rights" in the matter, yet he shared the doubts of Elihu Root and Attorney General Philander Knox that he had a "constitutional duty" to intervene in any way. Conceding that seizure would set an "evil precedent," he nonetheless concluded that the "emergency" was so grave that he must respond "as if we were in a state of war." Had management not decided to negotiate on learning of his intentions through a planned leak, he undoubtedly would have called out the troops.[11]

Roosevelt was never comfortable with his own inference that his war powers justified the seizure. He preferred to believe that the president possessed inherent powers in time of peace as well, and within the year he was describing the episode without reference to the Consititution. "Being for the moment the head of the nation," he wrote, "I obeyed the supreme law of duty to the republic in acting as I did."[12]

By 1913, when Roosevelt wrote his *Autobiography*, he formulated a constitutional doctrine—the stewardship theory—to justify his comportment, both actual and contemplated, in the Anthracite Strike. His intervention, he insisted, accorded with the Jackson-Lincoln theory of the presidency. That is, when great national crises call for "immediate and vigorous executive action," it becomes the duty of the president "to act upon the theory that he is the steward of the people, and ... that he has the legal right to do whatever the needs of the people demand, unless the Constitution or the laws explicitly forbid him to do it."[13]

The concept of stewardship reached to the essence of Roosevelt's political, social, and personal character. Philosophically, Roosevelt was both an absolutist and a pragmatist. He was obsessed with ultimate ends—especially "justice," about which he spoke with extraordinary certainty—and he did not regard process, including Constitution-ordained process, as an inviolable principle. Years before he became president, he warned against "attempting to establish invariable rules," and by the time he left that office the phrase "we should try this to see if it works" had become a virtual refrain. A nation, he insisted, "must be governed to the actual needs and capacities of its citizens, not according to any abstract theory or set of ideal principles."[14]

Predicably, Roosevelt regarded power creatively. He took great satisfaction in exercising it, and on a few unhappy occasions he abused it. "I don't think," he wrote shortly before he left the presidency, "that any harm comes from the concentration of power in one man's hands provided the holder does not keep it for more than a certain, definite time, and then returns to the people from whom he sprang." Few students of his career would challenge John Blum's statement that he, especially, "may have benefited from the limits on Presidential power which men who understood the problem in 1787 created." Yet neither would they deny that Roosevelt's compulsion to use power in what he conceived to be the public interest was one of the great sources of his strength.[15]

Roosevelt's feeling for power, along with his almost mystical attachment to "the people," virtually foreordained his strident support of centralized government. Gouverneur Morris, he had written in a biography of the Founding Father published in 1888, his thirtieth year, "championed a strong national government, wherein he was right; but he also championed a system of class representation, leaning toward aristocracy, wherein he was wrong." Other passages commended Morris for his clear-cut vigor in asserting that "state attachments and state importance had been the bane of the country."[16]

Nowhere, either in the work on Morris or in his hundreds of speeches and voluminous writings, did Roosevelt address specifically the Tenth Amendment's disposition of those powers not delegated to the federal government. His preferred reading of that Amendment—and this is an inference, though surely not an unreasonable one—emphasizes the phrase that assigns the undelegated powers "to the people" rather than the portion of the same sentence that assigns them "to the states." Roosevelt praised those who, like Hamilton, Washington, and Marshall, supported James Wilson's doctrine that "the National Government, representing all the people, should have complete power to act." And he derided those who cloaked their opposition to federal social or regulatory legislation in the mantle of states' rights. As he noted in a speech at Harvard in 1907, "There has been a curious revival of the doctrine of State rights. . . by the people who know that the States cannot with justice to both sides practically control the corporation and who therefore advocate such control because they do not venture to express their real wish, which is that there shall be no control at all."[17]

Roosevelt was no more disposed to interpret the First Amendment's protection of freedom of speech literally than he was to give an absolutist construction to the Constitution's references to states' rights. He believed, to be sure, that "it is a great deal better to err a little bit on the side of having too much discussion and having too virulent language used by the press." Yet he insisted that "freedom does not mean absence of all restraint," and he often challenged the right of anarchists and less extreme radicals to speak out. His celebrated attack on the Wilson administration's Sedition Act of 1918 was directed at a clause prohibiting criticism of public officials, not at its strictures against disloyalty. Shortly before leaving the presidency, moreover, Roosevelt sued the Pulitizer news interests for statements about his role in the acquisition of the Panama Canal Zone. "To my mind," wrote the federal district judge who dismissed one set of the resultant indictments, "that man has read the history of our institutions to very little purpose who does not look with very grave apprehension upon the possible success of a proceeding such as this." Or, as the editors of Roosevelt's *Letters* more plainly put it, a government victory "would. . . in the opinion of many men at the time and since, have placed the freedom of the press in jeopardy."[18]

All this was not without its ironies. As two recent studies of presidents and the press conclude, Roosevelt strove to control the press in his own political interest. But partly because he believed that an "enlightened and aroused" public opinion was essential to regeneration of the republic, he greatly increased the flow of information. He established a press room in the White House, cultivated friendly reporters, banished those who crossed him, and spoke with "incredible frankness" in carefully managed interviews.[19]

Roosevelt found the First Amendment's guarantee of religious freedom considerably more congenial than its provision for freedom of speech. He silently disapproved of the authoritarian structure of the Roman Catholic Church, and he openly asserted that parochial schools impeded Americanization. Yet he understood that religious conflict was incomparably more disruptive than religious diversity, and he pragmatically concluded that pluralism would best serve national unity. Thus he said in 1906 of a proposal, fostered by anti-Morman interests in Utah, to ban polygamy by constitutional amendment: "Nothing helps a creed so much as a foolish and futile persecution." Attacks during the campaign of 1908 on the Unitarianism of William Howard Taft, his chosen successor, forced Roosevelt to reflect directly on the constitutional issue. To require Taft to clarify his religious beliefs, the President wrote privately, "is to negative the first principles of our Government, which guarantee complete religious liberty, and the right to each man to act in religious affairs as his own conscience dictates." Reluctant to alienate "the bigoted, narrow-minded, honest," evangelicals from Taft during the campaign, Roosevelt said nothing publicly until after the election.[20]

Roosevelt's pragmatic, evolutionary strain also led him to conclude that judges made law. A decade before he came out for the recall of state judicial decisions in 1912, he was writing that "a layman who thought soberly" was competent to pass judgment on constitutional decisions because, at bottom, they should "express some public policy as well as law." The difference between Marshall and Taney had been "not in the technical propriety of their interpretation of law, but in their wisdom in what was really creating law." One reason "a wise court" would not put the Constitution in a straight jacket was the difficulty of formal amendment. It was essential, accordingly, that the Court itself provide for "growth and adjustment" through its decisions.[21]

This view of the Constitution as an organic body and of the Supreme Court as a policy-making institution gave Roosevelt's judicial appointments a distinctively political cast, despite his insistence that "high character,...good sense,...legal ability, and...broad-mindedness" were his first criteria. The chief justice, he wrote shortly after entering the White House, "should be not merely a learned lawyer but a constructive statesman." Remarking a few months later that Oliver Wendell Holmes' pro-labor decisions in Massachusetts strengthened his candidacy for an associate justiceship, Roosevelt added that he would like nonetheless to know whether Holmes was in "entire sympathy" with the views of his administration. "I should hold myself as guilty of an irreparable wrong to this nation if I should put in his place any man who was not absolutely sane and sound on the great national policies for which we stand in public life." Roosevelt was even more specific when Horace Harmon Lurton was under consideration. Lurton, the president explained to Elihu Root, "takes just the attitude we take as regards to the control of corporations, the checking of labor people when they go wrong, the right so to construe the constitution as to permit us properly to manage our insular affairs, and the propriety of the National Government doing what it can to secure certain elementary civil rights to the Negro."[22]

Although Roosevelt confined his heady appeal for the recall of judicial decisions during the Bull Moose Campaign to state courts, he obviously hoped to influence the federal judiciary. He referred repeatedly to Lincoln's attitude toward the Dred Scott decision. He noted that the Fourteenth Amendment had been applied "to a multitude of cases to which it is positive the people who passed the amendment had not the remotest idea of applying it." He observed that "no popular vote could reverse an earlier popular vote more completely than [did] ... the Supreme Court in the Legal Tender Cases and the Income Tax Cases." And he shrewdly reminded his audiences that he did not propose to make the legislature supreme as it was in England, Canada, Australia, and France. He further confounded the issue by calling the apparent tendency of state courts to overrule acts of the legislature, such as the New York State Workmen's Compensation Law, "a monstrous perversion of the constitution into an instrument for the perpetuation of social and industrial wrong and for the oppression of the weak and helpless." His purpose, he maintained in the face of enormous criticism, was to "make legislature and court alike responsible to the sober and deliberate judgement of the people, who are masters of both legislature and courts."[23]

Nowhere in government had the centralizing trends of the era kept pace with those in business. The intellectual authority of the Tenth Amendment's reservation of power to the states militated against legislation that impinged on states' rights, and the courts zealously defended their own prerogatives in any event. Not until 1886, for example, did the Supreme Court clear the way for Congress to confront railroad problems by ruling that states could not regulate interstate commerce directly. Nine years later, on the same day it ringingly affirmed one kind of national power in *Debs*, the Court declared in the Knight Sugar Trust Suit that the Sherman Antitrust Act of 1890 did not apply to manufacturing. This sharply inhibited the McKinley Administration, which instituted a total of three antitrust proceedings in four and one-half years. It also inhibited the Roosevelt administration, the new president's dramatic strike against the Northern Securities Company in 1902 notwithstanding. Only after the Court found in the beef trust case in 1905 that the "stream of commerce" allowed manufacturing to be regulated could the administration undertake antitrust action on a large scale.[24]

By the end of his presidency, Roosevelt had instituted more than forty antitrust proceedings. Yet he never regarded the Sherman Act as a viable means of controlling any but the most flagrant monopolies. Even as he revitalized the Sherman Law and strengthened the presidency in the process, he defended the economic advantages of large-scale organization. From his early months in office he urged upon Congress continuous regulation of big business by independent professional experts. A first imperative was knowledge and the right to obtain it. "It is no limitation upon property rights or freedom of contract," Roosevelt asserted in his first annual message, "to require that when men receive from government the privilege of doing business under corporate form...they shall do so upon absolute truthful representations as to the value of the property in which the capital is to be invested." A year and one-half later the president virtually forced reluctant Republican congressional leaders to create the Bureau of Corporations.[25]

Roosevelt quite understood, as the devolution of the Interstate Commerce Commission into little more than a statistic-gathering agency proved, that knowledge was not enough. "The early ICC," writes Stephen Skowroneck, "had been caught between the vitality of the electoral-representative system on one side and the vitality of judicial discipline on the other. A congress geared to guarantee the particular interests of all contending factions, coupled with a Supreme Court that had no patience for ambiguity in the delegation of legislative power to an administrative tribunal, stifled efforts to implement a Progressive theory of regulation and left the government with nothing new to offer in resolving the conflicts of the marketplace."[26]

In these circumstances, Roosevelt made reconstitution of the Interstate Commerce Commission the centerpiece of his legislative program, following his election to a full term in 1904. Specifically, he sought to win authority for the Commission to set maximum railroad rates subject to narrow, rather than broad, judicial review and to have the Commission's ruling go into force immediately, rather than after prolonged review. This, Roosevelt explained to Congress, was necessary in order to keep the great highways of commerce "open to all on equal terms." He added that Congress should not be deterred by philosophic objections to big government, for national supervision was the only means by which "an increase of the present evils. . .or a still more radical policy" could be prevented.[27]

In essence, Roosevelt was asking for a return of the power claimed by the ICC in 1887 but denied by the courts for almost two decades. As incorporated in the Hepburn Bill, his general recommendations passed the House overwhelmingly early in 1906. When, however, the measure reached the Senate, progressive Republicans tried to strengthen it and conservative Republicans to weaken it. This forced Roosevelt to take the offensive. By feinting and threatening, advancing and retreating, appealing to the public and cooperating with the opposition, he got a bill that left open the matter of broad or narrow review. But in so doing he hastened his slide into "lame duck" status. More significant still, if Skowroneck is correct, he "turned the regulatory debate into a constitutional test of wills over how the prerogatives of the executive, the legislature, and the judiciary were to develop in the new American state."[28]

Enactment in 1906 of two other regulatory measures—the Pure Food and Drug Bill and the Meat Inspection Amendment to the Agricultural Appropriations Bill—rounded out Roosevelt's legislative record. No major bills became law during his last two and one-half years in office, though he urged the need for a comprehensive federal regulatory program in speech after speech, and message after message. All inter-state business should be put under federal supervision, he told Congress in December 1907. "Centralization in business...cannot be avoided or undone, and...the public at large can only protect itself...by providing better methods...of control...."

The pure-food law was opposed so violently that its passage was delayed for a decade; yet it has worked unmixed and immediate good. The meat-inspection law was even more violently assailed; and the same men who now denounce the attitude of the National Government in seeking to oversee and control the workings of interstate common carriers and business concerns, then asserted that we were 'discrediting and ruining a great American industry.'[29]

Many sophisticated business interests agreed that revision of the antitrust laws was desirable. The House of Morgan, among other Wall Street offices, quietly supported Roosevelt's proposal to authorize the Bureau of Corporations to pass on mergers in advance. Smaller interests, such as those represented by the National Association of Manufacturers, feared however that "reasonable" restraints of trade would accelerate the rise of mammoth corporations like United States Steel, and business in general opposed Roosevelt's plan to provide effective regulation through government administrative agencies. As an analysis of the president's effort to revise the Sherman Law in 1908 concludes, "Roosevelt's view of the national interest and the need to keep a balance between the ideal and the reality was broader than that of the groups attempting to influence the pending legislation."[30]

The New Administrative State: Success and Failure

Roosevelt's program to regulate commerce and industry was but one part of his design for the new administrative state. His larger objective was to refashion all branches of the federal government into rational administrative units with independent executive controls. In addition to his rich practical experience, he brought to this task familiarity with the writings of ideas and most of the leading students of administration. Not surprisingly, as Skowroneck concludes, by the end of his presidency he had emerged as "the premier state builder of his age." Yet, for reasons that plagued his predecessors and successors alike, he failed in the end to consolidate his considerable achievements.[31]

As the struggle over the railroad and meat inspection legislation suggests, Roosevelt not only strove to inhibit the power of the courts, he sought to professionalize administration generally by supplanting men beholden to political parties or private interests with disinterested experts. His animating perception was the need to match the nation's administrative capacity to its economic and political capacity in the interest of "a more orderly system of controls." This required a career civil service grounded on merit, and to that end Roosevelt prevailed on Congress early in his administration to increase the Civil Service Commission's appropriation to the point that it could act as a true supervisory body. Then, in "gag" orders of 1902 and 1906, the president prohibited civil service employees from lobbying in their own behalf. Meanwhile, he used some of the political capital generated by his resounding victory in the election of 1904 to induce Congress to transfer the Forest Service from the General Land Office in the Department of Interior to the Department of Agriculture. This removed it from domination by lawyers accustomed to facilitating the movement of public lands into private hands to professional foresters prepared to manage the lands in the long-term public interest.[32]

The resultant vitalization of the Forest Service led to a bitter showdown between the president and Congress and, after Roosevelt left office, indirect affirmation of the stewardship theory by the Supreme Court. G.O.P. leaders had always resented Roosevelt's "accidental" ascendancy to the presidency. More important, a great many congressmen from both parties also resented his exuberance, his undisguised love of power, and his propensity to use the White House as a pulpit. On regulatory policies, it is true, Congress had divided more or less along traditional economic lines. But as Roosevelt's tenure lengthened and he came increasingly to act on the stewardship theory, policy conflicts tended to blur into institutional and personal conflicts. A bitter battle in 1907 prompted by the president's determination, as he later phrased it, to save sixteen million acres of forest lands "for the people...before the land-grabbers could get them," is illustrative.[33]

Responding to pressure from western business interests and resentful of the professionalization of the Forest Service and the administration's withdrawal of public lands from private entry under flimsy pretexts, Congress stipulated in 1907 that no forest reserve should be created thereafter in Oregon, Washington, Idaho, Montana, Colorado, or Wyoming. The stipulation took the form of an amendment to the Agricultural Appropriations Bill, a measure the president had to sign because funding for the Agriculture Department and all its subordinate agencies, including the Forest Service, depended on it. At the instance of Chief Forester Gifford Pinchot, Roosevelt withheld his signature for ten days while the Forest Service prepared papers to create twenty-one forest reserves in the six states affected. Then, just before signing the Appropriations Bill, the president formally proclaimed the new reserves.[34]

Roosevelt's cavalier remarks about the episode in his *Autobiography* demeaned both the political and constitutional issues. "The opponents of the forest service turned handsprings in their wrath," he wrote, "and dire were their threats against the Executive; but the threats could not be carried out, and were really only a tribute to the efficiency of our action." In truth, he was somewhat more sensitive at the time to the constitutional and other issues. "If I did not act...and if Congress differs from me in this position," he explained in a posterity memorandum, "it will have full opportunity in the future to take such position as it may desire." Congress, of course, took no further action, though both it and the Supreme Court did face the withdrawal question again during Taft's presidency.[35]

Transfer of the Forest Service from Interior to Agriculture had been a rare administrative advance. In 1905, on the urgent counsel of Bureau of Corporations Director James Garfield, Roosevelt formed the Commission on Department Methods, commonly known as the Keep Commission. The manner of its creation virtually guaranteed conflict. The president appointed the Commission without consulting Congress, bound its members to secrecy, and directed that it report directly to him. As one senator asserted, Congress regarded the Commission as a form of "executive encroachment" that threatened to make it "the victim of a bureaucratic advance to power." Angrily, in 1909, it rejected all of the Commission's recommendations, including those for centralized purchasing, creation of a national archives, and a government-funded pension system for public employees.[36]

By then the administration was grinding to an acrimonious conclusion. During the Panic of 1907, Roosevelt had acquiesced in the absorption of the Tennessee Coal and Iron Company by United States Steel. Four members of a Senate subcommittee to investigate whether the president had violated the Sherman Antitrust Law subsequently stated that he had lacked authority to authorize the merger. Others pointed out that he had simply stated that he would not "interpose any objection." No formal report was ever issued, though an important development occurred. In the course of its investigation, the subcommittee requested the head of the Bureau of Corporations to produce confidential information which had been voluntarily submitted by United States Steel. Asserting that the law creating the Bureau of Corporations provided that only the president could make public such information, Roosevelt directed that a portion of the documents be withheld on the ground that they had no bearing on the subject matter of the investigation. "I...told him [the chairman of the Judiciary Committee] they would not be given to the Senate, that I could not be forced to give them, and I did not see why they should make any effort to get them unless they were prepared...to have me impeached." The significance of this action, as Schlesinger concludes, is that it extended to domestic affairs the long practice in foreign policy of withholding from Congress limited amounts of information.[37]

Congress skirmished with Roosevelt almost to his last day in office. It refused to allow him to assign Secret Service agents to the Department of Justice for antitrust investigations. (Roosevelt charged that "congressmen themselves did not wish to be investigated," whereupon the House resolved that his special message on the Secret Service should be considered an invasion of its privileges.) Congress flouted the president's plan for carefully controlled development of electric power sites. It directed the secretary of the treasury to report all disbursements from the president's emergency fund. It refused to appropriate funds to publish the report of the Country Life Commission. Finally, it forebade the president to appoint commissions of inquiry without specific authority of Congress. "I replied to Congress," Roosevelt recalled, "that if I did not believe the Amendment to be unconstitutional,...and that if I remained in office I would refuse to obey it."[38]

Foreign Affairs

Many of the same forces that spurred centralization of the economy and civil government helped expand presidential power in foreign affairs. To be sure, control of foreign policy by the executive had long been the tradition in Europe, and partly to forestall such a development in America, the Founding Fathers had empowered Congress rather than the executive to declare war, raise and support an army and navy, and punish "offences against the law of nations." The Fathers had further specified that the Senate participate with the President in the making of treaties. But some of these safeguards had quickly fallen into disuse. In 1794, for example, the Senate refused to discuss the Jay Treaty with President Washington. It also allowed many administrative matters to be handled by executive agreement, a much more convenient and flexible device than treaties. Nonetheless, it bears emphasizing that it was the war against Spain and its colonial aftermath which prompted the first great transformation in the making and conduct of foreign policy.[39]

As for Roosevelt, no function of executive leadership fascinated him more than the conduct of foreign affairs. He accepted without reservation the responsibilities that were thrust upon him, and he gloried in the opportunities for national expression afforded by the United States' emergence as a world power. He acted with impetuosity and restraint, with bluster and sensitivity, with belligerence and with accommodation; and he acted always to advance the national interest as he conceived it. In so doing, he stamped his imprint on American foreign policy with a force exceeded by only a few wartime presidents and equalled, perhaps, by no peacetime president. He engaged in covert diplomacy backed by force or the threat of force. He used the executive agreement to formulate major policies. He sent American troops to Cuba. And he made a unilateral pronouncement in the manner of President Monroe. Concurrently, he interjected the Unites States self-consciously into European power politics. He took an assertive interest in the Pacific and parts of the Far East. He modernized its army and expanded the battle fleet. He facilitated negotiation of peace between Russia and Japan. And he extended a measure of self-government to the nation's new colonial dependencies.

Many of these policies rested constitutionally on the stewardship theory. But they also reflected Roosevelt's fervent conviction that self-defense was the first imperative of organized society, that the interests of advanced nations took precedence over those of backward peoples, and that a great power had a Kipling-like obligation to support the onward march of civilization. There was also a psychological component. More than once in the 1880s and 1890s Roosevelt had called for war in the ill-concealed hope that he might lead troops in battle, and as late as June 1897, four years before he became president of the United States, he wrote: "No qualities called out by a purely peaceful life stand on a level with those stern and virile virtues which move the men of stout heart and strong hand who uphold the honor of their flag in battle."[40]

In power, Roosevelt's realism and sense of responsibility softened the application of these values substantially. He continued, of course, to hold himself ready to invoke force in defense of the national interest; his maxim, "speak softly and carry a big stick," accurately characterizes his conduct of diplomacy with the great powers, if hardly the small ones. Moreover, his conception of the national interest became progressively more enlightened. He abandoned the notion that a far-flung empire was the hallmark of greatness even as he strengthened the United States' world position. He admitted an oriental country— Japan—into that privileged group of "superior" nations sanctioned to dominate the world. He repressed his near-obsession with glory. And he worked industriously to foster world peace, supporting a permanent court of international justice and even experimenting with compulsory arbitration.

Roosevelt's total performance was not without flaws. Some were compounded, furthermore, by his defiant language after the fact. In 1903, for example, he acquired the Panama Canal Zone under circumstances that raised grave doubts about the propriety of his methods. "Here again," he wrote in words similar to those he used to dismiss attacks on his conservation program, "there was much accusation about my having acted in an 'unconstitutional' manner...and 'usurped authority'—which meant, that when nobody else could or would exercise efficient authority, I exercised it."[41]

That same year Roosevelt took a first, tentative step toward formulating the "Roosevelt Corollary" to the Monroe Doctrine by secretly persuading Germany to halt military action against Venezuela for nonpayment of debts. (Afterwards, he rejected a German proposal for collective action in the future.) Fearful, two years later, that conditions in debt-ridden and revolution-wracked Santo Domingo would induce intervention by other European nations, he set forth the principles of what became known as the Roosevelt Corollary. "Brutal wrongdoing, or an impotence which results in a general loosening of the ties of civilizing society, may finally require intervention by some civilized nation," he said. "In the Western Hemisphere the United States cannot ignore this duty." Eleven months later, following discussions with Senate Republicans and the Democratic minority leader, Roosevelt arranged by protocol for the United States to take over Santo Domingo's customs office. The protocol failed twice to muster the necessary two-thirds majority of the Senate, and in the interim Roosevelt maintained control of the customs through what was, in effect, an executive agreement.[42]

By then, to paraphrase Schlesinger, the executive agreement was rushing into its own. Roosevelt had no compunction about acting on his personal conclusion that the United States should promote stability in the Far East, and in the summer of 1905 he strained his executive authority to the uttermost by having Senator Cabot Lodge and Secretary of War William Howard Taft, on separate visits to London and Japan respectively, pledge the United States to silent partnership in the Anglo-Japanese Naval Alliance. Although these arrangements were not binding legally, their import was clear: on the word of its president and without knowledge of its people, the United States government had agreed to act in concert with Great Britain and Japan in the event of a crisis in the Far East. Japan, Taft explained to Prime Minister Taro

Katsura, could count upon his government "quite as confidently as if the United States were under treaty obligations." Not until 1925, and then inadvertently, did this extraordinary circumvention of the treaty-making power become public.[43]

The most ironic and most far-reaching aspect of this new Anglo-American-Japanese accord was American recognition of Japan's suzerainty in Korea. Roosevelt further eased tension between the United States and Japan over California's discrimination against the Japanese with the famous face-saving "Gentlemen's Agreement." Meanwhile, he dispatched the American battle fleet around the world without consulting Congress. This prompted the chairman of the Naval Affairs Committee to threaten to withhold funds for supply en route. The president replied that he had enough money to get the fleet to the Pacific, that it would definitely go to the Pacific, and that it could then stay in the Pacific. "There was no further difficulty about money," he recalled.[44]

Yet even as the world cruise trumpeted the burgeoning of American power, Roosevelt perceived the limits of that power. In November 1908, with the fleet still on the high seas, Secretary of State Root and Baron Kogoro Takahira exchanged notes implicitly recognizing Japan's economic ascendancy in Manchuria. Two years later, perturbed by President Taft's attachment to "dollar diplomacy," Roosevelt sent his successor two compellingly realistic letters. The first urged Taft to abandon commercial ambitions in Manchuria and China in return for Japanese concessions on immigration. The second warned that to wage "a succesful war about Manchuria would require a fleet as good as that of England plus an army as good as that of Germany." It added that, although the "'open door' policy in China was an excellent thing..., it completely disappears as soon as a powerful nation determines to disregard it, and is willing to run the risk of war."[45]

Legacy

Roosevelt believed that, "in however small a way," his own presidency had been in the tradition of Washington and Lincoln. He further believed, as he phrased it in a valedictory letter to the British historian, George Otto Treveleyan, that effective government required a strong central executive and "a general recognition of the moral law." (He made no mention of constitutional restraints.) "I have felt...that...in showing the strength of, or in giving strength to, the executive, I was establishing a precedent of value....I believe in power; but I believe that responsibility should go with power, and that it is not well that the strong executive should be a perpetual executive."[46]

The continued growth of the executive under Presidents Taft and Wilson suggests that Roosevelt had in fact enlarged the precedential base for a strong presidency. As the earlier expansion of presidential power by Cleveland and McKinley suggests, however, the role of precedents is difficult to assess. The controlling assumptions of this paper, to wit, that the expansion and centralization of government were essentially, though not invariably, a reaction to centralizing developments in commerce, communications, and industry, implies that precedents were more apt to serve as a president's rationale of easiest convenience than as his energizing force. The conclusion, for example, that Roosevelt sent troops into Cuba in 1906 because of the precedent set by McKinley during the Boxer Revolt is an exercise in logic rather than history. So, too, the notion that Roosevelt's intervention in Cuba prompted Taft and Wilson to intervene elsewhere in the Caribbean. Yet, that having been said, the feeling persists that the cumulative actions of Roosevelt and his predecessors did influence Taft, Wilson, and their successors imperceptibly.

The matter also has its paradoxical aspects. Although both Taft and Wilson respected constitutionalism in ways that Roosevelt did not, both presided over marked expansions of presidential authority. Like Roosevelt, each sought stability in the Caribbean for essentially defensive reasons. But Taft, in particular, was enamored of the region's commercial possibilities, and partly on that account he fostered a policy of "dollar diplomacy" reinforced by the United States Marine Corps. Wilson's secondary purpose was more noble: the creation, or as some prefer, the imposition of democratic governments. Nonetheless, he continued Taft's support of a notoriously undemocratic regime in Nicaragua. As Wilson's eminent biographer, Arthur S. Link, observes, he also intervened elsewhere in Latin America "on a scale that had never before been contemplated."[47]

Two domestic episodes speak directly to the conflict inherent in Taft's and Wilson's concern for the separation of powers and the expansion of executive authority which their administrations actually fostered. In contradistinction to Roosevelt, Taft insisted that presidential power must "be reasonably and fairly traced" to a specific or "justly implied" grant of power by the Constitution or act of Congress. "There is no undefined residuum of power which he can exercise, because it seems to him to be in the public interest," he said in 1916 in a barely veiled attack on Roosevelt's stewardship theory. Taft had long nurtured reservations about the legal basis of Roosevelt's conservation program, especially, as he insisted, the withdrawal of lands from entry "beyond legal limitations." Rather than resort to pretexts, as Roosevelt had done through Gifford Pinchot, Taft asked for and received express authority from Congress in 1910 to withdraw lands. Five years later, in the *Midwest Oil Case*, the Supreme Court found, in effect, that the withdrawals by Roosevelt and others were constitutional and that the law passed at Taft's behest was unnecessary. Noting that the practice of withdrawal of public lands dated to the early years of the republic, the Court concluded that this long history gave weight "to the usage itself." It acknowledged that the executive cannot "by his course of action create a power," but it insisted that government was "a practical affair intended for practical men" and that, "by implication," Congress could grant a power to the executive to administer the public domain.[48]

The year after *Midwest* and three years after Roosevelt set forth the full stewardship theory in his *Autobiography*, Wilson almost brought the wheel full circle. In spite of his opposition until 1916 to federal child labor, rural credits, and other social and economic measures, Wilson was somewhat more a centralist than the juxtaposition of his New Freedom with Roosevelt's New Nationalism implies. Like Roosevelt, he conceived law organically, but unlike Roosevelt, he was strongly sensitive to due process. He once said, indeed, that Roosevelt's defiance of Congress's intent by creating sixteen million acres of forest reserves in 1907 was his "most arrogant single assertion of presidential power." By and large, Wilson's own first administration was marked by successful exertion of pressure on Congress. The prewar climax came in 1916 when, to avert a general railroad strike, Wilson persuaded Congress to grant a general wage increase in the guise of a reduction of hours to eight per day. He believed, as Roosevelt had believed in 1902, that seizure might be necessary; but unlike Roosevelt, who had assumed that he already had the power to seize, Wilson asked Congress for an express grant of power. He also requested authority to draft railroad managers and employees into the army. Congress readily approved the eight-hour principle, but it let both the seizure and draft proposals die. Then, three months before the United States entered the World War, a sharply divided Supreme Court upheld Congress's right to regulate wages, but only as an incident to its obligation to maintain railroad operations under the commerce clause.[49]

Meanwhile, for different reasons, Taft and Wilson failed to perpetuate the executive-professional coalitions that had been the crown of Roosevelt's administrative vision—and this despite the creation of a host of executive agencies including the Federal Trade Commission, Tariff Commission, Federal Law Board, and Federal Reserve Board. Taft, working through the Republican Old Guard, had tried to reconcile the new bureaucratic powers with a relatively static conception of the

Constitution. Wilson, more than either Roosevelt or Taft, set the modern pattern of agencies dividing allegiance between political philosophy and professionalism.[50]

Chapter 5

The Constitution of the Hoover and F. Roosevelt Presidency During the Depression Era, 1930-1939

————————————————————— Ellis W. Hawley

Ellis Hawley's paper describes the continuity and discontinuity of the constitutional development of the presidency in the 1930s. While the personality of FDR contributed much to that presidential growth, a more important explanation was the set of economic and social conditions that led a generation impressed by some past-managerial executive branch successes to demand major alterations. Yet the "political culture" continued to equate American constitutionalism with freedom and thus constrained presidential growth. Hawley traces the search for proper constitutional development of the presidency through five stages: the Hoover period; the 1st New Deal; the constitutional crisis period, 1935-37; the stage of executive reorganization, 1937-39; and the beginnings of a new security state, by 1939. Forrest McDonald, at Geneseo, had cautioned that while the twentieth century presidents under scrutiny, including Hoover and Franklin Roosevelt, were strong manipulative presidents, they themselves were frequently manipulated. Theodore Lowi agreed heartily with Hawley's assessment of the corporatist and managerial tracks of presidential growth in the 1930s, and the forms of change that had not previously been evidenced in presidential office. Hawley expressed appreciation for Lowi's agreement with his paper's assessment of the constitutional development of the presidency in the 1930s. He thought McDonald's "manipulator/manipulated" views of the presidency were too simplistically put.

For both the American Constitution and the American presidency, the years of the Great Depression, from 1930 through 1939, were an important period. For the Constitution they were important not only for the changes they brought, for what some scholars have called a "constitutional revolution," but also for its successful weathering of forces that destroyed constitutional government in a number of other nations. And for the presidency they were important for analogous reasons. For it, too, they brought major changes in powers exercised, functions performed, and resources available, changes that went along with those in the Constitution and were related primarily to the use of the office to create and set in motion the administrative machinery needed for a greatly enlarged regulatory and social service state. Yet a presidency restrained by a constitutional government of divided powers and intricate checks and balances did survive, a fact of considerable importance to the nation's future development and one especially noteworthy in a time when such institutions were under attack as being unsuited to the needs of modern nations.

To a degree, this mixture of change and continuity can be attributed to the personalities of the men who held presidential office during the period. Each had ideas about the Constitution and the presidency that helped determine the kinds of action taken, and each had personal traits that could render such action more effective or less so. These are matters that we shall note in more detail later. But the major emphasis in what follows is on the institutional problem created by the depression and the implications that the various efforts to solve that problem had for constitutional law and for constitutionally grounded constraints on presidential action. This is a story, it will be shown, that involved both Herbert Hoover and Franklin D. Roosevelt, and it is one that was central to the period's constitutional concerns and debates. Although at times these did encompass such issues as executive privilege, ceremonial behavior, and presidential power in the foreign policy sphere, they tended overwhelmingly to revolve around questions raised by the presidentially led search for new institutional formations capable of improving economic performance and meeting the demands for new social services.

It is this story, then, that I shall attempt to reconstruct and understand. In doing so, I want to focus first on the problem itself and the legal obstacles standing in the way of projected solutions; secondly on the successive efforts to solve it, noting the constitutional issues these raised and what was done about them; and finally on the mixture of change and continuity that had emerged from this process by 1939. In addition, I hope to convey some sense of the constitutional crisis that accompanied the economic one, of how differing perceptions of the work of the Founding Fathers were invoked in the ongoing debates, and of what the outcome meant for the subsequent course of American constitutional and presidential history.

The great national problem of the 1930s, as the historians Alfred Chandler and Louis Galambos have pointed out, was essentially one of faulty economic coordination.[1] It was a problem, in other words, of a malfunctioning set of markets and regulators that in their workings were leaving much of the labor force idle, much of the nation's productive capacity unutilized, and much of the American population living near or below the poverty line. According to classical economic theory, this was not supposed to happen; and one response to the problem was to stick with the theory, blame the situation on tamperings with the free market, and see the depression conditions as the inevitable results of a self-correcting process. Such a response, some would now say, should have been the one of all Americans. But this was the 1930s, not the 1890s. Perceptions of the problem had been strongly colored by the belief that industrial societies could develop and deploy capacities for economic and social management, a belief that seemed to be borne out by the nation's experience in World War I and by managerial successes in a variety of lesser arenas. And it was managerial solutions that quickly came to the fore, solutions, in other words, that would alter the workings of existing markets and regulators through the creation of new kinds of social and political machinery and the assignment to these of a part of the coordinative task.

The managerial solution eventually embraced would be an American version of the administrative state, empowered to create and enforce a new body of regulatory law and to administer an enlarged array of agencies engaged in providing public goods and services. But in the early 1930s this was not the obvious solution that it may now seem. At least three others were in the picture, and it cannot be fully understood without noting them. One was an associative or corporative state that would draw the needed social machinery from the group life and power centers of the private sector, using if necessary a degree of governmental power to do so. The notion that this could be done had developed a considerable following in the 1920s, and in the early 1930s was being attached to agitation for suspending or relaxing the antitrust laws.[2] Another solution with strong supporters was an emergency state, drawing administrative and programmatic resources from the private sector on a temporary basis and then giving them back when the emergency had passed. The model here was the World War I experience, the assumption being that the forces causing coordinative failure were analogous to those of a defeatable enemy causing temporary distress.[3] And still another solution was the localistic state, recognizing the need for new social machinery but seeking to provide it through new local or community agencies that presidential organizations might equip with a national outlook and induce to act as units in a national system.[4]

One major question, then, was how to go about erecting the new social machinery that seemed to be needed. Another was whether any of these managerial solutions could be carried out while preserving the restraints upon government imposed by the Constitution. The Framers, after all, had had no reason to envisage the needs of an industrial nation for managerial machinery. What managerial insights a few of them did have were confined to commerce, banking, and monetary policy.[5] And hence, it could be argued that they never intended for the American government to have a national managerial apparatus or to be involved in creating one. It could also be argued that sound legal reasoning applied to the words of the Framers had long since closed off the possibility of finding bendable or stretchable provisions that would allow a constitutional form of national economic and social management to be established. Standing in the way by 1930 were the doctrines of substantive due process, liberty of contract, dual federalism, and limited reach of the commerce power, all of them firmly established doctrines that tended to equate the preservation of constitutional liberties with the preservation of the existing system of economic coordination. And finally, it could be argued that the kind of governmental structure we had chosen to preserve our liberty, one of independent branches and divided powers was simply incompatible with these managerial designs, that it could not survive the kinds of power unification and concentration that were necessary to carry them out.

With these arguments, some proponents of the designs were in essential agreement, the result being that advocacy of them was sometimes accompanied by calls for remaking the Constitution or by attacks on constitutionalism itself. In the eyes of some, the rule of law would have to give way to the intelligent and flexible discretion of responsible directing minds.[6] But the more common view among advocates of a new managerial apparatus was that it could be constructed and made to work within a framework of continuing constitutional constraints grounded in the document written in 1787. One line of argument held that the Framers had built into the Constitution the powers needed to cope with future exigencies, particularly the means whereby fragmented power could be fused and residual power activated when national necessities demanded governmental action. These powers could be inferred from certain sections of Articles I and II.[7] A second and to some extent overlapping line of argument insisted that workable constitutions had to be living and growing documents capable of being adapted to and serving the legal needs of a nation's changing economic and social order. Behind this lay the legal outlooks that, by 1930, had become associated with sociological jurisprudence, legal realism, and judicial pragmatism. And building on this second line was a third, one that pointed to the potential for adaptation and growth in court rulings that had upheld a growing area of federal regulation, administrative lawmaking, and intervention to alter market-produced social outputs. The real need, it was said, was for resourceful and imaginative interpreters of the law, not for a new Constitution.[8]

It was within the context of these two ongoing debates then, one about managerial solutions and methods and the other about their constitutionality, that America's two depression presidents undertook the twin tasks of meeting new national needs and preserving as they did so the foundations of national liberty. Their methods and personal capacities would differ, as would their ideas about what the completion of these tasks required. But both recognized a need for action that had implications for the role and functions of the presidency and for the constitutional framework in general; and both, despite the allegations of their critics to the contrary, considered themselves constitutional presidents acting in ways that would preserve the foundations upon which American liberty rested. The mixture of change and continuity to be found in the transition from one to the other is part of the larger story of change and continuity with which we are concerned. And it is to their presidential activities having a bearing on this that we now turn.

The man occupying the White House in 1930, Herbert Clark Hoover, has traditionally been categorized as one of the "weak" presidents who interpreted the powers of his office narrowly, embraced laissez-faire economic prescriptions, and stood stubbornly against the emergence of a "positive state" resting on a new constitutional jurisprudence.[9] This is a view that is now being revised in works dealing with the Hoover presidency.[10] But before proceeding to what has been established in the revised view, it should be noted that the traditional view was not entirely in error. Hoover's thinking about government did contain a strong libertarian component, which saw liberty being preserved in part by arrangements that kept governmental power divided, kept the branches of government independent and coordinate, and kept government out of areas where it lacked and could not hope to develop competence. This was most explicitly stated in *The Challenge to Liberty*, a book expressing alarm about the tendencies of the New Deal.[11] But that Hoover held such views earlier seems evident from his reluctance to provide legislative leadership during the special session of Congress that he called in 1929, his reluctance to expand the federal regulatory power into new spheres, and his concern about judicial quality and independence when using his power to fill vacancies on the Supreme Court.[12] His record on these matters was consistent with his later claim to have viewed the "constitutional division of powers" as "the bastion of our liberties" rather than "a battleground to display the prowess of Presidents."[13]

This is not to say that Hoover was a "weak" president in the sense of being dominated by Congress or turned into someone else's puppet. He used the veto or threat of a veto to shape legislative output, most notably in the cases of the Agricultural Marketing Act of 1929, the Tariff Act of 1930, and the Relief and Construction Act of 1932.[14] He defended established executive prerogatives, notably in rejecting the Senate's request for confidential documents relating to the London Naval Treaty and in maintaining successfully that it could not take back its confirmation of appointments to the Federal Power Commission.[15] And while he seemed not to enjoy the ceremonial and social duties of the office, he resisted the idea that they should be curtailed.[16] But if he was not weak in these respects, he did not see himself as lawgiver, power accumulator, governmental expansionist, and tribune of the people in the sense that the nation's "strong" presidents have. His constitutional scruples and political philosophy kept him from doing so; and reinforcing them, one suspects, were personal traits and experiences that made him ill suited for the roles of legislative, party, or democratic leader. He lacked the political skills needed for these roles, tended to view this lack as a virtue rather than a defect, and had risen to prominence as the builder of businesslike economic and civic organizations rather than as a politician forging workable coalitions or a mass following.[17]

As recent scholarship has shown, however, Hoover's fears of the modern administrative state coexisted with a belief that the workings of the "invisible hand" of classical economics could be improved upon by developing institutions with managerial and regulatory capacities.[18] For him the answer to faulty economic coordination lay not in a managerial or regulatory state, but in a further extension and elaboration of the businesslike economic and civic organizations that he had been associated with in both his private and public careers. The needed national machinery, in other words, was to be drawn chiefly from the private sector; and the proper role of a government concerned with the maintenance of liberty was to assist in coaxing it forth, getting it established, and keeping it in operation. Economic forces, Hoover kept saying, could not be controlled by legislation. But "forward movement" could be organized and coordinated in ways making for a continuation of "progress" and, as the nation's leader, the president should be concerned with this kind of organization as well as with the organization of executive agencies. "By his position," Hoover told the

Gridiron Club in late 1929, the president "must, within his capacities, give leadership to the development of moral, social, and economic forces outside of government which make for the betterment of our country."[19]

In practice, moreover, the Hoover presidency did make strenuous and repeated efforts to develop the kind of extragovernmental machinery that could correct economic defects while preserving existing constraints on government. At the macroeconomic level, it helped to set up and gave its blessings to coalitions of business corporations and associations acting together to sustain consumer and investment spending.[20] At the micro level, it sought to bring appropriate forms of associational organization to such problem areas as agriculture, transportaion, banking, and the natural resource industries.[21] As another part of its organizational activities, it also created agencies working to stimulate appropriate forms of community organization and local governmental action.[22] And in conjunction with these organizational endeavors, it established a wide array of presidential commissions and study groups, the theory being that these would provide the informational and analytic base that would allow the machinery to work as intended. As Hoover explained it to the press, these commissions were needed only partly to make recommendations to Congress. The real need for them, the greater need, was to give proper guidance—or to allow the president to give proper guidance—to the development of forces outside of government. They were to be the intelligence agencies, in other words, for what Hoover called the "highest form" of self-government, a "self-government outside of government" that could act both as a safeguard of liberty and an initiator and forwarder of progress.[23]

Hoover had few doubts about the constitutionality of these kinds of action. The organizational endeavors, as he saw them, would help to preserve the governmental structure that the Framers had seen necessary to protect fundamental liberties; and in defending his creation and use of special commissions, he offered a line of argument similar to that of Theodore Roosevelt back in 1909. The right to create such agencies, he implied, rested on the rights of the president to seek advice and of public-spirited citizens with special expertise to give service to the people.[24] But on these matters Hoover's views did not coincide with those of a number of congressmen. He was accused of attempting to set up a government of "illegal and unauthorized" commissions as opposed to one functioning through duly constituted authorities, of helping to build trust and combines despite his constitutional duty to enforce the antitrust laws, and of making commitments that he had no authority to make.[25] He had, said Representative Joseph W. Byrns to the applause of congressional colleagues, "created more commissions and more independent boards, some of them without legal authority, . . . than any other president in the history of the entire country."[26] And while wits joked about his "sins of commission," the Congress meeting in 1932 took the position that his organization for unemployment relief had been created and given Commerce Department funds "without the slightest authority of law" and that consequently his request for an appropriation to keep it going should be rejected.[27]

Such criticisms did not lead Hoover to abandon his organization efforts. In the summer of 1932 he made another elaborate effort to erect banking and industrial committees that could reestablish and sustain the flow of spending.[28] But he was somewhat sensitive to the criticisms. He reacted, for example, by having lists compiled to show that earlier presidents had also made extensive use of special commissions; and by word and deed, he sought to make it clear that his organization of business collaboration to sustain spending did not mean that the antitrust barriers against forming restrictive cartels were to be removed.[29] He proved resistant, moreover, to the idea of delegating lawmaking and law enforcement powers to the machinery that was to be drawn from the private sector, as was now being proposed in both business and reformist circles. This he did regard as being both unconstitutional and conducive to the development of freedom-destroying trusts, a position made explicit in his responses to proposals emanating from the Chamber of Commerce and from Gerard Swope of General Electric.[30] Nor was he receptive to the idea of reviving the wartime Council of National Defense and using it to hatch another set of emergency economic organizations, as was being proposed in various other quarters. Although he did invoke war analogies in some of his own organizational work, particularly in 1932, he dismissed the calls for a new CND by saying that it was unneeded and that existing structures provided all the "economic council" that the president required.[31]

In these respects Hoover was now resisting, partly on constitutional grounds, the kind of corporative and emergency agencies that would become features of the early New Deal. He was also resisting, again partly on constitutional grounds, the growing demands that he step into the role of "legislative leader" and help produce a body of law authorizing federal regulatory and managerial bureaucracies to take over more of the tasks of economic coordination and social service provision. Only in the cases of three programs in 1932—that offering financial relief and emergency credit through agencies like the Reconstruction Finance Corporation, that seeking to narrow the gap between revenue and expenditure, and that seeking enhanced presidential authority to reorder and rationalize executive agencies— did Hoover attempt to exercise much legislative leadership; and in the first two of these, the constitutional bases for the laws being sought were clear and generally unchallenged.[32] In all three efforts, moreover, Hoover's experience tended to enhance his reluctance to move further along this route. It tended to bear out what he had said earlier about "the devil-and-deep-blue-sea trap," created by the penchant of those calling for such presidential initiatives to discover "meddling" with the separation-of-powers principle whenever the initiatives were attempted.[33]

In Hoover's hands, then, the presidency did not become an instrument to force major tests of constitutional powers and limitations. The rulings leading to the subsequent "constitutional crisis" and to the "constitutional revolution" that followed were not on laws that he had helped to produce; and when proposals met with constitutional objections from his legal experts, he tended to take these very seriously.[34] Yet his acceptance of and efforts to implement a form of managerial thinking about economic coordination and social services did lend encouragement to movements pushing for the kind of enlarged government that would force major tests of constitutional powers and limitations. They also helped to create a new set of popular expectations concerning the presidency, expectations that were probably more important than personal deficiencies in the increasingly negative assessments being made of his performance. And by putting excessive if not impossible burdens on private-sector organization, they contributed to a growing tendency to downgrade private-sector capacities while upgrading public-sector ones.[35]

It is also worth noting that three of the five Supreme Court justices who undertook the "constitutional revolution" of 1937 (Charles Evans Hughes, Owen J. Roberts, and Benjamin N. Cardozo) were Hoover appointees, and that a fourth (Harlan F. Stone) had Hoover's strong endorsement when initially appointed in 1925. Ironically, as some commentators have noted, Hoover's emphasis on juristic excellence and judicial independence in the appointment process helped to bring constitutional alterations that he would later denounce in no uncertain terms.[36]

With the coming to power of Franklin D. Roosevelt in 1933, the search of a depression-ridden nation for more effective forms of economic coordination and social service provision entered a new phase. Roosevelt, it seems, had no very concrete ideas as to what the new coordinative machinery should look like. Mixed with his willingness to create new bureaucratic structures was a lingering aversion to doing so, manifest in his support for emergency, corporatist, "people's," and communitarian mechanisms that were supposed to make such bureaucratization unnecessary.[37] But he was ready now to bring the full range of presidential powers to bear on the problem. He was also ready to expand presidential responsibilities in ways that Hoover regarded as dangerously subversive of the separation-of-powers principle. And despite what he had said in 1930 about the meddlesome "inverted pyramids" being erected on constitutional provisions, he was ready to champion the notion of an instrumentalist Constitution expandable to meet changing social and national needs.[38] In an often-quoted section of his inaugural address, he declared that "our Constitution is so simple and practical that it is possible always to meet extraordinary needs by changes in emphasis and arrangements without loss of essential form"; and as president, he said, he would ask Congress for "broad executive power to wage a war against the emergency, as great as the power that would be given me if we were in fact invaded by a foreign foe."[39]

This willingness to seek and use power, moreover, coexisted now with a set of crisis perceptions, personal and political capacitites, and popular and congressional expectations that allowed Roosevelt to do things that Hoover could not have done even if he had so desired. In particular, Roosevelt could become the nation's legislative leader, even more so than Woodrow Wilson was during his administration; and in this role he was able, during the so-called Hundred Days of 1933, to break down the normal barriers between Congress and the president, drastically shorten the legislative process, and secure statutory grants of power that he in turn could delegate to administrative creations or to appropriate private groups of subnational units. This, rather than the invocation of some stewardship or "national necessity" theory that would allow the president to act alone, was the basic route taken in producing new banking, agricultural, industrial, relief, and developmental mechanisms. Only the emergency banking proclamation issued before Congress convened might be regarded as falling outside this pattern, and even it was supposed to have a statutory base in a war measure still on the books.[40] Consequently, the constitutional tests posed by these 1933 measures were not, in any major way, tests of presidential powers grounded in Article II. They were tests, rather, of the kind of law that the national government could make and the extent to which the making of it could be delegated to agencies other than Congress.

In the crisis atmosphere that marked the Hundred Days, the drafters of these new measures gave relatively little consideration to matters of constitutionality and legal craftmanship. The general assumption, it seems, was that the war analogy would hold not only as to the action to be taken, but also as to constitutional challenges to it. And even among those considering the constitutional issue, little thought was given to the question of delegated power. Excessive or improper delegation, after all, had never been accepted as the basis for overturning a federal law. The major concern was with finding expandable clauses upon which to base the kind of detailed intervention in market processes that the measures authorized; and in practice two such clauses were found. One was the clause authorizing taxation to provide for the "general welfare." The other, and more important, was that authorizing Congress "to regulate commerce... among the several States." The narrow interpretation of this, New Deal theorists argued, was both incompatible with current national needs and a departure from what the Framers had intended. In the eighteenth century, it was claimed, the term "commerce" had been virtually synonymous with business transactions; and to the Framers, the argument continued, "commerce among the several states" had meant business transactions that concerned "more states than one." They had vested the power to control these in Congress, just as they had given Congress other powers that the states were incompetent to exercise. And by returning to what was originally intended, a meaning that would expand federal power even beyond what could be justified by the "current of commerce" arguments used in earlier affirmative rulings on federal controls, one could find constitutional ground for the kind of regulation that had now become a national imperative.[41]

In other respects, too, the New Dealers who became involved in public discourse about the legislative output of 1933 insisted that they were constitutionalists, not part of the political currents that would substitute government by men or groups for government by law. Admittedly, Attorney General Homer S. Cummings conceded, the sphere of administrative law was being vastly extended; government was now being guided by a sense of economic realism; and the making of law was now in the hands of those who saw it as "a living, vital, growing thing, fashioned for service and constantly refashioned for further service." But the "life, letter, and integrity of the Constitution" had not been impaired; "its checks and balances, its definition and division of authority, and its complete supremacy" remained inviolate; and every new power entrusted to the president had been conferred by the people, acting through their duly elected representatives. Nor had anything approaching a "dictatorship" been created. There had, said Cummings, been no usurpation of power, not substitution of executive will for national will, no resort to force or fear, no repression of dissenting thought or criticism, no pretensions of omniscience or omnipotence.[42] And in Roosevelt's own words, there had been "no actual surrender" of Congress's constitutional authority and not "the slightest desire to change the balance of these powers." "The only thing" that had been happening had been "to designate the President as the agency to carry out certain of the purposes of Congress," which was "in keeping with the past American tradition."[43]

Such was not the view, however, of the New Deal's political opponents or of those who felt themselves injured by the new administrative law being made under presidential auspices. As they saw it, the balance and separation of powers established by the Constitution were being destroyed by a power-seeking presidency gathering into itself the powers that should be exercised by Congress and the states. The constitutional foundations of liberty erected by the Framers and those who had correctly interpreted their intentions were thus being eroded, which, it was said, was opening the way for "personal government," bureaucratic tyranny, "democratic despotism," and undue centralization. And with a growing sense of alarm as the crisis atmosphere of the Hundred Days began to fade, those making such arguments began taking them not only to the judicial branch but to the court of public opinion. By 1935 they had become staples in a growing stream of criticism being articulated by business, legal, and Republican party leaders, by spokesmen for the "Constitution cults" that were a carry-over from the 1920s, and by a new group of business-supported organizations dedicated to preserving the "Constitution of the Fathers." Of greatest prominence among these new organizations was the American Liberty League, which in conjunction with its general defense of property rights proceeded to establish a National Lawyers Committee that depicted the Framers as having given constitutional sanction to laissez-faire economic doctrine, wrote and distributed adverse constitutional exegeses of reform proposals being considered in Congress, and promulgated legal opinions holding New Deal laws to be unconstitutional.[44]

It was in the context of this ongoing debate that cases involving the major laws of 1933 eventually reached the Supreme Court, the result being the rulings that produced the so-called "constitutional crisis" of the mid-1930s. Among the New Dealers there had been some hope that five of the nine Supreme Court justices might hold most of what had been done under the measures of 1933 to be constitutional.

This derived in particular from the affirmative rulings in 1934 in the *Blaisdell* and *Nebbia* cases, the first taking note of emergency conditions in upholding a Minnesota mortgage moratorium, the latter upholding a New York milk-pricing law against due process challenges.[45] But if there was any chance of this happening, it was dissipated by the sloppiness with which the 1933 measures had been drafted, the weakness and incoherence with which the government argued its legal case, and the growing evidence that the NRA codes, AAA committees, and other similar mechanisms were failing the test of workability.[46] A foreshadowing of what would happen came in early 1935, when an eight-to-one decision made the "hot-oil" section of the National Recovery Act the first federal law ever rejected as an unconstitutional delegation of legislative power.[47] And on May 27, 1935, subsequently to be known as "Black Monday," the Court's willingness to reject other measures became all too apparent. In three unanimous opinions, it held that Roosevelt had acted unconstitutionally in removing William E. Humphrey from the Federal Trade Commission, that the Frazier-Lemke Farm Bankruptcy Act violated constitutional guarantees of due process, and that the regulatory machinery created under the National Industrial Recovery Act had been unconstitutionally established and could have no basis in American constitutional law.[48]

These cases upheld constraints that Roosevelt and the New Dealers had hoped to see abandoned. The first denied a president removal power over appointees to the independent regulatory agencies, a power that Roosevelt and his legal experts thought had been affirmed in the *Myers* case of 1926.[49] The second made it clear that substantive due process was still alive, even in national emergencies. And the third and most important, the *Schechter* case, not only indicated again that there could be unconstitutional delegations of legislative power to the executive, but also that emergency conditions could not justify actions outside the sphere of constitutional authority, that the corporatist component in New Deal measures (i.e., the delegation of lawmaking power to private associations) was "unknown" to American law and "utterly inconsistent" with constitutional prerogatives and duties, and that the power to "regulate commerce...among the several states" could reach only those acts having "direct" effects on interstate trade.[50] All of these posed obstacles for those seeking to solve the problem of economic coordination and social service provision. But the first four of the constraints were ones that could be allowed to stand, especially since the New Deal's search for effective institutional machinery was, by 1935, already moving away from corporatist, emergency, and cooperative formulas toward more bureaucratic ones. It was only the last of the constraints, what Roosevelt called the "horse-and-buggy" definition of the commerce power, that threatened to derail the search itself.[51]

Despite this threat, however, the search did continue. In the summer of 1935, Congress enacted the measures of the Second New Deal, entrusting an enlarged complex of federal bureaus and boards with new regulatory and social tasks.[52] And the question now, given the penchant of the lower courts to issue injunctions against the implementation of these measures, became one of whether and how the Supreme Court could be induced to reconsider its legal position. One possibility, one that New Deal leaders were considering as early as 1934, was to change through legislation either the composition of the Court or the process of judicial review. There were a variety of proposals for doing this and had the early 1935 decisions in the gold cases gone against the government, Roosevelt might well have pushed for such legislation in the 1935 session.[53] The *Schechter* case, though, was not a good springboard for doing this. It struck down what had become an increasingly unpopular law, and the unanimity of the Court in doing so argued against efforts to solve the problem by increasing the number of justices. Accordingly, Roosevelt decided not to attempt any legislative solution. Instead, he would move other cases up, give the Court new opportunities to modify its interpretation, and wait for a more opportune set of circumstances should further action be required.[54]

In 1936, although given ample opportunity and much advice by New Deal lawyers and legal scholars, the Court did not modify its interpretive stance. On the contrary, in a series of negative decisions on the powers entrusted to such agencies as the Agricultural Adjustment Administration, the Securities and Exchange Commission, and the National Bituminous Coal Commission, it not only continued to apply the constraints specified in 1935, but also began invoking a doctrine of "dual federalism" as a further constraint on Congress's enumerated powers.[55] But the unanimity with which it had decided the *Schechter* case did not continue; New Dealers could take encouragement from powerful dissenting opinions and much public and scholarly criticism of the majority ones; and in the wake of the *Morehead v. Tipaldo* decision in June of 1936, a decision in which a five-man majority invalidated a New York minimum wage law for women on "liberty of contract" grounds, the commentary was strongly supportive of the view that something had to be done. Even Hoover was now calling for a constitutional amendment to restore to the states the power that they had believed they possessed. And while Roosevelt maintained a studied silence on the issue during the presidential campaign, these developments did seem to be creating the more opportune set of circumstances under which measures to alter the Court's composition or prerogatives might be taken. In view of them and in view of the election returns, Roosevelt was in no mood to become the president who had permitted "judicial usurpers" to impair the office of the executive and frustrate his efforts to deal with basic national problems.[56] He was ready to act and in doing so would usher in another phase in the ongoing debates concerning economic coordination and constitutional liberty.

The "court reform" plan that Roosevelt sent to Congress in February 1937 had been worked out by Attorney General Cummings and approved by the president some two months earlier. In essence, it would add six justices to the Supreme Court. But this essence was masked somewhat by making the additions dependent on the refusal of justices over seventy years of age to retire, by attaching it to a similar provision and various procedural reforms for the lower courts, and by adding a rationale expressing concern for the judicial workload. This very deviousness, it seems, was for Roosevelt part of the measure's attractiveness; and he also took mischievous pleasure in the fact that the major aspects of the scheme could be attributed to conservative justice James McReynolds. It had taken shape in Cummings' mind partly because he had been working on a history of the Justice Department and had discovered that McReynolds, when serving as Woodrow Wilson's Attorney General, had recommended to Congress the appointment of another lower court judge whenever an incumbent failed to retire at age seventy.[57]

According to Roosevelt and his legal experts, the measure proposed was clearly within the governmental framework established by the Constitution. It was a constitutionally legitimate remedy for a situation in which the judicial branch had departed from the intentions of the Framers and was misusing its power to block constitutionally valid policies adopted by the executive and legislative branches. It would, said Roosevelt, help to restore the basic form of American government, that of a "three-horse team" rather than one in which two of the horses were "pulling in unison" while the third was not.[58] But partly because Roosevelt had not laid the necessary groundwork in Congress, partly because the deviousness involved tended to backfire, partly because the Supreme Court was still a revered institution considered to be the bulwark of states' rights and civil liberties, challenges both to the wisdom and the constitutionality of the measure were quick to develop. And in the face of these challenges, Roosevelt did not fare well in his role as a legislative leader. A large group of southern and western Democrats joined the congressional opposition; personality and patronage could not be made to work as well as they had in 1933 and 1935; and lacking, despite efforts to create them, were the crisis perceptions existing earlier. These were particularly difficult to create after Justice Willis Van Devanter indicated an intention to retire and after decisions in the *West Coast Hotel* and *Jones & Laughlin Steel* cases, coming respectively in late March and early April of 1937, signaled that the old majority on the Court had given way to a new one.[59]

These cases proved to be the leading edge of what scholars would soon be calling the "constitutional revolution." In *West Coast Hotel*, upholding a minimum wage law for women in the state of Washington, the Court's new five-man majority began the process of reinvigorating state police power by removing the constraints associated with "liberty of contract" doctrine. And in *Jones & Laughlin*, the leading case upholding the regulatory structure authorized by the National Labor Relations Act of 1935, this same majority began the process of extending the reach of the commerce power to include intrastate activities having any effect at all on the workings of the national economic system. These processes would continue despite the fact that Congress, in August of 1937, would reject almost all of Roosevelt's "court reform" project. And joined with the new majority's simultaneous acceptance of taxation to provide for the "general welfare" and its rapid retreat from the delegation doctrine of the *Schechter* case, they produced an expanded constitutional framework that had room for the kind of national bureaucracy brought into being through the measures of the Second New Deal—a framework, so a number of New Deal legal theorists claimed, that amounted to a "restoration" of the intentions of the Framers rather than a departure from them.[60] After 1937, moreover, as the Court gradually became one dominated by Roosevelt appointees, the "revolution" became ever more secure and less and less likely to be reversed.[61]

Subsequently, Roosevelt was inclined to take credit for this "constitutional revolution" and its role in enabling America to have a modern administrative state. He had, he said, lost a battle but won the war. Yet the evidence now available seems to indicate that the battle need not have been fought, that any credit deserved was not for undertaking it but for helping to shape a national temper to which the "swing men" on the Court, Charles Evans Hughes and Owen Roberts, were already responding by the end of 1936. Hughes had abandoned the Court's old majority in the June 1936 ruling on the *Morehead* case and by that time, it now seems clear, was intent upon leading the Court into a more politically appropriate middle path. And Roberts's decision to do so in *West Coast Hotel* had actually been made by December 19, 1936. On that date, some two days after arguments in the case, he had voted with Hughes, Cardozo, and Brandeis rather than with the court's conservative bloc. As chief justice, however, Hughes had delayed announcement of the decision, initially to allow Stone to recover from an illness and join in the majority opinion, and then to avoid the appearance of an immediate capitulation to Roosevelt's "court reform" proposal. In the absence of such a proposal, it seems, the "revolution," or at least most of it, would still have taken place.[62]

It should be stressed, moreover, that while the "revolution" allowed the national government to grow in ways making for a stronger presidency, it did not mean the abandonment of a governmental structure featuring divided powers, checks and balances, and guarantees of individual liberty.[63] Although the Roosevelt Court moved to a position of judicial restraint on matters relating to the use and delegation of the commerce, taxing, and state police powers, it did not lose its capacity for exercising independent judgment or checking abuses of power by the other two branches of government. As subsequent developments would show, the actions of the modern presidency could still be contested on constitutional grounds; and far from turning Congress and the judiciary into "rubber stamps" for an all-powerful presidency, the events of 1937 actually helped to lay the basis for reviving and strengthening their institutional power. The judge-made "constitutional revolution" checked the erosion of the Supreme Court's institutional support in the political and legal culture and in the society at large, allowed it to gain new support as constitutionalism itself made a comeback, and thus permitted it to evolve into an effective instrument for expanding personal and minority rights. In these fields, it would soon be functioning again as an active policy-making institution. And "court-reform" became, in practice, the issue around which a congressional rebellion against presidential "dictatorship" could be organized, a rebellion that would have lasting effects in subsequent reassertions of congressional prerogatives and in the continuing power of a bipartisan coalition of congressional conservatives able to block presidential reform initiatives.[64]

The year 1937 is important, then, both for the "modernization" it brought to the American constitutional system and for the fact that the main features of that system did survive and persist. It is also important as the year in which the Roosevelt presidency began to mobilize its powers in the diplomatic sphere and use them in ways that ran counter to the "isolationism" that Congress had written into a series of neutrality measures. To some extent, the subsequent clash between "interventionists" and "isolationists" became a clash between the executive and legislative branches over control of foreign policy. And in this contest, Roosevelt operated from a strong constitutional position, which, ironically, had been made even stronger by the very Court that had become such a problem for him in the sphere of domestic action.

The major development in this regard had come in late 1936, when the Supreme Court, in the case of *U.S. v. Curtiss-Wright Export Corporation*, had upheld a 1934 measure authorizing the president to embargo the sale of arms to countries engaged in the Chaco War. The measure had been challenged as an unlawful delegation of authority, a view with which the district court had agreed. But in a somewhat surprising opinion, authored by conservative justice George Sutherland and having McReynolds as its lone dissenter, the Court had held that the president's powers in domestic and foreign matters were fundamentally different both in origin and nature. The latter, it said, was an inherent power held as a necessary concomitant of national sovereignty, not a power resting on the affirmative grants of the Constitution; it was therefore a "plenary and exclusive" power lodged in the "sole organ of the federal government in the field of international relations—a power which does not require as a basis for its exercise an act of Congress"; and its existence meant that legislation in foreign affairs could allow a degree of presidential discretion that "would not be admissible were domestic affairs alone involved." Just how much of these expansive contentions were in the nature of *obiter dicta* or could be challenged as resting on misunderstandings of history and sovereignty has remained a matter of dispute. But the case placed the Court's imprimatur on a doctrine that put few, if any, limits on presidential initiative in the making of foreign policy. And along with the *Belmont* decision in 1937, a case laying to rest any real doubts about the constitutionality of executive agreements, it made constitutional objections to Roosevelt's post-1937 actions in the foreign policy sphere exceedingly difficult to mount.[65]

The effects of World War II on the presidency and the Constitution are outside the scope of this paper. But is should be noted that as the war approached, Roosevelt not only sought new statutory grants of power to deal with a new national emergency, but also found ways to activate previous grants and began grounding some actions in what amounted to a merger of his powers as chief diplomat and military commander in chief. The presidency, he assumed, had the power to establish preparedness programs, to proclaim both "limited" and "unlimited" emergencies, to trade destroyers for naval bases, to create and assign administrative duties to new defense agencies, to organize informal sanctions against the "uncooperative," to wage an "undeclared war" against German submarines, to seize plants idled by labor disputes, and to do a variety of other things that often had little warrant in statutes or precedent.[66] As depression gave way to war, another expansion of presidential authority was underway, linked chiefly now to the creation of a national security and warfare state rather than a welfare one. Still to be seen was how far this would go, how much lasting change it would bring, and whether the constitutional system established in 1787 could find room for it as it had found room for the works of the second New Deal.

If there was now room for a modern administrative state, however, its place in the system was still an uneasy and unsettled one. In particular, its presence posed anew the old problem of how to give a governmental structure the power and coherence needed for effective performance without turning it into an instrument of tyranny uncontrollable by and unaccountable to the governed. Could this be done by giving the president new managerial powers and capacities and relying upon him, as the people's representative, to order, rationalize, and control the managerial bureaucracies that had become a necessary part of modern life? Could it be done by recognizing and accepting these bureaucracies as a "fourth branch" of government, constituted in its own uniquely suitable way and held in its proper place through an appropriately extended system of checks and balances? Could it be done by linking these bureaucracies to the group life of the private sector in such a way as to enhance their effectiveness while imposing checks on potential abuses of power? Or could it be done through a "constitutionalization" of public administration, a structuring of it, in other words, so that it had its own internal checks and could through its external relationships play a role of its own in maintaining constitutional balance? All of these approaches had their advocates in the late 1930s, and the debate begun then would be a continuing one.[67]

As Roosevelt saw it, the proper solution was the one calling for presidential ordering, control, and direction. Initially, this was less clear than it became later, partly because of the emergency and corporatist components in the early New Deal and partly because Roosevelt made relatively little use of the emergency reorganization powers granted him in 1933. But from the beginning, he was intent upon making the emerging national bureaucracy a presidential structure, not a fourth branch of government or a structure in which the constitutional relationships between separate powers were replicated in miniature. This was evident both in the moves designed to make the independent regulatory commissions more responsive to presidential leadership and in administrative arrangements intended to keep key positions in the hands of the "president's men" while keeping such men dependent on presidential action and support.[68] And as the bureaucracy kept getting larger and more complex and administrative difficulties kept growing and intensifying, these efforts to establish and maintain presidential control took on more overt forms and produced strenuously debated attempts to give the presidency new managerial powers and capacities while reducing both the power of Congress to shape the bureaucratic decisions and the capacity of bureaucrats to resist the role of presidential agents.

The most prominent attempt of this sort was that associated with the Executive Reorganization Bill recommended by the President's Committee for Administrative Management and sent to Congress on January 12, 1937. Under it, the president would be equipped with a new executive office, presidential assistants, reorganization powers, and formalized planning capacities. Congress would lose a good deal of its power over fiscal management, personnel matters, resource allocation, and regulatory implementation. And the bureaucracy would be made more manageable by rationalizing the departmental structure and integrating the independent commissions, except for their quasi-judicial functions, into it. In urging passage of the measure, Roosevelt took the position that the bureaucracy was part of an executive branch whose direction and control should be centered in the president if democracy was to work under modern conditions; and in support of this view, he could now cite a report based on expert study and reflection and purportedly representing the best social scientific thinking on the subject. The chairman of the Committee for Administrative Management, Louis Brownlow, had been a leading figure in the development and application of an "administrative science." So had the other two committee members, Luther Gulick and Charles E. Merriam.[69] And a list of the committee's staff members, one scholar has recently noted, would soon read like an honor roll of distinguished scholars in American political science.[70]

Roosevelt also argued publicly that he was not seeking more power, that he wanted only the tools of management that could help him discharge the powers already granted by the Constitution.[71] But evidence exists, particularly in Gulick's notes and memoranda, that the work of the Brownlow Committee was seen, both by the president and by the Committee's members, as somewhat analogous to the work of a constitutional convention.[72] And in the eyes of a broad array of critics, the proposed legislation became the "dictator bill," which, along with the "court packing" proposal being considered at the same time, was allegedly part of a presidential effort to subvert constitutional principles and establish "one-man rule." In Congress the measure became the subject of extended hearings and growing opposition, with congressional critics marshaling their own experts, defenders of bureaucratic turf mobilizing their "friends" and clienteles, and such organizations as the National Defenders, the American Guardian Society, and the National Committee to Uphold Constitutional Government expressing alarm about this new challenge to the foundations of national liberty. Little progress toward passage of the measure was made in 1937, and in 1938 the opposition seemed to grow even stronger. In the Senate a substanially revised version of the bill passed by a narrow margin. But in the House of Representatives, administration forces went down to defeat on a motion that recommitted the bill to committee.[73]

In 1939 an Administrative Reorganization Act was finally passed, one that did provide for new presidential assistants and did allow the president to initiate reorganization plans that would go into effect if Congress did not vote to disapprove them. Under the act, Roosevelt was successful in implementing a series of plans that did establish an Executive Office of the President, bring the Bureau of the Budget and National Resources Planning Board into it, create new administrative groupings of functionally related agencies, and transfer a number of units from one department to another. But this measure was a pale shadow of the one debated in 1937 and 1938. Gone were the sections calling for presidential-strengthening reform in budget and accounting practice, in the workings of the civil service system, in the cabinet and departmental structures, and in bureaucratic policy-making; and exempted from reorganization were the independent regulatory commissions and boards, and most of the bureaus that had resisted any loss of their traditional autonomy.[74]

Despite some claims to the contrary, Roosevelt had not really succeeded in implementing the "presidential control" solution to the problem of the new "administrative state" now operating in a policy committed to liberal and democratic values. His efforts to do so had encountered effective resistance from power centers outside his control, demonstrating, some would say, that the constitutional system was alive and working. And in subsequent years, there would be a continuing debate about the implications of his defeat on this issue. It would be deplored by critics who faulted America's governmental system for its lack of a strong planning and managerial capacity, for the resulting incoherence in its policy output, for its tendency toward governmental deadlock, and for the extent to which its bureaucracies had been "captured" or were "out of control." Yet at the same time, other students of the subject would come to see the defeat as one that had helped to move American governmental development in desirable directions, not only toward arrangements with more potential for needed administrative continuity but also toward an executive branch in which "counteracting" presidential and administrative "realms," the emergence of administrative pluralism and statesmanship, and the formulation of new procedural safeguards would provide the needed constitutional constraints. For some, the attorney general's *Report on Administrative Procedure* in 1941 and the Administrative Procedures Act of 1946 would be milestones in the movement toward "constitutionalizing" the new bureaucracy.[75]

Seen in retrospect, then, the depression period was both an interesting and important one in the history of American constitutionalism as it interacted with and affected presidential policy and behavior. It was a period in which the need for better economic coordination and social service provision emerged as the nation's central problem, one in which the president was expected to lead the quest for a solution, and one in which the answers attempted could not be fitted into the constitutional framework without intense controversy and the involvement of the presidency in battles over constitutional issues. During the Hoover administration, the solution that would pull the needed machinery from the group life and power centers of the private sector was tried and found wanting, generating in the process a critique that sometimes employed constitutional arguments. But it was the attempted solutions of the Roosevelt presidency, first through the grants of power secured in 1933 and later through the program of the Second New Deal in 1935, that provoked reactions leading to the "constitutional crisis," to the heated clash between competing conceptions of constitutional government and history, and to the mixture of change and continuity that has affected constitutional and presidential development since then.

In the end, the Roosevelt presidency had its way on the crucial constitutional issues. The controlling framework of constitutional constraints was altered to accommodate the New Deal's "administrative state" and "modern presidency"; they became legally constituted parts of the American governmental system; and their doing so has had major implications for the kind of government that Americans have lived under since 1937. Also important, although far less contested at the time, were the readings of the Constitution that strengthened presidential power in the foreign policy field and helped to create openings for what a later generation would call the "imperial presidency."

Yet these changes, important as they were, all took place within a larger pattern of continuity. There were for this period no major innovations to report in such areas as presidential ceremony, executive privilege, and Cabinet usage. And more importantly, the governmental system that emerged from presidential efforts to change our methods of economic coordination and social service provision was still one in which the judicial and legislative branches retained their institutional power and subnational units continued to make and enforce a large and important body of law. It was still, as the outcome of the battles over "court reform" and the "dictator bill" attested, a system in which presidential ambitions that appeared to threaten the larger constitutional design could be checked and frustrated;[76] and, most significantly of all perhaps, it was still a system in which commitments to constitutionalism in general and to the handiwork of the constitution makers of 1787 in particular remained strong and would endure. The America of the 1930s had its echoes of the kind of anticonstitutionalism found in various mass movements abroad. It also had people who continued to articulate the critique of the Founding Fathers that Charles Beard and others had developed earlier. But the heart of the period's constitutional debate was about "usurpations" of power, executive and judicial, not about the wisdom of continuing with the system begun in 1787. It was these appeals to constitutionalism that had the greatest mobilizing capacity among the American masses and the strongest resonance among those entrusted with the power to govern. The New Deal, as Jerold Auerbach has noted, was and remained a "lawyer's deal."[77]

Whether this mixture of change and continuity served the nation well is a matter that continues to be debated. Critiques of it persist, both by those who would return to the pre-1930 arrangements and by those deploring the continued rule of law made and interpreted by legal elites.[78] But what one can say with some assurance is that the American Constitution in the 1930s was a living one. It was alive in the sense of having support in the populace, the elites, and the culture. It was alive in the instrumentalist sense of being refashionable to meet newly perceived needs, the mechanism, as it turned out, being a Supreme Court that had absorbed and finally chose to exercise the amending function. And it was alive in the sense that it mattered, both in the calculations of those making public policy and as a check against courses of action that might otherwise have been taken.

Chapter 6

The Constitution of the Truman Presidency and the Post-World War II Era

_____ *Donald R. McCoy*

Here Donald McCoy describes how the Truman presidency was caught up in a variety of constitutional concerns, ranging from powers of Congress, the rights of citizens, and the executive, military, and foreign policy powers of the presidency. Two circumstances necessitated a change in government from the pre–New Deal low level of federal and presidential powers: the domestic needs of the nation, and the super power status of the United States in the world. Also at the heart of presidential development was President Truman's dynamic interpretation of the constitution, particularly the president's powers as chief diplomat and commander in chief. McCoy points out, however, that the Truman presidency had only limited success in developing civil rights and civil liberties programs, failed to resolve an emergency powers issue (Youngtown Sheet and Tube Case of 1952), and clashed frequently with Congress. Yet, concludes McCoy, both the constitutional process of the federal government, and within it the executive branch, were greatly enhanced during the Truman presidency.

About the McCoy paper, McDonald had raised the blanket charge that presidents, including Truman, were manipulated as well as manipulators. McCoy responded to McDonald by noting that everybody in Washington manipulates. It is the business of politics. Theodore Lowi, in his critical comments, argued that the constitutional growth of the presidency depends upon the institutionalizing of power. Such was not the case with nineteeth-century actions, for example Jackson's Bank Veto and Cleveland's Pullman Strike action. They were only small "coups d'etat." Manifestations of presidential powers in the Truman presidency were different, however. They were institutionalized, as illustrated by program budgeting, presidential clearance of legislation, employment measures, Keynesianism as the language of state, and national security.

The Constitution of the United States has stood on the high ground of American life from the beginning. Its words have shaped our government, our politics, and much of our everyday life. Yet its meaning has never been static, subject as the Constitution has been to amendment and especially interpretation. The document has been explicit enough never to have been radically changed in its meaning, but it has been adaptable enough to satisfy the nation's contestants for power. Except during the Civil War, the great majority of Americans have been content to settle their differences within the framework of the Constitution. It has been and remains, therefore, a vital instrument of government.

The presidency of Harry S Truman demonstrates this just as it marks a time of significant change in the use of the Constitution. The stage was set for serious discussions of the meaning of the Constitution when Truman succeeded to the presidency on April 12, 1945. There were those who were poised, upon the death of his predecessor, Franklin D. Roosevelt, to modify the interpretations of the document that had greatly enhanced executive powers since 1933. In particular, Congress stood ready to reclaim some of its lost authority. Not only had prosperity during World War II deflated the pressures for increasing federal economic and welfare powers, but it seemed clear that the president's wartime emergency powers could quickly be ended. Moreover, although most Americans agreed that their country should continue to play an important part in world affairs, no one realized how large that role would be. The seemingly mild-mannered Harry Truman was not thought to be a president who could have great say in what would happen. Who could have predicted that he would emerge as someone very different from what he seemed? Who could have predicted the bitter contests for world power that would quickly develop after the end of the war?

What occurred from 1945 until Truman left the White House in 1953 was of great constitutional significance, not only for that time but also to the present. Truman was central to this, regardless of whether he acted on his own, on advice, or in response to the challenges to his views and authority.[1] Let there be no mistake. Truman had views on the Constitution. Some of these he entered the presidency with, and some of them he acquired during his years in office. He may not have been a constitutional scholar, but there is much to Emmet Hughes's assessment of Truman and Woodrow Wilson as "the two twentieth-century presidents most sensitive to the constitutional origins of the Presidency." Truman could scarcely have avoided it, given the frequency with which he was forced to rely upon constitutional provisions and precedents to justify his actions. Thus he could say with conviction in 1959, "The longer I live, the more I am impressed with...our American Constitution....It's a plan, but not a strait jacket, flexible and short. Read it one hundred times, and you'll always find something new."[2]

Truman's philosophy of presidential power also derived from other than constitutional sources. These included experience, religion, history, and his general theory of life. Jonathan Daniels wrote correctly of Truman's belief, based on experience: "In the party organization system as as much a part of the organization of the American government—and as essential a part—as any of the devices, checks and balances, limitations and powers in the Constitution itself."[3] Then there was divine dictate which Truman referred to in 1948 when he declared that "in 1920 Almighty God expected us to assume the leadership of the world....I am trying my best to see that this Nation does assume that leadership."[4] Perhaps this was hyperbole, but I doubt it, given how often he referred in public and private to God.

Religion and experience squared in Truman's mind not only with the Constitution, but also with his view of life and his reading of history. But his emphasis on extra-constitutional things is significant. As he said in 1946, "I am guided by a simple formula: to do in all cases, from day to day, without regard to narrow political considerations, what seems to me to be best for the welfare of all our people."[5] In 1952 he put this even stronger when he asserted: "I like to do things that I think are right, I don't care whether any body likes it or not. If I think it is right, I am going to do it."[6] Of course, Truman exercised restraint in using his powers. He ascribed this in 1952 to his being a democrat as well as to his belief in the Magna Carta, the Bill of Rights, and, more important, the Bible—in short, to trying "to do what is right."[7]

It is not surprising that Truman believed a president needed to be assertive. This showed in his prediction about his successor, Dwight D. Eisenhower: "He'll sit right here and he'll say, 'Do this, do that,' and nothing will happen. Poor Ike. It won't be a bit like the Army. He'll find it very frustrating."[8] Truman believed that a chief executive needed push and courage. As he said in 1948 of Andrew Jackson and Andrew Johnson, they were not "pliant, supple" men, who might have let the Union be swept away. "Jackson did his duty in agony of mind as well as in agony of body." Johnson, Truman said, perhaps thinking of criticisms of himself, "was stubborn. He was tactless. Often he was ungracious to the point of being surly. The fact remains that he...defended...the principle that the Constitution...and not the desire of angry men is the supreme law of this land."[9] Truman believed that there was a mystique to all this. "The Presidency of the United

States," he wrote in his *Memoirs*, "carries with it a responsibility so personal as to be without parallel. . . . No one can know all the processes and stages of his thinking. . . . Even those closest to him. . . never know all the reasons why he does certain things and why he comes to certain conclusions."[10]

Nevertheless, the Constitution was important to Truman. He considered it to be subject to improvement, however. The government's job, he believed, is "to act as, say, an umpire, to see that everybody gets a square deal. That is the ideal situation sought by the Constitution. . . . It took us about 80 years to get a good start and to make it operate, and we are still trying to make it operate efficiently." His concern for it was selective, though. Indeed the Preamble was what he may have relied upon most in the Constitution in striving to do the "best for the welfare of all our people."[11] Truman made this explicit in 1949 when he declared that "the Constitution was established to 'promote the general welfare.' These are the words of its preamble. And that is the duty of our Government."[12] Of course, he did not use the Preamble to justify his actions constitutionally. If not Truman, then his advisers would have known that the Supreme Court had held that no statutory power is derived from it.[13]

Similarly, the Bill of Rights was the part of the Constitution Truman mentioned most often during his presidency. His regard for the personal liberties guaranteed in the Bill of Rights was seen throughout his administration. When, in 1945, Truman nominated Tom Clark to be attorney general, he "emphasized to him the need to be vigilant to mantain the rights of individuals under the provisions of the Bill of Rights," and he urged Clark to make this point clear to the United States attorneys.[14] Truman also on several occasions indicated the primacy of the Bill of Rights. As he declared in 1947, "I think that is the most important part of our Constitution—the right of the individual to go where he pleases, to do what he pleases, say what he pleases, as long as he is not materially injuring his neighbors."[15]

This is not to say that Harry Truman was ignorant of other aspects of the Constitution. It is just that there were certain parts of the document he emphasized, some because of his special interest in them and some, especially the provisions of Article II, because he largely found his authority there. He left it to Congress and the courts to stress those sections of the Constitution that were the foundations of their powers.

Truman began his administration hoping that he would have the cooperation of all officials, but he was soon disabused of that notion. With the election of a Republican Congress in November 1946, he took refuge in "the constitutional principle that the three branches of the Government are independent of each other." Although the president still talked of cooperation, he emphasized that "the duties and responsibilities of the Chief Executive and the executive branch of the Government are entrusted to me and my associates."[16] Truman proceeded along this line of independent powers as he received less cooperation than he desired from Congress during the next six years.

As for the judiciary, Truman had other plans. He hoped to rely on the Democrats who largely populated the federal district, appeals, and special courts. Moreover, he was able to appoint 116 judges of these courts. There is no significant evidence as to how satisfied Truman was with the results. If he was disappointed, he could look to the Supreme Court to set the most important things right. It was the Supreme Court that he had a splendid opportunity to shape, for he appointed four members to it. And he knew exactly what he wanted.[17] As Truman wrote in May 1945, "The Courts should be strictly judicial and not dabble in policy—except interpretation of the Constitution. It is not at all proper for courts to try to make laws or to read law school theories into the law and policy laid down by the Congress."[18] He also acted on more personal criteria for his Supreme Court appointees. All four of them had held high public office, and he knew them well and liked their politics.

Harold Burton was Truman's first nominee, to replace Justice Owen Roberts in 1945. Although a Republican, Burton had served effectively with the president in the Senate and on the Truman Committee to Investigate the National Defense Program. Probably more important was Truman's assessment of Burton as "someone who will do a thoroughly judicial job and not legislate."[19] The president followed a similar pattern for his other three appointments to the Supreme Court. In 1946 he nominated as chief justice Fred Vinson, a former congressman and his treasury secretary, whom he had described as a "straight shooter, knows Congress and how they think, a man to trust."[20] Truman appointed Tom Clark and Sherman Minton to the court in 1949. Clark was his attorney general and had worked with the Truman Committee; Minton, a federal appeals court judge at the time, had been closely associated with Truman in the Senate and had contributed to his nomination for vice president in 1944. Vinson had urged the appointment of Clark as a person who would agree with him. And Truman wrote to Clark of Minton that "he came of the same piece of cloth that you and the Chief Justice did."[21]

Thus, Truman tried to assure that the Supreme Court would be more of a lodestar for lesser courts than it had been since 1937 and that it would not become an activist body that would compete with the executive and legislative branches in making law. It is not surprising that an activist president wanted a passive Supreme Court, as well as a cooperative Congress. He was far from satisfied with what he got from the Court, thanks to the high level of its dissents and some contrary opinions from the new justices, particularly Clark and Burton.[22] As Truman said in 1959, "Packing the Supreme Court simply can't be done. . . . I've tried it and it won't work."[23] Yet scholars have argued persuasively that his appointees joined with others on the Court to create a restrained tribunal that was generally reluctant to challenge either congressional or executive authority.[24] The federal judiciary only voided three executive actions during Truman's presidency, and only one of these, the seizure of steel plants in 1952, was significant.[25] There is much in Glendon Schubert's comment that traditionally "the elected representatives of the people—the President and the Congress—must decide the great questions of constitutional law."[26]

A review of the use of constitutional powers during Harry Truman's presidency supports much of Schubert's thesis. Indeed one can say that it has usually been true since then, as most recently indicated in the Iran-Contra controversy. There is insufficient space here for a comprehensive discussion of the constitutional powers of the president during Truman's time. I shall, therefore, confine myself to the three most important areas—the president's powers as chief executive, as chief diplomat, and as commander in chief—subsuming his role as chief legislator under them.

Where did President Truman acquire his powers? The formal source for them was the Constitution, especially but not exclusively Article II. Therein lies the president's authority as head of the executive branch and commander in chief, as well as to reprieve and pardon, to appoint federal officials with the advice and consent of the Senate,[27] to make treaties subject to Senate ratification, to report to Congress and recommend legislative action, to execute the laws, to veto legislation, and, by interpretation, to do many other things in order to "preserve, protect and defend the Constitution of the United States." Under the Constitution, the president also acquires an immense amount of authority thanks to congressional actions. Without legislative action, the president has rather little to enforce and few means to do so. One fact that seems to be lost on many members of Congress is that they cannot confine presidential powers by passing more laws and ratifying more treaties for him to enforce. There are, however, other important sources of a president's authority. Not the least of these are the interpretations of executive authority—usually unchallenged by the courts[28]—by earlier presidents, many of whom thusly expanded executive powers. Harry Truman particularly benefited in this regard from the great extension by his immediate predecessor, Franklin Roosevelt, of presidential authority through interpretation. Another significant source of the expansion of executive powers is situational. During a time of crisis or a rise in the public's expectations, most importantly the Cold War in Truman's case, a president normally seeks to expand his power. He is usually successful, for Congress and especially the courts are then reluctant to deny him if the people expect action (which is often the result of a president's use of his political and ceremonial roles to drum up popular and congressional support).

Let us begin our review of Truman's presidential powers by examining his authority as chief executive. This was not as controversial or as significant as his powers as chief diplomat or commander in chief, but it was essential to the operation of the executive branch. Here Congress and Truman occasionally agreed on paring presidential authority, at least in terms of the funds, personnel, and number of programs at the chief executive's disposal. Congress even sometimes strengthened his authority by passing new laws for him to enforce.[29] It also tried, on occasion, to infringe upon his authority, actions which he usually resisted successfully.

The legislative assaults on Truman's prerogatives as chief executive were several. Of one of these, Truman wrote in his *Memoirs*: "Sometimes the Congress makes an effort to rob the president of his appointive powers. I would never stand for it."[30] An example of this was Truman's veto of a bill in 1948 that would have authorized a congressional committee to have the Federal Bureau of Investigation probe the president's nominees for service on the Atomic Energy Commission. He held this to be an infringement of his constitutional power of appointment.[31] Truman was equally forceful in other areas. In 1951 he vetoed a bill giving Congress some voice in the acquisition and disposal of land by the military services and the Civil Defense Administration. His reason was that it is the constitutional function of Congress to pass laws, but of the president to execute them.[32] In 1950 he distinguished between enforcing laws and spending appropriations, holding that the latter "is the discretionary power of the President. If he doesn't feel like the money should be spent, I don't think he can be forced to spend it."[33] Although controversial, this was not as bold as it seems, for Congress had given the president leeway to ignore its appropriation concerning, in this case, funds to expand the air force. Then there were laws that he decided sometimes to apply and sometimes not, labeling these permissive legislation. An example of this was Truman's use of the Taft-Hartley Labor Relations Act on ten occasions and his refusal to apply it otherwise, most notably during the steel strike of 1952.[34]

Where Truman encountered trouble concerned what we have come to call executive privilege. This arose in 1948 when the House Committee on Un-American Activities subpoenaed the Department of Commerce to deliver the security files on Edward U. Condon, the director of the National Bureau of Standards. Commerce Secretary Averell Harriman ignored the subpoena, citing as precedent the fact that no department head had ever responded affirmatively to a subpoena from a congressional committee. Truman soon ordered that any future requests from Congress for such confidential records must be referred to his office for determination. The House of Representatives then resolved to require the executive branch to disclose to House committees whatever information they needed.[35] Ironically in view of future events, Congressman Richard Nixon, speaking in support of the resolution, chastised the president for trying to deny Congress its constitutional "right to question the judgment of the President."[36] Truman ignored the resolution. When in 1950 the Senate pressured Truman to produce security files, after resisting he agreed in April to let a subcommittee review certain documents.[37] It was a draw, for the Senate did not get a free hand and the subcommittee members felt frustrated in trying to assess what had been opened to them. Truman returned to fight another day, vetoing as unconstitutional in June an act empowering congressional committees to examine executive records concerning alleged violations of the Hatch Act that regulated political activities by civil servants.[38] In 1951, in a related area, Truman contended without direct challenge that presidential conversations were confidential.[39] He struck one last blow against congressional infringement on executive privilege in 1953, after he had left office. Then he refused to respond to a subpoena to testify before the HUAC.[40]

As chief executive, Truman also worked to make the government more efficient, which among other things enhanced his presidential powers. In particular, he developed an advisory process in which policies came to him for decision instead of development. Vital in this respect was Truman's use and expansion of the Bureau of the Budget and his own staff to give him the information necessary to carry out his executive and legislative obligations. Even when he lost in pursuing his legislative program, as he often did on domestic matters, he maintained the president's power to try to fulfill his constitutional responsibilities.[41] Moreover, as Dorothy B. James has observed, "In fighting many unsuccessful battles...Truman helped to educate the American public, thereby laying a foundation that enabled his successors to accomplish his vision."[42] Truman had help from Congress in this institutionalization of the presidency, for example, in the establishment of the Council of Economic Advisers and the National Security Council, and in appropriating funds for larger staffs to assist him.

There was also Truman's use of ad hoc committees. These were not new devices, but he employed them more often than had his predecessors. One notable example with constitutional implications was the President's Committee on Civil Rights. This linked up with Truman's belief in the importance of the Bill of Rights. Although he was no zealot on the rights of racial minorities, he was relatively advanced on the question compared with many other officials. The PCCR's 1947 report was even more advanced, and Truman acted honorably in recommending legislative action based on it. Although Congress was basically unresponsive, Truman acted on his own in 1948 in the areas in which he had authority as chief executive. He then established committees to deal with discrimination and segregation in the civil service and the armed forces, the latter of which was an especially important step in promoting racial equality.[43]

There were also his administration's use of amicus curiae briefs in key civil rights cases, beginning in 1947, which contributed to several civil rights victories before the Supreme Court in the areas of housing, transportation, and education. Truman sought, too, to continue and then resurrect the wartime Fair Employment Practices Committee, finally settling for establishing a watered-down version of it under his emergency powers in 1951, the Committee on Government Contract Compliance. This was in effect continued by Eisenhower and strengthened by John F. Kennedy until it was regularized and broadened in the Civil Rights Act of 1964. Then there were the Truman administration's efforts, only partially successful, to effect desegregation in the District of Columbia.[44] All this gave meaning to Truman's words in his Civil Rights message of 1948 that "the Federal Government has a clear duty to see that Constitutional guarantees of individual liberties and of equal protection under the laws are not denied or abridged anywhere in our Union."[55] The joker in this was that Truman interpreted the extension of civil rights as "not protection of the people *against* the Government, but protection of the people *by* the Government."[46] Many Americans would rightly see the need for both, and the issue would give Harry Truman some agonizing moments during his presidency.

This was seen in the questions of domestic security that arose during Truman's administration. The federal government, during World War II, had reared a security apparatus to deal with threats of espionage, sabotage, and sedition. The concerns with subversion continued after the war as tensions quickly arose between the United States and the Soviet Union. Attorney General Clark and other officials in the administration and Congress urged better organization of activities against subversion. Important to this was the work of some clergy, and especially the United States Chamber of Commerce, in encouraging public support.[47] After the 1946 congressional elections, in which subversion was an issue, Truman as chief executive established an employee loyalty program to remove from and bar entry into federal employment when there were "reasonable grounds... for belief that the person involved is disloyal to the Government of the United States."[48]

Although the president's loyalty program led to some injustices as a result of overzealousness or sloppiness, it seemed almost fair compared to the unbridled investigations of some congressional committees and the loyalty laws enacted by several states. Truman contributed to this hysteria by following advice in 1947 to scare the hell out of the United States in order to get public and congressional approval of legislation to counter the perceived Soviet threat abroad. Once the administration had unleashed public concern to support anti-Communist foreign policy programs, it was easily exploited by others to win support for more drastic measures against possible subversion. Truman was on the spot, and would be throughout the rest of this presidency, to prove that his administration was coping with subversion and yet carrying out his duty to protect individual rights. If civil libertarians were often bothered by Truman's meanderings on these issues, they were furious with Congress and even irritated with the Supreme Court, which generally let stand state and federal loyalty-security programs. Only during the late 1950s and the 1960s would Congress calm down and the court significantly modify its position.[49]

Truman's main quarrel on anti-subversive measures was with Congress. Despite growing pressures from Congress and even from within the administration, he stalled in supporting or recommending legislation on subversive activities. In 1948 the president pointed out how difficult it was to draft a law on loyalty and espionage that "does not infringe the Bill of Rights." He added that he was "categorically opposed to any gestapo proposition that does infringe the Bill of Rights."[50] He could only stall for so long, especially after the Soviet explosion of an atomic bomb and the fall of China to Communist forces in 1949. By 1950 Congress began to move, further encouraged by the outbreak of McCarthyism in the Senate and of war in Korea. The result was the McCarran Internal Security bill, which virtually prohibited Communist political activity and authorized detention of suspected persons, without the safeguard of habeas corpus, in time of emergency. In August Truman lectured Congress against going too far. There was room for better legislation regarding spies, foreign agents, aliens, and the security of defense installations, but he warned against punishing dissent and establishing concentration camps.[51] After Congress overwhelmingly adopted the McCarran Act, Truman vetoed it, saying that the measure "would give Government Officials vast powers to harass all of our citizens in the exercise of their right of free speech. . . . It would make a mockery of the Bill of Rights."[52] Congress overrode the president's veto, but his statements were a stirring defense of individual rights for the time. Truman's veto of this act and of the McCarran-Walter Immigration Act of 1952 gave force to his conviction that, regardless of the odds of success, a president must veto any legislation that was out of harmony with the Bill of Rights. If this were not done consistently, he believed, further repressive thought and action would be encouraged. Truman's criticisms of the Internal Security Act were heeded with the passage of time, and the Supreme Court eventually eviscerated it.[53]

His veto of the McCarran Act fueled increased criticism of Truman for being soft on Communism. These attacks in turn encouraged Congress to deny Sumner T. Pike the chairmanship of the Atomic Energy Commission in 1950 and to force Edward U. Condon from office as director of the Bureau of Standards in 1951.[54] They perhaps reached their rhetorical peak during the 1952 election campaign when Republican vice presidential nominee Nixon attacked the Democratic presidential nominee, Adlai Stevenson, for carrying "a Ph.D. from Dean Acheson's cowardly college of Communist containment."[55] Truman felt compelled to attempt to develop a loyalty-security program that would be both more acceptable to his Red-baiting critics and consistent with the Bill of Rights. He tried this in 1951 by establishing the President's Commission on Internal Security and Individual Rights to study balancing the interests of national security and civil liberties. This venture turned into a fiasco when the Commission became mired in a fight with Congress over exemptions from conflict-of-interest laws. With pressure and criticism mounting, the president in April 1951 accepted the recommendation of his Loyalty Review Board that one could be removed from federal service when there was "reasonable doubt as to the loyalty of the person involved." Yet he was bothered by its adverse implications for civil liberties and asked the National Security Council to review the situation. In April 1952 the NSC devised guidelines designed to make the loyalty-security program more effective and yet fairer. Truman did not act on this until November, which was too late for it to become effective before he left office.[56] President Eisenhower in 1953 issued a more stringent, less fair executive order, but it was assailed by the Supreme Court in 1959. Eisenhower then issued a new executive order containing procedural safeguards for the accused.[57]

As already indicated, Truman took seriously his duties as chief legislator. He annually gave Congress the constitutionally mandated report on the state of the Union, adding to that in 1947 an annual report on the state of the economy. He showered Congress with recommendations for legislative action, and he often engaged in dialogue with its members as to what he thought they should or should not do. Truman also gave concentrated attention to his administration's legislative programs, mobilizing his staff and that of the Budget Bureau to review such programs as well as congressional enactments. This helped him to decide how to implement programs that were approved by Congress and strengthened his resolve to decide how to use congressional delegations of authority instead of giving in to pressures to negotiate them with committees of Congress.[58] Of course, Truman gave considerable attention to what he would veto or approve. With him, the veto was a vital instrument. He gave regular vetoes to 180 measures and pocket vetoes to another 70, a record exceeded only by Franklin Roosevelt and Grover Cleveland. Congress overrode twelve of Truman's vetoes, which tied him with Gerald Ford for second place after Andrew Johnson. Yet proportionately, he was overridden less often on his regular vetoes than had been Presidents Tyler, Pierce, Andrew Johnson, Grant, Hayes, Arthur, Wilson, Coolidge, Hoover, Nixon, and Ford.[59]

Among the president's most important powers are those pertaining to foreign relations. Few words are used in the Constitution to describe them. "He shall have the Power," the Constitution declares, "by and with the Advice and Consent of the Senate, to make Treaties, provided two thirds of the Senators present concur; and he shall nominate, and by and with the Advice and Consent of the Senate, shall appoint Ambassadors, other public Ministers and Consuls." How important these few words are, however. This is especially true because, under the Constitution, the president must "take Care that the Laws be faithfully executed" and that along with the Constitution and federal laws "all Treaties made...under the Authority of the United States, shall be the supreme Law of the Land." Thus, the president can constantly be negotiating treaties, and he also has the duty to enforce ratified treaties, thanks to his powers as chief executive and commander in chief. Congress has often supplemented these presidential powers, not only through treaty ratifications and approval of executive agreements with other nations, but also by establishing and funding appropriate executive enforcement agencies. The legislators did so generously during the Truman presidency. For example, the establishment of the Department of Defense, the Central Intelligence Agency, and the National Security Council in 1947 gave the president further sources regarding information, planning, and implementation of foreign policy. Congress made the CIA virtually immune from its inquiry, and in effect the legislators did not look into the work of the NSC.[60] Considering this, the president's control of the State Department and lesser agencies, and his stated constitutional powers, there is little wonder that Truman in 1948 told the Jewish War Veterans: "I make American foreign policy."[61]

This was a bold statement, but one well justified. After all, Truman had more power in the area of foreign relations than any of his predecessors. This had come about partly because of the unparalleled economic development of the United States on the world scene after the Second World War. With vastly increased international trade, commercial treaties and agreements took on new significance, giving the president much additional influence and power in the world. This was supplemented by American legislation, most notably the Marshall Plan of 1948, to assist the process of world economic reconstruction.[62]

There was much more, though. During World War II, American opinion had swung steadily in support of organized international action to undercut the possibility of another world war. The foundations had largely been laid by the time Truman became president to establish the United Nations for that purpose. In 1945 the Senate overwhelmingly ratified the United Nations Charter and Congress passed the United Nations Participation Act, which would subject the United States to certain decisions taken by the UN. This augmented the president's powers in foreign policy because of his treaty obligations to enforce those decisions. The UN was only the first of several postwar alliances entered into by the United States. In 1947 came the Rio Pact for western hemispheric defense, and in 1949 the North Atlantic Treaty, to mention two. If America's UN affiliation developed out of an overwhelming desire for "War No More" during World War II, the other security treaties came because of American fear of Soviet aggrandizement after the war. They all greatly increased the president's authority as chief diplomat to define them through interpretation and supplementary international agreements and as chief executive to implement them. Moreover, these treaties, along with such measures as the Truman Doctrine of 1947 and the Mutual Defense Assistance Act of 1949, very much enhanced the president's power as commander in chief because of their military provisions.

Americans generally accepted this concentration of foreign policy and military powers in the president's hands, even if there was often a division of opinion as to how well he used his authority. They did not have much alternative. The courts not only could not exercise such power, but were unwilling to question it. There was little sentiment for concentrating military power in the UN. As for Congress, its members knew that they could not effectively exercise foreign policy and military powers. Congress could deny presidential requests, but the times seemed too perilous for it to do that often. Usually the legislators could only try to shape the president's exercise of his powers, but that frequently turned into sniping with little effect. Truman occupied the constitutional roles of America's chief foreign policy-maker and commander in chief, which he used powerfully because of the public's responsiveness to the concept of "national security" that had emerged so gleamingly during World War II. Congress seldom had the ability to do more than quibble with him about America's foreign and military policies. After all, Truman had the prime sources of information, the planners and advisers, and the implementers—armies of them—at his beck and call. He could, moreover, point to international crises that Congress and most of the public agreed had to be dealt with.[63]

It is not surprising that Truman relied on both his foreign policy and military powers to respond to the time's most hostile challenge to America's treaty obligations. This came when he ordered military units into action after North Korea's invasion of South Korea in June 1950. Truman met this crisis with a decisiveness that made Franklin Roosevelt's actions of 1940 and 1941 seem dilatory. Truman cited precedents established by earlier commanders in chief to deploy American armed forces in combat situations. (Although all of these were minor, Truman did not know that Korea would be a full-scale war.) His primary justification was that, after the UN Security Council had called for action in Korea, he had a duty to respond under Articles 39 and 42 of the UN Charter. "We are," as he said later, "carrying out an obligation for the United Nations."[64] The president had consulted his advisers intensively, and he had informed some congressional leaders, but he did not ask for a declaration of war. He did not even ask Congress for something like the Gulf of Tonkin Resolution, as Lyndon Johnson would in 1964 regarding Vietnam. Truman had no doubt, whatever the criticism of his refusal to request a declaration of war, that his powers as chief diplomat—thanks to the UN Charter—and as commander in chief were constitutionally sufficient for meeting aggression in Korea. Moreover, as he said in March 1951, the "congressional power to declare war has [largely] fallen into abeyance because wars are no longer declared in advance."[65]

Truman would pay a price in increasing congressional sniping at his foreign and military policies as the war in Korea dragged on. And Republican Senator John W. Bricker of Ohio would offer an amendment to the Constitution in 1952 providing that the Constitution had primacy over treaties; that treaties and executive agreements could be effective as internal law only after the enactment of appropriate domestic legislation; and that Congress could regulate all agreements with foreign powers and international organizations. The Bricker amendment, somewhat watered down, did not come to a vote until 1954 when it was narrowly defeated by those bipartisan forces who believed that it would make a shambles of American foreign and military policy.[66] As Truman wrote as a private citizen in 1955, if the Bricker amendment were adopted "the country may as well readopt the Articles of Confederation and go back to a Greek city state."[67]

The North Atlantic Treaty of 1949 also augmented the president's powers as chief diplomat and commander in chief. It would lead to a full-scale debate in Congress in 1951 on foreign and military policy, although it was not the "Great Debate" that some fancied calling it. After Chinese Communist troops had entered the war in Korea with such devastating effect in the fall of 1950, it was increasingly asked whether American defenses should be so far flung and thus apparently vulnerable. This question had force because of the Truman administration's plans to commit additional troops to the defense of Europe, consonant with North Atlantic Treaty requirements. There were those who contended that the Senate had ratified the treaty with the understanding that that body would be consulted in meeting American obligations under the pact. Despite some confusion surrounding the ratification of the treaty, there was no firm basis to conclude that consultation had been agreed to. Beyond doubt was that, should American forces attached to the North Atlantic Treaty Organization be attacked, the United States would be at war. Truman's senatorial critics tried to head this off and to establish the right of consultation by limiting the president's power to assign troops to NATO. Truman was not concerned with the number of troops involved, for he had no reason to exceed the limit being discussed. His fight was to keep the Senate from infringing upon his powers.[68] As he declared in January 1951. "Under the President's constitutional powers as Commander in Chief of the Armed Forces he has the authority to send troops anywhere in the world. That power has been recognized repeatedly by the Congress and the courts."[69] What happened was a charade. The Senate let the president do what he had intended to do, and it indicated that in doing so—in a resolution that had no force of law—it had been consulted on the matter.

Truman's mixing of his powers as chief diplomat, commander in chief, and even chief executive was unavoidable. Truman believed that the situations he faced often called for exercising such a mixture, or at least rationalizing his actions with more than one set of constitutional powers. Be that as it may, let us now shift into high gear in considering his use of powers as commander in chief. If Truman's powers as chief diplomat gave rise to some of his most controversial actions, remember that he had broad powers purely as commander in chief, or as commander in chief and chief executive combined. One of these was his authority to remove military officers, which he importantly exercised twice. He removed Admiral Louis Denfeld as chief of naval operations in 1949 because of his criticism of the secretary of defense and the joint chiefs of staff before Congress. In a remarkably controversial action in 1951, Truman removed General Douglas MacArthur as the American commander in the Far East for his gross insubordination on policy matters. In both cases, the president had consulted top officials in the Department of Defense; only the ignorant or the politically ambitious could contend that he had not acted within his legitimate powers as commander in chief.[70]

Another aspect of Truman's role as commander in chief concerned his authority in occupied areas. There is little doubt that he and his subordinates would have acted as powerfully as they did in dealing with America's World War II enemies. Any question of their authority to do so, however, was removed by the Supreme Court in the case of *In re Yamashita* in 1946. This decision denied that a captured Japanese general sentenced to death by an American court martial had any constitutional rights.[71] Generally, this was interpreted as meaning that presidential activities were untouchable in occupied areas. A later related matter was unclear, though. This concerned the disciplinary powers of the commander in chief in areas occupied by American troops under the status of forces agreements concluded with allied countries beginning in 1951. It seemed clear that military personnel there would be subject to courts martial, but the question would arise as to the rights of American civilians. In 1949 Truman had said that the trials of civilians in those areas "should be conducted as we usually conduct them in this country."[72] This is not what happened, consonant with the provisions of the Uniform Code of Military Justice Act of 1950. In cases arising several years after Truman left office, the Supreme Court held that civilian dependents and employees had rights to regular constitutional trials.[73] This, of course, barely scratched the authority of the commander in chief.

One of the most controversial aspects of the commander in chief's authority during the Truman presidency regarded his emergency powers. The war powers of the president were, and remain, a murky area, one in which the courts have been reluctant to act. As Justice Robert Jackson wrote in 1944 about the war power: "I would not lead people to rely on this Court for a review that seems to me wholly delusive. . . . The chief restraint upon those who command the physical forces of the country, in the future as in the past, must be their responsibility to the political judgments of their contemporaries and to the moral judgments of history."[74] This issue arose with great force during the Truman administration with respect to the commander in chief's emergency powers. President Roosevelt had declared national emergencies in connection with World War II. These proclamations permitted the commander in chief to tap a vast reservoir of security and economic powers. This was augmented by wartime congressional grants of authority, especially regarding economic controls. Much use of the emergency powers was made, with, for example, Presidents Roosevelt and Truman ordering government seizure of business facilities in sixty instances during the years 1941–46.[75]

The tide of the commander in chief's emergency power receded only slowly after the war, largely because of the substantial residue of war-related problems. Although Truman and Congress cut back on these powers after the fighting ended in 1945, 103 emergency power provisions were still in effect in 1947, and Congress reinstated some others in 1947, 1948, and 1949. The Supreme Court upheld the president's emergency powers in principle in a 1948 case dealing with the Housing and Rent Control Act of 1947. Yet there was judicial disquiet. Justice William O. Douglas feared that the continuance of emergency powers would erode congressional authority and the Ninth and Tenth Amendments to the Constitution. Moreover, Justice Jackson warned that the president's emergency powers could be "as permanent as the war debts."[76]

Truman proclaimed a fresh national emergency in December 1950 during the darkest hours of the Korean War. This, partly bearing out

Jackson's warning, remained in effect until 1978! And the Truman, and later Nixon, emergency proclamations had only been replaced by the National Emergencies Act of 1976, which was a congressional attempt to restrain and regulate the president's emergency powers. It remains to be seen how successful this legislation—along with the War Powers Act of 1973, a better known effort to rein in the commander in chief's powers—will be. President Roosevelt's emergency proclamations remained partially in effect until 1952. Their termination did not affect Truman's 1950 emergency proclamation, which was specifically exempted and under which he exercised substantial emergency economic powers.[77]

It was unclear how far President Truman could proceed in using his emergency powers, especially since the conflict in Korea was an undeclared war. He was confident, however, how far he could go. Even before the war, he told the press that, according to the attorney general, he had the constitutional powers to deal with national emergency strikes. Truman declared, "Whenever there is an emergency, the President has immense powers to do what is right for the country." 'As chief executive, or commander in chief?" he was asked. "A combination of both," he replied.[78] Truman later modified this to add that the president determines whether there is a national emergency calling for use of his special powers unless Congress, when in session, so determines.[79] He held to that position until the Supreme Court corrected him in 1952.

This showdown came as a result of the great steel dispute of 1952, when the United Steel Workers demanded a large wage increase contrary to the government's anti-inflation program. In March, the matter was referred to the president's economic control system which, in order to avert a strike, recommended a substantial wage hike for the workers but with no price increases for steel. Management refused to accept this. Attempts to compromise the differences with management failed, and the steel workers called a strike. Truman refused to apply the cooling-off provisions of the Taft-Hartley Act because labor had been cooperative to that point. Instead, he decided on April 8 to seize the steel mills, for a "work stoppage would immediately jeopardize and imperil our national defense." In arriving at his decision, the president relied heavily on Tom Clark's 1949 statement as attorney general that "if crises arising from labor disputes in peacetime necessitate unusual steps, such as seizure, to prevent paralysis of the National economy, other inherent powers of the President may be expected to be found equal to the occasion." Moreover, Truman's good friend, Chief Justice Vinson, acting very unjudicially, advised him to proceed with the seizure. Truman justified seizing the steel mills on "the Constitution and laws of the United States, and as President and Commander in Chief." Yet he apparently had some qualms, partly because of contrary advice from several other close associates.[80] Perhaps this was demonstrated by his requests to congressional leaders for continuance of his emergency powers, specifically the authority to seize industries, which soon would lapse with the formal termination of hostilities with Japan.[81]

Nevertheless, Truman often reiterated that the president "has very great inherent powers to meet great national emergencies."[82] As he also wrote in a well-publicized letter, "The Constitution does not require me to endanger our national safety by letting all the steel mills shut down in this critical time." Truman pointed out that he had asked the other responsible parties to deal with the situation, Congress, labor, and management, but they had failed to act.[83] However forthright the president was, he found himself in a highly uncomfortable position. Defense Mobilization Director Charles E. Wilson resigned over the issue; labor refused to make further concessions; many in Congress criticized Truman for not using the Taft-Hartley Act—indeed, resolutions for his impeachment were introduced in the House; and business rallied around steel management's condemnation of his "unconstitutional" action.[84] Most important, management sought a judicial solution.

Federal Judge David Pine issued a temporary injunction against the government on April 29. The next day, after the steel workers had walked off their jobs, a federal appellate court stayed Pine's order. The government took the case to the Supreme Court and also persuaded the workers to return to work. The high court began its hearings on May 12, but as time passed things seemed less and less promising for the government.[85] In the middle of this, Truman told the press that no one could take emergency power "away from the President, because he is the Chief Executive of the Nation, and he has to be in a position to see that the welfare of the people is met." He did concede however, that he would abide by the Supreme Court's decision.[86] The Court announced its decision on June 2 in *Youngstown Sheet and Tube Co. v. Sawyer*. The justices held against the administration by a vote of six to three, declaring in effect that the president was not constitutionally empowered to seize the steel mills. Again the strike was on; again Truman sought labor-management agreement and, without success, appropriate legislation; and again he refused to use the Taft-Hartley Act. It was not until July 24 that labor and management reached an agreement, one which very much violated the government's anti-inflation guidelines on wages and prices.[87]

As for the Supreme Court's decision, it disabused Truman of his idea that he could do in a national emergency as he wished until Congress acted. Yet the Court had not struck a crippling blow to the president's powers as commander in chief. The six justices who had voted against him had disagreed as to why he had acted unconstitutionally, and a majority of the justices had agreed that the president still had wide latitude in exercising his powers. As Justice Clark, who had voted against the government, wrote, "the limits of presidential power are obscure. . . . The Constitution does grant to the President extensive authority in times of grave and imperative national emergency. In fact, to my thinking, such a grant may well be necessary to the very existence of the Constitution itself. . . . I care not whether one calls it 'residual,' 'inherent,' 'moral,' 'implied,' 'aggregate,' 'emergency,' or otherwise." Justice Jackson, who had also voted against the administration, cautioned that "We should not use this occasion to circumscribe, much less to contract, the lawful role of the President as Commander-in-Chief. I should indulge the widest latitude of interpretation to sustain his exclusive function to command the instruments of national force, at least when turned against the outside world for the security of our society." Only Justices Hugo Black and William O. Douglas broadly questioned the president's emergency powers in this case. As for the other four justices in the majority, their opinions applied only to the issue at hand. Indeed, they might have sustained Truman's seizure of the steel mills if it had not been for the existence of the Taft-Hartley Act or if the nation had faced a graver emergency.[88]

The Youngstown case demonstrated a number of things. One was that the president must be wiser in exercising his emergency powers, making sure that he has a better legal base and can make a better case for the dire consequences of inaction. This is all the more necessary when his critics, as was true with Truman in 1952, are gaining in strength in Congress and among the public. Yet the Supreme Court had shrunk from challenging Truman's authority as commander in chief in foreign and military matters in the steel seizure case. Thus, Truman and his presidential successors were able to continue exploiting the mystique of being commander in chief and the concept of the supremacy of national security very substantially. Indeed many of Truman's successors went further than had Truman, including infringing on the sovereign rights of other nations, exercising powers abroad that were denied the president at home, and using powers domestically that raised serious questions regarding the Bill of Rights. Despite the remedies prescribed during the 1970s by the courts and by Congress, depite hearings such as those on the Iran-Contra affair, the president's constitutional authority as commander in chief remains extensive, especially when used in conjuction with his powers as chief diplomat and chief executive. The issues of the Truman period, therefore, remain largely unresolved. One may raise the question, as Arthur M. Schlesinger, Jr., has, of whether Truman's seizure of the steel mills was an usurpation of power or an abuse of power. One can agree that it is better to have usurpation than abuse of power, for the former is based on no power and consequently sets no precedent. Abuse can be, and has been, justified as necessary to preserve the Constitution and the nation, which may encourage further abuses. We can ask, however, as Abraham Lincoln did in effect, are not such apparent abuses consistent with the spirit of the Constitution when they are essential to its preservation? Obviously, he thought so.[89]

Another question that arises with great force is, who is to decide? It is clear that during Truman's tenure of office the presidency grew significantly in its authority. There is also no doubt that then the president largely decided what his constitutional powers were. This occurred perhaps because Truman, as Emmet Hughes wrote, "may have been the only strongly aggressive president to have followed an equally aggressive predecessor."[90] It certainly happened because of the perceived international challenges of the post–World War II years, which led Congress, with great public support, to give the president much of the authority he requested. Occasionally, Congress even pressed it upon him. The judiciary, moreover, almost always endorsed these developments. Truman effectively exploited this situation to gain a dominant role in interpreting the Constitution by using invocations of "national security" and "general welfare," as well as his positions as chief executive, chief legislator, chief diplomat, and commander in chief. It is small wonder that some abuses occurred.

It is questionable to suggest, though, as Athan Theoharis has, that Truman's presidency was "indifferent to the law or the limitations imposed by the Constitution."[91] Neither the laws, treaties, nor the Constitution are self-executing; the president, like it or not, has the prime constitutional responsibility to enforce their provisions. Of course, one cannot rely solely on the president's self-restraint, however good the man, to prevent abuses or usurpation of power. This task primarily and constitutionally belongs to Congress, the courts, and the people. They have not done this job as satisfactorily as possible since 1945. They have, however, called the president to account, for example, in the steel seizure case, the loyalty-security program, the Vietnam War, the impeachment proceedings against Richard Nixon, the Iran-Contra affair, and arguably several elections. In considering the growth of presidential powers one must not ignore the contributions of Congress, the courts, and the people. If the presidents have erred, they have had an abundance of coconspirators outside the executive branch who have supported treaties, executive agreements, foreign adventures, additional federal domestic programs, and presidential interpretations of the Constitution, statutes, and treaties.

Harry Truman spoke to the overall issue in 1952 when he said, "The Constitution is a living force—it is a growing thing. The Constitution belongs to no one group of people and to no single branch of Government. We acknowledge our judges as the interpreters of the Constitution, but our executive branch and our legislative branch alike operate within its framework and must apply it and its principles in all they do."[92] I would add that, to achieve this, one must heed Thomas Jefferson's caveat, "Eternal vigilance is the price of Liberty." The Constitution will probably continue to evolve, subject to the interplay among the three branches of government and the people in response to their needs, fears, and ambitions. As Truman asserted in 1945, "Our Constitution came from a free and sometimes bitter exchange of conflicting opinions."[93] Villains, heroes, and ordinary folk have contributed to continuing that "sometimes bitter exchange." What makes it challenging is that it is not always clear who the villains and the heroes are. Thus presidents can be wrong and, therefore, occasionally threaten constitutional government. So can members of Congress, judges, and private citizens. What is important is that they sustain the debate over the interpretation of the Constitution. As long as the debate endures, the Constitution endures. The greatest danger lies in passivity, however alarming constitutional debate may seem at times. When any element in the American political system is aggressive, the other elements must be vigilant that neither it nor they go to irresponsible extremes. In this broadened concept of checks and balances lies not a guarantee but the best chance for perpetuating constitutional government in the United States.

PART II

The Constitution and the Modern Presidency:
Political Science Perspectives

Introduction to Part II

The essays by the five political science scholars on the modern presidency effectively demonstrate the historical continuity of the Madisonian-Hamiltonian interpretations of executive power. Domestic policy and formulation of the federal budget, as discussed by Jeffrey Tulis and Louis Fisher, focus on executive-legislative interdependence and tensions. In these two essays, the constitutional issue is whether or not the "executive power" found in Article II is a broad grant of authority to modernize the national economy and to set budgetary priorities; or, conversely, whether such "executive power" is constrained by the subsequent enumerated powers of Article II and the legislative powers found in Article I, Section 8 of the Constitution. Tulis and Fisher also deal with Madison's arguments over the separation of powers. Can the president interpret the Constitution alone in expanding executive authority, or is there a necessity to share power with the legislative branch?

Louis Koenig and Richard Pious focus upon the president's powers in foreign relations and the war power. They address several important constitutional issues related to the Hamiltonian concept of a "vigorous" chief executive. Is the president preeminent in conducting foreign policy? Is the treaty-making power still important in view of the modern use of executive agreements with other countries? How extensive is presidential authority under the commander-in-chief clause? Does the presidential oath imply the use of "emergency powers" and "executive prerogative" in national emergencies and military affairs? Does Congress maintain a role in declaring war, or have recent presidents superseded Congress with a general warmaking power? Does the War Powers Act of 1973 restrain presidents who commit U.S. armed forces in various foreign arenas?

Donald Robinson focuses upon the tensions between strong presidential leadership and the need for constraints when abuses occur. In his essay, Robinson updates the earlier constitutional debates concerning the desire to constrain executive authority (Madison) with the advocates of the Hamiltonian chief executive. Abuses such as Watergate and the Iran-Contra Affair may require a reexamination of executive-legislative relationships. Various reforms should be considered, although Robinson rejects "constitutional tinkering" and adaptation of the British parliamentary model to replace the Madisonian system of separation of powers and checks and balances. Instead, Robinson argues for more executive-legislative balance and cooperation to prevent executive abuse, while maintaining a vigorous presidency subject to democratic controls and accountability.

Theodore Lowi provides a summary overview of the presidency and the Constitution by emphasizing the paradox of presidential power and the ideological struggle over its interpretation. He contrasts the historians' emphasis on a heroic model of the presidency with political scientists divided between a liberal-oriented domestic necessity or deadlock model and conservatives who favor a war model of enhanced executive power. After analyzing each of the approaches, Lowi concludes by endorsing a radical constitutional viewpoint which emphasizes separation of powers and checks and balances. In agreeing with Donald Robinson's interpretation of presidential power, Lowi concurs that excessive executive authority needs to be checked in both domestic and foreign policy to restore the kind of balance originally envisioned by the Framers when they drafted the Constitution.

Chapter 7

The Constitutional Presidency in American Political Development

—————————————————— *Jeffrey K. Tulis*

Jeffrey Tulis argues that the post–New Deal presidency is wrongly thought to be a constitutional revolution. Instead, "big government" and the strong presidency are to be found in the 1787 Constitution, for example, in provisions dealing with a commercial economy, national taxation authority, and an independent chief executive. To make this case, Tulis sketches a framework for constitutional interpretation, which requires the identification and definition of core commitments, their philosophic presuppositions, and their institutional, cultural and policy implications. This approach suggests not only a new interpretation of American political development, but also a new way to conceptualize the "pathologies" associated with modern governance.

Geneseo Master Critic Theodore Lowi took exception to Tulis's provocative arguments. Lowi argued that the modern presidency and large national government are the products of historical discontinuities, such as war or economic crises, which fundamentally altered the balance of power between the states and the national government. In his rebuttal, Tulis claimed that a focus on historical discontinuities demonstrates both the expansion and repudiation of executive power. By focusing on the *Federalist Papers*, scholars can find Hamilton's emphasis on a strong presidency in the original Constitution.

It is now commonplace to observe that the New Deal represented a constitutional revolution in American governance. The establishment of a welfare state, the birth of a huge administrative apparatus for domestic affairs, the expansion of executive powers at the head of the national government, and the development of an unmediated, plebiscitary, relation between the president and the people are all said to mark a distinctively new America, born of this constitutional revolution.[1] In ordinary discourse these new policies and these new institutions are sometimes signified by the summary worry, "Big

Government." There can be no doubt that America has changed, that twentieth-century America is very different from the nineteenth-century polity in these respects, and that the twentieth-century political order contains trouble within it connected to these developments.

But the familiar argument that such change represents a constitutional revolution is wrong, or mostly wrong. Properly conceived, the Constitution is better understood as the generator of these developments rather than the repudiator of them, or most of them. Only the plebiscitary presidency can be shown to be radically inconsistent with the original Constitution, and even it might have been an unintended result of the Constitution, generated by institutional needs, if not the explicit plan, of the original regime. On this reading, big government and the modern presidency are not new at all, but rather implicit in commitments ratified two centuries ago. Their later emergence signifies the development of a constitutional logic, not the repudiation of constitutional principle.[2]

I do not mean to argue the prescriptive merits of this constitutional design here. To be sure, the Constitution has considerable flaws, and some of those, too, were built into the original arrangements. These and other problems that have developed later cannot be adequately described and assessed, however, before we recover a rudimentary constitutional logic, a constitutional frame of mind.

In this essay, I want to introduce that frame of mind by (1) reviewing the scope and character of several basic constitutional commitments, (2) discussing some of the formal features of this kind of constitutional interpretation, and (3) finally, contrasting this view of American political development and this kind of interpretation with the best argument I know that is opposed to it—that of Theodore Lowi, in his recent book, *The Personal President*.

Constitutional Commitments

The nationalization of American politics, big government, and a powerful presidency were all generated by the nineteenth-century constitutional order, prescribed by its most coherent partisans, and predicted by astute opponents of the constitutional polity. I will mainly draw upon *The Federalist* to sketch these commitments, but it is important to note at the outset how little disagreement there was regarding the meaning of the Constitution in these most fundamental respects during the ratification debates. Antifederalists warned of the dangers of centralized power, of a standing army, of a powerful executive, of the nationalization of policy—in short, they warned against adopting the

Constitution. Federalists defended the benefits of these very same features. Both sides, therefore, agreed on what the fundamental features of the regime would be. They disagreed over the desirability of the new regime, not over its logic. I will try to reiterate this important point by sketching the fundamental commitments that defined the regime—the commitment to the protection of individual rights, the commitment to Union, and the commitment to a large commercial republic.

Rights

In his influential book, *The Creation of the American Republic*, Gordon Wood argues that the adoption of the Constitution represented, to Federalists and Antifederalists alike, the abandonment of classical republicanism.[3] No longer dedicated to the cultivation of virtue as its own reward, or to the aspiration toward a common good, Americans adopted a form of government designed to protect individual rights. Gary Schmitt and Robert Webking have shown that this story is misleading. None of the American proponents of "classical republicanism" cited by Wood held the view or adopted the perspective that he attributes to them. None regarded virtue as its own reward. Rather, they regarded virtue, especially civic virtue, as an indispensable *means* toward the protection and security of individual rights. The political discourse of the era on all points of the viable political spectrum, they persuasively argue, was unequivocally "liberal" in the sense that rights trumped virtue in the hierarchy of legitimate governmental ends.[4] Antifederalists had opposed the Constitution not because they preferred virtue to rights, but because they feared that the new regime provided too little protection for rights. And after losing the battle over the original Constitution, they won a battle to amend the document not by adding a Bill of Virtues, but rather a Bill of Rights.

The debate over the constitution of America, then, began with a shared and settled commitment to the cornerstone of liberalism—individual rights. The great divisions of debate and contests of principle concerned the implications of this commitment and the relative merits of alternative constitutions to secure it.

Traditionally, republican government was thought possible only in a small nation possessed of a relatively homogeneous population and amenable to the inculcation of civic virtue. The Antifederalists believed that the states were, and could continue to be, modeled on that republican tradition. Large republics, they feared, would inevitably turn into monarchies, because only a monarch could extend the authority of government over a vast territory and discordant peoples, whereas a small republic could rely upon the attachment of the people themselves to their regime, to their principles, to ensure government's authority. The proposed Constitution committed Americans to a large republic. That commitment spawned two fundamental controversies that generated further commitments: a controversy over "states rights," and a controversy over the nature of the political economy implicit in the proposed Constitution.

Union

Both sides entered the debate over the Constitution prepared to amend the Articles of Confederation to strengthen the central government's authority to provide for a common defense for the several states. Under the Articles of Confederation the states were the sovereign entities, while under the Constitution the ratifiers all realized the national government would be sovereign. This feature of the Constitution is implicit in the idea of a constitution itself (as opposed to a treaty or compact) and is manifest in the supremacy clause, in the provisions for amendment, and in the Preamble. Hamilton's basic defense of this massive change was that the "central government" under the Articles was a government in name and responsibility, but not in structure and power. In short, it was not a government at all. "The great and radical vice in the construction of the existing Confederation," said Hamilton, "is in the principle of legislation for states or governments, in their corporate or collective capacities, and as contradistinguished from the individuals of whom they consist."[5]

Only the states were true governments under the Articles, and the central "authority," totally dependent upon them, was incapable of adequately carrying out even the most elementary functions of any government, such as defense. Hamilton delineated and defended the two features of the new government that would make it, truly, a government: (1) a direct, unmediated, coercive relation between the national government and individual citizens, and (2) the interpretive proposition (again evident to many opponents, although objectionable to them) that the new Constitution contained all the power necessary to accomplish its limited ends.[6]

The Antifederalists charged that the character of the new arrangement insured that, over time, the states would be absorbed into a national regime. The Federalists did not so much deny this as attempt to deflect attention away from it, and to highlight certain *mitigating* features of the new regime, such as the provision for state equality in the Senate.[7] It is ironic that modern day "states rights" advocates trace their lineage to the Antifederalists, because the Antifederalists stated the nationalist interpretation of the Constitution even more clearly than did Federalists. They realized that there is precious little support for the notion of "states rights" in the Constitution. This is not to say that their concerns for the political benefits of "federalism" are not persuasive. Smaller governments and associations sometimes can rectify problems born of excessive centralization.[8] But this concession was transformed by the Constitution from a matter of constitutive principle to one of discretionary policy. This characteristic of "federalism" is no more evident than in President Reagan's "New Federalism." The "New Federalism" is a *national* policy adopted by the national government and changeable in the future by the national government. Reversing the Articles, under the Constitution only the national government is a true government.

Political Economy

The second major commitment that stemmed from the decision to create a large republic rather than a confederacy of small ones was the development of a national commercial economy. In *Federalist Paper*, Number 10, James Madison articulated his well-known interpretation of the American political economy. His argument is very complex, but for our purposes several of its key points will suffice.

The characteristic political problem of all republics, according to Madison, is their tendency to factious dispute. Traditionally, this vice was constrained by civic virtue, homogeneity, in short, by narrowing and monitoring political difference. A large republic, he argued, held out the prospect of two new remedies to the problem of faction. First, size would necessitate representation rather than direct citizen democracy and thereby permit the refinement of political opinion through deliberation. He placed greater reliance on a second remedy, the extent of the nation itself, which would encourage the proliferation of factions so that no one might come to dominate and no few could easily combine. Crucial to this second solution were the kinds of factions that would be encouraged. The principle of equality would have the effect of delegitimizing religious factions by taming or secularizing them. And the development of a national economy would permit the proliferation of commercial pursuits. Commercial affairs would come to dominate the national character. Preoccupied with private commercial affairs, Americans would be depoliticized as their minds were drawn away from the great contests of political and religious principle to the smaller contentions of business. Government, too, could devote itself to the tasks of "administration" rather than the mediation of contending fundamental principles, such as oligarchy and democracy.

In the end, no change was more worrisome to many Antifederalists, particularly from the south, than the commitment to a commercial economy. Despite Hamilton's argument that agricultural and commercial economies had become interdependent and mutually supportive, agrarian Antifederalists knew that this commitment would ultimately change the private lives and associations, as well as explicit public policies of Americans.[9] The Federalists insisted, however, that the prior commitment to individual liberty would be better fostered by commercial than agrarian aspirations. Opportunities would be greater, and the prospect of substantial financial reward would tempt and preoccupy men of towering ambition who might otherwise have no outlet for it other than political tyranny.

Recalling the first constitutional commitment, to protect individual rights, the national economy was seen as a means to promote and reward individual talent. A commercial republic, by its nature, requires some protection for property rights, but it must be noted that the more fundamental commitment to individual liberty limits and directs that protection. Madison put the point this way:

> The diversity in the faculties of men, from which the rights
> of property originate, is not less an insuperable obstacle to a
> uniformity of interests. The protection of these faculties is the
> first object of government.[10]

From the protection of property, different kinds and amounts of property result. These differences are the source of the most common and durable sorts of factious dispute—those between the haves and the have-lesses. But because property is not the most fundamental commitment, *diverse faculties are*, governmental regulation is a logical extension of the decision to create a commercial republic in the first place. Writing two hundred years ago, Madison said, "The *regulation* of these various and interfering interests forms the *principal task* of modern legislation...."[11]

The commitments to Union and to a commercial economy come together in the *Federalist*'s discussion of taxation. The power of taxation in the new Constitution provoked heated debate because it captured, in one function, all of the basic commitments and their implications that I have discussed. Antifederalists worried that the power to tax implied "the power to destroy." The Federalists did not deny this, but urged that safety from the abuse of power did not rest with trimming power, but rather in the structure of the institutions charged with its exercise.[12] They conceded, indeed asserted, that a full authority to tax reveals the sovereign government's primordial power because it requires a direct coercive relation between the government and the individual. Under the Articles, that relation was mediated by the states, who held such coercive power. In establishing the Constitution, the ratifiers altered this most basic feature of American life.

The Presidency

The basic decisions sketched above committed the Founders to seek institutional innovations as well, partly to make power safe, as I just indicated, but also and more fundamentally to make power possible. The Articles, which lacked sovereign power, appropriately, lacked an executive too. Even the War was prosecuted through legislative committee, which experienced considerable difficulty.[13] The Constitution created an exceptionally strong executive. Many Antifederalists thought the executive too monarchic, and while Hamilton replied that the president would have less prerogatives than the British king, he conceded that the president would be stronger than the strongest state governor. Indeed, Hamilton went still further and offered the proposition that Americans had better hope that executive energy could be made compatible with republican principle, because executive power was indispensable to *any* government.[14]

The elements of the Constitution that established executive strength included an open-ended description of his power, which unlike the legislative article was barely specified. More significant, however, were the president's *structural properties*—unity, independence from the legislature, and reeligibility. Scholars today who do not attribute much significance to the Constitution in American political development often point unwittingly to these very structural features when they account for the dramatic increase in presidential responsibility and power in the twentieth century. In his influential book *Presidential Power*, Richard Neustadt concludes that a president's strategic advantages stem from the fact that "no one else sits where he sits," an unintended shorthand for the Constitution's structural properties.[15] Hamilton makes clear that these properties manifest a design, a purpose, to permit and encourage most aspects of leadership that have become so familiar to us.

I must note at this juncture that Hamilton did not recommend, and the Constitution gives little support to, "popular leadership," the routine appeal "over the heads" of Congress in support of executive initiatives. As Theodore Roosevelt was to argue much later, *occasional* popular appeals could be justified as logical extensions of the Constitution. The Founders feared, however, that there was no institutional means to prevent the *routinization* of popular appeals short of a general proscription.

Popular leadership was proscribed, but statesmanship was not. The Constitution encourages the president to initiate, plan, and direct, in addition to a more conservative role of withstanding popular pressure upon the government. These two roles are complementary, not contradictory. Structural properties of the Constitution (principally unity and independence) determined that presidents would inhabit a political position that would give them the institutional advantages that they have indeed come to display, although of course, they cannot determine that all presidents will use those advantages or that they will use them well.[16]

It has become common wisdom among presidency scholars that the administration of Franklin Roosevelt marked the emergence of a modern presidency, one which not only led and administered New Deal policies, but also embodied a more general "imperial" role. Among the prominent features of this new imperialism often mentioned are the growth of unilateral powers (such as the use of executive privilege), the use of the veto for policy purposes in addition to constitutional objection, and the development of a large White House staff.[17] The first two "new" functions are defended explicitly by Hamilton in *The Federalist*, while the third is an institutional implication of the growth of the nation and the government altogether, which I have tried to indicate was implicit in the original design.

This sketch suggests that we need to disconnect the problems of plebiscitary leadership from the development of big government. To be sure, big government requires a strong executive, but it is not clear that it entails a democratized presidency. Indeed, the original justification for presidential control of administration, argued by Madison in the first Congress's debate over the power of removal, rested upon the president's antidemocratic properties.[18] The development of independent regulatory commissions was, in part, a response to the democratization of the presidency.

This democratization (what I call the rhetorical presidency) was initially legitimized not by the New Deal, but by the comprehensive reinterpretation of the constitutional order articulated earlier by Woodrow Wilson. After attempting to formally amend the Constitution and failing, Wilson adopted a strategy of reinterpreting it and its institutional principles. The self-understanding of presidents, citizens, and scholars is now defined by that large view. For example, the common misperception that the Constitution adopted an *essentially* "checks-and-balances" view of separation of powers began with Wilson. Wilson offered new views of other fundamental properties, such as representation and independence, and these have had considerable influence as well. It is important to note that because his perspective was not inscribed by any structural changes of the Constitution, we now inhabit a polity whose presidency is governed *simultaneously* by the commitments and implications of the original design and the imperatives of a new plebiscitary perspective that has been superimposed upon the Constitution. It is in this political twilight that many of the dilemmas of modern governance may be seen.[19]

Policy Implications

I do not mean to argue that all the policies of the Progressive and New Deal eras occurred inevitably or that all agencies, programs, and regulations developed in the cause of big government were constitutional. For one thing, there is no single strand of policies that marks these eras. Many policies contradicted one another. More importantly, the arguments I have sketched cannot readily yield judgments regarding the wisdom or constitutionality of particular policies at particular times. Much more is needed for that. And arguments of the sort I have sketched cannot account for the precise timing of political developments like the New Deal. But these kinds of arguments do suffice, I think, to indicate that the broad defining features of New Deal liberalism are implicit in, and facilitated by, the original design. Americans had committed themselves to a national government, a national economy, and a strong executive long before the necessity of those attributes for our polity became fully manifest. They became manifest because of social, cultural, and political developments that the fundamental commitments initially set in motion.

One might argue, for example, against particular trust-busting policies. But once one has made the commitment to a political economy as a *means* toward eliminating factious tyranny by a minority or majority, can one deny the national government a constitutional authority to break up massive combinations of wealth? The same logic implies a power to *regulate*, indeed, in the proper circumstances and for proper purposes, to redistribute.

A Constitutional Frame of Mind

It is certainly obvious to all, if not unsettling, that I have sketched a constitutional argument with little attempt to analyze particular clauses of the document, or to trace the glosses on those clauses offered by courts. This is due partly to the need to cover a lot of ground in a short space—a full showing could stand much more attention to the Preamble, the Tenth Amendment, comparisons of Articles I and II and of other textual provisions. However, the basic argument and style of interpretation does not require, and might be subverted by, narrowly exegetical or legal analysis.

Consider the analysis of *Federalist Paper*, Number 10, widely regarded as a profound, perhaps the most profound, constitutional analysis of the character of American politics. No clauses of the Constitution are mentioned there. Madison displays a polity that seems to be both prior to, and beyond, a text. Of course, *The Federalist* as a whole makes repeated references to the text. But even these textual analyses are subservient to a larger constitutional frame of mind as exemplified in Number 10. One can describe that frame of mind as an openness to three rudimentary features of a constitutional logic: (1) constitutional commitments (2) the philosophic presuppositions of those commitments, and (3) the institutional and policy implications of those commitments.

The commitments themselves are rooted in and revealed by the text, but it is a text not confined to the page on which it is written. William F. Harris has shown clearly that the Constitution is both a signifier and that which is signified.[20] He describes these as the text and the working polity or text-analogue. Put simply, the Constitution's principles and propositions are not simply a set of "parchment distinctions" (to borrow Madison's pejorative characterization of the state constitutions); they are rather the organizers and generators of an actual polity. Federalists and Antifederalists alike possessed this understanding of the Constitution in the natural state of actual constitution makers (rather than the artificial one of self-conscious constitutional theorists). The Constitution is an attempt to create a whole polity, and the basic features of that polity are what I have labeled "constitutional commitments." A constitutional logic is the mutual relation of these commitments, their philosophic presuppositions, and their institutional and policy implications.

It may be useful to indicate what a constitutional frame of mind is not:

1. It is not "clause bound." Individual clauses need to be interpreted in light of the structure and purposes of the whole document and the polity that it signifies.

2. It is not dependent upon the intentions of the Framers. This proposition might seem troubling since I repeatedly refer to the

arguments of Federalists and Antifederalists. But I appealed to them as *indicators* of a constitutional logic, not as *authority* for the points I wish to press. The historical Framers offer considerable advantages to citizens today who wish to understand the Constitution. That is not because the Framers were *authoritative*. It is rather that the natural activity of framing provided them a *perspective* that has been lost after the Constitution took effect. Recovery of their perspective is extremely important, while particular Founders' conceptions and insights remain useful only as they remain coherent interpretations of the Constitution.

3. It is not a legal frame of mind, but rather a political perspective. As Sotirios A. Barber has recently shown, the decisions of the Supreme Court are only authoritative when they are adequate articulators of a constitutional frame of mind. If the Constitution is truly supreme, Barber shows, decisions of the Court can not *determine* (in the sense of make, or create) the Constitution's meaning, they can only attempt to discover it. It follows that they can, and often do, fail to articulate the meaning of the Constitution.[21]

4. Finally, because of its attention to implications, a constitutional frame of mind can not be constrained by particular historical practices, absent a larger interpretation of their place in constitutional logic. Just as a constitutionalist does not take clauses out of context, or peg meaning to particular intentions, so, too, it would be mistaken to simply survey nineteenth-century political practices and abstract from them alone fundamental constitutional commitments. The Constitution, after all, was adopted to *change* things, not to simply reflect custom. Consequently, the constitutional interpreter must attend to the aspirations toward which the polity was directed.[22]

Confirmation in Opposition

To return to the political themes of the paper, I have not detailed the connection between the original constitutional commitments and the varied and multiple institutions of contemporary governance in America. I have painted a picture with broad strokes and drawn very general conclusions from the implications of that constitutional picture. It would not be unreasonable to respond to my argument thus far by claiming that one could accept my account of the original design but doubt its inextricable connection to "big government" as we experience it today. Even granting my earlier remarks that my account of the original design does not automatically settle difficult particular questions regarding the constitutionality or politcal wisdom of specific policies and specialized institutions—the general connection between "big government" and the Constitution may still be in doubt. To be sure, it can be no more than a provocative showing rather than a definitive account, absent a detailed political history that I can not provide here.

But I may be a bit more persuasive in conclusion by pointing to one of the finest recent accounts of American governance which argues, contrary to me, that "big government" signals a constitutional transformation. Theodore Lowi's *The Personal President* offers a wide-ranging and probing critique of American politics today, seeing it burdened with pathologies traceable to developments that mark a fundamental discontinuity with the founding.[23] His analysis of the pathologies is especially interesting and often convincing, but it is the latter issue— the disconnection of "pathological" big government from the original Constitution—that I wish to discuss.

In order to make a case for the transformation of the founding, for the emergence of a "second republic," Lowi finds that he must deny most of the key commitments that I sketched earlier were America's commitments. Lowi's account is interesting precisely because he is driven to the most fundamental features of our constitutional logic, and he denies that they are so. Whereas I begin with commitments and extrapolate their implications, Lowi begins with "big government," discovers its necessary constitutional presuppositions, but denies they are our commitments. So if you accept my account of the commitments, Lowi's book will provide you more evidence of their inextricable connection to the broad features of modern governance in America.

Lowi constructs a striking contrast between the responsibilities of the state and national governments under the original Constitution. Beginning with the premise that the Constitution provides the national government with only *expressly* delegated powers, reserving all others to the states, Lowi derives a list of national responsibilities from the list of legislative powers adumbrated in Article I. He assigns a representative list of other governmental functions to the states. This division, reproduced below as Table One, shows clearly that the states, in Lowi's interpretation, do most of the governing. There are a number of problems with this depiction. First, there are several powers and responsibilities mentioned in Article I, Section 8, that Lowi does not mention, chief among them "to lay and collect taxes...to pay the debts and provide for the common defense and *general welfare* of the United States"; "to borrow money on the credit of the United States" and "to regulate commerce among the states." Second, by restricting the enumeration of legitimate national activity to the legislative article, he

Table One

Specialization of functions between national government and the states in the traditional system. From Lowi, *Personal President*, p. 24.

1. National govt. functions (domestic)	2. State government functions
Internal improvements	Property laws (incl. slavery)
Subsidies	Estate and inheritance laws
Tariffs	Commerce laws (ownership and
Public lands disposal	exchange)
Patents	Banking and credit laws
Coinage	Insurance laws
	Family laws
	Morals laws
	Public health and quarantine
	Education laws
	General penal laws
	Public works laws (incl.
	eminent domain)
	Construction codes
	Land-use laws
	Water and mineral resources laws
	Judiciary and criminal procedure
	Electoral laws
	Local government laws
	Civil Service laws
	Occupations and professions laws
	Etc.

violates the terms of the very section he employs which concludes with the provision "to make all Laws which shall be necessary and proper for carrying into Execution the foregoing powers, *and all other Powers vested by this Constitution in the Government of the United States, or in any Department or Officer thereof.*" Third, Lowi asserts without argument that constitutions may only contain expressly granted powers. Neither Federalists, like Publius, nor Antifederalists, like Brutus, held this view. Indeed, as is well known, Hamilton spells out in considerable detail a means-ends logic that compels the conclusion that there are implied powers in the Constitution.[24]

More significant than the clause-bound interpretation, however, is the fundamental commitment that is abstracted from it. Lowi argues that the Constitution meant to make "the state laws...more fundamental than the national laws." Contrary to my interpretation of

The Federalist and the worry of almost all the Antifederalists, Lowi argues that the Constitution is, in effect, a set of amendments to the Articles of Confederation.

He sees the implications of this strikingly original claim quite clearly. In his account, the New Deal established for *the first time* the fact of, and principle behind, a new relation between the national government and the people: "For the first time the national government *established a direct and coercive relationship between itself and individual citizens.*"[25] This is, of course, not factually true, but it is true that such a claim is constitutionally consistent with the case Lowi wishes to build. While I don't think he has faced up to political history here, (e.g., the Civil War) there is something laudable in his willingness to follow so faithfully the logic in the claim that the New Deal marked a constitutional revolution.

This logic is extended to some of the institutional commitments I have discussed. For example, Lowi argues that the original Constitution embraced legislative supremacy and that the president was intended to be in fact, if not in name, "an essentially parliamentary office."[26]

Why does Lowi reach such different conclusions about America's fundamental commitments? Part of the reason for this very different reading of the Constitution must be that Lowi adopts strategies of constitutional interpretation different from my own. Lowi embraces a clause- or article-bound interpretivism, an appeal to concrete states of minds or original intentions, and finally, to an identification of constitutional design with original contemporaneous practice. These provide some evidence for commitments opposite those I sketched.

But the most striking feature of *The Personal President* is the larger constitutional logic that it reveals and evidences: an intimate connection between the principles of liberty, Union, a national economy, a strong presidency, and the legacies of the New Deal.

Chapter 8

The Constitution and Presidential Budget Powers: The Modern Era

————————————————— *Louis K. Fisher*

According to Louis Fisher, budgeting is central to constitutional government, but the present system is so complex that it hinders executive-legislative accountability. Fisher traces this problem to the 1974 Congressional Budget Act, under which Congress sought parity with the president in preparing budgets. This was a significant departure from the 1921 Budget and Accounting Act, where the President prepared the budget and Congress implemented it through authorization and appropriation bills. Fisher claims that the 1974 law produced spending increases, soaring deficits, and the inability to approve appropriations on time. The 1985 Gramm-Rudman-Hollings Act showed that Congress could not control the deficit problem. Geneseo Master Critic Theodore Lowi observed that Fisher placed too much blame on Congress. Fisher disagreed. The 1981 Reagan tax cuts and military increases required Congress to discover new revenue sources or to increase deficits. Simultaneously, Congress has become so enmeshed in interchamber and partisan dissension that budgets have not been approved on time. Fisher dismisses proposals for an executive line-item veto or a balanced budget amendment as unworkable. Instead, he urges repeal of the 1974 law and the return of full budget preparation authority to the president.

The Constitution vests in Congress the ultimate power of the purse: the power to appropriate and the power to tax. Our system of government also places important budgetary responsibilities and spending decisions in the president. How do we reconcile these institutional rivalries? Can this natural competition and conflict be channeled in a constructive direction to serve the public interest?

Budgeting is central to constitutional government. From English history we know that the power of the purse is intimately associated with major struggles between the executive and legislative branches. The triumph of the legislature is directly connected to the protection

147

of individual rights and liberties. Our system of government must deliver not only basic needs and services, but do so with accountability. To hold government accountable, citizens must be able to understand the processes and activities of budgeting.

Unfortunately, the present system is excruciatingly difficult for everyone: for executive officials, for legislators, and for the general public. In 1984, Congressman John Dingell said this about our budget process: "What we have done over the past decade is to create a budget process that is so complex as to be incomprehensible to almost everyone. Most of the Members do not understand it beyond a super-ficial level. The press does not understand it. The business community does not understand it. The financial community does not understand it. And most important of all, the public does not understand it."[1]

This paper explores the relationship between the budget and constitutional values, with special attention to the twentieth century. We need to understand contemporary issues, such as Gramm-Rudman, but to do that we must create a broader context. To know where we are, and where we are going, we have to build a foundation.

The topics in this paper include the "executive budget," as adopted in the Budget and Accounting Act of 1921; the effort to reassert congressional control in the Budget Act of 1974; the Gramm-Rudman Act of 1985, including its travails in the federal courts; and the proposal to grant the president a line-item veto. The paper ends with an appeal to think deeply about constitutional requirements and institutional capabilities.

Basic Institutional Structures

Article I, Section 9, of the Constitution provides that "No Money shall be drawn from the Treasury, but in Consequence of Appropriations made by Law." This is the source of Congress' power of the purse. The details of that power, together with the institutional apparatus for budgeting, had to await statutory action and the adoption of congres-sional rules. The Constitution makes no mention of appropriations committees. It does not distinguish between appropriations and authorizations. Nothing in the Constitution requires a budget. For almost a century, tax committees (Ways and Means in the House, and Finance in the Senate) handled both appropriations bills and revenue measures.

Although the president was not directed to prepare a budget in the form we know it today, the first secretary of the treasury, Alexander Hamilton, wanted to exercise power along the lines of the British parliamentary model. He was active in formulating policy and shepherding it through Congress. A number of legislators regarded his activity as an improper encroachment on congressional prerogatives. Investigations in 1793 and 1794 were so fierce that Hamilton resigned from office.[2]

The custom at that time was for executive agencies to transmit their budget requests to Congress in a "Book of Estimates." Neither the secretary of the treasury nor the president was formally responsible for the contents of this document, but several presidents intervened to revise budget estimates before they went to Congress. Their secretaries of the treasury assisted them in that task. Some presidents entered office with exceptional qualifications for budgeting. For example, James K. Polk had been chairman of the House Ways and Means Committee.[3]

For most of the nineteenth century there was little difficulty in adopting and implementing a budget. Customs revenues usually covered the modest expenditures of the federal government. In fact, there were periods of surplus when excess funds were used to liquidate the national debt or to distribute funds to the states. Deficits increased sharply at the time of the Civil War, forcing Congress to restructure its committee system. In 1865, the house reduced the jurisdiction of the Ways and Means Committee to revenue bills. Its other responsibilities were parceled out to two new committees: an Appropriations Committee and a Committee on Banking and Currency. Two years later the Senate created an Appropriations Committee.

Although the president received no new statutory powers over the budget, public perceptions changed. At both a state and national level, legislators were viewed as corrupt spenders. The post–Civil War period was "marked by excesses of freebooting entrepreneurs and political spoilsmen that led to constitutional, statutory, and judicial restraints designed to protect the victims of what seemed an age of greed, grab, and gain."[4]

Reformers looked to the executive office as the source of economy and efficiency. Presidents, not Congress, held the role of guardian of the purse. Political cartoons captured this change in perceptions. After Congress overrode President Arthur's veto of a rivers and harbors bill, which Arthur condemned as a vehicle for wasteful log-rolling, the cartoonist Thomas Nast came to the rescue. Arthur, holding a rifle, is seen watching an oversized vulture perched on the Capitol consuming his veto message. The cartoon contained these words of encouragement: "President Arthur, hit him again! Don't let the vulture become our national bird."[5]

President Cleveland penned a number of blistering veto messages to protest what seemed to him totally meritless pension bills for veterans. In another Nast cartoon, Cleveland is shown manfully blocking the door to the U.S. Treasury while thwarted pension agents slink from his presence.[6] If Nast were alive today, I suspect he would have both Congress and the president perched atop the Capitol, with both branches making unseemly raids on the treasury.

Under the pressure of mounting budget deficits at the end of the nineteenth century and the early twentieth century, Congress established committees and commissions to recommend more efficient practices by executive agencies. At Taft's request, Congress appropriated $100,000 in 1910 to encourage studies into more efficient ways of conducting the government's business. Taft used the money to set up a commission. Two years later he submitted the commission's proposal for a national budget. The idea was to make the president responsible for reviewing departmental estimates and organizing them to form a coherent document.[7]

On June 10, 1912, Taft directed departmental heads to prepare two sets of estimates: one for the customary Book of Estimates and a second for the national budget recommended by his commission. Since the budgetary situation had improved and there was little likelihood that Taft would be reelected that year, Congress passed legislation to block his plans. A statute directed agency personnel to prepare estimates and to submit them to Congress only in the form required by law.[8] Congress believed that the budget format was part of its spending prerogative. For his part, Taft regarded the form in which he transmitted recommendations to Congress as purely an executive matter. He therefore told department heads to prepare two sets of estimates:

> Under the constitution the President is entrusted with the executive power and is responsible for the acts of heads of departments and their subordinates as his agents, and he can use them to assist him in his constitutional duties, one of which is to recommend measures to Congress and to advise it as [to] the existing conditions and their betterment.... If the President is to assume a responsibility for either the manner in which business of the government is transacted or result obtained, it is evident that he cannot be limited by Congress to such information as that branch may think sufficient for his purposes. In my opinion, *it is entirely competent for the President to submit a budget,* and Congress can not forbid or prevent it.[9]

Congress could not forbid it, but neither did legislators have to pay any attention to the budget when it arrived. His model was almost completely ignored. After leaving office, Taft lamented the dust accumulating on the reports of his commission.[10]

Budget and Accounting Act

Just as Civil War debts had forced Congress to make fundamental changes in its committee system, so did the costs of World War I precipitate a move to a modern budget system at the national level. Federal spending climbed from about $700 million before the war to $12.7 billion by 1918, and to $18.5 billion by 1919. The national debt, which stood at about one billion dollars in 1916, leaped to over $25 billion by 1919. Members of Congress realized that new powers would have to be delegated to the president to respond to these developments.

In 1919 the House of Representatives created the Select Committee on the Budget. The objective was not to devise the theoretical ideal. The Committee was expected to recommend a system "in complete harmony with our constitutional form of government." Changes were needed in three areas: formulation of the budget, congressional action on the budget, and supervision and control of the execution of the budget. Statutory action was required for the first and third areas. The second could be accomplished by changing the rules of the House and the Senate.[11]

The Select Committee identified a multitude of problems: spending was not considered in connection with revenues; Congress did not require the president to present a carefully thought-out financial program; spending estimates submitted to Congress represented only the desires of the individual departments, establishments, and bureaus; and these requests were not revised by a superior officer to bring them into harmony, eliminate duplication, or make them conform to the needs of the nation. The committee condemned the lack of accountabililty in the system:

> Practically everyone familiar with its workings agrees that its failure lies in the fact that no one is made responsible for the extravagance. The estimates are a patchwork and not a structure. As a result, a great deal of the time of the committees of Congress is taken up in exploding the visionary schemes of bureau chiefs for which no administration would be willing to stand responsible.[12]

The committee concluded that responsibility would have to be concentrated in the White House to subject bureau and departmental estimates to "scrutiny, revision, and correlation." If duplication, waste, extravagance, and inefficiency existed within the executive branch, "the President will be responsible for them if he includes in his budget an estimate for their continuance." In fixing executive responsibility, however, the select committee did not intend to subordinate Congress to the president. The plan provided for executive initiative of the budget, "but the President's responsibility ends when he has prepared the budget and transmitted it to Congress." Only in that sense was it an "executive budget." The president's submission did not change "in the slightest degree the duty of Congress to make the minutest examination of the budget and to adopt the budget only to the extent that it is found to be economical."[13] Increases could be made in committee or on the floor by simple majority vote.

Some of the budget reformers wanted to copy the British parliamentary model by concentrating power in the executive and prohibiting legislators from adding funds to the president's budget. Congressman John J. Fitzgerald supported restrictions on congressional power. As chairman of the House Appropriations Committee, he believed that Congress should be prohibited from appropriating any money "unless it has been requested by the head of the department, unless by a two-thirds vote, or unless it was to pay a claim against the government or for its own expenses." David Houston, secretary of the treasury under President Woodrow Wilson, asked Congress in 1920 not to add to the president's budget unless requested by the secretary of the treasury or approved by a two-thirds vote of Congress.[14]

Charles Wallace Collins, a budget reformer, urged the adoption of the British model. "Our institutions," he said, "being more nearly akin to those of England, it is to the English budget system that we more naturally look for the purpose of illustration." He noted that Parliament usually passed the budget without alteration. Budget reform in America, according to Collins, required "the relinquishing of the initiative in financial legislation to the executive by the Congress.... The President would possess the functions of a Prime Minister in relation to public finance."[15]

Congress rejected this version of an executive budget. The budget was to be executive only in the sense that the president was responsible for the estimates submitted. It was legislative in the sense that Congress had full power to increase or reduce the president's estimates. The bill was not meant to "impair either the authority or the responsibility of Congress."[16]

The Budget and Accounting Act created a Bureau of the Budget, to be located in the Treasury Department, and authorized the president to appoint his own budget director. The Budget Bureau was given authority to "assemble, correlate, revise, reduce, or increase the estimates for Congress and the Supreme Court which are included in the budget without revision.[17] Both Houses of Congress changed their committee systems. In 1920, immediately after passage of the bill on the House side, the House put jurisdiction over all appropriations in a single committee. In 1922 the Senate adopted the same reform.

Under the rules, the Appropriations Committees retained formal control over all appropriations. Because of developments after 1922, however, their jurisdiction gradually declined. To understand the reforms adopted in the Budget Act of 1974 and the Gramm-Rudman Act of 1985, it is necessary to review this period.

The Appropriations Committees were undermined by what we call "backdoor spending." Instead of funds being approved explicitly and directly by the Appropriations Committees, they could be provided implicitly and indirectly by the authorization committees. There were two major forces of backdoor spending: borrowing authority and contract authority.

Borrowing authority allows a federal agency to operate without appropriated funds. An agency is given authority to enter into financial obligations and make payments from borrowed monies. Funds could be borrowed either from the Treasury Department or from the public. That was one way to circumvent the Appropriations Committees.

The other way was contract authority, which allowed agencies to enter into obligations before they received an appropriation. Once an obligation was made, the Appropriations Committees had to provide whatever funds were necessary to "liquidate" the obligations. This was merely a clerical task of determining how much had been obligated. The real control was with other committees that had given the agencies contract authority.

Authorization committees also passed "mandatory entitlements" in the form of veterans' benefits, social security, revenue sharing, and other social programs. Once these benefit levels were established by authorization bills, the federal government was obligated to make payments to eligible individuals or state governments. Almost all of these entitlements bypassed the Appropriations Committees. By the 1960s, a large portion of the budget was uncontrollable in a given year because of various open-ended entitlements and fixed costs.

The congressional budget process was subject to other criticisms. When the president's budget arrived on Capitol Hill, it was immediately carved up into thirteen separate appropriations bills handled by different subcommittees. The combined spending of these appropriations and backdoors was not coordinated in any systematic way with revenue bills.

In 1972, President Nixon and Congress clashed head-on with the "Battle of the Budget." Nixon wanted to impose a spending ceiling of $250 billion for fiscal 1973, giving him complete discretion to cut wherever needed to preserve the ceiling. Congress refused to grant him this discretionary authority, but the confrontation precipitated the Budget Act of 1974.

When Congress denied Nixon the spending ceiling and the discretion to cut programs, the administration imposed a ceiling anyway. Secretary of the Treasury George Shultz announced that the president had reviewed the budget and "now feels sure that he can hold the outlays in the fiscal 1973 budget to $250 billion, and he is determined to do so."[18] The administration impounded massive amounts for domestic programs.[19] Through these unilateral actions the waters between the two branches were poisoned. Nixon had asked Congress for power to cut spending. Denied that authority, he announced through his treasury secretary that he had the power anyway. Speaker Carl Albert protested that the president had made a "monkey out of the legislative process."[20]

Although Nixon had condemned Congress for losing control over the budget, the record does not support his charge of legislative irresponsibility. From fiscal 1969 through fiscal 1973, appropriations bills passed by Congress were $30.9 billion below Nixon's requests. Over the same five-year period, backdoors and mandatory entitlements exceeded his budgets by $30.4 billion.[21] In aggregate terms, it was pretty much even. Through its own informal and decentralized system, Congress had stayed within the totals proposed by Nixon. Congress was able to adhere to the president's totals while altering his priorities.[22]

Budget Act of 1974

The Budget Act of 1974 is a statute of immense complexity. The first nine titles deal with a new congressional budget process; the last title creates a system for dealing with presidential impoundments. Only the bare essentials of the statute need be discussed here.

The statute made major changes in the congressional budget process. It established Budget Committees in both Houses, with the responsibility for preparing at least two "budget resolutions" a year. The purpose of a budget resolution is to permit Congress to act on the budget as a whole. The resolution contains five aggregates: total outlays, total budget authority, total revenues, the deficit or surplus expected for the year, and the accumulated public debt for all years. Outlays and budget authority are divided into major functional categories (national defense, agriculture, transportation, etc.) to permit debate on budget priorities.

Under the terms of the Budget Act of 1974, the first resolution was supposed to be passed in the spring to guide congressional action on appropriations bills and other legislation. It served as a nonbinding "target." The second resolution, scheduled for the fall, supplied a binding ceiling on spending and a floor on revenues. If a mismatch existed between the totals in the fall resolution and the individual actions by Congress, a "reconciliation" bill could be passed to direct committees to come up with additional savings. The reconciliation process was later moved to the spring to permit cuts on entitlement programs.

The Budget Act established a Congressional Budget Office (CBO) to give legislators technical support. A revised fiscal year, to begin October 1 instead of July 1, gave Congress three extra months to complete action on appropriations bills. The hope was to avoid continuing resolutions that Congress used as stopgap vehicles until passage of the regular appropriations bills. Other sections of the statute placed restrictions on backdoors and set new deadlines for authorizing committees.

Title X of the Budget Act established new procedures to deal with impoundment. If the president decides to withhold funds, he must submit a report to Congress. There are two kinds of impoundments. If the withholding is temporary (a "deferral"), either House may disapprove the deferral at any time. The funds must then be released for obligation by the agencies. If the withholding is to be permanent (a "rescission"), the president must obtain the support of both Houses within 45 days of continuous session. Otherwise, the funds must be released.

As a result of the legislative veto case of 1983 (*INS v. Chadha*), little remains of the impoundment title. The Supreme Court struck down all forms of the legislative veto as unconstitutional, including the two-House, one-House, and committee versions. This eliminated the one-House veto used by Congress to disapprove deferrals. Nevertheless, as a way of preserving peace between the branches, OMB Director David Stockman entered into an agreement with the Appropriations Committees. The understanding was that President Reagan would not abuse the deferral power, now stripped of the legislative veto.

When Congress passed the Gramm-Rudman Act in 1985, requiring stringent cuts to conform to the deficit targets, the Reagan administration made heavy use of the deferral authority. Members of Congress and groups affected by the impoundments immediately went to court and claimed that the president no longer had authority to defer funds. They argued that the history of the Budget Act of 1974 clearly indicated that the president's deferral authority was linked inextricably to the legislative veto. If one went, so did the other—because they were "inseverable."

A district court and appellate court accepted this line of reasoning. The district judge concluded that Congress would have preferred no statute to one without the legislative veto. To eliminate the one-House veto while retaining the deferral authority would allow the president to use the statutory procedure "in effect, as a 'line-item veto' (which is, of course, anathema to Congress)."[23]

Some of the provisions of the Budget Act have been worthwhile. Title IV has been effective in restricting new backdoors. CBO has established itself as a useful agency for estimating the cost of pending legislation, performing scorekeeping functions, and making macroeconomic projections. Despite these gains, the congressional budget process is in worse condition than it was in 1974. Appropriations bills are enacted later than ever, if at all. Before the Budget Act it was highly unususal for all twelve months of a fiscal year to go by without passing the regular appropriations bills. It is now a common practice. From fiscal 1968 through fiscal 1975, only two appropriations bills remained under a continuing resolution for an entire fiscal year. From fiscal 1976 through fiscal 1985, that figure jumped to twenty-seven.[24] For both fiscal 1986 and fiscal 1987, the fiscal year began without a single appropriations bill enacted into law.

Deficits are larger, far larger, than they were before passage of the Budget Act of 1974. In the ten years from fiscal 1966 through fiscal 1975, deficits averaged $14.8 billion a year. For the decade from fiscal 1976 through fiscal 1985, the average annual deficit increased to about $100 billion a year. Budgets submitted by presidents and budget resolutions passed by Congress have been chronically unreliable and deceptive, regularly underestimating spending and overestimating revenues. The result, year after year, are deficits far beyond presidential and congressional projections.[25]

There have been other problems with the congressional process. More and more is added to continuing resolutions, converting them into massive vehicles for general legislation. The continuing resolution enacted on October 18, 1986, was 385 pages long. In previous years, CRs were routine measures about six pages in length. The deadlines imposed by the Budget Act have been habitually ignored.

Congress found it so difficult to pass the second budget resolution that it figured out how to automatically spring it into place, without congressional action. Eventually it was eliminated. Adoption of the first budget resolution has been delayed for months as both Houses struggled for compromises. Because of these delays, action was postponed on authorization and appropriations bills.

Did the Budget Act fail? Members of Congress were reluctant to make that announcement. They feared that constituents would dismiss Congress as inherently incapable of acting responsibly on the budget. Members claimed there was a strong need for a "process." Even members who voted consistently against budget resolutions said nice things about the Act. They praised the process while condemning the product.[26]

Why stay with a process that regularly yields deplorable results? Trent Lott, Republican from Mississippi, gave this answer for the Budget Act's survival: "The primary reason is that it is worthwhile politically. Members of Congress use the budget process to give the appearance that they are doing something about the deficits or dealing with the budget. In my judgement, they are using it as political cover so that they can continue to be fiscally irresponsible."[27]

The Budget Act was defended on other grounds. "Give it time," was one justification. After a few years this appeal grew stale. Congress seemed to have a promising process that kept making promises. When budget totals became too dreadful for anyone to defend, the results were attributed not to the process, but to exteral political and economic events. Supporters of the Budget Act announced: "The process is not the problem; the problem is the problem." If that were the case, why did Congress go to the trouble of changing the process in 1974, or again in 1985 with the Gramm-Rudman bill? Clearly, processes do count, and they are expected to deal with events internal and external.

The Budget Act of 1974 spawned two side effects of immense importance for executive-legislative relations: (1) budget resolutions gave presidents the ability to gain control of the legislative process, and (2) reliance on budget resolutions reduced the president's responsibility for submitting a budget. Paradoxically, the president's power increased but his responsibility declined.

Why comprehensive action favors the president. Budget resolutions are praised because they permit centralized, systematic, and coherent legislative action. The premise of the Budget Act is that members of Congress will behave more responsibly if they have to vote explicitly on budget aggregates and face up to totals, rather than deciding spending actions in piecemeal fashion by passing separate appropriations and legislative bills. In 1974, as now, it was difficult to defend fragmentation, splintering, and decentralization when reformers pressed eagerly for "coordination" and a "unified budget process."

The model of the executive budget looks appealing. The Budget and Accounting Act assumed that presidential control and responsibility would be improved by centralizing the budget process in the executive branch. However, advantages for the president do not necessarily apply to Congress. It is a mistake for Congress, with its unique institutional qualities, to try to emulate the executive branch.

The Budget Act of 1974 promised a choice between two budgets: presidential and congressional. The analogy is weak because the president is head of an executive branch fortified by a central budget office. There is no head in Congress, and there are no comparable powers for CBO. Congress is inherently decentralized, and no amount of procedural tinkering can disguise that reality. It is fixed by the nature of the institution.

In 1974, no one anticipated that the right president at the right time could exploit the budget resolution and use it to advance executive goals. However, that is what happened in 1981. President Reagan had the votes to gain control over the budget resolution in the House and the Senate. He used the budget resolution as a blueprint to retrench domestic programs, increase military spending, and cut taxes. This radical change in budgetary policies brought about an explosion in budget deficits and laid the groundwork for the Gramm-Rudman Act. It is highly unlikely that an error of that magnitude could have occured with the previous decentralized, fragmented process.[28]

The incrementalism of the former budgetary process operated as a brake on radical changes. In contrast, the Budget Act of 1974 strengthened Reagan's hand by requiring Congress to vote on an overall budget policy. The White House had to do three things: gain control of the first budget resolution; pass the tax-cut bill; and use reconciliation to reduce entitlements and domestic spending. David Stockman, Reagan's OMB Director from 1981 to 1985, explained how the congressional budget process became a convenient handle to promote administration goals. The constitutional prerogatives of Congress "would have to be, in effect, suspended. Enacting the Reagan administration's economic program meant rubber stamp approval, nothing less. The world's so-called greatest deliberative body would have to be reduced to the status of a ministerial arm of the White House."[29]

The White House did not understand what it was doing. To compensate for the tax cut, unprecedented controls had to be placed on spending. Instead, defense spending shot up and the reductions in domestic programs were never enough to compensate for the tax and military policies. The result was a stunning pattern of record deficits. When Reagan entered office, the total national debt was about one trillion dollars, accumulated over a period of almost two centuries. Within five years the national debt had doubled. Within a few more years it will have tripled. After leaving office, the wunderkind Stockman admitted: "a plan for radical and abrupt changes required deep comprehension—and we had none of it."[30]

The results of 1981 revealed serious weaknesses within Congress. Instead of adopting CBO's projections, or substituting an economic forecast of its own, Congress accepted the administration's assumptions. Although the Budget Act supposedly gives Congress an independent technical capability, in 1981 Congress chose to accept the administration's flawed and false premises.

A loss of presidential accountability. President Reagan effectively exploited the congressional budget process in 1981, but the overall effect of the Budget Act of 1974 has been to undermine the president's budget as a target on aggregates. Before 1974 there was only one budget: the president's. The performance of Congress could be measured by comparing committee actions with presidential requests. The Joint Committee on Reduction of Federal Expenditures prepared "scorekeeping results" and circulated them on a regular basis. These reports were printed in the *Congressional Record*. Members of Congress therefore knew, from month to month, how legislative actions compared to the president's budget. Through informal techniques, Congress managed to coordinate its actions and change the shape of the president's budget without exceeding its size.

The Budget Act of 1974 changed these dynamics. There are now a multitude of budgets: the president's, the first budget resolution, the second budget resolution, the second budget resolution revised (passed the following the spring), and a dizzying number of other budgets to reflect changing baselines, reestimates, and updates. The phrase "below budget" and "above budget" lost its meaning. There is no longer an understandable benchmark to judge congressional action.

This confusion produces a substantial cost to democratic government. Voters cannot fix responsibility. Members claim that amendments to an appropriations bill "are well within the budgeted figures."[31] The question, of course, is *whose* budgeted figures? The president's? The budget resolution? Instead of staying within the president's aggregates, members of Congress can vote generous ceilings in a budget resolution and then announce to their constituents that they have "stayed within the budget."[32] This convention has found acceptance within the White House. In 1985 President Reagan indicated that he "would accept appropriations bills, even if above my budget, that were within the limits set by Congress's own budget resolution."[33]

How responsible are budget resolutions? Do they discipline the spending appetites of Congress by forcing members to vote on totals? The record is not encouraging. Congressman David Obey, a member of the House Appropriations Committee, offered this assessment: "under the existing conditions the only kind of budget resolution you can pass today is one that lies. We did it under Carter, we have done it under Reagan, and we are going to do it under every President for as long as any of us are here, unless we change the system, because you cannot get Members under the existing system to face up to what the real numbers do. You always wind up having phony economic assumptions and all kinds of phony numbers on estimating."[34]

The decline in presidential responsibility for budget estimates has been dramatic. After forcing major changes in tax rates, defense spending, and domestic programs in 1981, President Reagan submitted budgets that were almost totally ignored by both Houses. He remained a player by opposing tax increases and any defense cutbacks, but he did not present a budget that he was willing to defend. The responsibility for putting together a national budget fell to Congress by default. It may seem heroic for Congress to accept this assignment, but the voters cannot hold accountable an inherently decentralized legislative body the way they can fix responsibility on a single president.

Gramm-Rudman-Hollings

The growth of budget deficits after 1981, combined with Reagan's refusal to propose a solution, set in motion the forces for the Gramm-Rudman-Hollings Act of 1985. This statute symbolizes many things: the futility of relying on the congressional budget process created in 1974; a recognition that the political stalemate between President Reagan and Congress required a statutory framework with strong sanctions; and an unwillingness to delegate any additional authorities or powers to the executive branch.

Gramm-Rudman creates a statutory schedule to eliminate deficits by fiscal 1991. Beginning with a deficit of $171.9 billion for fiscal 1986, the statute decreases that level by about $36 billion each year over a five-year period. In an effort to create a compact between the two branches, the president's budget and the congressional budget resolution must adhere to those targets. If in any fiscal year the projected deficit exceeds the statutory allowance by more than $10 billion, a "sequestration process" is triggered to make across-the-board cuts to meet the statutory target. Half of those cuts come from the defense; a number of social programs were exempted.

Under Gramm-Rudman, the sequestration process depended on decisions by the comptroller general. OMB and CBO would estimate the amount of deficit for the upcoming fiscal year. If their deficit projection exceeded the statutory target by more than $10 billion, each agency would calculate the budget reductions necessary on a program-by-program basis. Their reports would then go to the comptroller general. After reviewing the OMB and CBO reports, the comptroller general would make whatever adjustments he considered necessary and report his conclusions to the president. The president was required to issue this sequestration order without change, mandating a series of spending reductions throughout the government.

Recognizing that this process had grave constitutional problems, Congress provided for a "fallback" deficit reduction process in the event the courts invalidated the role of the comptroller general. Under the substitute process, the OMB and CBO reports would go to a specially created Temporary Joint Committee on Deficit Reduction consisting of the full membership of both budget committees. The joint committee would report the sequestration bill for floor action and, if passed by both houses, it would go to the president for his signature or veto.

Gramm-Rudman provided for an expedited process to test the constitutionality of the bill. A three-judge court held the comptroller general's role invalid on February 7, 1986. In *Bowsher v. Synar*, handed down on July 7, 1986, the Supreme Court sustained the lower court. Both decisions concluded that the sequestration process violated the separation of powers doctrine by vesting executive functions in an officer removable by Congress. Although the comptroller general is appointed by the president with the advice and consent of the Senate, he is removable only by a joint resolution of Congress or by impeachment.

The removal process was an easy way out for the Court. The most offensive feature of Gramm-Rudman, in terms of constitutionality, was the provision that allowed the comptroller general to draft a presidential sequestration order that the president himself could not alter. He had to issue an order under his name with no ability to control the content. This procedure is repugnant both to separation of powers and the principle of presidential responsibility.[35]

In *Bowsher v. Synar*, the Supreme Court resorted to simplistic doctrines and distorted the writings of Montesquieu, Madison, and Justice Jackson. In keeping with the strict separation of power theory announced in *Chadha*, the Court noted that Madison in *Federalist Paper*, Number 47 had quoted Montesquieu's warning that "there can be no liberty where the legislative and executive powers are united in the same person, or body of magistrates...."[36] This fragment from Montesquieu is misleading, for Madison went on to explain that Montesquieu did not mean that "these departments ought to have no *partial agency* in, or no *control* over, the acts of each other." The meaning of Montesquieu, said Madison, "can amount to no more than this, that where the *whole* power of one department is exercised by the same hands which possess the *whole* power of another department, the fundamental principles of a free constitution are subverted." Clearly the Gramm-Rudman Act did not attempt that concentration of power.

In *Bowsher*, the Court preferred strict separation over checks and balances. It said that the Framers provided for a legislative "and a separate and wholly independent executive branch." The Constitution, according to the Court, did not "contemplate an active role for Congress in the supervision of officers charged with the execution of laws it enacts." It quoted approvingly from *Humphrey's Executor* (1935) that the three branches of government must be "entirely free from the control or coercive influence, direct or indirect, of either of the others." Once Congress enacts a bill "its participation ends" until it passes new legislation.[37]

This is a highly inaccurate picture of American government. It is absurd to say that the three branches are to be "entirely free from the control or coercive influence, direct or indirect, of either of the others." Under this doctrine, how could we have checks and balances? How could one branch prevent abuses in another? We would have three separate branches spinning independently in their orbits, making effective government impossible.

Despite *Chadha* and *Bowsher*, Congress continues to be involved in administrative matters. Supervision of the agencies has not changed. When officials in the executive branch decide to confront Congress and tell it to stay away from administrative matters, they usually learn that pristine theories of government are to no one's advantage. I will give you two examples.

In 1984, while signing an appropriations bill, President Reagan objected to the inclusion of a number of committee vetoes. He said that they were invalid under *Chadha* and that he would advise the agencies to ignore statutory provisions that require agencies to obtain the approval of congressional committees before implementing certain actions.[38]

The House Appropriations Committee responded to Reagan's threat by reviewing an agreement it had entered into with the National Aeronautics and Space Administration. The Appropriations Committees had agreed to let NASA exceed spending caps, or ceilings, that are placed in appropriations bills, provided the agency obtained the approval of the Appropriations Committees. In view of Reagan's signing statement, House Appropriations now said it would eliminate the committee veto and repeal, at the same time, NASA's authority to exceed caps. In the future, whenever NASA wanted to spend in excess of a cap, it would have to come to Congress and have a new law passed, just as *Chadha* ordained.[39]

NASA did not want this rigidity. The administrator of NASA, James M. Beggs, wrote to both Appropriations Committees and suggested that the funding ceilings be placed outside the law, in the conference report, and the agency would agree to seek the approval of both Appropriations Committees before exceeding a ceiling. In short, an executive agency and a congressional committee would continue with a legislative veto, but of an informal and nonstatutory nature.[40]

The second example comes from 1987. OMB complained about a committee veto that had appeared for more than ten years in a foreign assistance bill. The law prohibited the administration from transferring funds among various foreign aid accounts unless it received prior, written approval from the Appropriations Committees. It was a standard quid pro quo. In return for additional flexibility in spending funds, the agency agreed to share decisions with their review committees.

OMB Director James C. Miller III objected to the procedure, advising the Committees that it violated *Chadha*. David R. Obey, chairman of the House Appropriations Subcommittee on Foreign Operations, told Miller that the administration would lose not only the committee veto but transfer authority as well. Obey said that the letter from OMB "means we don't have an accommodation any more, so the hell with it, spend the money like we appropriated it. It's just dumb on their part." Obey's position was supported by Mickey Edwards, ranking Republican on the subcommittee.[41]

The Item Veto

Among the many budget reform proposals considered in recent years is the item veto, which would permit the president to veto individual items within an appropriations bill. This proposal has been a perennial flower since 1876, when it was first offered as a constitutional amendment. Floor action did not occur until 1938. The House of Representatives voted to give the president item-veto authority by statute, but no action was taken by the Senate.[42]

The issue went no further until 1984 and 1985. At that point Senator Mack Mattingly proposed that the president be given item-veto authority by statute. His first attempt was rejected by the Senate as an unconstitutional amendment to a pending bill.[43] The next year his bill was withdrawn after a lengthy filibuster.[44] In the midst of these debates the Reagan administration had made a concerted effort to obtain item-veto authority. The idea appeared regularly in the State of the Union Messages. For example, President Reagan told Congress in his Message in 1986: "Tonight I ask you to give me what forty-three Governors have: Give me a line-item veto this year. Give me the authority to veto waste, and I'll take the responsibility, I'll take the cuts, I'll take the heat."[45]

Although the states function as "laboratories" to test social and economic programs, the item veto is not easily plucked from the states and engrafted onto the national government. The item veto is sustained by a unique culture in the states and cannot be severed from it. State constitutions differ markedly from the federal Constitution, especially in their distribution of executive and legislative powers. A much greater bias exists against legislators in the states than at the national level. State budget procedures differ substantially from congressional procedures. Appropriations bills in the states are highly detailed to facilitate item vetoes by governors. In contrast, appropriations bills passed by Congress contain few items. Appropriations are made in lump sum. Finally, state judges have encountered chronic problems in discovering a coherent and principled theory for item-veto power. These conceptual problems might be duplicated and possibly compounded at the national level.[46]

The "item veto" is a simple phrase but a very complicated idea. It is more of an umbrella term that envelopes many variations. The basic form provides authority to veto individual items in appropriations bills. This power becomes controversial when used to strike not merely appropriation (dollar) amounts but substantive law (conditions and qualifications) as well. Another variation is the "item-reduction" veto. Ten states allow their governors to *reduce* the level of an item. A third variation is the "amendatory veto," which allows a governor to condition his approval of a bill by returning it to the legislature with suggestions for change. Seven states authorize some form of the amendatory veto.

The Reagan administration wanted a broadly defined item veto. An OMB study called item-reduction authority "vital" and urged that the president be given authority to veto substantive provisions ("riders") attached to appropriations bills.[47] State courts have wrestled valiantly, but unsuccessfully, with this issue. May governors veto conditions in an appropriations bill while keeping the funds? By using the item veto, can governors convert a conditional appropriation into an unconditional appropriation? Can they strike legislative language, or is it inseverable from the dollar amount? If they can cut and sever, does this give them not only enhanced executive power but legislative power as well? Are they essentially rewriting the bill?

This issue has confounded state courts for over a century. No bright lines have yet to emerge. An early effort came from a Mississippi court in 1898, which decided that the governor should not have the power to veto objectionable conditions on appropriations. Allowing the governor to strike the condition would produce a law that had never received the legislature's assent:

> The executive, in every republican form of government, has only a qualified and destructive legislative function and never creative legislative power. If the governor may select, dissect, and dissever, where is the limit of his right? Must it be a sentence or a clause, or a word? Must it be a section, or any part of a section, that may meet with executive disapprobation? May the governor transform a conditional or contingent appropriation into an absolute one in disregard and defiance of the legislative will? That would be the enactment of law by executive authority without the concurrence of the legislative will and in the face of it.[48]

These questions recurred in subsequent cases. A 1915 decision illustrates the mischief of an item veto. The governor struck from a biennial appropriation the words "per annum" from the phrase "$2500 per annum." The effect was to reduce a two-year amount from $5000 to $2500, allowing the governor to exercise not only item-veto power but item-reduction power as well. The court ruled that he exceeded his authority.[49] Another governor, also without success, attempted to exercise his item-veto authority by striking the digit "2" from a $25 million bond authorization.[50]

Some judges decided that a governor could sever sections from a bill if the veto is merely "negative" in effect.[51] Other judges regarded these vetoes as "affirmative" because they created "a result different from that intended, and arrived at, by the legislature."[52] A Virginia court in 1940 looked to the medical community for helpful analogies. It defined an "item" as something that could be taken out of a bill without affecting its other purposes or provisions: "It is something which can be lifted bodily from it rather than cut out. No damage can be done to the surrounding legislative tissue, nor should any scar tissue result therefrom."[53] If a provision or condition was "intimately interlocked" with other portions, an item veto was impermissible.[54] Such tests proved to be too abstract and subjective to apply.

State judges in recent years have become increasingly skeptical about their ability to distinguish between negative and affirmative vetoes. They fear that such tests plunge the courts in "disingenuous semantic games" that are unworkable in practice no matter how appealing in theory.[55]

In addition to these conceptual difficulties, the analogy between Congress and state legislatures is weak. State constitutions are filled with detailed prescriptions and proscriptions on the authorization-appropriation process. Many states direct that general appropriations bills shall embrace nothing but appropriations, in effect prohibiting the addition of substantive legislation. State legislatures are not supposed to use appropriations bills to create, amend, or repeal substantive legislation.[56] The Louisiana constitution requires that the general appropriations bill "shall be itemized."[57] State constitutions even prescribe the form and style of bills.[58]

These policies protect the governor's item-veto authority, but the U.S. Constitution is virtually silent on such matters. It contains nothing on the style and form of appropriations bills. There are no requirements for itemizing appropriations bills and no effort to prohibit legislation on appropriations bills. These issues are left exclusively to the rules of the House and the Senate.

State appropriations bills are highly detailed. They identify individual projects, giving the governor a clear opportunity to exercise his item veto. Congress appropriates in lump sums. Specific projects and activities are not identified in the bill presented to the president. They are placed in committee reports as part of the nonstatutory system of controls. Executive agencies prefer this system because it gives them substantial discretion in allocating lump-sum amounts, provided they "keep faith" with their review committees.

This point needs constant reemphasis. Item-veto authority would give the president little additional power under the current system for the simple reason that appropriations bills do not contain items. This rock-bottom fact continues to escape many advocates of the item veto. Take an example from the Energy and Water Development Appropriations Act for fiscal 1985, which included $864.5 million for the general construction account for the Corps of Engineers. Surely ths account teems with "pork-barrel" projects, inviting the president's item veto. However, individual projects are not mentioned in the public law. They are found only in committee reports and agency budget justification documents.[59] Other than a few projects that are earmarked in the account, the only "item" for the president's veto is the lump sum of $864.5 million.

If Congress followed state practice by itemizing appropriations bills, the results might not be all that appealing. Agencies would lose their discretion to move funds between items. An item veto might make Congress more irresponsible. To satisfy constituent demands, even of the most indefensible nature, a member need only add extraneous material to a bill and tell colleagues that the president is free to strike the offending amendment. The prospect of an item veto could make logrolling worse.

Would presidents use item-veto authority to curb spending? No one knows. Presidents, White House aides, and agency officials would have a potent weapon to influence spending, but the direction could be upwards or downwards. Senator Mark Hatfield warned about the complex ramifications: "We have all witnessed the power of the President when he lobbies Congress by telephone. It does not take much imagination to consider how much more persuasive he would be if his words were buttressed with a veto stamp over individual projects and activities within our States or districts."[60]

The threat of an item veto might force legislators to delete or scale back a project, but that can be done now with the regular veto. On the other hand, White House lobbyists could advise a member of Congress that certain projects in their district or state are being considered for an item veto. At the same time, the member could be asked ("unrelated," of course) how he or she plans to vote on the administration's bill scheduled for the following week. A minor project might survive in return for the legislator's willingness to support a costly administration program. Both sides would prevail in this accommodation, pushing budget totals upward. Projects could also be held hostage in return for a member's support for a nominee or some other presidential objective.

The item veto has significance beyond the particular budgetary savings that may, or may not, be realized. At stake are the power relationships between the executive and legislative branches, the exercise of Congress' historic power of the purse, and the relative abilities of each branch to impose their version of budgetary priorities. A radical restructuring of constitutional power could flow from what appears to be a relatively minor reform proposal.

The president's budget would have enhanced status. Under the Budget and Accounting Act, the executive budget can be amended up or down by Congress. The final judgment rests with Congress, subject to presidential veto of the entire bill. The item veto would alter this equation. The president could strike what Congress had added to his budget; rarely could Congress attract a two-thirds majority in each House to override him.

Administration officials candidly admit that the item veto would be used to delete congressional initiatives and add-ons.[61] The president's Economic Report issued in 1985 explains that the adoption of the item veto "may not have a substantial effect on total Federal expenditures" but may be used by the president "to change the composition of Federal expenditures—from activities preferred by the Congress to activities preferred by the President."[62]

Conclusions

The enactment of Gramm-Rudman was a clear signal that the budget process had seriously failed. Even so, the deficit projections in Gramm-Rudman will not be met. Both branches concede that the yearly targets for maximum deficits, with the deficit brought to zero by fiscal 1991, will not and should not be complied with.

In searching for substitutes and improvements, we need to restore a budget system that takes advantage of the institutional strengths of both branches. For the last decade we seem to have appealed to institutional weaknesses rather than institutional strengths. By looking to Congress for comprehensive action, we unwittingly weakened the unity and leadership that must come from the president. By creating a system of many budgets, we opened the door to escapism, confusion, and unaccountability. In an effort to force Congress to act in a comprehensive manner, we inadvertently supplied a tool for centralizing power in the executive branch.

When Congress launched the modern budget system in 1921, it did a good job in understanding the unique roles of the two branches. The Budget and Accounting Act fixed responsibility on the president by holding him accountable for agency estimates. As a single executive officer assisted by a central budget bureau, the president was ideally situated to do that. The 1921 Act preserved the institutional strengths of Congress by giving it full freedom to modify the president's budget and impose its own sense of priorities. Each branch was given a mission it could efffectively discharge.

The Budget Act of 1974, as amended by Gramm-Rudman, offers an entirely different model. Congress assumed the responsibility for making a budget. The president is no longer responsible for the budget he submits, at least not as he was between 1921 and 1974. The current political system does not hold him accountable.

How to instill in the budget process a clear sense of institutional responsibility and capability is a central issue for the coming decade. The budget process is not merely the heart of the legislative process. Exercising control over the public purse is the essense of self-government. The power of the purse is part and parcel of constitutional government. We need to protect and preserve this precious heritage.

Chapter 9

The Modern Presidency and the Constitution: Foreign Policy

Louis W. Koenig

Louis Koenig notes that the constitutional provisions for foreign affairs are an "invitation to struggle" between the executive and Congress since both branches are given substantial powers. This reflected the Framers' intentions to maintain the principles of separation of powers and checks and balances in the conduct of foreign policy. However, the modern presidency demonstrates a two-track system. Koenig labels these as *Track One* and *Track Two*. In the first track (or what Master Critic Lowi called the "fast track"), the executive has nearly complete autonomy to declare and conduct war, negotiate and implement executive agreements (rather than treaties), and to conduct covert operations. Track Two requires executive-legislative collaboration in committing U.S. troops, ratifying treaties, and appropriating funds for foreign policy. The president prefers Track One since it promotes executive control. However, it could lead to executive abuses such as in Watergate and the Iran-Contra Affair. Koenig suggests that executive-legislative harmony might be restored by a joint executive-legislative cabinet, by enlarging the input of civilian and political advisors into foreign policy, and by appropriate presidential balance between management of policy details with delegation of foreign policy responsibilities to others.

The Framers of the Constitution struggled with the dilemma of power and responsibility, of creating an office such as the presidency, amply endowed with means to cope with a demanding environment, and yet one that might not in time afflict society with the scourge of tyranny. Few of the Framers were confident that their craftsmanship laid this problem to rest. They expected it to persist, leaving future generations to struggle with the issue. Thus far, no generation has provided answers superior to those of the Framers. If anything, the basic tools the Framers devised to have foreign policy made and conducted with ample power, and also with responsibility befitting a republic, remain, in their essential characteristics, just as the Constitution originally provided.

The Framers had strong incentives to vest substantial powers in the presidency for conducting foreign relations. The mightiest nations of Europe all were at our borders—Britain, France, and Spain. The lack of substantial executive power in the Articles of Confederation had hampered the conduct of the Revolution and the management of foreign relations in the post-Revolution period. With little hesitation, the Framers commenced Article II, establishing the presidency, with the sweeping mandate: "The executive power is vested in a President of the United States." A similar generosity was not bestowed upon Congress, whose powers were limited to those "herein granted." Unlike Congress, the president is not limited to powers expressly enumerated, but is endowed with all of "the executive power...to determine," as Hamilton puts it, "the condition of the nation" in its foreign relations.[1] Whatever enumerations that followed the general grant were mere emphasis, although several modified the general grant of power.

Other influences affirmed the proddings of experience to vest substantial powers in the presidency in foreign affiars. The principal political thinkers who were well known to the Framers were united in the view that the function of foreign relations should be committed to the executive alone. Blackstone, Montesquieu, and Locke were all of this persuasion. Locke, for example, separated what he termed *the federative power* from ordinary executive power. The federative power encompassed both foreign and military affairs and, in Locke's analysis, were the exclusive province of the executive. The Framers, who feared concentrated powers as a likely caldron of tyranny, stopped well short of this prescription and dispersed power over foreign relations among the branches and between the houses of Congress. George Washington, hero of the revolution and presider of the Constitutional Convention, the presumed first president of the new government, spurred the tendency to vest imposing power in the executive.

In their efforts to undergird the presidency with power, while avoiding the excesses of tyranny or irresponsibility, the Framers utilized two basic tools of constitutional architecture—separation of powers, and checks and balances. Separation of powers established three distinct branches, in providing for executive, legislative, and judicial functions. Each branch, endowed with substantial power, and with different powers in different sets of hands, could check the other by withholding its cooperation. Lawmaking, appointments, appropriations, and treaty-making are illustrative of matters that are at the core of foreign relations and are divided between the president and House or the president and the Senate. The Framers left open the question of which branch was to have the decisive voice in foreign affairs, and seemed even to imply that predominance might sometimes shift between the branches. With ample justification, Edward S. Corwin concluded that "The Constitution, considered only for its affirmative grants of power, . . . is an invitation to struggle for the privilege of directing American foreign policy."[2]

But the Framers did not always conform to the ideal of evenhandedness in allotting power between the branches. By vesting command of the armed forces with the presidency and superintendency of the department that conducts foreign relations, the Constitution-makers endowed him with the principal instruments of initiative and action. The power to act directly in response to events and opportunity established for the president a formidable advantage over Congress, which can act only indirectly by legislating its interest and preferences, but which depends on the executive for their effectuation. Furthermore, perceptive Framers, such as the authors of the *Federalist Papers*, saw the presidency as possessing characteristics that would contribute powerfully to its advantage. Better than the other branches, the executive was capable of unity, secrecy, and dispatch, prime assets for conducting foreign relations.

The Presidency of George Washington

Clues to the intentions of the Framers are not limited to the Constitutional Convention and ratification debates, but are also discoverable in several early presidencies whose incumbents were themselves delegates to the Convention. Of these, the principal clue-provider is George Washington, who believed that the Constitution vests the conduct of foreign relations in the president, that he and his office are the sole channels of official intercourse with foreign governments.

Washington viewed the presidency as analogous to the European monarch. Like the monarch, the president could conduct diplomatic relations directly or act through deputies. An early sign of Washington's belief was his use of Gouverneur Morris as his private diplomatic agent in 1789 to negotiate with Britain concerning her performance of her obligations under the peace treaty. Faced with a situation where the Senate had adjourned and the post of secretary of state had not been filled, and eager to avoid delay, Washington by his own decision chose Morris for the mission and prepared his instructions.[3]

But Washington's view of executive power, while most readily acceptable in his selection of aides and emissaries, encountered doubt and resistance when he proclaimed United States neutrality in the war between Britain and France in 1793. The episode touched off a debate between Hamilton ("Pacificus"), who resolved the ambiguities of the Constitution in the president's favor, and Madison ("Helvidius"), who saw the congressional war function to imply that Congress also was empowered to keep the nation at peace. Madison contended that the congressional war-declaring function must be interpreted broadly to include the keeping of peace and that any exceptions in behalf of executive power must be strictly construed. That two key providers of the Constitution, Hamilton and Madison, were in public disagreement, reveals the depth of confusion over the Framers' intent.[4]

Hamilton contended that the conduct of foreign relations is, in its nature, an executive function and, therefore, except where the Constitution provides otherwise, belongs to the president, on whom the Constitution bestows "the executive power." The fact that the legislature possesses the power to declare war and other powers does not diminish the discretion of the president in the exercise of powers that constitutionally belong to him. In effect, Hamilton argued in further elaboration, the president has all powers that the facts of international relations may at any time make conveniently applicable unless the Constitution clearly vests them elsewhere. Consequently, the president possesses the initiative in foreign affairs, and can confront Congress with faits accomplis at will, although Congress has no constitutional obligation to follow the president's lead or support his policies.

In his counter-theory, Madison argued that Congress is empowered to determine foreign policy because of its constitutional power to declare war. The president's diplomatic powers are instrumental only and involve, at most, no greater discretion than the determination of "matters of fact." Madison belittled Hamilton's suggestion of concurrent discretionary powers in the hands of the two branches as inevitably productive of inconvenience and confusion.[5] As will be seen, the Hamilton-Madison debate has persisted to this day through two centuries of constitutional experience. Although the context changes, the arguments remain essentially the same. Simultaneously, Hamilton's thesis that the president has a monopoloy of diplomatic intercourse was echoed by John Marshall in the House of Representatives in 1789: "The President is the sole organ of the nation in its external relations, and its sole representative with foreign nations." In effect, Marshall was saying that the president is the instrument of communication with other governments. Madison, however, would add that what the president communicates may be the decision of Congress.

Treaties and Executive Agreements

The two areas of foreign relations on which the Framers most concentrated were treaties and war, which they considered the most consequential instruments of that domain. The Framers' distrust of monopolistic power was well evident in the treaty provisions of the Constitution, according to which the Senate can offer its advice at every step of negotiation, not merely at the point of the president's submission of the final document for the Senate's action. The requirement of Senate approval had no counterpart in the constitutions of other nations where treaties were the monopoly of the executive. The two-thirds vote necessary for the Senate's consent is traceable to the two-thirds vote required in the Articles of Confederation when the individual states made treaties. The new Constitution's two-thirds vote served to reassure the small states who feared the predominance of the large states under the future government.

President Washington, in faithful adherence to constitutional prescription, visited the Senate seeking its advice on questions arising during treaty negotiations with the southern Indian tribes. When Senators objected that they ought to deliberate privately, without the chief executive present, an annoyed Washington withdrew. Both he and his presidential successors have shunned face-to-face consultations with the full Senate. The sheer growth of the Senate militates against the participation of all its members in treaty negotiations. Instead, presidents have developed informal substitutes. For example, they may brief individual senators on the progress of negotiations. Not infrequently, senators have joined executive officials in negotiating treaties. Senators Arthur Vandenberg and Tom Connally, then the upper chamber's leading Republican and Democrat in foreign affairs, were members of the United States delegation to San Francisco to draft the United Nations Charter. Presidents value the senators for contributing their sense of what the Senate will accept and their capabilities in the Senate's ultimate deliberations in rallying support and staving off opposition. With a Democratic president, Truman, and a Republican controlled Senate, Vandenberg provided invaluable support in successfully promoting a resolution, expressing the sense of the Senate, that what eventually became the North Atlantic Treaty should be undertaken. Such a treaty was also a prime project of President Truman.

The two-thirds vote, which originally was reassuring to the small states, has been transformed by the march of experience into the imperative of bipartisanship in treaty-making. Without bipartisan support, a treaty has scant chance of adoption under the two-thirds rule. It also makes the president vulnerable to pockets of opposition as he patches together the formidable two-thirds majority. A few Senators can force their most cherished views on the president. In promoting two treaties committing the United States to turn over the Panama Canal to Panama, President Carter, who prevailed in the Senate by only a single vote, had to accept a reservation to the initial treaty, introduced by Senator Dennis DeConcini (D.-Ariz.), asserting the right of the United States to send troops into Panama to keep the canal open. The president simultaneously had to soothe the Panamanians angered by the reservation.[6] To gain his hairline victory, Carter had to make not only this and other concessions, but to plead abjectly that his ability to conduct foreign affairs in the eyes of other nations hung in the balance.

The treaty power is a prime example of how the silences and omissions of the original Constitution are clarified by experience and practice. The Constitution says nothing concerning the termination of treaties, but according to practice, the president's power to terminate is coequal with that of Congress.[7] The possibilities are illustrated by the redefinition of United States relations with Taiwan, transpiring in the Carter years. As a step toward establishing full diplomatic relations with the People's Republic of China, President Carter terminated a mutual defense treaty with Taiwan while asserting that "Taiwan is part of China."[8] Subsequently, Congress joined in the task of redefining relations by adopting the Taiwan Relations Act, which provided for some military relationships in lieu of the terminated defense treaty. Carter approved the act.

Practice has also conjured up a potent competitor to treaties—the international executive agreement. The president may enter into executive agreements free from senatorial review and the two-thirds vote of the treaty power. The Constitution does not provide specifically for presidentially negotiated executive agreements. It does, however, provide for "agreements or compacts" between individual states and foreign governments with congressional consent.

Most likely the Framers paid little heed to executive ageements because at the time, they were dwarfed in numbers and importance by treaties, the principal means of contract between nations. Nonetheless, executive agreements were employed promptly once the Constitution was put into operation. The earliest known use of the executive agreement centered on arrangements made by the postmaster general with foreign postmasters for the reciprocal receipt and delivery of letters and packets through the post offices. Among the early milestones were the Louisiana Purchase, arranged by executive agreement, and an agreement of 1817 with Great Britain concerning naval armaments to be maintained by each country on the Great Lakes and Lake Champlain.

Executive agreements have grown enormously in numbers and importance, especially in the twentieth century. Practice and circumstance have weighed heavily in their favor. They thrive most in times of international stress. As American involvement in both world wars loomed, executive agreements were devised for intergovernmental loans, rationing, and shipping, reflecting the importance of the economy in modern warfare. As military relations with another country deepen, they are expressed in executive agreements—for example, Britain's exchange of bases in the western hemisphere for "obsolescent" American destroyers in World War II. Territory has been annexed by executive agreement—Texas, Hawaii, and American Samoa.

Agreements can be negotiated in secrecy and then bypass the two-thirds Senate vote required for treaties. Leading United States foreign policies have been made via executive agreements: the Open Door Policy, Theodore Roosevelt's "Gentleman's Agreement" with Japan to limit immigration to the United States, Richard Nixon's agreement with Japan to curb her exports of textiles, and Ronald Reagan's agreement to curb her automobiles. Executive agreements negotiated at Yalta, Teheran, and Potsdam delineated basic relationships of the great powers after World War II. World War II and the wars in Korea and Vietnam all were ended not by grand treaties of peace, but by executive agreements.

The speed of negotiations, plasticity of method, secrecy, and avoidance of the Senate and its uncertainties have made the executive agreement highly appealing to presidents. Agreements have also burgeoned in response to forces external to government, such as scientific and technological change. The rise, for example, of motion pictures, the telephone, radio, and television have produced executive agreements in fulfillment of the international dimensions of those devices.

Any cataloguing of executive agreements encounters difficulty because of their elusiveness in being defined, or even described with any precision. They range from shadowy statements by presidents to explicit documents. Their scope, frequency, and importance have increased enormously since the Second World War. A sequence of agreements drew the United States, step-by-step, into military commitments in Southeast Asia and eventually into full-scale war. Indicative of the growing reach of the executive agreement were President Nixon's assurances to President Thieu of South Vietnam, in an exchange of private letters, that if North Vietnam should ever violate a peace settlement just negotiated, the United States would respond with "full force." The agreement was not reported to Congress,[9] which had a stake in the matter, given its constitutional power to declare war.

The prevailing sentiment among constitutional law scholars is that executive agreements can be used interchangeably with treaties.[10] The obvious appeal of executive agreements to the president is that they enable him to conduct foreign relations with greater freedom from congressional control, permitting his pursuit of what legislators might consider over-audacious, potentially costly executive adventures. Illustrative of the possibilities is President Reagan's agreement with Kuwait to bring her tankers under the American flag and American naval protection as they plied the Persian Gulf amidst the Iran-Iraq war. The outcry of legislators, including those of the president's own party, against the risk of hostilities with Iran did not deter the president.

Despite their shadowy character, executive agreements can be categorized into several varieties. Some are "presidential agreements," that the president or his deputies make pursuant to his own constitutionally granted authority as possessor of the "executive power" and as commander in chief. What became known as *Irangate*—the sale of arms to Iran and the diversion of proceeds to the Nicaragua contras— was the product of a series of presidential agreements made by executive aides with private individuals, some with sullied reputations, as well as with officials of other governments. Presidential agreements may be encouraged or authorized by Congress, even though the president may choose to pursue them under his own constitutional authority. Likewise, he can disregard a Senate or congressional veto and consummate an agreement independently.[11]

A second category consists of congressional-executive agreements, which the president or his deputies negotiate pursuant to authority conferred by Congress through a statute or joint resolution, or in effectuation of a general policy enumerated in legislation. Similarly, a treaty may provide authorization, and an executive agreement may be sanctioned by Congress after the fact of its negotiation.[12]

Altogether, the executive agreement has attained through usage a scope and importance far beyond any anticipation of the Framers. In the twentieth century, and especially since World War II, the numbers of executive agreements have far exceeded treaties, and the habit of presidents has been increasingly to use agreements for matters that are important and controversial, and treaties for lesser business that readily evokes consensus.

In the 1970s and 1980s, executive agreements have been increasingly viewed as a threat to the constitutional balance between Congress and the executive. A recurrent concern is that the president may make a serious military or foreign policy commitment without Congress's knowledge or participation. After congressional investigations exposed secret military agreements with Ethiopia, Laos, Thailand, Spain, and Portugal, Congress adopted the Case Act of 1972, requiring that all executive agreements be reported to Congress within sixty days. Agreements concerned with sensitive national security matters are submitted as classified documents to the House and Senate foreign affairs committees. The effectiveness of this legislation has been bedeviled by the vagaries of defining executive agreements. Not suprisingly, presidents take a far more restrictive view than Congress of what these instruments encompass.

Ambassadors and Special Agents

In providing that the president shall appoint ambassadors and ministers with the Senate's advice and consent, the Framers reflected the reality experienced in the revolution and under the Articles of Confederation: that foreign relations are conducted by emissaries continuously posted in foreign capitals and entrusted with the tasks of diplomatic representation and negotiation. Promptly after the Constitution was instituted, the United States became represented abroad by ministers whose power and competence compared favorably with other diplomats.

Believing that a regular diplomatic structure did not preclude a more personal one for the chief executive, President Washington instituted the practice of employing special agents to conduct diplomatic negotiations in which he was particularly interested. Monroe, Jay, and Gouverneur Morris all served Washington as special agents.

The practice has been commonly followed by other presidents. Jefferson sent Monroe to the court of Napoleon to help Robert Livingston arrange the Louisiana Purchase. Colonel Edward House and Harry Hopkins served Wilson and Franklin Roosevelt as their principal liaisons with allied leaders in the two world wars. Phillip Habbib was President Reagan's special envoy to the Middle East early in the Lebanese crisis, to the Philippines in the replacement of Marcos by Aquino, and to Central America.

Unlike ambassadors and ministers, special agents are appointed solely by the president, without referral to the Senate since they are not appointed to permanent "offices," do not serve indefinitely, and do not have the emoluments of office or duties prescribed by the constitution or legislation.[13] Although special agents are not provided for specifically in the Constitution, their use is implied by the treaty power and the all-purpose "executive power" clause. Special agents maximize the president's personal role in foreign affairs. Discharging business which to him is often of crucial importance, they command his confidence and trust, which ambassadors do not always evoke. Special agents know better than anyone the latest intentions of the president, and they command prestige in foreign capitals by coming directly from the White House.

But the use of special agents is not without flaw. Some may be rank amateurs at diplomacy, whose ignorance and naiveté may lead to stumblings, as the workmanship of President Reagan's special agents' journeys to Iran to sell arms and secure the release of American hostages suggests. Special agents short-circuit normal institutional scrutiny and review in the executive branch, which enlarges the danger of error. Agents undercut the resident ambassador, a potential morale-draining experience.

Making War

Although the power to initiate hostilities, or "war," is one of the most controversial aspects of the Constitution and the presidency today, it was far from being a major concern of the Framers. The principal report of the one debate that explicitly considered the warmaking power occupies little more than one page out of 1,273 that contain the printed records of the Philadelphia Convention. In a debate on August 17, 1787, the delegates considered the clause of the draft Constitution reported by the Committee on Detail which gave Congress the power "to make war." Charles Pinckney of South Carolina objected that the legislature was too cumbersome to exercise that power, and urged that it be vested in the smaller Senate which by dint of its custody of the treaty power would develop an informed judgment about foreign affairs. Madison and Elbridge Gerry of Massachusetts moved successfully to insert the word *declare* instead of *make*, in order to endow the executive with the power to repel sudden attacks. Madison's notes suggest a desire to broaden the executive's power in the warmaking area. Reportage of the debate also discloses confusion among the delegates concerning the import of the change moved by Madison and Gerry.[14]

Yet for any power at all to be vested in Congress over war was a clear departure from the prevailing practice of European nations which regarded war as the province of the executive—the monarch. Nonetheless, the Framers chose to break new ground by involving the legislature in decisions of war. As in their other decisions, they were scrupulous to avoid concentrating power in any one branch and the temptations of abuse such structuring would create. Hence, once again, they chose to divide the war power between Congress and the executive. Their choice is all the more striking when it is recalled that in the era in which they labored, nations commonly conducted hostilities without a declaration of war. The Seven Years War between Britain and France, waged principally in North America, was an undeclared war. In the American Revolution, British-French hostilities never evolved into an expressly declared war. In the seventeenth and eighteenth centuries, the habit of European powers was to engage in naval reprisals that sometimes resulted in outright, although undeclared, wars.[15]

In the era since World War II, the formula implanted by the Framers in the Constitution—of Congress as the initiator of war and the president its conductor—has been all but reversed, with the president becoming both the initiator of war and its conductor. Even in the five instances in American history where war has been declared, the president initially requested it, and no such request, when the president has chosen to make it, has been denied by Congress. All of the country's major wars were the outcome of presidential policies, in the making of which Congress had at most only a minor part. The presidents have clearly rebuffed the Framers and their intention that Congress play a major role in the war process by possessing the power to declare war. Instead, the president has dominated the war power through his capacity to launch policy initiatives and control the direction of evolving policy.

Other factors have contributed to the president's ascendance. Declaring war has become something of an anachronism and a rarity. Reasons have not been lacking for a disinclination to declare war. A war declaration risks misunderstanding and overreaction to the limited objectives of the initiator of combat. Diplomatic embarrassment may lurk in a war declaration since it may recognize non-recognized guerilla opponents or inhibit the possibilities of obtaining a settlement of the dispute. A war declaration might trigger the enforcement of many statutes and unnecessarily increase the president's domestic authority.[16]

In addition to the practicalities of situations, the president's war power has been aided by expansive theories. Hamilton, in his debate with Madison, for example, contended that the president can use force in repelling "a sudden attack." Hamilton's proposition is based on the notion that the president, in responding, is exercising an inherent right of national self-defense, although his statement leaves unanswered such questions as what defines a "sudden attack," whether it must be directed against the United States, and who determines when an attack has occured.[17]

Expansive theories, when coupled with critical events, have speeded the enlargement of presidential power. For the nation's most threatening war, the Civil War, Lincoln and his legal advisors claimed for the president what they termed "the war power," an amalgam of his authority as commander in chief and the duty "to take care that the laws be faithfully executed." In twelve weeks between the attack of Fort Sumter and the convening of Congress in special session, Lincoln employed these two clauses to sanction measures sufficient to wage full-scale war. Subsequently, Lincoln invited Congress to "ratify" certain of his most far-reaching actions, such as his enlargement of the armed forces and suspension of the writ of habeas corpus. Modern-day presidents are far less prone to seek congressional ratification, relying instead on the authority they deem derived from the executive power clause and as commander in chief.

A second major force in the expansion of the president's war power derives from the United States' numerous involvements in minor hostilities. These have been principally with our Latin American neighbors, and typically involve violence of brief duration and few casualties—landings of United States marines to protect United States property and citizens perceived as endangered in weak nations by civil unrest and the inability of local authorities to provide sufficient protection. A recent example was President Bush's dispatch of 26,000 troops to capture General Noriega in 1989. Equally commonplace are the pursuit of pirates, aid to a recognized government, and alleged humanitarian intervention. Episodes like these inspired presidents to claim a similar, although greatly expanded, authority to employ the armed forces in Korea and Vietnam, both protracted struggles with heavy casualties, that rank among the major wars of American history.

Events and environment, including changes in the nature and dimensions of warfare, have also combined to extend the president's war power. The two world wars transformed national security into world security, and the concept of collective self-defense materialized, with explicit recognition in the United Nations Charter. The concept was also embodied in a great web of regional and bilateral alliances whose prevailing formula was that the United States agreed to regard an attack on a member nation as threatening its own safety, and its response was to include assistance in defensive measures. The principal wars the United States has undertaken since World War II—Korea and Vietnam—were justified by their presidential administrations as necessary under existing bilateral and multilateral commitments. It is not unusual for contemporary presidents to shift their justificatory theses for undertaking hostilities. President Johnson, for example, originally justified his landing of marines in the Dominican Republic in 1965 as necessary to protect the safety of the United States citizens. Subsequently, he cited the need to preserve the security of the western hemisphere in accordance with the provisions of the Organization of American States Treaty.

Congress's war power has also been eroded in recent decades by the rapidly increasing involvement of the military in the tasks of diplomacy. Using the armed forces has indeed become the conduct of diplomacy by other means. President Reagan's dispatch of the marines to Lebanon, his invasion of Grenada, and ordering of a naval escort in the Persian Gulf, are all substitutes of military action for historic diplomacy. The military's expanded foreign policy role is made possible by the creation of a huge standing army, a development that many of the Framers abhorred. Since the Second World War and the Cold War that set in close on its heels, the president has had available, and has aggressively used, armed forces that are sufficiently large and equipped, and mobile to fight on short notice, at any place in the world, including conflicts whose eventual dimensions are unforseeable.

Equally important, contemporary presidents, in committing the forces to combat, although they readily cite the precedents of their predecessors in resorting to combat, have increasingly ignored the constraining procedures observed by their predecessors which helped maintain the balance between the branches for the war power. Consequently, where Jefferson and Lincoln, after committing the armed forces to combat, formally and promptly reported their actions to Congress and the public and invited legislative ratification or approval of their acts, contemporary presidents tend to skip those democracy-serving amenities. President Truman, for example, when the Korean war broke out, believed that a swift American response was necessary or South Korea would be overrun. The fast-dissolving events, he concluded, did not allow enough time to consult Congress. Instead, he invoked powers he considered already available such as provisions of the United Nations Charter, which the Senate had earlier approved, and, building on the practice of his predecessors, he cited his power and obligation to protect the "broad interests of American foreign policy."[18] In characterizing the full-scale combat in Korea, the Truman administration spoke not of war, but of "police action," inventive phraseology that implied that the president, by his own decision, could protect those interests of the United States by military action definable as being short of war.

The president's self-serving determination of the rules of the game for use of the armed forces has been eased by the lack of significant judicial intervention in defining the respective roles of the executive and Congress in matters of war. The landmark *Prize Cases*[19] in the Civil War accorded blanket approval to the president to make war without a prior authorization to do so. The court upheld Lincoln's proclamation of a blockade of Southern ports on the theory that the president possesses unlimited power to wage war in defending the nation against war, whether by invasion or rebellion. Furthermore, according to the Court, the president is the sole judge of what acts amounted to "war," a finding that enormously expanded his power. The Court accepted the argument of Richard Henry Dana in the case that "war is a state of things," and not an act of the legislature.[20]

The United States' most recent wars have not been seriously challenged in the courts. The Korean War was reviewed in its domestic context only—the president's seizure of the steel mills, whose output he deemed essential, in a labor-management dispute, to support the armed forces in combat. Although the Court ruled against the president, it did so not on the basis of the respective war powers of the president and Congress, but on the president's violation of separation of powers and Congress's role in lawmaking in seizing the mills. The effect of the case was weakened by the lack of consensus in the reasoning of the Court's majority. Each of the six justices who comprised the majority gave a distinct opinion. Although in the Vietnam War many cases were litigated on its constitutionality in lower federal courts, the Supreme Court avoided making an authoritative ruling, and even lower court rulings did not provide a coherent legacy.[21]

The Efforts to Modernize the War-Declaring Power

Paradoxically, it was the president who made the initial move to update the war power when President Eisenhower became convinced that President Truman had taken too much on his shoulders politically in making the Korean War a presidential war by excluding Congress from the decision to go to war. Consequently, when Communist China threatened nationalist China, Eisenhower proposed that Congress adopt a resolution authorizing the president "to employ the Armed Forces of the United States as he deems necessary for the specific purpose of securing and protecting Formosa and the Pescadores against armed attack." Although Eisenhower simultaneously contended that "the authority for some of the actions which might be required would be inherent in the authority of the Commander-in-Chief," he also believed that by associating Congress with his purpose, his declaration of his readiness to fight for Formosa would have greater impact on the Communist Chinese. Congress responded positively and Eisenhower successfully repeated the procedure in a subsequent crisis in Lebanon.[22]

Eisenhower's formula for modernizing the war-declaring power foundered in the Vietnam War. In 1964, following a reported attack on American destroyers by North Vietnamese small naval craft in the Gulf of Tonkin, President Johnson, in the Eisenhower manner, requested and secured from Congress a resolution authorizing the president to take "all necessary measures" to "repel any armed attack" against United States forces and "to prevent further aggression." But as the war in Indochina expanded, congressional critics contended that the president had exceeded the intent of the resolution and that the original triggering incident had not been accurately reported. As the war dragged on and opposition to it grew, Congress eventually repealed the resolution.

With the onset of Watergate and the deepening impasse of the Indochina war, Congress enacted its version of an updated war declaring power, the War Powers Resolution of 1973, and sustained it over a presidential veto. According to the Resolution, the president can initiate emergency military action in the absence of a declaration of war, but within forty-eight hours after committing the armed forces to combat, he must report that occurrence to Congress in writing. The Resolution requires that "in every possible instance" the president must consult with Congress prior to his combat decision and in situations where the involvement of the armed forces in hostilities is likely. The combat action must end in sixty days, unless Congress authorizes the commitment. That deadline can be extended for thirty days if the president certifies that the additional time is necessary for the forces' safety. Within the sixty-day or ninety-day period, Congress can order the immediate removal of the forces by adopting a concurrent resolution, which is not subject to presidential veto. In 1983, the law's constitutionality became dubious when the Supreme Court held in *Immigration and Naturalization Service v. Chadha*,[23] that the legislative veto, exercised through a concurrent resolution, was unconstitutional since it deprived the president of his constitutional role in lawmaking.

In nearly a decade and a half of experience, the War Powers Resolution has been of only slight consequence. Its first major testing occurred in 1975 when Cambodia seized the Mayaguez, an American container ship, and at President Ford's order, American forces, by ground and air attacks, freed the vessel and its crew. Although congressional leaders complained that instead of being consulted they were merely informed of a presidential decision already taken, there was widely expressed congressional approval of his action. The Resolution also had little impact in the Carter years, since the president submitted only one report under its terms concerning the hostage rescue effort. Both Ford and Carter disregarded the consultation provisions before commencing combat operations. Both also emphasized, in filing reports, that that step in no way acknowledged the Resolution's constitutionality.[24]

In invading Grenada, in dispatching marines to Lebanon as part of a multinational peacekeeping force, and in committing military aircraft to aid Chad against rebel and Libyan forces, President Reagan also shunned consultation and regarded the reports called for by the War Powers Resolution as optional rather than mandatory. But when the marines suffered casualties in Lebanon in 1983 and public support declined, Congress adopted, and the president approved, a joint resolution authorizing the marines to remain there for eighteen months. Both the executive and legislative branches chose this longer period than that provided in the War Powers Resolution from a shared desire not to have Lebanon become an issue in the 1984 elections. Nonetheless, in approving the joint resolution, Reagan questioned its constitutionality, although in signing it, he accorded the War Powers Resolution the most consequential status it has yet achieved.[25] Yet in approving the Lebanon Resolution, the president declared that he might, through his own constitutional powers, continue military operations beyond the eighteen-month period without congressional reauthorization. In his 1987 commitment of naval forces to protect former Kuwaiti oil tankers that had been reflagged as American vessels, Reagan considered the War Powers Resolution inapplicable despite the high risk of hostilities.

Congress has derived its best leverage against the presidential war phenomenon from its appropriations power, particularly in its exercise in the post-Vietnam era. In the 1970s President Ford, faced with expanding Soviet and Cuban intervention in Africa with arms and troops, urgently appealed for funds to aid a pro-American faction in Angola. Congress rebuffed him. President Ford was rejected more sweepingly when the Senate adopted a 1976 amendment to the Arms

Export Act, sponsored by Senator Dick Clark (D.-Iowa), prohibiting "any kind" of assistance for military operations in Angola. The Clark amendment was subsequently repealed, and the Reagan administration reinvoked limited military aid to the pro-American forces in Angola.

In the Reagan era, Congress employed appropriations to prohibit particular kinds of aid and to exact concessions for policies it favored. For example, it stipulated that El Salvador should manifest progress on human rights and land reform, and on the trials of national guardsmen accused of murdering four American churchwomen.[26] In his administration's early years, Reagan obtained funding for the Nicaraguan Contras and their efforts to destabilize the Sandinista government, but in his second term Congress, fearful of United States military involvement, sharply curtailed that aid. In its several versions, the Boland amendment, sponsored by Congressman Edward Boland (D.-Mass.), limited the executive to "humanitarian aid." The Reagan administration's counterthrusts, which eventuated in the "Irangate" scandals, became a constitutional crisis of the first magnitude. The administration chose to circumvent the Boland amendment through arms sales to Iran, with profits transferred to the Nicaraguan Contras for their military needs. Foreign governments, private individuals, and lesser officers of the National Security Council manipulated the transfers of funds despite the Boland amendment's prohibition of support for the Contras from any "funds available to...any agency or entity of the United States involved in intelligence activities." As congressional committee hearings established, the NSC had been covertly turned into an operational intelligence unit in order to sidestep congressional restrictions on the Central Intelligence Agency.

In the perspective of the Framers, Irangate perpetrated a constitutional crisis. Article 1, Section 9, requires that all funds raised by the government or its agents must be received or expended only in accord with laws passed by Congress—the historic "control of the purse-strings"—a cardinal principle of democratic states. Irangate created a shadow treasury, the repository of an executive slush-fund, whose employment could render totally meaningless the appropriations function devised by the Framers as a bastion against executive tyranny.[27]

The President's Staff for Foreign Policy-Making

Apart from its provisions for the presidency, the Constitution contains little structuring of the executive branch. Unlike many foreign democratic constitutions, it does not establish a cabinet or specify the constituent departments to complement the president. The American Constitution provides only that "he may require the opinion, in writing, of the principal officer in each of the executive departments, upon any subject relating to the duties of their respective offices...." Nonetheless, promptly after the first presidency commenced in 1789, executive departments—State, Treasury, War—and the post of attorney general were created. Faced with a crisis in foreign affairs—war between Britain and France and the imperative of American neutrality—Washington instituted the cabinet, consisting of his department heads, for joint consideration of policy-making. The cabinet meeting appealed to Washington by permitting the testing of the opinions of his counselors in the presence of their peers.

The department head, such as the secretary of state, is appointed through the constitutionally prescribed Senate review of his credentials for his office. His performance is subject to congressional examination, particularly through its lawmaking and investigative committees. He holds news conferences and is otherwise accessible to the press. He manages an institutional staff or departmental bureaucracy, which mobilizes the vast quantities of information and diverse expertise required for the making of modern-day foreign policy. Secretaries of state such as Hughes, Dulles, and Kissinger have wielded premier influence in the presidential administrations in which they served.

But presidents are sometimes less inclined to accord a substantial role to the secretary of state and the State Department. According to the cliché, these presidents prefer to be "their own Secretaries of State." The Roosevelts, Wilson, and John Kennedy, for example, were all of this persuasion. Reagan's initial secretary of state, Alexander Haig, resigned after a short tenure, and his successor, George Shultz, was sometimes bypassed or overruled, as in the Irangate Affair. Presidents are prone to regard the State Department's staff as unduly devoted to establish policy at the expense of alternatives and prone to a pained reluctance in carrying out presidential decisions. Presidents, faced with a brief tenure, are impatient for results and tend to discount the bureaucracy's struggles with complex problems, governmental size, and the plodding efforts necessary to forge a consensus among the diverse agencies of foreign affairs.

In a move uncontemplated by the Framers, presidents have, over time, built up their own staffs to the point that all presidents since Kennedy have used the White House staff to maximize their own involvements in foreign affairs. Where once the national security assistant had worked within a modest compass as a general aide to the National Security Council, created by the National Security Act of 1947, the office was transformed into a post whose incumbents rivaled and sometimes outpaced the secretaries of states and defense in influence and impact. Kennedy's initial national security assistant, McGeorge Bundy, and a cadre of aides monitored foreign policy and national security problems and the progress of decision-making and implementation throughout the executive branch.

During Henry Kissinger's incumbency in the Nixon and Ford administrations, the role of the national security assistant came into fullest flower. Kissinger not only helped create policy but, unlike his predecessors, conducted diplomatic negotiations to carry it out. He quadrupled the assistant's staff to some fifty-four "substantive officers," chaired half a dozen interagency committees covering the full range of foreign policy, and managed "working groups" that prepared staff studies for top-level policy-making and formulated options for presidential decision. Like other national security assistants, both before and after his time, Kissinger was the perfect instrument to effect the preference of contemporary presidents to make the presidency, rather than the departments, the center of policy-making.[28]

President Carter, consequently, sanctioned an expansive role for his national security assistant, Zbigniew Brzezinski, who also directed a miniature bureaucracy capable of moving faster than its competitor, the State Department. Brzezinski gained leverage from the daily briefing he provided the president on the foreign-affairs–national-security scene and generally enjoyed ready access to his chief. No foreign policy matter reached Carter without being filtered through Brzezinski and NSC processes.[29] Like Kissinger, Brzezinski became a highly visible policy spokesman. The totality of power amassed by both assistants frustrated their respective secretaries of state to the point that both these senior cabinet officials resigned.

President Reagan, who resolved to avoid the power-centered national security assistant by limiting the role to that of policy coordinator and by excluding him from direct access to the president, eventually abandoned that formula as a procession of five appointees held the post. The fourth incumbent, Frank Carlucci, reverted toward the power model of the national security assistant and revived the frustrations of the secretary of state, whose influence was often overshadowed.[30] Doubtless the powerful national security assistant would offend many Framers, with their suspicion of concentrated power and the immunity of the post from the normal play of checks and balances. The assistant is not subject to Senate confirmation and is ordinarily exempt from public appearances before congressional committees—

by pleading the necessity of protecting his confidential relationship with the president. The assistant short-circuits the expertise and informa- tion resources of the State Department and sows confusion among foreign governments when his articulations of foreign policy contradict those of the secretary of state. Irangate illuminates the potentialities for abuse in a national security system, which at the presidential level can elude external accountability and is held only to those standards the chief executive is disposed to impose.

The presidency's foreign affairs staff also includes the Central Intelligence Agency which, although somewhat more accountable to Congress, operates with wide latitude, and, as Irangate also illustrates, sometimes strays into abuse. Intelligence, overt and covert, spying, subversion, lawbreaking, all deeds of the contemporary presidency, are doubtless alien to the most imaginative projections of the Founding Fathers.

The Courts

Over the nearly two centuries in which the Constitution has been operative, the courts have been extraordinarily supportive of the president's powers in foreign affairs. Generally, the courts have applied the doctrine of political questions to this field, holding that it will not decide issues which, by their nature, are not fitting for judicial resolu- tion or which have been delegated to the other branches under the Constitution's provisions for separation of powers. A spur to the court's reticence when questions of military judgment or foreign policy are involved is that such issues have distinctly political consequences and are, by their nature, beyond judicial competence. Edward Corwin contended that the doctrine of political questions reflected the lack of definite legal criteria for determining the scope of presidential powers in foreign affairs, and for deciding contests between the president and Congress.[31]

Nonetheless, some scholars perceive a weakening of judicial deference since World War II.[32] The mere availability of judicial review lurks as a threat in the backround to an excessively free use of presi- dential power. The Supreme Court's expanded support for the Bill of Rights focused interest on that sector of the Constitution as a likely fulcrum for judicial intervention in the exercise of presidential power.

In the principal instances when it has cast off its reticence, the Supreme Court has been generously supportive of presidential power. In *United States v. Belmont*,[33] for example, the Court ruled that the president may negotiate executive agreements on his own authority to implement his decision to recognize a foreign government. Although the Court rejected President Nixon's claim of executive privilege for the Watergate tapes, it recognized for the first time, in *Nixon v. United States*, the validity of executive privilege for foreign affairs and national security matters.[34] In *United States v. Curtiss-Wright Export Corp.*,[35] the Court upheld a congressional delegation of authority to the president of discretion to impose an embargo on the shipment of arms.

Curtiss-Wright provides a most sweeping affirmation of the president's power in foreign affairs. Justice Sutherland, whose opinion was joined by six other justices, delineated the doctrine that the foreign affairs powers of the Constitution derive from the sovereignty of the United States as a nation. Such powers, therefore, would exist even without an explicit conferral by the Constitution. In effect, "sovereignty" assures that no federal exercise of foreign power can fail for lack of constitutional support. But sovereignty is not a doctrine for everyday application across the board of foreign relations. It does not overcome the formal safeguards, such as the Bill of Rights, implanted by the Framers to ward off abuses of power.

The Two-Track System

With the now lengthy historical experience under the Constitution and its illumination of the Constitution's general language, it is demonstrable that the Framers provided for a two-track system in foreign affairs.

What might be designated the first track consists of a set of powers and practices, in whose employment the president enjoys high, if not complete, autonomy. Here many of his acts are concealed in secrecy, beyond the sight and awareness of Congress and the public. If, subsequently, his conduct does become known, the hour is already so late, and commitment so far ventured, that little opportunity remains to check or reverse the president's actions. More likely, passivity and acquiescence are the lot of those outside the president's circle. Presidential autonomy is nurtured by the nature of both the office and foreign affairs. Secrecy, dispatch, unity—the virtues of the presidency noted in *The Federalist*—enable the chief executive to eclipse the slower-paced legislature, whose decision-making is fragmented among members' votes, committees and subcommittees, and elaborate procedural rules that facilitate procrastination.

This little-restricted presidency has emerged most fully since the Second World War. It is evident in President Truman's response to the sudden outbreak of war in Korea in 1950, in the secret war in

Cambodia from 1969 until 1973, in the abortive Bay of Pigs invasion of Cuba in 1961, in the confrontation of the Soviet Union in the Cuban missile crisis in 1962, in Reagan's dispatch of the armed forces to the Persian Gulf in 1987, and Bush's invasion of Panama in 1989. As these examples suggest, the first track, with its high degree of autonomy, permits the president to make the most consequential decisions of foreign affairs, those that actually or potentially can replace peace with war, that can be horrendously costly in lives and treasure or, in the nuclear age, even fatal to mankind.

The second track, painstakingly laid by the Framers and affirmed in two centuries of experience, is characterized by substantial interaction between the branches, with the President dependent upon his success in gaining approval and support from Congress and the public, including public opinion, understanding, and approval. Interacting with Congress and courting its approval, the president and his aides manifest more receptivity to accommodation and collaboration. Especially when appropriations or new laws are required, or new administrative structures must be created, this dependent presidency is more likely to interact constructively with Congress. This track is commonly used for foreign aid programs and policies, which require recurrent appropriations from Congress. Treaties of alliance and peace, as well as those dealing with other matters, necessitate the Senate's advice and consent, as do appointments to the principal diplomatic posts. An assertive Congress can provide or withhold its approval or attach conditions restricting the president's freedom to act, such as requiring his finding periodically that human rights are being sufficiently protected, or showing manifest gains, before foreign aid can be continued.

The two tracks traverse the entire domain of foreign policy-making, and parallel each other so extensively that, as a practical matter, they provide the president a choice: whether to pursue a particular policy action by the first track, or to achieve it on the second, which fosters his solicitude for congressional and public approval.

The components of the two tracks include the principal instruments the president employs in dealing with foreign affairs. Thus the president can make executive agreements, which often have the characterisitics of the first track. His parallel choice of the second track is to make treaties requiring the advice and consent of the Senate, a shared power. Similarly, the president, choosing the first track, can commit the armed forces to combat simply by his own decision. Or, on the second track he can consult Congress and secure its approval under the terms of the War Powers Resolution. Again, he can conduct foreign policy largely through ambassadors whose appointment has been approved by the Senate, or bypass them by relying on special agents whom he alone selected.

The first track with its opportunities for autonomous decision can often assure swift and firm decision, secrecy and surprise, and capitalize on the fleeting opportunities of international affairs. By its nature, it is most difficult to reconcile with the democratic ideals of legislative participation and an informed public. Its worst manifestations are the secret war in Cambodia and the privatizing of foreign policy in Irangate, with its deceptions of Congress and the public, flouting of accountability, and possible criminality. As these occurrences attest, the dilemma faced by the Framers remains unresolved: how to provide for a powerful presidency in foreign affairs while avoiding the abuses of power.

Chapter 10

Presidential War Powers, the War Powers Resolution, and the Persian Gulf

————————————————— *Richard M. Pious*

Richard Pious notes that the constitutional provisions of warmaking authority are "ambiguous, underdefined, or incomplete." Before World War II, Congress declared war in major conflicts and the president conducted them under his authority as commander in chief. However, Pious identifies more than two hundred minor conflicts where the president dispatched U.S. troops without a congressional declaration of war. Geneseo Master Critic Theodore Lowi found that executive warmaking power has expanded in modern times. Forrest McDonald agreed by stating that governmental and executive powers have expanded, particularly since World War II. Pious argues that the 1973 War Powers Resolution has been a symbolic effort by Congress to regain warmaking authority with the president. It has failed to achieve its substantive goals since most presidents have ignored WPR provisions with impunity. Through a series of case examples, Pious demonstrates that the WPR is no check on the president. He argues that the WPR was poorly drafted and that Congress is more likely to defer to executive initiatives. The record since World War II, particularly in the Korean War, the Vietnam War, and the Persian Gulf conflict, demonstrates presidential control over foreign military actions.

Do presidents exceed their constitutional and statutory authority when they unilaterally use the armed forces of the United States in hostilities? This is not a hypothetical issue. Since 1789, when the national government began operating under the Constitution, Congress has passed eight declarations of war involving five hostilities (the War of 1812, the Mexican-American War, the Spanish-American War, and the First and Second World Wars). Yet as early as 1798 President John Adams used the navy against French ships in an undeclared naval war, an action which the Supreme Court (perhaps recogniding the fact that Congress had favored hostilities and had pushed a reluctant Adams into them) upheld, holding that there could be "perfect" wars declared by Congress as well as "imperfect" undeclared wars.[1]

Since then, our armed forces have been used more than two hundred times without declarations of war. Many of these involved small operations: antiterrorist actions, protection of American lives and property in civil disturbance, evacuations of Americans and third-party nationals, participation in international policing or peacekeeping efforts, covert operations designed to destabilize or overthrow foreign governments, airlifts or sealifts of supplies to neutral or friendly nations involved in hostilities, convoying ships of neutral or friendly nations, convoying in disputed waters to assert freedom of navigation, and the imposition of blockades and quarantines.[2] Even though these operations usually risked few American lives, some have involved us in direct or indirect confrontation with important regional powers or with the Soviet Union, risking much wider hostilities. In addition, since World War II presidents have involved our nation in two undeclared wars (in Korea and Indochina), in which more than one hundred thousand American servicemen and servicewomen were killed, more than half a million were injured, and hundreds of billions of dollars were expended. Were these presidental wars constitutional and lawful?

Debates over the reach of presidential war powers cannot be settled conclusively by analyzing the intentions of the Framers of the Constitution of 1787. Neither presidents nor members of Congress limit themselves to these intentions: presidential warmaking remains entangled in constitutional and legal thickets, and debates over war powers have not been settled by the judiciary. Thus, warmaking abroad is paralleled by constitutional warmaking at home: a two-pronged attack against both the viability of the White House policy making and its legitimacy.

Warmaking: Who Decides?

Who should decide when and how the United States would use force in its relations with other nations was one of the most contentious issues debated at the Constitutional Convention. Pierce Butler argued for a powerful president who would have the power to make war. James Madison and James Wilson, fearful of executive tyranny, opposed giving the president the prerogatives exercised by the British Crown. They wanted Congress to continue to exercise war powers, just as it had during the revolutionary war under the Articles of Confederation.[3]

The result was an uneasy compromise. At first glance, the plain meaning of the Constitution seems to divide war powers.[4] Article I, Section 8, grants Congress the power "to declare war," raise the Armed Forces, organize and regulate them, grant letters of marque and reprisal, and punish piracy and other offenses against the law of nations—what today we would call an "antiterrorist capability." The appropriations power funds the military, and the "necessary and proper" clause gives Congress broad legislative powers for war-waging. Article II names the president commander in chief of the armed forces (and of the state militias when called into national service). He has the executive power of the United States, and the oath of office and responsibility to see that the laws are faithfully executed (including international law and the treaty or other commitments entered into by the United States). By and with the advice and consent of the Senate, the president appoints military officers. But these presidential powers, taken on their face, do not grant the president plenary warmaking authority. As James Wilson put it at the Pennsylvania ratifying convention, "This system will not hurry us into war." He then added, "It is calculated to guard against it."[5] Nor do they require the legislature to subordinate its own power to that of the executive.

These grants of power are ambiguous, underdefined, or incomplete. They do not cover the entire field of war powers, and their loose construction virtually invites the president and Congress into boundary disputes. What is the scope of the commander-in-chief clause, for example? An early draft of the New Jersey Plan at the Convention granted a plural executive the power "to direct all military operations," but also prohibited any of the executives from taking "command of any troops, so as personally to conduct any enterprise as General or in any capacity." Neither the grant of power nor the restriction remained in the final version of the Constitution, and so the commander-in-chief clause remains a general term which can be interpreted in an open-ended way.[6] Alexander Hamilton, in *Federalist Paper, Number 69*, argued that the title "would amount to nothing more than the supreme command and direction of the military and naval forces," but that formulation is itself ambiguous (and presumably allows for personal direction of forces). The president can claim implied war-waging powers that "fill in the blanks" and expand on ambiguous terms. For example, the Constitution makes no mention of aggressive war, acquisition of territory, interventions and interpositions, police actions, truces, armistices, proclamations of neutrality, convoying in sea lanes, undeclared naval wars, or covert operations. Nonetheless, all these are acts of sovereign nations, and presidents have engaged in them without obtaining advance congressional approval. Presidents fuse powers (such as the commander-in-chief clause and the executive power) and combine obligations (the oath and the duty to faithfully executive the laws), to create a set of "resulting powers" that enable them to unilaterally set in motion and supervise all sorts of military operations.

Consider the powers of Congress, which are also loose and ambiguous and provide ample opportunity for expansion. The early Convention drafts gave it the power "to make war," but this was changed to "declare" because some delegates argued that the original wording would have prevented the government from repelling an invasion unless and until Congress assembled (which might not be possible if an enemy launched a surprise attack which cut off north from south).[7] Does this imply that the power "to make war" goes to the president? Or is it shared with Congress through the exercise of its other powers, specifically the power to legislate on military matters and appropriate funds for war? Justice William Paterson (a delegate to the Convention) later held in a case that "there is a manifest distinction between our going to war with a nation at peace, and a war being made against us by an actual invasion. . . . In the former case, it is the exclusive province of Congress to change a state of peace into a state of war."[8] May the declaration itself become more than a simple statement "changing a state of peace into a state of war"? Can it be used to define war aims? To prescribe how a war is to be conducted? To limit the president's discretion in using force? These are unanswered questions, and perhaps unanswerable by textual analysis and attempts to explicate the original intent of the Framers. Although it is often argued that all defensive uses of the military are to be initiated by the president, an equally persuasive case can be made that the power is concurrently held, since it is Congress which issues "letters of marque and reprisal" authorizing privateers to take military action on behalf of the United States.[9]

Constitutional ambiguities continue to provoke commentators into disparate interpretations of executive and legislative war powers, which have led to fierce debates over the legitimacy of presidential war-making. During the Mexican-American War, President Polk's actions in sending troops into disputed territories to provoke a Mexican response were roundly condemned in his maiden speech to the House of Representatives by an obscure first-term member of the Whig party named Abraham Lincoln. The Whigs even managed to pass a resolution in Congress which condemned that war as "illegally and unconstitutionally begun."[10] Later, Lincoln was on the receiving end of this kind of criticism, as northern Democrats attacked his conduct in provoking and prosecuting the Civil War in much the same terms. Indeed, much of the 1864 Democratic party platform involved an attack on the prerogatives asserted by Lincoln.[11] Today the debates over war powers are carried on in much the same terms as these nineteenth-century disputes: those who worry chiefly about how effectively our nation can use its armed forces to project its power abroad tend to advocate presidential war powers; those concerned about constitutional balance, or about the arrogance of presidential power at home and abroad, seek to expand the congressional role.

No stable structure of presidential-congressional relations for war-waging has been distilled from the course of American political development. While war-waging powers have evolved through custom, practice, implementing legislation, and federal court cases, the two branches continue to struggle over the scope of their war powers. However many specific powers Congress is granted by the Constitution, in their aggregate they do not add up to plenary authority to make war. Nor do powers granted to the executive by the Constitution or recognized by judicial interpretation add up to plenary warmaking authority.

Proponents of presidential power argue that each power granted to Congress can be treated as a limited exception to the war powers confided by the Constitution in the commander in chief.[12] The president, the argument goes, can unilaterally send American forces into combat as part of his duty to see laws faithfully executed—in this case international law. He may use the armed forces to uphold treaty commitments of the United States without obtaining further congressional approval. He may use the military in a nuclear crisis as part of the understanding that he "preserves, protects, and defends" the constitution. Alternatively, partisans of Congress argue that legislative powers add up to a war-waging power to be exercised by a sovereign Congress over a compliant president.[13] They can also be considered a set of checks that the president must surmount, a form of political constraint that requires him to seek support in Congress in order to gain a national consensus for his war aims. Even presidential orders for the use of nuclear weapons, from this perspective, must be preceded by consultation with congressional leaders.[14]

Consider the impact which these formal powers have on the way we wage war. Congressional powers have a discrete "stop-go" quality to them: either the legislature chooses to declare war, or it does not; either it grants legislative and budgetary authority to draft troops and pay them to fight, or it does not; either it insists that hostilities be ended, or it does not; either it consents to a peace treaty, or it does not. These constitutional powers provide Congress with only an intermittent and sporadic influence over war-waging. They do not add up to a continuous process involving consultation and cooperation with the executive branch: no timetables or action-forcing deadlines are established. The Constitution does not require presidential consultation with legislators, or reporting to Congress on executive actions, or for other continuous collaboration; it assumes that the president will have to get statutory and budgetary authority from Congress at discrete intervals.[15]

In contrast, the president's constitutional war-waging powers permit him to exercise continuous direction and supervision over the armed forces. He may deploy forces to "signal" other nations, he may engage in total war, or he may do anything in between in his attempt to calibrate means and ends and comply with the international law of proportionality in the use of armed force, as well as with strategic and tactical doctrines.

The War Powers Resolution

To see how the intermittent exercise of legislative power intersects with the continuous obligations of executive power, let us consider how presidents have used the armed forces in hostilities since passage of the War Powers Resolution in 1973 over President Nixon's veto. "At long last," proclaimed its sponsor, Senator Jacob Javits, "Congress is determined to recapture the awesome power to make war."[16] But did it?

The purpose of the WPR is to "insure that the collective judgment of both the Congress and the president will apply to the introduction of United States armed forces into hostilities" or into situations in which hostilities might be imminent.[17] Section 2(c) restricted presidential warmaking to situations in which Congress had declared war or given specific statutory authorization, or in which the United States, its territories or possessions or armed forces, had been attacked. (The insistence on "specific" statutory authorization was designed to prevent the White House from using selective service or military procurement appropriations as evidence that Congress supported an undeclared war). Section 3 required the president "in every possible instance" to consult with Congress before introducing American forces into hostilities. And after every such introduction he was to "consult regularly with the Congress until United States Armed Forces are no longer engaged in hostilities or have been removed from such situations." Section 4 required the president to report to Congress within forty-eight hours of such introduction of forces, and every six months thereafter. (He was also required to report to Congress if he introduced the armed forces, when equipped for combat, into the territory, airspace, or waters of another nation, or enlarged the deployment of such forces.)

Presidential use of force in hostilities triggered a sixty-day period, (under Section 5 of the WPR), at the end of which time the president would have to remove troops unless he obtained one of the following from Congress: a declaration of war; specific statutory authorization to continue fighting; or an extension of the time limit. Unless the president obtained congressional approval, he would have thirty days to remove the forces. Moreover, at any time that the president used force without a declaration of war or specific statutory authorization, Congress could by concurrent resolution (not subject to presidental veto) order him to withdraw within thirty days.

The WPR has had limited impact. Presidents from Ford (the Mayaguez rescue attempt of 1975) through Bush (troop movements to Panama during a 1989 coup attempt against Noriega) have routinely minimized, evaded or ignored its provisions, arguing that it is an unconstitutional infringement on their powers as commander in chief, that it weakens the certainty of collective security arrangements, and that it fails to consider important security interests of the nation.[18] They ignore the prior consultation clause. The WPR did not specify with whom the president should consult. Clearly it would be impracticable to meet with all members of Congress, but no alternative was specified. Consultation was not required in all cases, but only if the president thought it "feasible." Nor did the language define "consult." Presidents assume that they are complying with the WPR if they simply brief several senior members of Congress after the fact, not while decision is pending on the use of force.

Presidents sometimes ignore the reporting requirements. Congress, after all, cannot compel a president to issue a report within forty-eight hours of using force, particularly if the president denies that the use of force constitutes "hostilities" and instead claims it involves "peacekeeping" or "covert operations" or an antiterrorist" action.[19] Even when presidents do issue reports, it is in the form of a two-page letter, with less information about the incident than can be found in the evening's network news. Presidential reports are not issued "under" the WPR, and do not refer to it, nor to the sixty-day "clock" which is supposed to limit their use of the armed forces without subsequent legislative approval. Thus, if Congress wishes to set a time limit, it must do so itself, just when the crisis is heating up and the American people are likely to "rally round the flag" and support the administration and its version of events—making it extremely unlikely it will oppose the presidential decision.[20]

Presidents can ignore the WPR's congressional sanctions with impunity. The provision allowing Congress to end presidential warmaking by concurrent resolution is probably unconstitutional, given the Supreme Court holding in the *INS v. Chadha* case that such "legislative veto" resolutions which are not in turn presented to the president for *his* signature or veto are unconstitutional.[21] Thus, the only way Congress could check the president would be by a *joint* resolution which is subject to presidential veto—and Congress has yet to amend the WPR to provide for such a mechanism. Even if it did, a president who retained the support of as few as one-third of the members of either chamber of Congress could use *his* veto against a congressional veto resolution ordering him to withdraw the troops, confident that his veto would not be overturned. And even if it were, the president could ignore such a resolution, because it is likely the federal courts would refuse to hear any court challenge against him if he continued the hostilities (using the doctrine of political questions), or hold that the issue was either not ripe for adjudication or was mooted by events, or hold that other congressional legislation or actions demonstrated an intent to support the president's policy, or determine that the president's powers as commander in chief had been infringed upon. In *Crockett v. Reagan*, for example, the court of appeals upheld a lower court decision holding that the issuance of a report under the WPR was a political question, and indicated that the court would not act to set a sixty-day clock if the president refused to do so.[22]

Presidents have no incentive to make the WPR work. On the contrary, they have every incentive to sabotage or ignore it. Consider the Mayaguez crisis during the Ford administration. In 1975 the Khmer Rouge government in Cambodia seized the American merchant ship U.S.S. Mayaguez in international waters. It was taken to the island of Kho Tang. President Ford demanded that the ship be released, but the message, relayed through Peking, was slow in getting to Cambodia. Two days later, without consulting members of Congress in advance, Ford ordered U.S. planes to attack Cambodian patrol boats. The next day, again without advance consultation, the president ordered to marines to rescue the crew. They stormed onto the wrong island, ran into an ambush, and suffered heavy casualties before withdrawing. Yet shortly before the operation was launched, Cambodians in another sector had released the crew in a boat which was picked up by the navy, which also retrieved their abandoned ship. Had Ford taken the extra time to consult members of Congress, the operation would have been delayed, the news of the crew's release would have reached Washington—and forty-one marines might not have died, nor fifty have been wounded.[23]

President Carter also ignored the WPR. He sent the aircraft carrier Constellation as part of a task force of thirty naval vessels near Iran as a demonstration of force without reporting to Congress. He sent four AWAC planes and 96 airmen to Saudi Arabia, and when these planes were sent over North Yemen during armed clashes between it and South Yemen, the administration again did not report, even though the planes might have drawn hostile fire. When U.S. planes airlifted Morrocan troops into Shaba province of Zaire to put down a insurrection, the administration said no report was necessary because the planes did not land directly in the battle zone—in spite of clear language in the law that covered the transport of foreign troops into battle.[24] (And it is absurd to assume that the WPR only covered planes landing directly on the field of battle). Finally, President Carter did not consult with Congress prior to attempting the rescue of American hostages in Iran, which prompted the resignation of Secretary of State Cyrus Vance, who had promised the Senate at his confirmation hearing that the administration would consult Congress before committing American armed forces in a rescue attempt.

President Reagan also ignored key provisions of the WPR, delayed complying with others, and narrowed the reach of the act. The invasion of Grenada provides an illustration. The administration sent 1,900 marines and 4,000 airborne rangers into Grenada in 1983 in the midst of a civil war involving rival Marxist factions of the government, with instructions to evacuate American medical students, "forestall further chaos," and "help in the restoration of democratic institutions in Grenada." Reagan did not consult Congress or obtain its prior approval. His final orders for the invasion were issued three hours before five leaders of Congress were given a briefing. Twelve hours after the invasion, Reagan sent a letter to Congress in lieu of a formal report, but did not activate the sixty-day clock—although in putting down the resistance eighteen American soldiers were killed and thirty-nine wounded. Congress thereupon decided to start the sixty-day clock itself: by a vote of 403 to 23 in the House and 64 to 20 in the Senate, with a majority of both houses voting in favor—but did so in separate legislative vehicles which did not trigger the clock.[25] The popularity of the invasion with the American people, as well as the quick victory which made withdrawal of most American forces possible within the week, forestalled any conflict between president and Congress.

Even when Reagan seemed to comply with the WPR, it was simply a public relations ploy. Consider the compromise which the president reached with Congress in 1983 on the peacekeeping force sent to Lebanon. In September 1982 Reagan ordered 1,200 marines to Beirut at the invitation of the Lebanese government to help police the city. The marines became a symbol of American backing for the government, which soon embroiled them in internal Lebanese politics, because the government was opposed by a coalition of Muslim, Palestinian, and Druse forces, backed by Syrians. The Reagan administration did not consult with Congress under the WPR. For a year, while marines were subjected to snipings, bombings, landmines, and other attacks, Reagan issued no report nor did he begin the sixty-day clock. So Congress decided to start the clock itself. When Congress passed the Beirut Resolution in October 1983, invoking the WPR, it gave the president authority to keep the forces in Lebanon for eighteen months (which would take Congress past the 1984 elections). Moreover, it did so in the form of a joint resolution, subject to presidential veto, establishing the precedent when Congress intended to invoke the WPR, it would do so by joint rather than concurrent resolution—enabling the president to stop any congressional action if he could get one-third of one house of Congress to back his veto of a joint resolution.[26]

Reagan won a a great public relations victory by making it appear that, when Congress invoked the WPR, it was doing so to back the administration. Reagan signed the Beirut Resolution in a White House ceremony. But at the same time, the White House released a statement which said that Congress could not set any time limits on his use of force nor limit their deployment. He argued that "the initiation of isolated or infrequent acts of violence against United States armed forces does not necessarily constitute actual or imminent involvement in hostilities, even if casualties to those forces result." Finally, Reagan insisted that, by signing the resolution, he was not giving up any of his powers, nor could it "be interpreted to revise the President's constitutional authority to deploy United States Armed Forces."[27]

For a time in Reagan's second term, the WPR became completely inoperative. The administration decided to punish the regime of Colonel Muammar Khadaffi for its support of international terrorism. On March 25, 1986, in operation Prairie Fire, A–7 and A–6 naval attack planes armed wth Harm and Harpoon missiles hit a Libyan missile site and two patrol boats after six Sam–5 missles were launched at American aircraft on routine patrol over the Gulf of Sidra. Although the operation had been decided upon on March 14, Congress was never briefed—even though the Soviet Union was given advance warning so it could evacuate its technicians from Libyan missile sites to avoid a great power confrontation. State Department legal advisor Abraham Sofaer argued that no consultation was required if American forces were operating in international waters or airspace—even if their location might expose them to hostile fire, further restricting the reach of the WPR.[28]

The WPR was also ignored in a second reprisal against Libya. On April 14, responding to evidence that Libya had backed terrorists who had bombed a West Berlin discotheque and killed American military personnel, the United States launched Operation El Dorado Canyon. Eighteen F–111s based in England and fifteen A–6 and A–7 carrier-based fighters hit five targets in Libya described as terrorist installations: the raid also injured Khadaffi and members of his family (there are conflicting reports as to the death of an adopted daughter). During the planning for the raid, there were no consultations with Congress. On the day of the operation, at 4:00 p.m., a group of legislative leaders was summoned to the White House and briefed by the president and the secretaries of state and defense. At 6:30 p.m., they were told by National Security Advisor John Poindexter that the raid was about to commence, but that if they objected "unanimously and strongly" it could be called off—because the planes were still forty minutes away from Libyan airspace. Thus members were notified about a decision that had already been taken and an operation already begun.[29]

Case Study:
War Powers in the Persian Gulf, 1987-1988

American naval convoying in the Persian Gulf in the late 1980s demonstrates continued congressional impotence and judicial evasion in dealing with presidential war powers. Our nation's regional interests in the Persian Gulf are to ensure the stability of friendly oil-producing countries, maintain freedom of navigation in international waters, and promote a balanced settlement of the Iran-Iraq conflict. Our strategic interests are to increase our influence in the region at the expense of the Soviet Union, for as President Carter put it in his address of January 23, 1980, "any attempt by any outside force to gain control of the Persian Gulf region will be regarded as an assault on the vital interests of the United States, and such an assault will be repelled by any means necessary, including military force."[30]

Early in 1981 the Pentagon announced plans to use the Rapid Deployment Force and a naval task force to defend U.S. interests in the Gulf. Bases in Kenya and Diego Garcia provided the Navy with logistical support. In May 1984 U.S. warships in the gulf began escorting oil tankers chartered by the navy's Military Sealift Command to provide fuel for our naval forces in the area. And in late May 1987, the Defense Department announced that President Reagan had acceded to a Kuwaiti request to reflag eleven of its tankers and provide naval protection for them, a move directed against Iran, which had been attacking ships heading toward Kuwait and other gulf nations, and designed to preempt an offer by the Soviet Union to provide such protection for supertankers in the Gulf. This decision was made in late February without congressional collaboration, and communicated to the Kuwaitis on March 7. It was not until March 19 that the Senate Foreign Relations Committee received its first word of the decision.

American warships sailed in dangerous waters. On May 17, while on routine patrol, the destroyer U.S.S. Stark was severely damaged by an Iraqi missile, and thirty-seven sailors were killed. Three days later, the Pentagon announced new rules of engagement which put American warships on a high state of alert, with permission to shoot at Iraqi or Iranian aircraft approaching in a threatening manner (an action taken that August against an Iranian aircraft). Through 1987 and into early 1988, American warships convoyed the reflagged Kuwaiti tankers and other American flagships through the Gulf with great success. Our ships were rarely attacked, and the only damage sustained came from mines, most of which were neutralized by minesweepers. Meanwhile, ships of other nations not protected by American and European convoying operations had to brave magnetic mines, silkworm missiles, bombing and strafing by airplanes, and rocket-propelled grenades launched from speedboats. Most observers gave the administration high marks for its tactical successes, and the convoying no doubt contributed to Iran's decision to enter into negotiations with Iraq in 1988.

Did the president act constitutionally and lawfully in putting American ships into the Gulf in situations of imminent hostilities? In approving rules of engagement which enabled them to fire at their own discretion on planes or ships approaching them? The president, of course, as commander in chief, has great discretion to place the armed forces where he wishes and to determine their mission and how they will perform it. But are there limits to these powers? And what about Congress and *its* constitutional and statutory war powers?

After the president announced the decision to convoy the reflagged vessels, some officials (Defense Secretary Weinberger, Secretary of State Shultz, NSC advisor Carlucci) claimed that the War Powers Resolution did not apply since their intention was to deter further military action. They held to that position even after the Stark was damaged by the Iraqis. Yet a military convoy operation (complete with minesweeping) is clearly a risky venture, in which fighting may occur. Shouldn't Congress have been in on that decision? Other officials in the Reagan administration (Chief of Staff Howard Baker, Attorney General Edwin Meese, and Treasury Secretary James Baker), argued that Congress should be brought in under the War Powers Act, but they were overruled. The hardliners argued that the Act was unconstitutional and that the administration need not make even a pretense of obeying it. Liberal Democrats in the House (110 of them) thereupon brought suit in federal court to direct the president to obey the WPR requirements, a suit which was dismissed immediately by the federal district court in which it was filed on the grounds that compliance with this law involved "a political question."

Congress itself did little to ensure a role in decision-making. The Senate voted 91–5 to require the administration to inform Congress of its assessment of the situation in the Gulf, prior to actually reflagging the Kuwaiti ships. Reagan complied with this meaningless provision even before it had passed the House, but refused to issue a report to Congress under provisions of the WPR, claiming that escort duty and minesweeping in international waters involved neither hostilities nor the possibility of imminent hositilites.

The administration held a strong hand. It had enough supporters in the Senate to prevent Congress from taking any action against its policy. Thus when the House voted early on for a ninety-day delay in the reflagging (200 Democrats and 22 Republicans in favor, 38 Democrats and 146 Republicans against), a similar proposal was filibustered in the Senate. To break that filibuster would have required sixty votes, but supporters of the president were able to muster forty-four votes, and so the attempt to end the debate failed, and with it all chance to delay reflagging of ships for ninety days. Later, an effort in the Senate to require the president to act under provisions of the War Powers Resolution also failed because some southern Democrats, led by Georgia's Sam Nunn, argued that the Senate would be undercutting the president. (Two days after that vote an American helicopter attacked an Iranian ship laying mines, killing three of the crew, seizing the others as well as the ship). Yet another proposal, this one by Democratic Majority Leader Robert Byrd and Georgia Senator Sam Nunn to apply a ninety-day limit on reflagging Kuwaiti tankers (unless the Senate and House approved a continuation) also could not round up the sixty votes needed to defeat a filibuster. The mood in Congress was volatile and sometimes bellicose: when American forces destroyed an Iranian oil platform which had been used to coordinate attacks on shipping, the Senate voted 92–1 in favor of a resolution supporting the action.

Anyone who thinks that Congress can develop a coherent policy on the use of military force is invited to examine Senate Resolution 194, the Nunn-Warner resolution, adopted by a 54–44 vote. It required Reagan to report within thirty days on his policy, and thirty days after that the Senate could vote on a joint resolution framing policy for the Gulf under a special rule which would preclude a filibuster. Thus the Byrd-Warner resolution guaranteed opponents of the president's policy that there could be some kind of vote on it. But the resolution also contained a statement of policy which supported "a continued U.S. presence in the Persian Gulf," while expressing "reservations about the convoy and escort operations of the U.S. naval vessels." It included an amendment offered by Minority Leader Robert Dole that specified that nothing in the resolution should be construed as limiting the president's constitutional powers as the commander in chief of the armed forces to use American forces in self-defense. It also included an amendment offered by Jesse Helms which authorized the navy to sink any Iranian ship or destroy any Iranian installation threatening an Americn warship. Thus, the Senate resolution incorporated the most bellicose aspects of the convoy operations and took the most extreme positions on the president's war powers to satisfy hawks, while at the same time provided for a vote in future on the entire convoying operation to satisfy doves.

The Byrd-Warner resolution also specified that further votes under its provisions would not be linked to the WPR. For unlike the WPR (which ends military operations unless Congress votes to continue them within sixty days), any new resolution would have required Congress to take an affirmative vote to cut off the operation. (Even so, the House failed to pass the Byrd-Warner joint resolution and so no vote under its provisions was ever scheduled).

Eventually the administration decided on limited consultation. When the U.S. frigate Samuel B. Roberts suffered extensive damage and casualties after hitting a mine laid by the Iranian navy, congressional leaders were summoned to the White House for consultations on a possible American reprisal. "For the first time, we were consulted before the 'executive' order was sent out and before it was decided," said Senate Majority Leader Robert Byrd, agreeing that a reprisal would be "a legitimate response."[31] The U.S. cruiser Wainwright and frigate Simpson and destroyer Joseph Strauss and A–6 jets from the carrier Enterprise thereupon sank or damaged three Iranian warships (the

Joshan, Sahand, and Sabalan), and three motor boats, and damaged the Sassan and Sirri oil platforms. On April 20 Reagan sent a report to Congress, "consistent with" provisions of the WPR.

Because congressional leaders had been in on the decision, there was no discussion on the floor of Congress in the days immediately following the attack. On April 19, Senator Robert Dole observed: "Having attended a number of 'consultations,' I have found over the years that they primarily have been notifications, not consultations, but I think that in this instance, to the credit of the administration, there were consultations."[32] "There won't be a fight, so long as they keep consulting," Democratic House Whip Tony Coelho promised.[33] On June 7, the a majority of the Senate (by a 51–31 vote) upheld a parliamentary maneuver to block a vote on keeping forces in the Gulf, further acquiescing in (or legitimizing, depending on your point of view) the president's policy.

Congressional reactions to the administration policy are perhaps best understood in the context of American public opinion. Americans don't like the armed forces being sent to faraway places to act as the world's police force. They don't want casualties in small scale military operations. But they also rally round the president and the military when it is perceived to be under attack. Thus, after the navy attacked and captured an Iranian minesweeper in the Gulf, a NYT/CBS news poll found that 78 percent of the public approved while only 8 percent disapproved. Moreover, 64 percent favored an attack on Iran if it attacked U.S. ships, only 24 percent were opposed.[34] Yet, as public opinion in the Vietnam War and in the Lebanon peacekeeping operation demonstrates, the public mood is volatile. Support can drop sharply if casualties are high.

For the most part in the convoying operation, the president missed an opportunity to use the WPR. As Alan Cranston put it, "Like his Democratic and Republican predecessors, Reagan has failed to strengthen his hand by seizing the opportunity that war powers requirements can offer for enlisting congressional support."[35] Instead, by ignoring the War Powers Resolution, the president simply alienated members of Congress, gave opponents of his policy leverage by allowing them to raise constitutional and legal issues and fault the legitimacy of his actions.

On all counts, the WPR has been a failure. Presidents have ignored its requirements with impunity, confident that its provisions would never stand up in court. Members of Congress have used it as a convenient way to distance themselves from the administration—unless it turns out that the operations are successful, in which case they drop their objections and ignore the WPR. Congress has not insisted that the administration adhere to the terms of the WPR, and there is no reason to think it will be anything more than a dead letter in the future.

"It is not a lack of power which has prevented the Congress from ending the war in Indochina," Senator William J. Fulbright observed in 1972, "But a lack of will."[36] The same could well be said of the reason why Congress cannot get presidents to collaborate effectively on decisions involving peace and war. Given the ambiguities and silences of the Constitution of 1787, the realities of constitutional interpretation are created "on the ground," when presidents and Congress interact. The only way for Congress to play an important role in decisions about peace or war is to insist on it, and then to do so. The record to date gives little indication that Congress will defend either its constitutional prerogatives or its statutory powers under the WPR. And if Congress will not stand up for itself, is there any reason to suppose that either the president or the judiciary will stand up for it?

Chapter 11

The Presidency and the Future of Constitutional Government

Donald L. Robinson

Donald Robinson argues that the presidency, as established in the Constitution and as it has evolved in the modern context, poses a dire and immediate threat to constitutional government. He is concerned with the abuses of executive power in the Iran-Contra Affair and the more persistent problems of executive-legislative stalemate and disharmony. Geneseo Master Critic Forrest McDonald agreed. In the electoral arena, the presidency has been dominated by the Republicans and the House by the Democrats, while the Senate has a pattern of relatively close two-party competition. He also identified the lame-duck syndrome of a second-term president who cannot work effectively with Congress so that an adversarial relationship develops. Robinson proposes several reforms that, in his opinion, would provide the necessary checks and balances to monitor executive decisions and to prevent abuses of power. These include expanding the membership of the National Security Council to include federal legislators, special elections and dissolution of the two branches, and party reform. Lowi disagreed with the special election proposal, calling it the wrong solution for the wrong problem. Robinson replied by arguing that he was trying to find solutions for both executive-legislative stalemate and the executive tendency toward autocracy in crisis situations.

I have been asked to speak about the future of the American constitutional order. Thinking about the future is a little like thinking about the past. One looks both for continuities and for breaks in the pattern of events. The difference, of course, is that one's thoughts about the future are not pinned to facts. One is dealing in the realm of probabilities, of hopes and fears. There is a powerful urge to assume that the future will be merely an extension to the present, that constitutional government, having survived for two centuries, will muddle through future difficulties as well.

211

As citizens of a republic, however, it is especially important that we be aware of other possibilities, ranging from collapse to creative renewal. The health of a republic depends ultimately on the commitment of believing, caring men and women. We need to consider whether our constitutional system may now be imperiled after its two hundred years of development and by changes in its environment.

Rather than attempt to maintain suspense, let me state right at the outset the perspective on constitutional form that has emerged from my own studies and analysis. I believe that the presidency, as it has evolved since the middle of the twentieth century, poses a dire threat to constitutional government in this country. Unless we come to grips with these changes and make adjustments to compensate for them, we shall meanly lose the hope that has borne America through two turbulent centuries.

The summer of the bicentennial of the Constitution was a time of testing for the American political system. In November 1986, it came to light almost by accident that our government for over a year had been secretly engaged in selling weapons to a terrorist government in the Middle East. When the president asked the attorney general to look into the situation, it further developed that the profits from this wretched scheme were being used to support a guerilla movement in Central America, in violation of several laws. A series of investigations— by a presidentially appointed board headed by former Senator John Tower (R-Tex.); by a special prosecutor, Lawrence Walsh, appointed by a panel of federal judges at the request of the attorney general; and by a joint congressional committee cochaired by Senator Daniel Inouye (D-Hawaii) and Representative Lee Hamilton (D-Ind.)—exposed an appalling set of operations, running "outside the constitutional fence."[1]

It was dismaying to confront these revelations during the bicentennial summer. It presented a spectacle of abuse in high places that had few precedents in American history. It left our Middle East policy in a shambles, and the intelligence services of other nations were reluctant to cooperate with a government that managed its own affairs so badly.

Yet the affair was not without its redeeming features. Wrongdoers were exposed and punished; in that sense at least, the system could be said to be "working." Several key officials, including George Shultz, secretary of state, and Caspar Weinberger, secretary of defense, as well as several lawmakers—besides Hamilton and Inouye, Senators Warren Rudman (R-N.H.), Sam Nunn (D-Ga.), George Mitchell (D-Me.), and William Cohen (R-Me.), and Representatives Louis Stokes (D-Ohio), Richard Cheney (R-Wyo.) and Tom Foley (D-Wash.)—inspired new confidence in the system. And the nation got a much-needed civics lesson.

There was a tendency, as the Iran-Contra investigations wound down, to breathe a sigh of relief. No "smoking gun" had been found in the president's hand, and it would not be necessary to endure the ordeal of an impeachment proceeding. James Reston, writing his last regular editorials in a distinguished career at the *New York Times*, took the view that it would "probably be a long time before the CIA and the NSC. . . run wild over or around the President and the Congress, and a long time too before the Constitution is violated in the name of conservative principles." He acknowledged that the secretary of state in his testimony had told "an alarming story of corruption at the top of the government," that "unelected, unconfirmed and virtually unknown staff officers in the White House" had been making major foreign policy decisions on their own, lying to Congress and apparently not even obtaining the president's informed approval for some of their initiatives. Nevertheless, he drew comfort from what he saw as evidence that "this system of separate and equal powers can be manipulated only so far before it rallies under stress."[2]

In constitutional terms, the Tower Board reached a similarly comforting conclusion: that the Iran-Contra fiasco was "a policy blunder caused, not by institutions, but by individuals."[3] It took, as the epigraph of its report, the rhetorical question propounded by the Roman poet, Juvenal: "Who shall guard the guardians?" Presumably, by the Tower Commission's lights, this question was virtually unanswerable. Commissioner Edmund Muskie, a former senator and secretary of state, remarked as the report was being issued that it was up to the president to make the system work. It was made for his use, and "by actions, by his leadership, [he] determines the quality of its performance."[4] It seemed almost a counsel of despair.

When Reston wrote that it would be "a long time" before any future president's men would be tempted to perpetrate a similar fiasco, it brought to mind the Watergate scandal and how quickly the impression of that episode had lost its monitory effect. Why were Reston and the Tower Board so loath to see a pattern in these recurrent crises? Why were they so reluctant to see implications for reform?

The answer is rooted in the prevailing conception of the role of the chief executive in constitutional government. At the beginning of its section entitled "Recommendations," the Tower Board indicated its disposition by citing the opinion of Justice George Sutherland in the famous case of *United States v. Curtiss-Wright Export Corporation*.[5] This opinion has become the charter of presidential power in foreign affairs. It is built on the theory that the power to conduct foreign relations is inherent in a nation's sovereignty and is by nature an executive power. It therefore exists, as an executive power, from the moment the nation asserts its sovereignty. It is in that sense extra- or pre-constitutional, in a way even more fundamental than the Constitution itself. (Contrast James Madison's observation made in 1792: "In Europe, charters of liberty have been granted by power. America has set the example...of charters of power granted by liberty."[6])

All that a constitution can do, according to Justice Sutherland's theory, is to indicate certain exceptions to the general principle that the nation's power of foreign relations, vested in the executive, is plenary. Thus, the Constitution of the United States provides that the Senate must ratify treaties and confirm the appointment of the president's ambassadors and that Congress must declare war and raise and maintain armed forces. With these specific exceptions noted, however, the rest of the foreign policy power must be assumed to be the province of the executive. So, at any rate, runs the doctrine that Sutherland presents in *U.S. v. Curtiss-Wright*.[7]

The Tower Board took this theory as its authority in considering what lessons to draw from the Iran-Contra Affair. In fact, it embellished it. Quoting Sutherland's view that "the President alone has the power to speak and listen as a representative of the nation," the Board added that, "whereas the ultimate power to formulate domestic policy resides in the Congress, the primary responsibility for the formulation and implementation of national security policy falls on the President."[8]

Not suprisingly, given this point of departure, former Senator Tower and his associates came up empty, as far as institutional reforms are concerned. Not only should the president remain untrammeled by legislative interference, they concluded; so should his staff. The purpose of the NSC and its staff is to advise the president and to coordinate the activity of the department in service of the president's policies. "As a general matter," the NSC ought not to "engage in the implementation of policy or the conduct of operations." At the same time, however, "the inflexibility of a legislative restriction should be avoided," because a "legislative proscription might preclude some future president from making a very constructive use of the NSC staff."[9]

To assess this conclusion, we must return to the sources of the American constitutional tradition. We should do so modestly, for, as Justice Robert Jackson warned in assessing President Truman's seizure of the steel mills in 1952, "Just what our forefathers did envision, or would have envisioned had they foreseen modern conditions, must be divined from materials almost as enigmatic as the dreams Joseph was called upon to interpret for the Pharoah."[10] This is particularly true for the executive, since the Framers had so little experience themselves with that part of the constitutional structure and their phrasing of Article II was so spare. Nevertheless, a candid consultation of the Framers' pronouncements on this subject does yield a few important clues about their intentions.

There was no executive at the national level under the Articles of Confederation. Congress administered its own affairs through ad hoc boards, and it had only a very limited bureaucracy to assist with administrative tasks. Thus Article II of the Constitution of 1787 established something new, and its Framers, whose experience with "the executive power" had been confined to state governments, had only a sketchy idea of the power they were vesting in the president.

By analogy with the state governments, the powers of the federal chief executive centered on the enforcement and implementation of the laws, including the appointment of officers to help him carry out these functions. In addition they included such responsibilities as giving information to the Congress on the state of the Union, granting reprieves and pardons, and vetoing legislation.

Beyond these powers which the president received by analogy with the state executives, however, the president was given responsibility for foreign relations. With the consent of two-thirds of the Senate, he could "make" treaties and, with the Senate majority's consent, appoint ambassadors; and he was directed to "receive ambassadors." He was also, of course, made commander in chief of the armed forces. (Some of the governors at that time were commanders in chief of state militia, but the new president's powers in the field were obviously more awesome.)

In sum, though the text of the Constitution does not say so explicitly, John Marshall was drawing a fair inference when he declared that "the president is the sole organ of the nation in its external relations and its sole representative with foreign nations." Sometimes, however, this oft-quoted sentence is made the basis for assertions that go far beyond Marshall's meaning. He was not arguing that presidents were free to make their own foreign policy, much less that they were free to ignore laws by which Congress sought to direct their actions in foreign relations. In fact, in the same speech, he commented that Congress was constitutionally free to "prescribe the mode" by which the laws, including treaties, might be carried out, was free in fact to "devolve on others [beside the president] the whole execution of the contract," but that "til this be done," it was the duty of the executive department to carry out the treaty "by any means he possesses."[11]

It seems clear that the principal intention of the system of separated and checked powers established by the Constitution is to force the executive and legislative branches to cooperate. The sharing of power keeps the branches in contact and often brings them into conflict. That is indeed the Framers' most fundamental intent.

Note also that the Framers did not distribute the shares of power randomly. To Congress they gave the making of policy. To the executive they gave enforcement and administration. The assignments were not pure, of course. Each branch had a hand in the other's affairs, to keep a check on it. The executive could recommend measures, and he or she could veto enactments of which he or she disapproved and thereby require that only special majorities could enact them over his objections. Congress also had a hand in administration, by its power of the purse and authority to structure departments through legislation and set their assignments, and by the Senate's power to confirm the appointment of all major administrative officers.

Despite this mixing, however, the centers of gravity were clear. Congress, representing the various regions, occupations, and classes in the Union, would by its deliberations ascertain and establish the nation's will. The president, a single individual, would decisively and vigorously carry that will into execution.

So far there is no distinction between foreign and domestic affairs. With Senate consent, the executive makes treaties, which is a kind of lawmaking. But once made, the executive has the same obligation toward treaties as toward any other form of law: the obligation to "take care" that they are "faithfully" executed.

In assigning these roles, the Framers paid careful attention to the differing relationship of the two branches in the operation of "factions." Factions were unavoidable in republican political life. That is the point of Madison's argument in *Federalist Paper*, Number 10. Factions were groups of people ("men," in those days) who came together to promote their own interests. According to the Framers' doctrine of man, if people were free to form such combinations, they would always do so. Many theorists thought this tendency was fatal to republican government. Madison thought not. He believed that in a large republic there would be enough variety that no single group could form a majority by itself. So long as majorities ruled, no single "faction"—at any rate none based on economic interests—could gain control, certainly not for long.

Thus it was safe, in legislative assemblies, to give free rein to factions. They would check one another.

Note, however, that Madison's famous theory does not apply to the executive. In the legislature many factions could be represented, but there was to be just one chief executive. Both the process by which he was selected and his mode of operation in office were thus utterly different from those pertaining to Congress. His election was rigged so as to minimize the likelihood that any single group of "designing men" could manipulate the process for partisan ends. Furthermore, according to Alexander Hamilton, his unique responsibilities required him to be capable of decisiveness and secrecy. Also, the electorate had to be able to focus accountability on him personally for the vigorous enforcement of the law.

Hamilton was perfectly clear on this point. He agreed with Madison that factions would inevitably arise in republican politics, but he insisted that their operation be confined to the legislature. It was imperative to keep their "baneful" effects out of the executive branch.[12]

Hamilton spelled this position out in *Federalist Paper*, Number 70. Wherever two or more people were involved in a political enterprise, there was always the danger of bitter dissensions and animosity. "Whenever these happen," he wrote, "they lessen the respectability, weaken the authority, and distract the plans and operations of those whom they divide." Such "inconveniences" were unavoidable in the legislature; in fact, "differences of opinion and the jarring of parties" in the legislature "often promote deliberation and circumspection, and serve to check the excesses of the majority" in the legislative arena. But it was far different where "the supreme executive magistracy of a country" was concerned. Here the disadvantages of dissension were "pure and unmixed." They constantly counteracted those qualities which were most necessary to the effective performance of the executive function, vigor and expedition, and without any counter-balancing good. Hamilton gave just one example of this operation: "In the conduct of war, in which the energy of the executive is the bulwark of the national security, everything would be apprehended from its plurality [that is, from vesting the executive power in the hands of a council, rather than a single individual]."[13] On the basis of this understanding, the Framers vested the executive power in a single individual and designed an electoral process to enable presidents to come to office without mortgaging their authority to factions.

Thus, the Framers' reason for preferring "unity" in the executive is clear. So also, unfortunately, is their failure to consider the two leading threats to the perpetuation of a "republican executive": the difference between domestic and foreign affairs, and the impact that a maturing bureaucracy would have on the balance of the branches.

The Difference Between Domestic
and Foreign Affairs

The Constitution provides just one method for governance. Congress makes the laws; the president executes them. There is no authority in the Constitution for the president to spend any money or establish any new functions of government without prior congressional enactment.

In domestic governance, this procedure is adequate except in the most unususal circumstances. President Lincoln took money from the Treasury without authorization to quell a civil war, but the desperation of those circumstances served to underline the general rule.

In foreign relations, on the other hand, the president operates routinely without lawful guidance. Jefferson purchased Louisiana and responded to military attacks without prior legislative authorization.[14] Polk stationed troops in disputed territory in southern Texas, provoking the Mexican War. Modern presidents, building on these precedents, deploy troops all over the globe. Often they draw a measure of legal authority from treaty commitments and congressional resolutions, but it is obvious that they have enormous leeway in interpreting their responsibilities under the enactments. Their discretion apparently extends from abrogating treaties which they deem to have served their purpose (as President Carter did in relation to Taiwan) to applying military force in the face of a contrary judgement by allies with whom we share a treaty obligation (as President Reagan did in Grenada and the Persian Gulf). In short, presidents have a degree of discretion in foreign affairs which would be utterly inadmissible in domestic affairs, and it extends not just to implementation, but to policy-making.

In foreign relations, the president has become the principal policy-maker and often acts alone. He develops the nation's negotiating position on arms reductions, what we will try to achieve and what we will not accept; he strikes deals with Japan about trade in automobiles and electronics; he determines whether we will support the Central American presidents' plan for that region. These are policies of the greatest consequences for the nation. In coming to them, presidents are not carrying out a determination made elsewhere. They may be affected by many things, including the disposition of leading members of Congress and the advice of specialists in the State Department. But in the end, presidents decide for themselves. They appoint the responsible people in the departments. They determine which advice to listen to.

I have asserted that the Framers did not think very carefully about this difference between foreign and domestic governance. Hamilton, as we have seen, was an exception. Another was John Jay. (Jay was not a Framer in the strict sense, not having been a delegate to the Federal Convention in 1787. But his influence was felt there, and as an author of *The Federalist*, he virtually qualifies.) With Hamilton and Gouverneur Morris, Jay had helped to draft the constitution of New York state in 1777, with its high-mounted executive. He had been foreign secretary under the Articles of Confederation, and he was the author of some of *The Federalist* papers dealing with foreign relations (Numbers 3, 4, 5, and 64). Both he and Hamilton foresaw that the conduct of foreign relations would involve delicate judgments, and they wanted those who made these decisions to be free from accountability to factions in the legislature. Jay had had his fill of legislative interference during the negotiations with Spain over navigation of the Mississippi River in the mid-1780s.[15]

But even if it might be argued that Hamilton and Jay stood for executive prerogative in foreign relations, their position would, I believe, have met strenuous resistance in the Federal Convention as a whole. The royal prerogative, by which the British monarch had power to declare war as well as raise and regulate fleets and armies,[16] was not a popular concept at the Convention. James Wilson and other advocates of a strong executive had to be very careful to assure their fellow delegates that they had no intention of bringing prerogative to America. The doubly emphatic language of the take-care clause in Article II seems designed to insure that presidents would stick closely to the law, and it made no distinction between domestic and foreign affairs.

The Enlargement of the Executive Branch

Most constitutional traditions (Great Britain's, France's, Japan's) begin with an effort to put boundaries on the power of the administrative apparatus of the government. In America's case, the constitutional tradition begins with a need and desire to *create* a national government.

By 1787, the nation had been independent for a decade, but its administrative bureaucracy was still extremely primitive. There were few officials serving in its ranks, and neither the government as a whole nor any of its component boards had independent standing. Administrative capabilities were created more or less ad hoc, to serve the congressional sense of need.

One of the great achievements of the federal and ratifying conventions was to establish a separate, independent existence for the executive power. In doing so, however, they were opening a path to the creation of a federal bureaucracy, under the management of a chief executive. What is most remarkable is how little attention they gave to this prospect and its significance for the emerging Constitution. Of course, Americans had little direct experience with public bureaucracy in the eighteenth century. They had read William Blackstone's and David Hume's reflections on the threat of bureaucratic power,[17] but few of them seemed to have learned much about bureaucratic power from these works. Some commentators (Benjamin Wright, Charles Thach) seem proud that the Founders relied so little on theoretical writings, but in this case their work suffered from selective learning.

The affairs of the colonies and state governments did not require much administration. The principal experience of Americans was as clients of the colonial administration in London, which had produced mostly an emotional aversion. The military effort during the revolutionary war required administration, but that seemed only a temporary necessity and had ended in 1783. Given the conception of national government in the late eighteenth century, which focused mainly on running the post office, conducting foreign relations, defending borders, paying off the national debt, maintaining a national currency, and providing government for the capital city, it is easy to see how the Framers might not have anticipated the need for an elaborate federal bureaucracy. Departments of State, Treasury, War and the Post Office were created during George Washington's administration, and a separate Department of the Navy in 1798. But there was no Department of the Interior until 1849, not even a Department of Justice until 1870.

Beginning in the late nineteenth century, however, growth in the complexity of organization and in sheer numbers of federal employees began to gain momentum. In 1901 there were 239,476 civilian employees of the federal government. Fifty years later the number had increased tenfold. The executive branch grew during the twentieth century not only in size and complexity, but in its powers of initiation and in the exercise of "delegated powers." For example, it was not until Franklin Roosevelt's administration that the practice developed of drafting major pieces of legislation at the White House or in administrative bureaus. By President Nixon's time, a Congress controlled by the Democrats was willing to delegate far-reaching powers over wages and prices to a Republican president.[18]

With these developments, the transformation of the Framers' system was complete. Whereas the Framers had expected Congress, the legislative assembly, to declare the regime's will through laws, primacy now lay in both domestic and foreign relations with the solitary executive and people who served at his pleasure. The president had become not only the initiator of policy ideas and the articulator of an integrated outlook on the nation's affairs (roles foreseen by the Constitution), but, by the exercise of delegated powers, the "chief legislator" and, by prerogative, the maker of the nation's foreign policy. Congress remained the most independent and in some ways the most powerful legislature in the world, but it had lost the centrality which led Woodrow Wilson as late as 1885 to assert that ours was a "congressional government."

As Hamilton's analysis makes clear, the president's constitutional position and the electoral foundations of his office are entirely unsuited to these new responsibilities. It is incompatible with a republican form of government for one person, who is elected once every four years and whose tenure is invulnerable to political discipline, to exercise such extensive discretion. The rule of law cannot restrain him; its prescripts have of necessity become too broad to guide him in the application of principles to specific circumstances, and they are in any case inapplicable to vast areas of his discretion, particularly in the field of foreign policy.

Nor can the regime's "checks" bring him decisively to account, so long as he avoids conviction for "treason, bribery, or other high crimes and misdemeanors." Virulent opposition in the press and in Congress can cripple him, render him contemptible and politically impotent, but it cannot dislodge him without traversing the impeachment process. And even if a move for impeachment should produce a conviction (which it has not yet done for an American president), the office would devolve upon his hand-picked successor, the vice president. While contemplating these wretched alternatives, his critics are confronted with the choice of emasculating "the only president we've got" or finding some basis for cooperating with him.

In an essay first published in 1948, entitled "Our Constitutional Revolution and How to Round it Out," Edward S. Corwin wrote, "Unless we are prepared to forgo altogether the values on constitutionalism, we need to give some deliberate attention to that element of the Constitution which has remained comparatively unresponsive to crisis; I mean the structural element."[19] Corwin noted that recurring crises had led Congress to delegate vast powers to the executive and caused presidents to stretch precedent and assume responsibilities that were undreamed of by their predecessors. There had of course been many adjustments in governmental structure to equip the presidency for these new roles, among the most important of which were the establishment of the Executive Office of the President, the National Security Council and staff, the Council of Economic Advisers, and the

Office of Management and Budget, to strengthen his personal staff; a spectacular increase in the number and sophistication of media specialists and opinion samplers at the White House, to help him mold popular support for his leadership; and a tremendous apparatus at the White House and in the departments to see that people of sympathetic views were recruited to help formulate and implement the administration's policies (in the executive branch, in the so-called independent regulatory agencies, and even in the courts). In addition, the expansion of primaries, the provision of public financing, and the introduction of new technologies (television, computer assisted mailings, and polling) gravely weakened the ties between presidents and their parties.

Yet, despite these revolutionary changes in the political system, the basic constitutional structure stubbornly persisted. We still elected the legislature and executive separately. We still adhered to a rigid electoral schedule. Meanwhile, the courts resisted informal adaptations in constitutional process, insisting that lawful powers be established the old-fashioned way, by congressional enactment followed by presidential signature, not the other way round (*INS v. Chadha*); and reserving to presidents exclusively the power to administer the laws (*Buckley v. Valeo* and *Bowsher v. Synar*).

In these circumstances—unless, as Corwin said, we are prepared to forgo the values of constitutionalism—we need to do two things. The first is to clarify our thinking. We have to recognize that checks and balances, rather than the rule of law, are the principal reliance in our system for holding power accountable and that the Constitution's checks need to be adjusted to the new realities of American national governance.

Recently there have been some imaginative efforts to strengthen the checks within the existing system, such as provisions enacted within the past decade for giving timely notice to congressional intelligence committees whenever the government embarked on covert activities abroad (unless the president found that national security required that notification be delayed), and the naming of a bipartisan senatorial committee under the chairmanship of Senator Chris Dodd (D-Conn.) to monitor the peace process in Central America initiated by Costa Rican President Arias. However, the Iran-Contra Affair showed how much these controls depend on the competence, alertness, and goodwill of the president and his top aides, qualities which were in short supply in the Reagan White House at the start of his second term. Thus, when President Reagan assured the cochairs of the Senate Intelligence Committee of his "determination to return to proper procedures, including consultation with the Congress," and smoothly indicated his agreement with the principle that "we all benefit when we have an opportunity to confer in advance about important decisions affecting our national security," not everyone was convinced that we had fashioned an adequate remedy for the abuses so recently unearthed. Misgivings seemed to be confirmed when the president gave assurance that he would insist that his NSC staff provide "timely notification to Congress," as required by law, "in all but the most exceptional circumstances."[20] Presumably he alone would determine how "exceptional" any given set of circumstances were.

In the president's eyes, discretion in interpreting the laws' requirements remained with him. He promised that "maximum consultation and notification is and will be the firm policy of this administration," but he could not speak for future administrations. Even in his own case, we were left finally to trust him, rather than depend on countervailing institutions to restrain the abuse of power.

Clearly this was inadequate. If modern governance is to reflect the Framers' commmitment to shared power, there had to be fundamental alterations. Some observers believed that it might come through amendments in the laws—if, for example, members of Congress were added to the National Security Council (and if presidents could somehow be induced to rely exclusively upon the regular channels of the NSC to coordinate policy, rather than using agencies and persons, public and private, outside of the NSC system). Such an amendment to the NSC Act of 1947 could probably be drafted to skirt Article I, Section 6, of the Constitution, which prohibits a person who holds "any office under the United States" from being a member of Congress. The NSC is strictly advisory, and its staff is supposed to focus on "advice and management, not implementation and execution," in the words of the Tower Report.[21] If the NSC Act as currently enacted were judged insufficiently clear in removing the NSC per se from operations, and thus made membership virtually an "office" under the Constitution, perhaps it could be further amended to bring it into line with the conception set forth in the Tower Report, which was so enthusiastically embraced by a chastened Reagan administration.

Statutory adjustments alone, however, will not be adequate. Even if they were deemed compatible with the doctrine of separation, they would still depend on the determination of the president to abide by them in good faith and on his capacity to insure that his administration carried out his intention in this regard. But "if men were angels, no government would be necessary." In carrying any system of laws and institutions into effect, there is an inescapable measure of trust required in the good faith and capacity of individuals. But constitutions ought not to rely too much on good faith.

This brings us to the second need: a change in the system of incentives set up by the Constitution to govern interactions between the president and Congress. The dynamic now favors confrontation. It thus leads to an excess of political posturing, governing by mutual finger-pointing, rather than responsible, coordinated action by legislators and executives on such problems as deficit reduction. Ominously, it leads responsible people in the executive branch to acts of evasion when the law imposes unwanted constraints or burdens or responsibilities. The present system also prevents the electorate from holding anyone accountable for these failures.

Rather than confrontation, our system needs to encourage cooperation, and when the existing elected officials cannot find a basis for cooperation, it ought to give the nation a chance to resolve the disagreement through elections. Elections in a large republic are primarily about the personnel of government, rather than its policies. Nevertheless, in choosing leaders voters sometimes make a statement about policy, too, as in 1860, 1896, 1932, and 1980. In those instances, deadlocks were resolved by putting new leadership in place. The elections were not a referendum on policy; they were a repudiation of failed leadership and a declaration of willingness to empower a new team.

When the government disgraces itself or falls into stalemate, there needs to be an opportunity for renewal. Such crises do not occur regularly, every two or four years. Nor is the impeachment process an adequate remedy for failed leadership. When policy is failing or the branches are deadlocked, it is beside the point to inquire whether one individual has committed "high crimes and misdemeanors." And even if a conviction can be gained (none has, during our first two centuries), it results only in the removal of the president and his replacement by a person of his own choosing. What the nation needs in those instances is renewal, not the purging of one individual.

In another place, I have spelled out a plan for dissolution and special elections when the political branches are deadlocked or when the government is weakened by scandal or demonstrated incapacity.[22] I will not repeat that argument here, except to say that a carefully regulated system of special elections would not weaken one branch at the expense of the other. It would not disturb the existing balances. It would give point and purpose to disagreements between them and provide a mechanism for resolving them, if the people so determined.

Woodrow Wilson pointed out that, between presidential elections,[23] the public often ignores political debates because they have no climax, no decisive result. In a parliamentary system, on the other hand, the attentive public pays heed, because catastrophe may befall an unwary government at any moment. Wilson's point may be overdrawn as applied to parliamentary systems today, but it nevertheless suggests an important feature of a system where, when a serious crisis develops, the public has reason to hope for a timely resolution, via elections.

We need not adopt a parliamentary system in order to enjoy the benefits that would come from borrowing one of its features. Indeed, there is great merit for us in a system of separated powers, if we can rid ourselves of the difficulties that arise from the extreme form it takes in our system. We have occasionally been saved from serious problems by the operation of independently elected branches that are able to check each other's excesses.

There is a difference, however, between salutary checks and persistent deadlock. It may be difficult to draw that line in the turmoil of everyday politics, and there is some risk that the government might resort to dissolution too often. But there is risk, too, in a system that cannot move for renewal under any circumstances, save on a regular, four-year cycle. The very regularity of that provision tends to undermine its usefulness as an occasion for genuine renewal. Candidates prepare for it years in advance, without knowing what qualifications or what sort of person will be needed when election day finally arrives. Also, renewal is short-lived, because the system tends to settle back into deadlock soon after the elections, as everyone begins to feel the system's incentives for confrontation and recalls that it will be four long years before there is another chance for a fresh start.

The best way to honor the Framers is to follow their example. That means being willing to take a hard look at the situation in which we find ourselves, courageously and carefully measuring our performance against the standard of our ideals. It also means overcoming inertia, summoning up the effort to think and act creatively, taking pains to adapt the shared ideals of the American political tradition to human and political realities. Because of the Framers' good work and (as Justice Thurgood Marshall has reminded us) the determination and sacrifices of those who were left out of the original design, we do not need to invent first principles of self-government. We do need to think afresh about how to realize those principles under modern conditions. Thinking about how to bring the presidency within the ambit of constitutional restraint is the right place to start.

AFTERWORD
Presidential Power and the
Ideological Struggle Over its Interpretation

—————————————— *Theodore J. Lowi*

> Those who lead the country into the abyss
> Call ruling too difficult for ordinary men.
> *Bertolt Brecht*[1]

If presidential supremacy was written into Article II and was full-blown in the hearts and minds of the Founders, and if the presidency had been growing steadily through each of the heroic presidents, in response to economic and national growth, why was the office so impoverished in 1933 when we needed it most?

The story of the presidency can be told in heroic terms. Examples can be found in each and every one of the chapters in this book. After all, a heroic view was made to order by the choice of presidents around which the book was organized: Jefferson, Jackson, Lincoln, Theodore Roosevelt, Franklin Roosevelt, Truman. Whether gods or devils, these are presidents of heroic size and heroic action. Each presidency is a story about the personal strength of the president and about the power each president called upon. Each presidency is a story of success in meeting the needs of the nation at that particular point in time, usually involving some kind of potentially debilitating crisis. Most, not all but most, were crises involving foreigners, either on our soil or abroad.

If each heroic presidency were in a line of continuity, and if that line of continuity were a line of development, what a gigantic office it would have been by the end of the nineteenth century, not to speak of 1933. But in reality the presidency in 1933 was impoverished in at least three ways. It was, first, lacking in constitutional authority. Assertions made by previous presidents were either of doubtful credibility or were in the foreign affairs field and provided little if any rationale for concomitant authority in the domestic field. Second, the presidency was even more noticeably impoverished in management

227

capacity. The Bureau of the Budget was only a decade old at the time of Roosevelt's election, and it was going to remain a relatively obscure office in the Treasury Department for still another seven years before it would become a real instrument of management. There was almost no White House staff, except for a few cronies and a couple of secretaries. There was no "institutional presidency" in something we got and called the Executive Office of the President at the end of the 1930s. And third, there was no mass public capacity. The heroic presidents spoke frequently enough in the grand rhetoric of which Tulis speaks so eloquently in his book on the subject, but most of that grand rhetoric had to do with the president's war powers or freedom to operate in international waters. Woodrow Wilson began to speak of the president as representative of all the people, but as one of the few presidents ever elected by a distinct minority of the electorate, Wilson's assertions to that effect would have had little credibility had he not been president during the world's first total war.

If these heroic presidents were all part of a process of development, then the only way to understand the outcome in those terms is with a concept on *non*-development. That may be difficult to grasp inasmuch as so many other features of our polity and economy did develop in a way as to confirm a developmental thesis. But non-development is the only way to be able to accept the truth of everything else reported by the authors of these chapters.

A few specific examples of development and non-development are called for. Jefferson, according to Professor Ketcham, was a great president who believed in presidential leadership in the terms expressed over a century later by President Wilson, that the principle of government empowered by consent could transform the often tyrannical executive into, in Wilson's words, "the servant and friend of the people" (p. 18). However, if Jefferson believed in a presidency of leadership based on mass consent, his actions befitting a great president were largely the Louisiana Purchase and the Embargo (pp. 21–26). Professor Ketcham suggests that these reveal "his earnest willingness to use the powers of government on behalf of the public good." However, both were done within a war and emergency context, in a public opinion vacuum, and not as a consistent and normal expression of a constitution amply equipped for the routinization of great presidents. It may well be that the real Thomas Jefferson was the president who doubted even the constitutional power of the national government to build internal improvements! In any case, if Jefferson expanded the presidency to a point that enabled him to be the great president Professor Ketcham believed him to be, then this same man presided over the dismantling of that greatness before the end of his office. How can we know this? Because his three successors, Madison, Monroe, and John Qunicy Adams, were weak presidents, unassertive presidents, failures as president, and consistently under the thumb of an assertive Congress. By the time the next great president arrived, Andrew Jackson, he had to build his heroic presidency virtually from scratch.

Having done so successfully, Andy Jackson, according to Professor Remini, turned out to be "the first modern president" (p. 30). And for him, this is the beginning of "the growth of presidential power" (p. 30), as though there were a linear development beginning with Jackson and ending at some recent indeterminate point, or perhaps not ending at all. So, if the growth began with Jackson, and if Jackson is the "revolutionary" president Professor Remini claims he is, then that means that there had been no development between Jefferson and Jackson as far as the presidency is concerned.

And how much did Jackson contribute? Jackson was indeed a great communicator and an activist, but his communication was charismatic, and charisma is something that cannot be handed down to successors, or institutionalized. Moreover, his activism was mainly negative. Chief Justice Marshall in cases like *McCulloch v. Maryland* (1819) and *Gibbons v. Ogden* (1824) had issued an open invitation to all presidents and to Congress to take a strong and expansive national role into the economy. But what did Jackson do? He declared war on the national bank, which was Hamilton's favorite instrument of national leadership, and he actively and frequently vetoed other congressional enactments. He ended up confirming the strict, very narrow construction of the Constitution favoring states' rights and favoring a very small role for the national government. As it turns out, Jackson was more like Jefferson than unlike him, inasmuch as both of them were dubious of the constitutional power of the national government to engage in internal improvements, and both stood by and watched while Congress committed the national government to a tremendous program of internal improvements. Ironically, the one positive change brought about by the Jacksonian presidency that was institutionalized and did eventually contribute to a particular development in the presidency was the establishment of the national convention system of nominating presidents. This gave the presidency a popular constituency independent of Congress and was eventually, but not immediately, to provide presidents a base for popular leadership. Nevertheless, a whole line of presidents after Jackson returned to a very small presidency, a miniscule version of the Jackson presidency. Non-development once again.

Little needs to be said about the presidency of Abraham Lincoln, because it was a war presidency and to that extent is definitely an exception, apart from anybody's theory of development. It is not ironic but ideological that so many historians and political scientists today look to Lincoln as a model or a precursor or a justification of the strong and rhetorical presidency. I'll have more to say below about the War Model of the presidency. Suffice it here to endorse strongly an observation made by Professor Benedict in the latter part of his paper, that the "congressional government" and "the hegemony of the Senate" of the late nineteenth century were "to a large extent. . . merely a return to normal after the abnormal years of the Civil War and Reconstruction" (p. 59). That is a reasonable context for the long succession of presidencies following Lincoln and a reasonable confirmation of a non-developmental thesis about the presidency.

Teddy Roosevelt may be the most interesting case among the whole group, because all the conditions were right at the turn of the century for big national government, a powerful centralized presidency, a big and positive bureaucratic/professional state. But conditions, even when they can be seen as part of a long line of development, did not have their own results built within them. As Barrington Moore put it, "The inevitable is seldom what anybody expected." If the theory of development tells us the results that ought to have happened, given certain conditions, and if nevertheless they didn't happen, then it's wrong to go on talking about causes, conditions, or development. Neither the national government nor the presidency grew significantly during or immediately after the Theodore Roosevelt presidency. There was a flurry of activity, but it was not consolidated, nor did it produce precedent. Thus, William Harbaugh opens his analysis with recognition that "the growth of executive power in the late nineteenth and early twentieth century reflected in great measure changes induced by the industrial revolution" (p. 66). Yet, Harbaugh goes on throughout his paper to demonstrate the converse, that the executive power really did not grow, and in fact actually shrank in relation to the development and growth of other parts of the government and of the corporate world. The fact is, until the small spurt in the Wilson period and then in the 1930s, all three branches of the national government probably show a net shrinkage in comparison to the growth of industry and of interstate commerce. The real political growth in that period was not in the institutions of national government but in the rise of interest groups and the expansion of their presence at the national level. What little growth that is supposed to constitute "the creation of a new American state" in that period was the first efforts by Congress to regulate the interstate economy. But even here, Congress did everything it possibly could to keep that from becoming a contribution to the growth of the presidency. In fact, the utilization of the Independent Regulatory Commission was Congress's means of arranging for the administrative implementation of regulations without handing the authority directly over to the president. The only advance in constitutional power in regard to the presidency was probably *In Re Neagle* (1890), and here again, it contributed only to the War Model of the presidency, recognizing the president had implied powers to defend "peace in the United States" (p. 64). And the only big event displaying presidential power potential was the Pullman strike, and that's not much of a constitutional precedent. No "inherent power" was recognized; nor was any "emergency power" or the power to "guaranty a republican form of government" recognized as a source of new authority. The authority exerted was the authority to deliver the mails, and the breaking of the strike was done under a broad injunction to cease and desist, such that the executive was actually intervening to defend *judicial authority*. Once the strike was over, it left no constitutional tracks.

Most of the Theodore Roosevelt presidency was puffery. He may have been the first rhetorical president, but the rhetoric was mainly empty. He talked a lot about the rise of big corporate industry, but he did relatively little about it. Harbaugh quotes with approval an observation made by Skowronek that Theodore Roosevelt had emerged as "the premier state builder of his age." Yet, he goes on, "For reasons that plagued all his predecessors and all his successors, [Roosevelt] failed in the end to consolidate his considerable achievements" (p. 73). Again a case of non-development. What's most remembered and admired about Roosevelt is associated with warmaking. As Harbaugh puts it, "It was the war against Spain and its colonial aftermath which prompted the first great transformation in the making and conduct of foreign policy" (p. 76). Teddy Roosevelt was a product of, as well as a maker of, that war, and its contribution to the presidency was to the War Model of the presidency. The other two important moments in his presidency were the acquisition of the Panama Canal Zone "under circumstances that left a legacy of . . . grave doubt in the United States about the propriety of his methods," (p. 78), and his dispatching of the American Battle Fleet around the world without consulting Congress and, by that action, forcing Congress to come up with the money. The only point about all of this is a non-developmental point, that *the presidency can be as big as the size of the war that calls upon his actions. Or, the presidency can be as big as the president can make the international threat appear to be.*

The non-developmental history of the presidency within a general development pattern that fits almost every other area of American society can best be seen by the time we reach the crisis of the 1930s. Even before Franklin Roosevelt was elected, there was a general consensus, according to Hawley, that the economic problem was one of poor coordination and that the need was for a government capable of a "managerial solution." As mentioned earlier, it is terribly significant that there was no management capacity fifty years after conditions were ripe for it. And, again in agreement with Hawley, another big question then was whether there was any constitutional authority for the management capacity. Despite all the so-called growth in the presidency, it was terribly clear in the early 1930s that the constitutional question had to be settled before there could be much managerial capacity.

The Roosevelt administration started out on both paths simultaneously, pushing for an expansion of the executive branch while preparing a constitutional defense for what they were trying to do. The managerial side was completely improvisational, ranging from the corporate state approach of NRA, to a cooperative but almost syndicalist approach in agriculture, to an independent agency ("alphabetocracy") approach to regulation, to a "command and control" approach to fiscal policy and welfare. But so weak was the constitutional basis for any of these management approaches, even after 150 years of so-called development and growth in the presidency, that most of the New Deal approaches were declared unconstitutional. Two lines of constitutional decision making were required: (1) one to establish the constitutionality of the regulatory power and the administrative approach to it, culminating in *NLRB v. Jones & Laughlin Steel Corporation*, and (2) to validate the welfare and fiscal aspects of administration, culminating in *Helvering v. Davis* and *Steward Machine Co. v. Davis*, both in 1937. And once these cases opened the constitutional gates, the managerial capacity was still so inadequate that the most important presidential commission in history, the President's Committee on Administrative Management, opened its report with the famous plea, "The president needs help." This was 1939.

The Truman story really confirms my own personal contention that "development" and "growth" in the presidency did not begin until after the F. Roosevelt presidency and the establishment of a constitutional and an institutional foundation for growth. Until Truman's succession, there was precisely so little constitutional or institutional foundation that each "great" president had to be "as big as he could"; whatever bigness he gained, he could not consolidate and leave as a legacy for his successor. Even if a few precedents were established, that is not the same as growth and development. Until Truman, each strong president had to gain his strength and size through a virtual coup d'etat or a whole series of coups d'etat. From Truman onward, every president was a strong president; President Eisenhower proved that even a person who did not want to be a strong president was a strong president. This is because each post-FDR president inherited an institutional base and then added substantially to that base in ways that suited his own style of operation. But it was rare for succeeding presidents to wipe out any of the previous contributions; each of those was accepted as a given, and each was built upon, even when there might be some inconsistency between the established and the added. There is no need to go into the details of Truman's contribution in this respect, but it was quite substantial in a number of areas.

The papers by the political scientists in this volume help to explain why the historians tend to adopt a heroic/developmental theory as though it were the self-evident truth. Political scientists are not immune to the tendency to tell the presidential story in heroic terms; in fact, they may reinforce the heroic and the developmental by their more analytic and multi-presidential approach, as contrasted with the single-case approach taken by the historians here, and by many other historians. Nevertheless, the best way to enter into an explanation of the heroic/developmental presidency and perhaps to find an alternative, is to adopt a functional, political approach to intellectual history: Of what use is the heroic/developmental presidency to those who use it? My effort to answer this question will not be limited to the political scientists in this volume, nor are they consistently illustrative of all the points being made. My role here is to make issues.

First let me repeat that I am not against a developmental approach. On the contrary, my argument is that development is the best attitude because it forces political scientists to look at the historical, and therefore the institutional, dimension of politics. But the development approach must allow for non-development, and if development is imposed on something that is not developing, then there must be some underlying, if unexplored, values in the analysis. When in the context of the presidency the heroic is added to the developmental, then underlying values are almost certainly present. The heroic can be true, and it can be good. But heroes are the materials myths are made of, and social science must always be sensitive to myths and examine them skeptically.

Now let us return to the question, of what use is the heroic and the developmental presidency? There are at least two important uses, and both are ideological. One is liberal and the other is conservative, or better, neo-conservative.

For a long time the liberals dominated the writing on the presidency. From Schlesinger and Burns to Neustadt, the liberal historians and political scientists provided most of the research and virtually all of the developmental and analytic work on the presidency. Liberals were, in fact, the authors of the presidency in fact as well as the authors of the presidency in theory. For the liberal intellectuals, the analyses all led toward the *need* for presidential power to get America going again, to keep America going, to coordinate the highly pluralistic parts of the American democracy, to fulfill the American dream of social justice. Their model was, in effect, a Domestic Necessity Model, or a deadlock model, with the president as the only sure way to meet the need or to overcome the deadlock. For Schlesinger, the paradigm presidency was Andy Jackson. For James MacGregor Burns, the president and the "presidential party" was the only way to overcome "the deadlock of democracy," not only a problem but the title of a book he published in 1963.[2] Richard Neustadt, in the most important single work published on the presidency, could say in his opening statement, "My theme is personal power and its politics: what it is, how to get it, how to keep it, how to use it. My interest is in what a president can do to make his own will felt. . . to carry his own choices through that maze of personalities and institutions called the government of the United States."[3]

For the liberals, the presidency is indeed a developmental phenomenon, but it was never a matter of natural and inevitable growth. Each president must meet the needs of society and use the government to prevail over them. Presidents who make a valiant stab at it are good presidents, presidents who succeed at it are great presidents, and presidents who fail or don't try are the lowest of the low. Each president is a heroic figure, because each president meets the social need in defiance of Congress and "the interests." More recently, presidents were understood to be better off working in conjunction with the interests to get the interests to join him in meeting social needs, but the liberals never got over their appreciation of a president working in defiance of Congress. A president who expanded the Constitution was on the way to being a great president. When the courts on occasion stepped in to approve, that was sufficient indication for presidential defiance and heroic action. Thus, the Constitution is either a source of the power the president needs, or the president has to be a revolutionist whose defiance makes the Constitution all the office needs it to be. In this context, the purpose of the modern liberal president is to complete the unfinished tasks of the New Deal. And the liberal assumption has been that presidents *ought* to have "power commensurate with their responsibilities" because presidents would choose to do good things if they had the power to do so. This Deadlock Model or Domestic Emergency Model of the presidency is the liberal model. Such a model clearly needs a heroic presidency and can certainly benefit from a developmental theory of the presidency.

Conservatives, or neo-conservatives, buy a surprising amount of the liberal model. It didn't start out that way in the Republican party, because the Republican party until virtually the 1970s was dominated not by conservatives, but by libertarians who opposed strong or heroic presidents as part of their general opposition to big and strong government. But during the 1970s, beginning with Richard Nixon and culminating with Ronald Reagan, the conservative point of view took over the leadership in the Republican party, and conservative or neo-conservative intellectuals came into their own.

There was a point not too long ago when liberals enjoyed using "conservative intellectual" as an example of an oxymoron, along with military intelligence, jumbo shrimp, and political science. But liberals would live to eat those words, because some of the leading intellectuals, ideology notwithstanding, are now conservatives, or neo-conservatives. In brief, the conservatives share the liberal view that the presidency has been developmental and heroic, and presidential growth, not being natural, came largely from a series of heroic defiances of Congress. Where the liberals have viewed Congress as a source of deadlock and a problem to be overcome, conservatives go many steps farther into the realm of viewing Congress as a hateful, corrupt institution. Congress-bashing is one of the favorite pastimes of conservatives. But its use goes far beyond cocktail party enjoyment; Congress-bashing is a fundamental part of the upgrading of the presidency as an instrument of conservative goals.

What has happened to people we once called conservatives, that they should now be so committed to the heroic presidency after years of opposition to strong presidents as part of their opposition to big government and to New Deal liberalism? The fact is that those people weren't truly conservatives; they were free-market libertarians who are consistently against big government, including the big presidency. It was always incorrect to call them conservatives; they got saddled with the conservative terminology because they were an older type of liberalism, displaced by New Deal liberalism. An entirely new breed of genuine conservative has emerged, and they took their place as leading members of the Reagan Administration and, more importantly, as extremely influential academics and journalists writing about, among other things, presidential power. They thrill to the heroic presidency, just as much as the New Deal liberals, but they seek to use the image and the reality of the heroic presidency for different purposes altogether.

Conservative scholarship is making a determined effort to capture the presidency for conservatism. Like the liberals, they admire those presidents who were heroic, and they take particular pleasure in the stories of presidents defying Congress and discovering new constitutional sources of presidential power. Many conservatives have become prodigiously hardworking and productive students of the Founding, attempting first of all to redefine and therefore to capture the Founding for conservatism. Leaving aside the particulars of the conservative interpretation of the Founding, I will take time only to look at the presidential aspects of that reinterpretation. I don't have to go any further than Tulis's paper, which with only slight exaggeration can stand as a representative statement. At the outset, Tulis asserts, without developing the proposition, that "big government and the modern presidency are not new at all, but rather implicit in commitments ratified two centuries ago" (p. 134). A few pages later he adds the assertion that "the Constitution created an exceptionally strong executive" (p. 139). Most students of the presidency, including virtually all the authors in this volume, would agree that the acorn of the strong presidency was planted in the original Constitution. Tulis is unique in this group and rare among presidential scholars to argue that not merely the acorn but the mighty oak itself was already there.

I find the documentation for this original intent thesis very flimsy indeed. But that is of little concern here, just as it is of little concern that the documentation for a liberal position toward the intent of the Constitution regarding the strong presidency is also flimsy. The point once again is in the question of what use this original intent argument, or any other conservative argument about the heroic presidency, is to conservatives.

If the liberal use is lodged in the Domestic Necessity Model, or the Deadlock Model, the conservative need is lodged in the War Model of the presidency.

In brief, war was always, and for persons of all ideological persuasions, the one condition supporting the strong, heroic presidency. The Founders understood this to be the case and, with Washington, opposed "foreign entanglements" precisely because that was the only way to keep from developing presidential supremacy (the normal condition being *legislative* supremacy). Today, conservatives, particularly neo-conservatives,[4] are not proposing foreign entanglements in order to get a strong presidency. On the contrary, in their War Model they assume a condition of war—or constant threat of some sort to national security—that makes aggrandizement of the presidency urgently necessary. As long as there was a Cold War the constant communist threat was sufficient to meet the assumptions of the War Model Presidency. But the Cold War was not a necessary factor at all. Its alleged end in 1989–90 made the War Model and its real foundation much clearer. First, conservatives were quick to celebrate the collapse of the Soviet satellite empire in Eastern Europe with the argument that the collapse, which they embraced as genuine, had fully confirmed U.S. Cold War policies, in particular the Reagan policy of crash program Pentagon expansion to give us safety and to spend the Russians into bankruptcy. Second, the most conservative of conservatives were equally quick to embrace a post-Cold War U.S. emphasis on national security. They denounced U.S. "Gorbymania," doubtful that Gorbachev or his successors had given up on world communist commitments. As the right-wing International Security Council put it, the surrender of the Soviet Union could be a fake and it left open the question of "whether we are witnessing a tactical zig in Soviet policies intended to bolster the grand strategy of achieving global hegemony." Third, threats of atomic attack sufficient even to sustain the Strategic Defense Initiative (SDI or "Star Wars") as well as the surface and undersea fleets, could come from a number of other hostile but non-communist nations. It is hard, for example, to disregard the timing of the so-called discovery of the sale by Western advanced nations of atomic and other strategic materials to Arab countries. Fourth, the collapse of the communist system created a potential threat to American security in the unification of the two Germanys, all the more threatening because it was worked out by Gorbachev and Kohl without U.S. involvement in the "speeding unification steam engine."

Finally, the War Model presidency is a domestic necessity for those who embrace it. One might even call it the Solzhenitsyn Model or the Whittaker Chambers Model, which would propose, in effect, that the West will eventually fall (Fall?) not because communism is a superior doctrine but because the West is too weak from self-indulgence and greed. Like the liberals with their Domestic Necessity Model, the conservatives embrace the Bully Pulpit—but they go much further. Whereas liberals generally embrace the Bully Pulpit for the practical utilitarian purpose of transcending the interests and achieving programmatic goals presumably in service to the public, conservatives take the pulpit idea much more literally as a source of moral teaching and hands-on guidance. The flag-burning amendment effort went well beyond partisanship: its purpose was to make patriotism an issue in its own right, with or without a communist enemy. And there are indeed ample enemies against which to re-arm. The War on Drugs is a handy replacment for a Soviet threat. Invasions of Panama and Peru, infiltration of countries like Venezuela, and continued fear of Cuba are not the only evidence of the easy interchangeability of enemies. As in the days of McCarthy, drugs can be shown to be transposable from international security to internal security. William Bennett's qualification to lead the War on Drugs was based upon his years as a fearless conservative leader of cultural causes. It turned out to be a short step from there to drug scams, compulsory drug testing where no clear issue of public safety exists, and the denial of jobs to those who refuse to take the drug test—reminiscent of 1950's loyalty/security investigation. The culmination of moral-rearmament-without-Cold War may be the Bennett prediction in the Spring of 1990 that the war on drugs would soon produce a "dramatic increase in orphanages." This is a throwback to a 19th century epoch when Americans felt, as today, under siege by the poor in the cities. Mr. Bennett's authoritative paternalism was expressed in a remark associated with his prediction about orphanages: "sometimes you need Mother Teresa, and sometimes you need Dirty Harry," seemingly offering his own services for both. Bennett's authoritarianism was not lost on President Bush who proposed no new programs for supporting the poor or homeless but swore to wage the war on drugs "neighborhood by neighborhood, block by block, child by child."[5]

In the War Model, Congress is not merely the obstruction and the focus of specialized interest, as it is seen by so many adherents of the Domestic Necessity Model. Congress is literally hated by conservatives because of its efforts to intervene and to oppose presidential supremacy by various laws and resolutions which, under the assumptions of the War Model, are tantamount to treason. I share with Koenig the view that the Constitution implicitly provided for President and Congress to "share" the war powers. Koenig nicely underscores this with the observation that, since most wars up to 1787 were fought without benefit of any formal declaration of war, the constitutional provision for sharing war powers, which required Congress to make a formal declaration of war, was a novelty and therefore a sign of original intent (pp. 180–181). In trying to come to some kind of concordance with the War Model (although not using this term) Koenig identifies a two-track system which, for short, I take the liberty of calling the Fast Track and the Slow Track. The Fast Track is the track of secrecy, unilateral action, energy, commitment, decisiveness, where time is always of the essence. The Slow Track is a Separation of Powers Track, permitted by a longer time horizon, and desirable wherever time permits, yet highly unpredictable, uncontrollable, public, full of leaky holes, and dominated not merely by the legislature but by a large and pluralistic process fueled by greed, otherwise called the pursuit of happiness. Unfortunately, the distinction of the two tracks, while logical, is breaking down because conservative drivers on the Fast Track are like Pac-Man characters eating up the pedestrians of the Slow Track. Tulis offers a wonderful example of the attitude of the drivers on the Fast Track with his observation that "the common misperception that the Constitution adopted an *essentially* 'checks and balances' view of separation of powers began with Wilson" (p. 141). No matter that this flies in the face of most constitutional interpretation (see, for example, Koenig, p. 172: "The Framers utilized two basic tools of constitutional architecture—separation of powers and checks and balances").

Cases of heroic and defiant actions that feed the War Model abound in conservative writing, with Lincoln leading the way. But why not, given that he was president during the only war in which the Union itself was at stake. Jefferson provides cases like the emergency opportunity to purchase the Louisiana Territory and the unilateral imposition of the Embargo. Teddy Roosevelt is also a great source of defiant presidential actions as well as defiant-sounding presidential rhetoric. President Jackson doesn't figure much in the conservative discourse because, despite being one of the generals to serve as president, he had an unusual "respect of the prerogatives of Congress in foreign affairs" (Remini p. 41).

Why are the conservatives unable to rest easy with a concordance like Koenig's, in theory or in practice? First, under assumptions of the War Model, the president needs access to, if not control over, increasing numbers and types of resources in the domestic part of society that ought to be operating under the Slow Track, and control over those types of people and groups and political actors capable of effective political obstruction. But second, and far beyond that instrumental need, there is a moral need for the Fast Track to encroach on the Slow Track: The president must be in as strong a position as possible to alarm and morally to rearm Americans against external and internal threats.

Is there a possibility of revision toward softening of the War Model with President Bush? He seems less conservative than Reagan, more the professional politician, and more willing to negotiate with Congressional leaders as well as the Germans and the Russians. There is always that possibility, but the concrete signs are not altogether positive. Bush's actions in regard to Panama, China, Iraq, Gorbachev, NATO, and German unification all seem to indicate that he not only keeps close personal control over foreign policy but feels no obligation whatsoever to keep Congress informed. Perhaps he has been lucky that foreign policy issues have broken in favor of the United States totally without regard to actions we have taken. Nevertheless, his behavior idicates his intention to be a virtually unilateral president in foreign policy. His approach to the domestic presidency has been at least as forthrightly conservative as Reagan's, and he has demonstrated that one can be a strong domestic president without having a program and without relying constantly on television. He went beyond Reagan on patriotism with the flag-burning issue, and he went far beyond Reagan with Willy Horton on civil rights. He has gone beyond Reagan as a moral leader also on the issues of abortion and drugs. In an epoch of mounting deficits, where there is almost no prospect of new domestic programs anyway, national rearmament against mortal moral enemies has the great advantage of being inexpensive.

One of the most significant expressions of the current conservative mentality is the title of George Will's book, *Statecraft as Soulcraft*. This is not a small-state pro-market attitude. A true libertarian (erroneously called a conservative) would have difficulty even saying the words in Will's title, much less entertain the idea for one moment that the state ought to be responsible for shaping the soul. Genuine conservatives look to strong government in the hands of good people led by a president elected to do good things. Conservatives seem to share with liberals the assumption that presidents with great power will choose to do good. They differ only in their concept of the good.

As for these two schools of thought, liberal and conservative, with their deep ideological stake in the heroic presidency, I say a plague on both their houses. I propose that we look for another house altogether, with an ideology but without such a heavy stake in any sort of heroic presidency. Two other houses do exist, and the welcome mat is at their door. These houses are (1) radical libertarianism and (2) radical constitutionalism, with *radical* defined as simply getting at the roots. The radical libertarian view has already been identified and its special virtues noted. One of the most interesting and learned occupants of this house is Forrest McDonald, a conservative on a number of things but definitely a radical libertarian on the modern national government and the presidency. The invitation to enter their house, tantalizing though it is, I cannot accept because, along with its overwhelming consistency, libertarianism is glaringly anachronistic.

We need an approach that joins liberal and conservative schools in recognizing the irreversible reality of big government and the big president, without falling into either ideological trap. The only apparent alternative is radical constitutionalism. It is constitutionalism because it prefers the Slow Track to the Fast Track, and it is radical because it is willing to sustain some losses, if losses are necessary to sustain constitutionalism. It is ideological first because there is no way to prove that the separation of powers is a virtue, and second because there is no way to prove that the losses would not be irreparable. But if Solzhenitsyn is one of the poets of the conservative school of thought, radical constitutionalism has its poets, one of whom is Justice Robert Jackson, particularly in his dissent in the famous *Korematsu* case:

> When an area is so beset that it must be put under military control at all, the paramount consideration is that its measures be successful, rather than legal. The armed services must protect a society, not merely its constitution. . . . But even if [the orders of General DeWitt] were permissible military procedures, I deny that it follows that they are constitutional. . . . Much is said of the danger to liberty from the Army program for deporting and detaining these citizens of Japanese extraction. But a judicial construction of the due process clause that will sustain this order is a far more subtle blow to liberty than the promulgation of the order itself. A military order, however unconstitutional, is not apt to last longer than the military emergency. Even during that period a succeeding commander may revoke it all. But once a judicial opinion rationalizes such an order to show that it conforms to the Constitution. . . the Court for all time has validated the principle [in this case the principle of racial discrimination]. The principle lies about like a loaded weapon ready for the hand of any authority that can bring forward a plausible claim of an urgent need. . . .[6]

Four of the five political scientists in this volume tend to agree, to varying degrees, with the radical constitutionalist position. Although Koenig is too conciliatory for my tastes toward both heroic schools, he nevertheless holds tight to the principle of sharing and finds ample justification for a place for Congress equal to that of the president in matters of war and foreign affairs. And he displays little concern for the costs or risks of Congress's sharing the war or foreign policy powers. *Putting concern for forms as equal to or above concern for power is the litmus test of the radical constitutionalist.*

Fisher at first does some Congress-bashing befitting the heroic schools, but it is quickly apparent that his purpose is to restore the separation of powers rather than to bury it under a pile of reconciliation resolutions. After describing the post-1974 budget process and President Reagan's use of it to dominate Congress, he goes on to recognize that "it is highly unlikely that an error of that magnitude [of the explosion in budget deficits] could have occurred with the previous decentralized, fragmented process" (p. 158). That observation becomes a premise for an argument strongly favorable not only to "presidential accountability" (p. 159) but to reforms that would "restore a budget system that takes advantage of the institutional strengths of both branches." (p. 168).

Robinson is a good ending, not only because he shares my constitutionalism but because he is as radical about it as I am. As with any radical constitutionalist, his first and major premise is the dependency of the system on the separation of powers and checks and balances, and he makes it his premise without regard to whether we are talking about foreign policy or domestic affairs. He quotes with approval an observation first made in 1948 by the distinguished constitutionalist Edward S. Corwin, "Unless we are prepared to forgo altogether the values of constitutionalism, we need to give some deliberate attention to that element of the Constitution which has remained comparatively unresponsive to crisis; I mean the structural element" (quoted in Robinson on p. 221). He goes on to support strongly my often-published contention that the delegation by Congress of its vast powers to the executive produced a deep structural discontinuity with constitutional traditions. Such a recognition leads with inexorable logic to efforts to restore the balance between Congress and the president. In this matter, Robinson goes as far as anyone I know. To him, statutory adjustments to redress the balance between president and Congress are inadequate, because they depend for implementation on the president, who is most likely to prefer the imbalance as the best way to be heroic (pp. 223–224). According to Robinson, a constitutional rather than a statutory approach is needed, not only to redress the balance between the two branches but also to provide "a system of incentives" to help president and Congress overcome the confrontational relationship that now prevails and replace it with a more cooperative relationship. Robinson then takes a truly radical step, a proposal for a constitutional means of controlling president *and* Congress, making both more politically accountable. Impeachment is inadequate, first because it is applicable only in extremes, and second because it merely replaces one leader with one other. What he proposes is a plan for "dissolution and special elections when the political branches are deadlocked or when the government is weakened by scandal or demonstrated incapacity" (p. 224). Whether this is a wise or appropriate reform is not the issue. It simply provides an illustration of an alternative to presidential power that does not begin or end on the heroic and that does not make assumptions about the capacity of any president under any circumstances to coordinate the whole economy or to set the world to rights.

Because the dominant views of the presidency in the past thirty or more years, the liberal and then the conservative, have been in such complete agreement on the need and justification for the heroic presidency, there has been a blotting out of alternative views. The presence of a constitutionalist school and perhaps also a libertarian school might encourage some reexamination of the premises of the heroic. Reflection ought also to be encouraged by the fact that presidents of both liberal and conservative persuasion in the past thirty years have gone out of office widely considered to be failures. This could be attributable to their model of operation just as much as it might be attributable to bad luck or bad judgment. Failures, scandals, and disgraces ought to lead to some sober reflection.

First, liberals and conservatives alike must recognize that the power of the presidency, no matter how well justified, won't necessarily be used for good. The assumption that men are not angels is undeniably basic to the American Constitution. Second, both heroic schools must recognize that even if presidents wish only to do good, all the power we could ever give them would be insufficient to enable one person in one office with no matter how much help to coordinate the economy *or* to set the world to rights. Economies have their own way of prospering or of fouling up, and nations, regardless of their affiliation with which great power, are going to have their civil wars no matter what American presidents decide to do. The libertarian recognizes the inherent limits of what governments mustn't try. The constitutionalist also recognizes the severity of the limits on government, but recognizes that governments, especially democratic governments, are going to try to do something, no matter how much mischief they may cause. The threat to our society from politics comes just as much from goodwill as it does from greed and malevolence. The purpose of the Constitution is to contain the goodwill, the greed, *and* the malevolence, not in order to keep anything from happening, but to sublimate all those energies toward a loyalty to the process that enables them to live together. In other words, the purpose of the Constitution, including such parts of it as the presidency, is not to facilitate a particular programmatic outcome at home or abroad. The purpose of the Constitution is, more modestly, to keep the process itself alive. The presidency has gotten too big for the Constitution. Our choices under the circumstanses are (1) to follow the *Korematsu* majority and to find a new congressional justification for that size, or (2) to follow the *Korematsu* dissent and to reduce the presidency to constitutional scale in the vast range of decisions that have to be made and to formulate a rule to cover the few exceptional cases. Yes, there are exceptional cases, to repeat Justice Jackson, where for the government, "the paramount consideration is that its measures be successful, rather than legal." But that covers the exceptional cases. No institution can, or should, be built on or for the exceptional cases.

AN HISTORIAN'S LAST WORD

——————————————————— *Martin L. Fausold*

How do historians react generally to the near-universal view of political scientists that since World War II we have uniquely had in America a "deadlock of democracy"; and specifically to Theodore Lowi's contention that since the Schechter case was for all practical purposes overturned in 1937, the American presidency has become too big for the Constitution, resulting in what Lowi calls, in a book by the same name, *The End of Liberalism.*

Most historians in the Geneseo program do not agree that the American presidency in the post-World War II period jumped almost full blown into "deadlock" and into an institution too big for the Constitution. The president's executive power, separation of power, interest in "national welfare," ceremonial and administrative roles, and war and foreign powers evolved rather geometrically over two hundred years into the present condition. It is not without reason that historians of the presidencies addressed in this book—Jefferson, Jackson, Lincoln, T. Roosevelt, F. Roosevelt and Truman—see their presidents frequently in heroic terms. They do not conclude, as does Theodore Lowi, that the fact that comparatively weak presidents followed their strong presidents points to little constitutional development of the presidency until the post-World War II period. They would argue, on the contrary, that the strong presidents are almost inevitably followed by weak presidents. Lacking a crisis and given the American propensity to cyclical ideological arrangements, how could the immediate successors of Jefferson, Jackson, Lincoln, T. Roosevelt, F. Roosevelt and Truman match their initiatives? The ideological downturn following these strong presidents required that there be far fewer strong presidents to bow to the more conservative manifestations of congressional strength. Such is not to say that the strong presidents did not contribute to the constitutional initiatives and development of their successor strong presidents. Jackson surely drew from Jefferson's belief in states rights and his use of party; Lincoln

245

drew from Jackson's levelling of America and his assertion of executive prerogative; T. Roosevelt's "square deal" was constitutionally consistent with Lincoln's "emancipation" and transformed the "War Model" presidency into a "Domestic Model" presidency; F. Roosevelt greatly expanded T. R.'s idea of a positive state as implemented by mimicking the latter's artful manipulation of Congress; Truman capitalized on F. Roosevelt's New Deal, codifying it in such a way as to prepare the groundwork for Lyndon Johnson's Great Society—and for Ronald Reagan's subsequent "supply-side" dismantling of it. Historians have to believe that Johnson's Great Society did not spring from a blank surface.

Historians frequently respond to the political scientists' particular excitement about the post-War presidency by noting that the nation has often been in comparably dire constitutional straits in the 150 years before the Second World War—and that presidents were known to have frequently and heroically met the challenges of those straits. Jefferson torturously shifted away from his narrow interpretation of the Constitution to purchase Louisiana and thus make less likely the swallowing of United States by foreign powers on its border. Jackson fended off a "corrupt" plutocracy by using the constitutionally provided veto for political purposes. Lincoln faced a constitutional crisis that dwarfed the alleged "deadlock" and the problem of bigger-than-Constitution presidencies of the post-World War II period. T. Roosevelt introduced the positive state to ward off the "Great Barbecue" of the 1870s and the industrialism of the turn of the century. Franklin Roosevelt faced a labor force decimated by a 25% unemployment of its workers. It took Harry S Truman to make permanent the New Deal before a powerful Congress could reduce it. Interestingly, while political scientists today fear an inordinately strong presidency, they say little about those long periods when the nation suffered inordinately strong Congresses which deadlocked democracy until heroic presidents fought them for the larger good. The fact that Reagan successfully fought the deadlocked democracy—whatever one may think of his reasons—demonstrates well that it can happen again.

In summary, most historians believe that tensions in the American constitutional system are to be expected. Without question the tensions do reflect disturbing problems in the nation. Historians, however, are not inclined to see that tensions or attendant problems can be significantly lessened by new constitutional arrangements. Such does not gainsay some modest constitutional repairs. Rather than being constitutional, America's quandaries are far more political ones embedded in the current economic, social, cultural, religious and international context of the nation.

A POLITICAL SCIENCE PERSPECTIVE

—————————————— *Alan Shank*

Unlike the "Historian's Last Word," I have no quarrel with either the "heroic model" of the pre-1950's presidency or with Lowi's anti-heroic portrayal of the more recent presidents. It all depends on one's perspective of the presidency in a constitutional context.

The historical presidency considers how individual chief executives responded to various constitutional challenges. The six historians are primarily interested in showing how their particular presidents did well in fulfilling their constitutional responsibilities.

The five political scientists are less concerned with individual presidents. They are more concerned with analyzing the constitutional dilemmas of the more recent chief executives. The two most prominent deal with executive-legislative conflict and concentration of presidential authority in foreign policy and warmaking powers.

Using historical precedents, the political scientists agree there is an evolutionary constitutional development of the presidency. But they no longer find heroes in the White House. Instead, all the recent presidents, from Eisenhower to Bush, have had, with few exceptions, enormous problems in working with Congress on domestic policy. They have also tended toward exercising exclusive power in conducting foreign policy and have acted imperially in various military adventures.

Political scientists find recurring patterns of constitutional conflict in the Cold War (from 1945–1989) and in domestic policy stagnation (at least since Johnson's Great Society). Cold War tensions with the Soviet Union produced the "imperial presidency." Presidents Johnson and Nixon conducted the Vietnam War in a spirit of autocracy and non-consultation with Congress. When Richard Nixon also became the first president in history to resign from office as a result of the Watergate fisaco, the confidence of Congress and the American public toward the presidency took a nosedive.

This distrust did not result in a cyclical pattern of strong and weak presidents. Instead, all presidents had considerable difficulties since 1974. Louis Fisher shows that the battle of the budget became so stalemated that President Reagan and Congress decided to delegate solutions to a formula. The Gramm-Rudman-Hollings law is an abdication of constitutional responsibility. Others have described it more harshly as a "smoke and mirrors" solution to reducing the largest budget deficits in our nation's history.

Similarly, congressional efforts to diminish the imperial Cold War presidency through the War Powers Resolution of 1973 failed miserably. Richard Pious and Louis Koenig correctly show that all presidents since Richard Nixon consider the WPR to be unconstitutional. Consequently, presidents remain on the "fast track" of foreign policy, choosing to ignore Congress, except when they seek its support.

No one would argue that Donald Robinson's portrayal of the Iran-Contra Affair is inaccurate. Never before had a president sought to establish a privatized foreign policy to defy Congress and deceive the American people. Power was delegated by President Reagan to the National Security Adviser (McFarlane and Poindexter), the NSC Staff (Oliver North), and two non-government individuals (Richard Secord and Albert Hakim) to trade U.S. missiles to Iran for the release of American hostages in Lebanon.

Then, as Robinson indicates, part of the proceeds of the arms sales to Iran were illegally diverted to provide military assistance to the Nicaraguan Contras. This was done in defiance of various prohibitions enacted by Congress, the so-called Boland Amendments. The obvious conclusion is that Iran-Contra produced both constitutional stalemate between the branches and an abuse of the foreign policy power by the Chief Executive.

I disagree that President Reagan successfully fought the deadlocked democracy. The better example is Lyndon Johnson's enormous domestic policy achievements with Congress in the 1964–65 period, when civil rights, voting rights, and the Great Society antipoverty programs were enacted.

In contrast, President Reagan had one cooperative year with Congress in 1981 for a downsized domestic federal government—$35 billion of budget cuts, a $225 billion tax cut, and a trillion dollar increase in the defense budget. By his second term, Reagan was uninterested in the deficit or domestic policy. His major achievement was the 1988 INF treaty with the Soviet Union. Also, Congress was cutting back the military.

The point is that the modern presidency is no longer judged by significant executive-congressional achievements. Instead, we have a recurring pattern over the last forty years of constitutional disharmony between the two branches in domestic and foreign policy. These stalemates have prompted many calls for constitutional reform, thereby echoing earlier eras of the presidency when structural and institutional changes were made to improve our political system.

CONTRIBUTORS

Michael Les Benedict

Michael Les Benedict was born in Chicago in 1945 and received his bachelor's and master's degrees in history from the University of Illinois, Urbana-Champaign, and his doctorate from Rice University, where he worked under Harold Hyman. His entire academic career has been at Ohio State University, where he is currently a full professor. Professor Benedict has had numerous awards, most especially as a visiting member of the Institute of Advanced Study at Princeton University, and a Fellow of the Guggenheim Foundation and the Woodrow Wilson Center. His specialization is the American Civil War and Reconstruction, and American legal and constitutional history. He has written prolifically: articles, textbooks, and scholarly monographs. His book, *The Impeachment and Trial of Andrew Johnson* (1973) was heavily relied upon by House of Representatives Judiciary Committee Chairman Peter Rodino in the 1974 hearings on the impeachment of Richard Nixon. Because of his specialization on constitutional development in the Civil War and post–Civil War period, Professor Benedict was unusually well equipped to assess the constitutional aspects of the Lincoln presidency.

Louis K. Fisher

Louis K. Fisher is American National Government Specialist at the Congressional Research Service of the Library of Congress, having received a Ph.D. in Political Science from the New School for Social Research (1967). For the past nine years, he has been adjunct professor at Catholic University, with previous teaching experience at American University and Georgetown University. In 1976, Fisher received the Louis Brownlow book award by the National Academy of Public Administration for *Presidential Spending Power*. He has contributed chapters for nineteen books, ranging on topics of executive-legislative relations, presidential powers, and the federal budget. Fisher has written seventy articles appearing in scholarly journals, law reviews, magazines, newspapers, and various congressional committee documents. His five books include *The Politics of Shared Power* (1981, 1987) and *Constitutional Conflicts between Congress and the President* (1985).

William Henry Harbaugh

Born in New Jersey in 1920, William Harbaugh received his A.B. from the University of Alabama, his M.A. from Columbia University, and his Ph.D. from Northwestern University. He has taught variously at the University of Connecticut, University of Maryland, Rutgers University, and Bucknell University, and since 1966 he has been at the University of Virginia, where in 1977 he was made Commonwealth Professor of History. He has had numerous honors, and has demonstrated eclectic scholarship, working in biographic areas of differing time periods of the first half of the twentieth century. His book, *Power and Responsibility: The Life and Times of Theodore Roosevelt* (1961) is considered by most scholars to be the best single volume on Theodore Roosevelt. His second major work, *Lawyer's Lawyer: The Life and Times of John W. Davis* (1973) was nominee for the *National Book Award* in 1974. Because of his Roosevelt biography and his immersion in constitutional law to prepare himself for writing the Davis biography, William Harbaugh was particularly equipped to address the twentieth century context of the Theodore Roosevelt presidency.

Ellis W. Hawley

Born in Kansas in 1929, Ellis Hawley received his undergraduate education at the University of Wichita and his M.A. in history from the University of Kansas. He received his Ph.D. from the University of Wisconsin. Professor Hawley taught at North Texas State University for eleven years before he was appointed Professor of History at Ohio State University. In order to have access to the newly opened Herbert Hoover Presidential Library, and because of the reputation of the University of Iowa's history program, he accepted a professorship at Iowa. He is currently chairman of the History Department there. His first published monograph, *The New Deal and the Problem of Monopoly* (1966) earned Hawley a national reputation. This book and his numerous publications on the 1920s and the 1930s, all masterfully documented, have earned for him the accolade as one of the finest scholars of the inter-war period. No scholar in the nation was better prepared to address the continuity of the constitutional development of the presidency of the Hoover and the F. Roosevelt administrations. Professor Hawley, as with most historians in this NEH program, has made numerous scholarly presentations at SUNY-Geneseo.

Ralph Louis Ketcham

Ralph Louis Ketcham was born in Berea, Ohio, on October 28, 1927. He received his A,B. from Allegheny College, his M.A. from Colgate University, and his Ph.D. from Syracuse University. Although Professor Ketcham has been a member of the Syracuse University faculty since receiving his doctorate there, he has held numerous visiting lectureships and professorships in this country and abroad. His research specialties are American intellectual history and political theory, and American revolutionary and early national period. He has published prolifically. Professor Ketcham coedited the papers of James Madison and of Benjamin Franklin. Principal among his authored works are *James Madison, A Biography* (1971) and *From Colony to Country: The Revolution in American Thought, 1750–1820* (1974). His most recently published work, in 1984, is *Presidents Above Party: The First American Presidency, 1789–1829*. All books have been highly acclaimed. Because of his research interests and writing, Professor Ketcham was particularly well equipped to address the constitutional aspects of the Jefferson presidency. Just prior to his participation in the Geneseo program, Professor Ketcham was named the nation's College Professor of the Year by the Council for the Advancement and Support of Education.

Louis W. Koenig

Louis W. Koenig is Professor Emeritus at New York University, Visiting Distinguished Professor at Long Island University, having also taught at Columbia University and Bard College. Koenig has a distinguished career of governmental service, including the Office of Price Administration (1944), State Department (1950), and Bureau of the Budget (1941). He has worked for the Ford Foundation and the Rockefeller Foundation. Koenig developed educational materials for NBC television, "Our Legal Profile" (1965), and was special commentator for NBC for the 1969 presidential inauguration. Koenig is the author of twelve scholarly studies and texts which have been used widely throughout the country. His principal research has focused on the American presidency in five editions of *The Chief Executive*.

Theodore J. Lowi

Theodore J. Lowi has been John L. Senior Professor of American Institutions at Cornell University since 1972. Before this appointment he was on the political science faculty of the University of Chicago, after receiving his Ph.D. from Yale University in 1961. Professor Lowi has made distinguished contributions in political theory, public policy analysis, and political behavior. He has written or edited a dozen books, including *The Pursuit of Justice* (with Robert F. Kennedy) and the highly influential *The End of Liberalism*. In 1988, Lowi received the annual Burton Feldman Award from the Gordon Public Policy Center for outstanding contributions to public policy. Lowi has been president of the Policy Studies Organization and vice president of the American Political Science Association in 1985–86. His most recent book, *The Personal President* (1985), won the 1986 Neustadt Prize for the best book on the presidency published in 1985. In 1988, Lowi received an honorary degree, Doctor of Letters, from the State University of New York at Stony Brook.

Donald R. McCoy

Donald R. McCoy was born in Chicago in 1928 and received his degrees in history respectively from University of Denver (B.A.), University of Chicago (M.A.) and American University (Ph.D.). Beginning his teaching career at the State University of New York College at Cortland, Professor McCoy has since been a member of the history department of the University of Kansas. In 1974 he was made University Distinguished Professor of History. His research interest ranges across political history of the 1920–1950 period. He has written celebrated biographies sequentially in the period, notably *Calvin Coolidge, The Quiet President* (1967), *Landon of Kansas* (1966), and *The Presidency of Harry S Truman* (1984). Among other numerous publications, in 1957 he edited, with Martin L. Fausold, *Student Guide to the American Story II*. He has published significantly in the area of archives, most importantly, *The National Archives: America's Ministry of Documents* (1978). Early in his career Professor McCoy served as an alderman in the City of Cortland. The codirectors of the Geneseo NEH program frequently used the good services of Donald McCoy in their construction and implementation of the project, including the publication of these papers.

Forrest McDonald

Forrest McDonald was born in Texas in 1927. He received his three degrees in history (B.A., M.A., Ph.D.) from the University of Texas. In 1961 he received an M.A. degree in history from Brown University. Forrest McDonald was respectively a member of the history departments of Brown University (1958–67), Wayne State University (1967–76), and the University of Alabama (1976–pres.). His research interests are constitutional history before 1800 and economic and business history, 1890 to the present. Professor McDonald first gained national attention with his *We the People* (1958), which was the principal refutation of Charles Beard's classic work, *An Economic Interpretation of the Constitution*. Very few historians have written so much and so profoundly as Forest McDonald. His expertise in the early constitutional development of the American presidency was manifested by *The Presidency of George Washington* (1973) and *The Presidency of Thomas Jefferson* (1976). Testimony to his scholarship was evidenced by his appointment as the Bicentennial Year Jefferson Lecturer, the U.S. government's highest honor paid to an academic person. Professor McDonald was the logical choice for Master Historian Critic of the Geneseo program. In 1989 he was awarded the degree of Doctor of Humane Letters by SUNY-Geneseo.

Richard M. Pious

Richard M. Pious is professor of political science at Barnard College, where he has taught since 1973, having received a Ph.D. from Columbia University in 1971. He also serves as Professor of the Columbia University Graduate Faculties. Professor Pious has contributed numerous articles dealing with the American presidency, the Constitution, electoral politics, Congress, and public policy. His books include *The President, Congress, and the Constitution* (1984) and *The American Presidency* (1979). He has lectured widely throughout the country at various colleges and universities. Professor Pious has made numerous media appearances and has served as consultant to the Japanese and Soviet media on the American presidential primaries (1987, 1988) and to *Time Magazine* on war powers and presidential powers (1987).

Robert Vincent Remini

Born in New York, New York, in 1921, Robert Remini received his B.S. degree from Fordham University and his master's and Ph.D. degrees (in history) from Columbia University. Following eighteen years as a member of the history department at Fordham University, he has been professor of history at the University of Illinois (Chicago Circle). Almost without exception he is considered the nation's foremost Andrew Jackson scholar and has had numerous awards to attest to that fact. His research interest, however, ranges beyond the Jackson era to the whole of the 1789–1877 period. His first writing, in fact, was outside the Jackson period. It was *Martin Van Buren and the Making of the Democratic Party*, published in 1959. But his writing on Jackson is prolific and profound, the most significant being two volumes, *Andrew Jackson and the Course of American Empire* (1978, 1981). Because of his eclectic scholarly interest, Professor Remini was particularly well equipped to place the Jackson presidency in the constitutional aspect of presidential development in the 1820–40 period.

Donald L. Robinson

Donald L. Robinson is Professor of Political Science at Smith College, having received a Ph.D. from Cornell University under the supervision of Clinton Rossiter. In 1983 he appeared on public television in a series of programs called "The Constitution: That Delicate Balance." He was panelist and senor consultant to PBS for a series of programs on the presidency in 1987. Since 1983, Robinson has been director of research for the Committee on the Constitutional System, a group of two hundred leaders assessing the operation of American government and the possibility of constitutional changes. His most recent book, *"To The Best of My Ability": The Presidency and the Constitution* (1987) focuses on executive development and the suggestion for constitutional reform.

Jeffrey K. Tulis

Jeffrey K. Tulis is associate professor of government at the University of Texas at Austin, having previously taught at Princeton University (1982–87). He served as a Fellow in Law and Politics at Harvard Law School (1986–87). He holds a Ph.D. in Political Science from the University of Chicago. Tulis has received fellowships and grants from the National Endowment for the Humanities, American Council of Learned Societies, and John Olin Foundation. He has lectured widely on topics including the *Federalist Papers* and constitutional issues of the presidency. His books include *The Presidency in the Constitutional Order*, coedited with Joseph Bessette (1981), and *The Rhetorical Presidency* (1987).

NOTES

Introduction: The Presidency and Constitutional Development

1. The following discussion on the competing interpretations of executive power in the Constitution and the *Federalist Papers* is based upon the editor's introduction and collection of essays compiled in *The Federalist Papers*, edited by Isaac Kramnick (New York: Viking Penguin, 1987).

2. Comments of Forrest McDonald at "The Constitution and The Presidency Conference," held at SUNY-Geneseo, April 16, 1988.

3. James MacGregor Burns, *The Deadlock of Democracy* (Englewood Cliffs, N.J.: Prentice-Hall, 1963).

4. Comments of Forrest McDonald at "The Constitution and The Presidency Conference," held at SUNY-Geneseo, April 16, 1988.

5. Arthur M. Schlesinger, Jr., *The Imperial Presidency* (Boston: Houghton Mifflin, 1973).

6. *Immigration and Naturalization Service v. Chadha*, 77 L. Ed. 2d, (1983), 317. For a further discussion on the implications of the *Chadha* decision as it affects the War Powers Resolution, see James L. Sundquist, "The Implications of *Chadha*," in *Reforming American Government*, edited by Donald L. Robinson (Boulder, Col.: Westview Press, 1985), 248-53.

Chapter 1: The Jefferson Presidency and Constitutional Beginnings

1. First Inaugural Address, March 4, 1801: Merrill Peterson, ed., *The Portable Thomas Jefferson* New York: Viking Press, 1975), 290-95.

2. Jefferson to Henry Lee, May 8, 1825: Henry A. Washington, ed., *The Works of Thomas Jefferson* (New York: Lippincott, 1884), VII, p. 407.

3. Quoted in R. Ketcham, *James Madison, A Biography* (New York: Macmillan, 1971), p. 28.

4. Aristotle, *Politics*, Book I, Chapt. II.

5. David Hume, "That Politics May Be Reduced to a Science," *Political Essays* (1741); C W Hendel, ed. (Indianapolis: Bobbs-Merrill, 1953), p. 20.

6. Alexander Pope, "Essay on Man," Epistle III, lines 303–304.

7. All quoted from Gordon Wood, *Creation of the Republic, 1776–1787* (Chapel Hill, N.C.:, 1969), p. 406.

8. Madison to Washington, April 16, 1787; R.A. Rutland et al., eds., *The Papers of James Madison* (Charlottesville,: University Press of Virginia, 1978), IX, p. 161.

9. Max Farrand, ed., *The Records of the Federal Convention* (New Haven, Conn.: Yale University Press, 1937), II, p. 301 (August 15, 1787).

10. Madison, "Vices of the Political System," April 1787, and Madison to Jefferson, Oct. 17, 1788: *Papers of Madison*, IX, p. 354, and XI, p. 298.

11. Farrand, *Records*, II, 52–54 (July 19, 1787).

12. Speeches of January 1790; quoted in Geoffrey Seed, *James Wilson* (Millwood, N.Y.: KTO Press, 1978), 134–37.

13. Farrand, *Records*, II, 30–31, 56 (July 17, 19, 1787).

14. Ibid., II, 202–03 (August 7, 1787).

15. Ibid., II, 203–05 (August 7, 10, 1787).

16. Ibid., II, 249, 236–37 (August 9, 10, 1787).

17. "Information for Those Who Would Remove to America" (1782); R. Ketcham, ed., *The Political Thought of Benjamin Franklin* (Indianapolis: Bobbs-Merrill, 1965), 336–46.

18. Farrand, *Records*, 204–05, 249 (August 7, 10, 1787).

19. Jefferson to W.C. Jarvis, Sept. 28, 1820; E. Dumbauld, ed., *The Political Writings of Thomas Jefferson* (Indianapolis: Bobbs-Merrill, 1953), p. 93.

20. Jefferson to F. Hopkinson, March 13, 1789; *Portable Jefferson*, 436–37.

21. Hamilton to J.A. Bayard, Jan. 16, 1801; H.C. Syrett et al., eds., *The Papers of Alexander Hamilton* (New York: Columbia University Press, 1975), XXV, p. 319.

22. Jefferson to Ellen Collidge, August 27, 1825; A. Koch and W. Peden, eds., *The Life and Selected Writings of Thomas Jefferson* (New York: Modern Library, 1944), p. 721.

23. Jefferson to Walter Jones, March 31, 1801, and to Garland Jefferson, Jan. 25, 1810; P.L. Ford, ed., *The Writings of Thomas Jefferson* (New York: Putnam,

1892), VIII, 29, 210. Jefferson to Elbridge Gerry, Jan. 26, 1799; Koch and Peden, *Writings of Jefferson*, p. 545.

24. "Sixth Annual Message," Dec. 2, 1806; Peterson, *Portable Jefferson*, p. 326; Jefferson to B. Bidwell, July 5, 1806, quoted in Noble Cunningham, *The Process of Government Under Jefferson* (Princeton, N.J.: Princeton University Press, 1978), p. 189.

25. Jefferson to R.R. Livingston, April 18, 1802; Peterson, *Portable Jefferson*, 485–86.

26. To J. Breckenridge, August 12, 1803; Ibid., p. 497.

27. To W.C. Nicholas, Sept., 7, 1803; Ford, ed., *Writings of Jefferson*, VIII, p. 248.

28. To J. Breckenridge, Aug. 12, 1803, Peterson, ed., *Portable Jefferson*, p. 496.

29. Jefferson to Madison, April 27, 1809; *Papers of Madison* (Presidential Series), I, 139–140.

30. Jefferson to Gallatin, Dec. 3, 1807; quoted in Dumas Malone, *Jefferson the President, Second Term, 1805–1809* (New York: Little-Brown, 1974), V, p. 476. The account of Jefferson and the Embargo depends heavily on Malone's narrative.

31. Jefferson, "Address," March 4, 1809; quoted in Ibid., p. 668.

32. Edward Livermore, *Annals of Congress*, Jan., 1808; quoted in Ibid., p. 563.

33. Jefferson to Gallatin, May 5, 1808 and August 11, 1808; quoted in Ibid., 589, 601.

34. Jefferson to J.C. Cabell, Feb. 2, 1816; quoted in Ibid., p. 613.

35. Jefferson to John Tyler, June 28, 1804, and to John Norvell, June 11, 1807; Koch and Peden, *Writings of Jefferson*, 576, 481–582.

Chapter 2: The Constitution and the Presidencies: The Jackson Era

1. James Parton, *Life of Andrew Jackson* (Boston: Mason Bros., 1866), III, p. 695.

2. Robert V. Remini, *Andrew Jackson and the Bank War* (New York: Twayne, 1967).

3. Michael Chevalier, *Society, Manners and Politics in the United States* (Boston: Weeks, Jordan, 1839), p. 181.

4. J. D. Richardson, *Compilation of the Messages and Papers of the Presidents* (Washington, D.C.: Gov't Printing Off., 1908), II, 1152, 1153, 1154.

5. It can be argued, of course, that the Supreme Court decision-making process may be "democratic" in a different sense, namely that they protect minority or individual rights when they maintain the Constitution as basic law. Such a process may be fairer and more in keeping with our constitutional system, but I do not believe it can be called "democratic." It is for this very reason, I suspect, that Aristotle felt that an oligarchic system was superior to any other system of government.

6. "Taking Another Look at the Constitutional Blueprint," in *American Heritage*, May/June 1987, Vol. 38, No. 4, p. 60.

7. November 22, 1834.

8. Daniel Webster, *The Works of Daniel Webster* (Boston: Little, Brown, Brown:, 1864), III, p. 434.

9. Ibid.

10. Thomas Hart Benton, *Thirty Years View* (New York: D. Appleton and Co., 1865), I, p. 411; *Register of Debates*, 23rd Congress, 1st Session, p. 220.

11. For a discussion of this tour and its meaning, see Robert V. Remini, *Andrew Jackson and the Course of American Democracy, 1833–1845* (New York: Harper & Row, 1984), pp. 60–83.

12. *National Intelligencer*, November 2, 1833.

13. Webster, *The Works of Daniel Webster*, VII, 143–144.

14. *Register of Debates*, 23rd Congress, 1st Session, 1835.

15. Ibid., p. 1375.

16. August 27, 1987,. The article concerned the nomination of Justice Robert Bork to the Supreme Court.

17. Richardson, *Messages and Papers*, II, 1304, 1305.

18. Jackson to Andrew Jackson Donelson, May 12, 1835, Donelson Papers, Library of Congress.

19. Ibid., II, 1011.

20. Ibid.

21. Richardson, *Messages and Papers*, II, 1011.

22. Manuscript Ledger, George Bancroft Papers, Massachusetts Historical Society.

23. Kermit L. Hall, *The Politics of Justice: Lower Federal Judicial Section and the Second Party System, 1829–61* (Lincoln, Nebraska: University of Nebraska, 1986), p. 3.

24. Richardson, *Messages and Papers,* II, 1395; Robert V. Remini, *Andrew Jackson and the Course of American Democracy,* III, 262–263; Leonard D. White, *The Jacksonians: A Study in Administrative History, 1829–1861* (New York: Macmillan, 1954), p. 520 note.

25. Thomas Donaldson, *The Public Domain, Its History, with Statistics* (Washington, D.C.: Government Printing Office, 1884), p. 21.

26. Horace Greeley, *The American Conflict: A History of the Great Rebellion in the United States of America 1860–64* (Hartford, Conneticut: O.D. Case & Co., 1865), I, p. 106.

27. Jackson to Coffee, April 7, 1832, Coffee Papers, Tennessee Historical Society.

28. Richard P. Longaker, "Andrew Jackson and the Judiciary," *Political Science Quarterly,* 1956, LXXI, p. 350.

29. William W. Freehling, *Prelude to Civil War: The Nullification Movement in South Carolina, 1816–1836* (New York: Harper & Row, 1966), p. 530.

30. Martin Van Buren to Jackson, December 22, 1832, Van Buren Papers, Library of Congress; Benjamin F. Butler to Wilson Lumpkin, December 17, 1832, Gratz Collection, Historical Society of Pennsylvania; Marvin R. Cain, "William Wirt against Andrew Jackson: Reflection of an Era," *Mid-America* (1965), XLVII, p. 113ff.

31. Richardson, *Messages and Papers,* II, p. 1006.

32. Jackson's address to the foreign ministers, April 6, 1829, U.S. Presidents, A. Jackson Papers, New York Public Library.

33. Richardson, *Messages and Papers,* II, p. 1206.

34. Kenneth M. Stampp, *The Imperiled Union: Essays on the Background of the Civil War* (New York: Oxford Univeristy Press, 1980), p. 33.

35. Richardson, *Messages and Papers,* II, 1211, 1213; Remini, *Andrew Jackson and the Course of American Democracy,* III, p. 21.

36. Ibid., pp. 22, 23.

37. Hall, *The Politics of Justice,* p. 26.

Chapter 3: The Constitution of the
Lincoln Presidency and the Republican Era

1. Address Before the Young Men's Lyceum of Springfield, Illinois, January 27, 1838, in Roy F. Basler (ed.), *The Collected Works of Abraham Lincoln* (9 vols., New Brunswick, N.J.: Rutgers University Press, 1953-1955), I: 108-15 (hereafter Lincoln, *Collected Works*).

2. Daniel Walker Howe, *The Political Culture of the American Whigs* (Chicago: University of Chicago Press, 1979), 87-95; Arthur M. Schlesinger, Jr., *The Age of Jackson* (Boston: Little, Brown, 1945), 38, 275-77.

3. James D. Richardson, *A Compilation of the Messages and Papers of the Presidents* (9 vols., Washington, D.C.: Government Printing Office, 1896-98), IV: p. 665; Daniel Webster, *The Works of Daniel Webster* (12th ed., Boston: Little, Brown, 1860), IV: p. 144; Reverdy Johnson in the *Congressional Globe, 30 Congress, 1 Session*, 671-76 (May 10, 12, 1848). As Charles Warren recognized, "The idea appeared to be prevalent at the time . . . that it was rather the Executive which was active in usurpation of power." Charles Warren, "Presidential Declarations of Independence," *Boston University Law Review* 10 (January 1930): p. 17.

4. Fragment of suggestions to Taylor, March 1848, in Lincoln, *Collected Works*, I: p. 454; ibid., p. 504.

5. W.E. Binkley, *The Powers of the President: Problems of American Democracy* (Garden City, N.Y.: Doubleday, Doran & Co., 1937), 116, 133; George Fort Milton, *The Use of Presidential Power, 1789-1943* (Boston: Little, Brown, 1944), p. 107. Although William Archibald Dunning referred to Lincoln's "temporary dictatorship" as early as 1898 and William B. Weeden claimed in 1906 he "reached the powers of a dictator", the notion of Lincoln as "constitutional dictator" was most fully developed by Clinton Rossiter in his book *Constitutional Dictatorship* in 1948. See Dunning, *Essays on the Civil War and Reconstruction* (New York: Macmillan, 1897), 20-21; William B. Weeden, *War Government, Federal and State in Massachusetts, New York, Pennsylvania and Indiana, 1861-1865* (Boston: Houghton Mifflin, 1906), p. x; Clinton L. Rossiter, *Constitutional Dictatorship: Crisis Government in the Modern Democracies* (Princeton, N.J.: Princeton University Press, 1948). Edward S. Corwin referred to "Lincoln's 'Dictatorship' " in his classic *The President: Office and Powers, 1787-1957* (4th rev. ed., New York: New York University Press, 1957), p. 20, and described Lincoln as scorning Congress and claiming unlimited executive powers to cope with military emergencies and to pursue war aims. Ibid., 21-22, 229-33. James McGregor Burns referred to Lincoln's "constitutional usurpations" in his *Presidential Government: The Crucible of Leadership* (Boston: Houghton Mifflin, 1965), p. 36, while Richard M. Pious refers to Lincoln's "constitutional dictatorship" in his standard text *The American Presidency* (New York: Basic Books, 1979), p. 57. It is quite common for political scientists and lawyers to claim Lincoln acted illegally during his presidency in order to save the Union.

See, for example, Gottfried Dietze, *America's Political Dilemma: From Limited to Unlimited Democracy* (Baltimore: Johns Hopkins University Press, 1968), 17–62; Ferdinand Lundberg, *Cracks in the Constitution* (Seacaucus, N.J.: Lyle Stuart, Inc., 1980), p. 25; Dwight G. Anderson, *Abraham Lincoln: The Quest for Immortality* (New York: Knopf, 1982), 8, 10–11, 166, 219. Francis D. Wormuth and Edwin B. Firmage, *To Chain the Dog of War: The War Power in Congress in History and Law* (Dallas: Southern Methodist University Press, 1986), p. vii. Arthur Selwyn Miller, *Democratic Dictatorship: The Emergent Constitution of Control* (Westport, Conn.: Greenwood Press, 1981), 77–80. Arthur M. Schlesinger interprets Lincoln's actions to have been extra-constitutional, despite Lincoln's effort to constitutionalize them under the rubric of "war powers." Schlesinger, *The Imperial Presidency* (Boston: Houghton Mifflin, 1973), 58–67. Schlesinger refers to him as a "despot." Ibid., p. 59.

6. See for example, David Donald, "Abraham Lincoln: Whig in the White House," in Donald, *Lincoln Reconsidered: Essays on the Civil War Era* (New York: Vintage Books, 1961), 187–208; Harold M. Hyman, *A More Perfect Union: The Impact of the Civil War and Reconstruction on the Constitution* (New York: Alfred A. Knopf, 1973), p. 76 and passim; Herman Belz, *Lincoln and the Constitution: The Dictatorship Question Reconsidered* (Fort Wayne, Ind.: Louis A. Warren Lincoln Library and Museum, 1984); Don E. Fehrenbacher, "Lincoln and the Constitution" and "The Paradoxes of Freedom" in Fehrenbacher, *Lincoln in Text and Context: Collected Essays* (Stanford, Cal.: Stanford University Press, 1984), 113–42.

7. Marcus Cunliffe, *American Presidents and the Presidency* (New York: American Heritage Press, 1968), p. 64. Binkley titled his chapter "The Jacksonian View of the Executive Prevails" in Binkley, *Powers of the President*, p. 89.

8. Richard P. McCormick, *The Second Party System: Party Formation in the Jacksonian Era* (New York: W.W. Norton, 1966; Michael Les Benedict, "The Party, Going Strong: Congressional Elections in the Mid-Nineteenth Century," *Congress and the Presidency* 9 (Winter, 1981–82): 37–60.

9. Norman A. Graebner, "James K. Polk: A Study in Federal Patronage," *Mississippi Valley Historical Review* 38 (June 1951): 613–32; David Meerse, "Buchana's Patronage Policy: An Attempt to Achieve Political Strength," *Pennsylvania History* 40 (January 1973): 37–58; Roy Franklin Nichols, *The Disruption of American Democracy* (New York: Macmillan, 1948), 243–49. For a brief general discussion, see Leonard D. White, *The Jacksonians: A Study in Administrative History, 1829–1861* (New York: Macmillan, 1954), 11–13, 300–46.

10. James K. Polk, *The Diary of James K. Polk During His Presidency, 1845 to 1849*, ed. Milo Milton Quaife (4 vols., Chicago: A.C. McClurg, 1910), I: p. 373.

11. George Bancroft to J.G. Wilson, March 8, 1888, quoted in Binkley, *Powers of the President*, p. 105; letter fragment from Phillips to Moncure Conway, sent in spring 1865. McKim-Garrison Mss., New York Public Library.

12. For the policy behind Buchanan's deference to the Supreme Court, see Don E. Fehrenbacher, *The Dred Scott Case: Its Significance in American Law and Politics* (New York: Oxford University Press, 1978), 307–14. For the political implications of Buchanan's inactivity during the secession crisis, see Kenneth M. Stampp, *And the War Came: The North and the Secession Crisis, 1860–1861* (Baton Rouge: Louisiana State University Press, 1950), 46–62.

13. The Marquis de Chambrun, after spending the war and Reconstruction years in Washington, explained that the president "sends to Congress each year... a message containing... a complete exposition of his policy... and suggesting such action as the public service seems to require. It is accompanied by special reports of almost all of the secretaries, who recommend in general the passage of certain laws, and transmit, in support of their opinion, an immense mass of documents. ...These communications are soon followed by others.... [T]he members of the committee... hold frequent conferences with the different secretaries, and the latter furnish... explanations, sometimes by writing, but in most instances orally, as special inquiries are made." Thus important pieces of legislation "are the result of this long and elaborate examination and interchange of views." Adolphe de Chambrun, *The Executive Power of the United States: A Study of Constitution Law*, trans. Madeleine Vinton Dahlgren (Lancaster, Penn.: Inquirer Printing and Publishing Co., 1874), 95–96. See also Leonard D. White, *The Republican Era: A Study in Administrative History, 1869–1901* (New York: Free Press, 1958), passim, and White, *The Jacksonians*, 124–62. When relations between committee chairmen and department heads broke down, the chairmen's positions were in jeopardy. See, for example, Richard H. Sewell, *John P. Hale and the Politics of Abolition* (Cambridge, Mass.: Harvard University Press, 1965), 196–207; David Donald, *Charles Sumner and the Rights of Man* (New York: Knopf, 1970), 374–497; Allan Nevins, *Hamilton Fish: The Inner History of the Grant Administration* (New York: Dodd Mead & Co., 1936), 449–65.

14. There are specialized studies of how particular presidents handled patronage matters—for example, Graebner, "James K. Polk: A Study in Federal Patronage"; Meerse, "Buchanan's Patronage Policy"; Harry J. Carman and Reihard H. Luthin, *Lincoln and the Patronage* (New York: Columbia University Press, 1943); Michael Les Benedict, *A Compromise of Principle: Congressional Republicans and Reconstruction. 1863–1869* (New York: W.W. Norton & Co., 1974), 59–69 and passim. But none provide a systematic account of how the system operated. For an initial overview, see Michael Les Benedict, "Factionalism and Representation: Some Insight from the Nineteenth Century United States," *Social Science History* 9 (Fall 1985): 361–98. See also White, *The Jacksonians*, 72–75, 104–24; White, *The Republican Era*, 26–27, 122–23, 223–24, 309.

15. For example, while Congress retained control of general financial policy after the Civil War, it delegated broad authority to the secretary of the treasury to buy and sell gold and United States securities. Since the maintenance of financial stability was crucial to the economic well-being of the country, the

secretary was exercising one of the most important responsibilities of the government, fraught with both economic and political consequences. See Walter T.K. Nugent, *The Money Question During Reconstruction* (New York: W.W. Norton, 1967), 21–38; Irwin Unger, *The Greenback Era: A Social and Political History of American Finance, 1865–1879* (Princeton, N.J.: Princeton University Press, 1964); Milton Friedman and Anna Jacobson Schwartz, *A Monetary History of the United States, 1867–1960* (Princeton, N.J.: Princeton University Press, 1963), 15–88; George S. Boutwell, *Reminiscences of Sixty Years in Public Affairs by George S. Boutwell* (New York: McClure, Phillips & Co., 1902), II: 125–202.

16. Lincoln, First Inaugural Address, in Richardson, *Messages and Papers*, VI: p. 7.

17. Ibid., 13–14.

18. Ibid., 14–15.

19. Ibid., pp. 18, 19, 39.

20. Charles P. Poland, Jr., "Abraham Lincoln and Civil Liberties: A Reappraisal," *Lincoln Herald* 76 (Fall, 1974): 119–32; Randall, *Constitutional Problems Under Lincoln*, 147–57; Hyman, *A More Perfect Union*, 73–76.

21. Richardson, *Messages and Papers*, VI: 15–16.

22. Ex parte Merryman, 17 Federal Cases 144 (C.C.D.Md. 1861) (No. 9787). Quoted at 149.

23. Lincoln, Message to the Special Session of Congress, Richardson, *Messages and Papers*, VI: p. 25.

24. Ibid. See also William Whiting, *War Powers Under the Constitution of the United States* (10th ed., Boston: Little, Brown, 1864), p. 27. Whiting, Solicitor of the War Department, was recognized as an administration theorist of presidential war powers.

25. Suspension of the Privilege of the Writ of Habeas Corpus, *Opinions of the Attorneys General* 10 (1861): p. 82.

26. Ibid., 81–82.

27. Ibid., p. 83.

28. Richardson, *Messages and Papers*, VI: 24.

29. Ibid., p. 25.

30. Lincoln to Albert G. Hodges, April 4, 1864, in Lincoln, *Collected Works*, VII: p. 281.

31. Michael Les Benedict, "Preserving the Constitution: The Conservative Basis of Radical Reconstruction," *Journal of American History* 61 (June 1974): p. 67.

32. Richardson, *Messages and Papers*, VI: p. 25.

33. R.H. Dana, Brief for the United States and Captors, *The Prize Cases*, in Philip B. Kurland and Gerhard Casper (eds.), *Landmark Briefs and Arguments of the Supreme Court of the United States: Constitutional Law* (80 vols., Washington, D.C.: University Publications of America, 1978–pres.), III: 514–17; William M. Evarts, Brief for the United States, *The Prize Cases*, ibid., 30–34. Dana's argument is published with the report of the decision. Prize Cases, 67 U.S. (2 Black) 637 (1863). At page 660, Dana referred to "Overwhelming reasons of necessity," but he meant that the disastrous consequence of a narrow construction of executive power sustained the logic of a broader construction, as is clear from the argument he presented in the preceding pages.

34. Theodore Roosevelt, *Theodore Roosevelt: An Autobiography* (New York: Charles Scribner's Sons, 1924), p. 357.

35. Alexander Hamilton, Opinion as to the Constitutionality of the Bank of the United States, in Harold C. Syrett (ed.), *The Papers of Alexander Hamilton* (27 vols., New York: Columbia University Press, 1961–87), VIII: 99–134.

36. *Opinions of the Attorneys General* 10 (1861): 85–92, quoted at p. 85 and p. 91.

37. Paul M. Angle (ed.), *Created Equal?: The Complete Lincoln-Douglas Debates of 1858* (Chicago: University of Chicago Press, 1958), 36–37, 77–79, 309–10. For efforts to make sense of Lincoln's views, see Gary J. Jacobsohn, "Abraham Lincoln 'on this question of judicial authority': The Theory of Constitutional Aspiration," *Western Political Quarterly* 36 (March 1983): 52–70; Don E. Fehrenbacher, "The Galena Speech: A Problem in Historical Method," in Fehrenbacher, *Lincoln in Text and Context*, 15–23; Fehrenbacher, "Lincoln and the Constitution," ibid., 122–26.

38. Hyman, *A More Perfect Union*, 88–89.

39. Prize Cases, 67 U.S. (2 Black) 635 at 668 (1863).

40. Ibid., p. 670.

41. Ibid., 682–99, especially 690–93 (Nelson, dissenting). Quoted material at p. 693.

42. Ex parte Vallandigham, 68 U.S. (1 Wallace) 243 (1864).

43. Ex parte Milligan, 71 U.S. (4 Wallace) 2 (1866).

44. Mississippi v. Johnson, 71 U.S. (4 Wallace) 475 at 484 (1867).

45. Ibid., 487–86.

46. Southerners tried to enjoin the secretary of war from enforcing the law in *Georgia v. Stanton*, 73 U.S. (6 Wall.) 50 (1867), but both the administration

and the majority of the justices agreed the case raised the same question and the Court confirmed its prior ruling.

47. President Richard Nixon appears to have contemplated defying a decision of the Supreme Court sustaining the Watergate special prosecutor's subpoena of relevant materials. See Leon Jaworski, *The Right and the Power* (New York: Reader's Digest Press, 1976), p. 164.

48. Thomas and Hyman, *Stanton*.

49. The most clearly organized discussion of Lincoln's use of presidential war powers is Randall's *Constitutional Problems Under Lincoln* (New York: D. Appleton and Co., 1926).

50. Corwin, *The President*, p. 227.

51. For example, Binkley, *Powers of the President*; Burns, *Presidential Government*, 34–45, 282–83, and passim; Corwin, *The President*; Pious, *American Presidency*; Clinton Rossiter, *The American Presidency* (rev. ed., New York: Harcourt, Brace and World, 1960); Richard P. Longaker, *The Presidency and Individual Liberties* (Ithaca, N.Y.: Cornell University Press, 1961), 18–26; Louis W. Koenig, *The Chief Executive* (New York: Harcourt Brace and World, 1964); Joseph E. Kallenbach, *The American Chief Executive: The Presidency and the Governorship* (New York: Harper & Row, 1966), passim, especially 524–61; Rexford G. Tugwell and Thomas E. Cronin (eds.), *The Presidency Reappraised* (New York: Praeger, 1974); R. Gordon Hoxie, *Command Decisions and the Presidency: A Study in National Security Policy and Organization* (New York: Reader's Digest Press, 1977); Arthur S. Miller, *Presidential Power in a Nutshell* (St. Paul, Minn.: West Publishing Co., 1977), esp. 166–67, 170–74, 211–12.

53. As exposited by present-day advocates of broad executive power, the inherent powers of the presidency carve exceptions to clearly delegated powers of Congress. For a recent example, some Republicans have insisted that the president's inherent authority to conduct foreign policy would justify him in spending money in pursuit of his policy, despite congressional refusal to authorize the expenditure as required by the Constitution. See Patrick H. Buchanan in the *Washington Post*, July 20, 1987, section C, page 1; Jeanne J. Kirkpatrick in the *New York Times*, July 26, 1987, section E, p. 3.

Likewise, President Richard Nixon claimed an inherent power to refuse to expend congressionally appropriated funds, to refuse information requested by Congress and the courts, and to ignore statutes and court decisions that impeded him in protecting national security. Schlesinger, *The Imperial Presidency*, 232–72; Alfred H. Kelly, Winfred A. Harbison, and Herman Belz, *The American Constitution: Its Origins and Development* (6th ed., New York: W.W. Norton & Co., 1983), 682–97. See also Ralph S. Abascal and John R. Kramer, "Presidential Impoundments, Part 1: Historical Genesis and Constitutional Framework," *Georgetown Law Journal* 62 (July 1974): 1549–1618; Note, "The Impoundment of Funds," *Harvard Law Review* 86 (June 1973): 1505–35; Erwin

Griswold, Brief for the United States, U.S. v. U.S. District Court, Kurland and Casper (eds.), *Landmark Briefs* 72: 569–624; James D. Sinclair et al., Brief for the Respondent, Richard M. Nixon, *U.S. v. Nixon*, Kurland and Casper (eds.), *Landmark Briefs* 79: 463–614. See Frank J. Donner, *The Age of Surveillance: The Aims and Methods of America's Political Intelligence System* (New York: Knopf, 1980), 243–48.

54. Whiting, *War Powers*, p. 27.

55. Richardson, *Messages and Papers*, VI: p. 24.

56. Ibid., p. 25.

57. Thomas and Hyman, *Stanton*, 147–49; Hans L. Trefousee, "The Joint Committee on the Conduct of the War: A Reassessment," *Civil War History* 10 (March 1964): 5–19; Herman Wolkinson, "Demands of Congressional Committees for Executive Papers," *Federal Bar Journal* 10 (April 1949): 95–150. Wolkinson noted Lincoln as refusing a Senate request for copies of messages from Fort Sumter in March 1861 (p. 148). However, the Senate requested Lincoln to provide the information only if compatible in his opinion with the national interest. Lincoln merely responded that he did not feel it would be compatible with the national interest to make the messages public at that time. Richardson, *Messages and Papers*, VI: 12–13.

58. Richardson, *Messages and Papers*, VI: 223–24.

59. *Congressional Globe*, 38 Congress, 2 Session, 970 (February 21, 1965). See Benedict, *A Compromise of Principle*, 84–97.

60. U.S. Statutes at Large, 12: p. 354 (March 13, 1862); 589–92 (July 17, 1862).

61. Randall, *Constitutional Problems Under Lincoln*, 357–63.

62. Richardson, *Messages and Papers*, VI: 96–98, 157–59.

63. Ibid., 97–98.

64. Whiting, *War Powers*, i–ii.

65. Richardson, *Messages and Papers*, VI: 213–14.

66. Ibid., p. 223. According to Lincoln's secretary, John Hay, agitated Republicans objected that the provision was no different in effect from Lincoln's own action. Hay recorded Lincoln as responding that he might "in an emergency do things on military grounds which cannot be done constitutionally by Congress." If he said it, it is hard to know precisely what he meant by it. He was not exercising "emergency power" but "war power," and he had, as already demonstrated, recognized similar power in Congress. More likely Hay misconstrued his words, and he meant that his action, based on wartime necessity, was different in kind from Congress's effort to dictate provisions

of state constitutions. It seems unlikely that he could have objected to a resolution of Congress that had announced that it would receive no representatives from a restored state government whose constitution was inconsistent with the provisions of the amnesty oath. John Hay, *Lincoln and the Civil War in the Diaries and Letters of John Hay*, ed. Tyler Dennett (New York: Dodd, Mead, & Co., 1939), p. 204; John G. Nicolay and John Hay, *Abraham Lincoln: A History* (10 vols., New York: Century Co., 1890), IX: p. 120.

67. Lincoln to Butler, August 9, 1864, in Lincoln, *Collected Works*, VII: 487–88.

68. Lincoln to Chase, September 2, 1863, ibid., VI: 428–29.

69. Binkley, *Powers of the President*, p. 135.

70. Michael Les Benedict, *The Impeachment and Trial of Andrew Johnson* (New York: W.W. Norton & Co., 1973).

71. These are chapter titles from Cunliffe, *American Presidents*, and Binkley, *Powers of the President*. See also Milton, *Use of Presidential Power*, 137–53; Corwin, *The President*, 24–34; Pious, *The American Presidency*, p. 74; Harold J. Laski, *The American Presidency: An Interpretation* (New York: Harper & Brothers, 1940), p. 127; White, *The Republican Era*, 46–48.

72. For the expansion of congressional power, see Hyman, *A More Perfect Union*, 171–87 and passim; Leonard P. Curry, *Blueprint for Modern America: Nonmilitary Legislation of the First Civil War Congress* (Nashville, Tenn.: Vanderbilt University Press, 1968).

73. Richardson, *Messages and Papers*, VII: p. 6.

74. William B. Hesseltine, *Ulysses S. Grant, Politician* (New York: Dodd-Mead, 1935), 159–68; Matthew T. Downey, "The Rebirth of Reform: A Study of Liberal Reform Movements, 1865–1871" (unpublished Ph.D. dissertation, Princeton University, 1963), 197–202.

75. Downey, "Rebirth of Reform," 266–315; Jacqueline Bell Tusa, "Power, Priorities, and Political Insurgency: The Liberal Republican Movement, 1869–1872" (unpublished Ph.D. dissertation, Pennsylvania State University, 1970), 31–78, Ari Hoogenboom, *Outlawing the Spoils: A History of the Civil Service Reform Movement, 1865–1883* (Urbana, Ill.: University of Illinois Press, 1961), 50–110.

76. Charles Sumner, *Republicanism vs. Grantism*, in *The Works of Charles Sumner* (15 vols., Boston: Lee & Shepard, 1883), XV: 83–171; E.I. Sears, "Grantism vs. Caesarism," *National Quarterly Review* 29 (September 1874): 256–67; George W. Julian, "The Death Struggle of the Republican Party," *North American Review* 126 (March–April 1878): 262–92, at 271–80; Jeremiah S. Black, "General Grant and Strong Government," ibid., vol. 130 (May 1880): 417–37,

at 430–37. For the Liberal Republican bolt of 1872, see Earle Dudley Ross, *The Liberal Republican Movement* (New York: Rumford Press, 1919); Downey, "Rebirth of Reform"; Tusa, "Power, Priorities, and Political Insurgency."

77. Carl Schurz, Speech at St. Louis, reported in the Springfield *Weekly Republican*, July 26, 1872, p. 6.

78. Richardson, *Messages and Papers*, VII: 450–51.

79. Hoogenboom, *Outlawing the Spoils*, 149–78.

80. Richardson, *Messages and Papers*, VII: 447–49, 489–90; Kenneth E. Davison, *The Presidency of Rutherford B. Hayes* (Westport, Conn.: Greenwood Press, 1972), 136–44; Vincent P. DeSantis, "President Hayes' Southern Policy," *Journal of Southern History* 20 (Nov, 1955): 476–94.

81. Davison, *Presidency of Rutherford B. Hayes*, 145–54.

82. Richardson, *Messages and Papers*, VII: 523–44; Davison, *Presidency of Rutherford B. Hayes*, 162–63; Carlton Jackson, *Presidential Vetoes, 1792–1945* (Athens, Ga.: University of Georgia Press, 1967), 141–44.

83. Allan Peskin, *Garfield* (Kent, Ohio: Kent State University Press, 1978), 556–65, 567–72; H. Wayne Morgan, *From Hayes to McKinley: National Party Politics, 1877–1896* (Syracuse, N.Y.: Syracuse University Press, 1969, 249–54.

84. Woodrow Wilson, *Congressional Government: A Study in American Politics* (Boston: Houghton Mifflin, 1900; originally published 1885). See also Gamaliel Bradford, *The Lesson of Popular Government* (2 vols., New York: Macmillan Co., 1899), I: 349–81.

85. Henry Jones Ford, *The Rise and Growth of American Politics: A Sketch of Constitutional Development* (New York: Macmillan, 1898), 279–93. See also Simeon E. Baldwin, *Modern Political Institutions (Boston: Little, Brown, 1898), 84#116; Chambrun, *The Executive Power in the United States*, 149–54.

86. Henry C. Lockwood, *The Abolition of the Presidency* (New York: R. Worthington, 1884).

87. Bryce, *The American Commonwealth* (2 vols., London: Macmillan 1889), I: 61–64; Cooley, "Some Checks and Balances in Government," *International Review* 3 (May 1876): 319–20.

Chapter 4: The Constitution of the Theodore Roosevelt Presidency and the Progressive Era

1. This essay draws heavily on my *Power and Responsibility: The Life and Times of Theodore Roosevelt* (New York: Farrar, Straus & Cudahy, 1961). Except as noted, all quotations are taken from it. I subsequently refined and synthesized my

views on Roosevelt in the Introduction to William H. Harbaugh (ed.), *The Writings of Theodore Roosevelt* (Indianapolis: Bobbs-Merrill, 1967).

2. For *Neagle* see Arthur Schlesinger, Jr., *The Imperial Presidency* (Boston: Houghton Mifflin, 1973), 82–83.

3. Allan Nevins, *Grover Cleveland: A Study in Courage* (New York: Dodd, Mead, 1932), 611–28. For the exchanges between Cleveland and Governor John P. Altgeld of Illinois, as well as the judicial decisions, see Henry Steele Commager (ed.), *Documents of American History* (New York: Appleton-Century, 7th Ed., 1963), 609–16.

4. Quoted in Lewis Gould, *The Presidency of William McKinley* (Lawrence, Kan.: University of Kansas Press, 1980), p. 243. Also, see Gould generally.

5. Schlesinger, *Imperial Presidency*, 88–89.

6. Quoted in Ibid., p. 82

7. See generally, Harbaugh, *Writings*, and John Morton Blum, *The Republican Roosevelt* (Cambridge, Mass.: Harvard University Press, 1954).

8. Hermann Hagedorn (ed.), *The Works of Theodore Roosevelt*, 20 vols. (New York: Charles Scribner's Sons, 1926), National Edition, Vol. XV, State Papers as Governor and President 1899–1909, p. 92).

9. Harbaugh, *Power and Responsibility*, 149–65.

10. Roosevelt to Winthrop Murray Crane, October 22, 1902, Elting Morison and John M. Blum (eds.), *The Letters of Theodore Roosevelt* (Cambridge, Mass.: Harvard University Press, 1951–54), III, 359–66.

12. Roosevelt to Lyman Abbott, September 5, 1903, *ibid.*, p. 592.

13. Theodore Roosevelt, *An Autobiography*, XX, National Edition, p. 455.

14. See generally Harbaugh, *Writings* and *Power and Responsibility*.

15. See Roosevelt's moving letter to George Otto Trevelyan, June 19, 1908, *Letters*, VI 1085–90; Blum, *Republican Roosevelt*, p. 123.

16. Theodore Roosevelt, *Gouverneur Morris*, VII, National Edition, p. 328, 330.

17. Theodore Roosevelt, "Legislative Actions and Judicial Decisions," Address at Harrisburg, Pennsylvania, October 4, 1906, *American Problems*, XVI, National Edition, p. 70; Theodore Roosevelt, *Presidential Addresses and State Papers*, 8 vols. (New York, The Review of Reviews Company, 1910), VI, p. 1175.

18. 219 U.S1 I, 31 SCT 212, 55 LEd 65; *Letters*, VI, fn. p. 1426.

19. George Juergens, *News From The White House* (Chicago: University of Chicago Press, 1981), and Robert C. Hilderbrand, *Power and the People* (Chapel Hill, N.C.: University of North Carolina Press, 1981).

20. Roosevelt to Hannah Kent Schoff, May 7, 1906, *Letters*, V, p. 259, and to J. C. Martin, November 6, 1908, *ibid.*, VI, 1333–35; Harbaugh, *Power and Responsibility*, 339–41.

21. Roosevelt to Frederick Getman Fincke, June 7, 1901, *Letters*, III, 88–89.

22. Roosevelt to Mark Sullivan, May 13, 1907, ibid., 6, pp. 665–69; to Benjamin Ide Wheeler, December 12, 1901, ibid., III, p. 205; to Henry Cabot Lodge, July 10, 1902, ibid., III, pp. 288–89; and to Elihu Root, August 18, 1906, ibid., V, 367–69.

23. Harbaugh, *Power and Responsibility*, Chaps. 23–27; George E. Mowry, *Theodore Roosevelt and the Progressive Movement* (Madison, Wis.: University of Wisconsin Press, 1946); John Allen Gable, *The Bull Moose Years* (Port Washington, N.Y.: Kennikat Press, 1978).

24. Naomi R. Lamoreaux, *The Great Merger Movement in American Business, 1895–1904* (Cambridge: Cambridge University Press, 1985), for background.

25. Theodore Roosevelt, *State Papers as Governor and President*, XV, National Edition, p. 91.

26. Stephen Skowronek, *Building a New American State: The Expansion of National Administrative Capacities, 1877–1920* (Cambridge, England: Cambridge University Press, 1982).

27. Harbaugh, *Power and Responsibility*. Also see generally Blum, *Republican Roosevelt*, and George E. Mowry, *The Era of Theodore Roosevelt* (New York: Harper, 1958).

28. Ibid.; Skowronek, *Building*, p. 257.

29. Harbaugh, *Power and Responsibility*, pp. 249–51; Roosevelt, *State Papers*, XV, p. 423.

30. Arthur M. Johnson, "Theodore Roosevelt and the Bureau of Corporations," *Mississippi Valley Historical Review* 45 (1959) 571–90.

31. See Skowronek, *Building*, 172–79, for insights into and a new synthetic view of Roosevelt and his efforts to create a new administrative capacity.

32. Ibid., p. 180. Samuel P. Hays, *Conservation and the Gospel of Efficiency: The Progressive Conservation Movement, 1890–1920* (Cambridge, Mass.: 1959), is still the basic book on the subject.

33. Roosevelt, *An Autobiography*, p. 396. See also my account of the G.O.P., "The Republican Party, 1893–1932," in Arthur M. Schlesinger, Jr., *History of U.S. Political Parties*, III (New York: Chelsea House 1973), 2069–2255.

34. Roosevelt, *Autobiography*, p. 395.

35. Ibid., p. 396.

36. See Oscar Kraines, "The President versus Congress: The Keep Commission, 1905-1909—First Comprehensive Presidential Inquiry into Administration, *Western Political Quarterly* 23 (1970): 5-54.

37. Roosevelt to Kermit Roosevelt, January 23, 1909, *Letters*, 6, p. 1481; Schlesinger, *Imperial Presidency*, p. 84.

38. Harbaugh, *Power and Responsibility*, pp. 343-51.

39. This section of foreign policy is drawn basically from the paperback edition of my biography of Roosevelt. It reflects the influence of Howard K. Beale, *Theodore Roosevelt and the Rise of America to World Power* (Baltimore: The Johns Hopkins Press, 1956). For a recent and highly favorable reinterpretation of Roosevelt's conduct of foreign policy, see Frederick W. Marks III, *Velvet on Iron: The Diplomacy of Theodore Roosevelt* (Lincoln, Neb.: University of Nebraska Press, 1982).

40. Theodore Roosevelt, "Captain Mahan's 'Life of Nelson,' " *The Bookman*, 5 (June, 1897), 333.

41. Roosevelt, *Autobiography*, p. 501.

42. Roosevelt to Elihu Root, May 20, 1904, *Letters*, IV, 801; Harbaugh, *Power and Responsibility*, pp. 193-97.

43. Schlesinger, *Imperial Presidency*, pp. 85-89.

44. Roosevelt, *Autobiography*, p. 540.

45. Roosevelt to William Howard Taft, December 8, 22, 1910, *Letters*, VII, 180-81, 189-92.

46. Roosevelt to George Otto Trevelyan, June 19, 1908, *Letters*, VI, 1084-1090.

47. For a perceptive revisionist treatment of both Wilson and Roosevelt, considerably more favorable to Wilson than to Roosevelt, see John Milton Cooper, Jr., *The Warrior and the Priest* (Cambridge, Mass.: Harvard University Press, 1983). Paolo E. Coletta, *The Presidency of William Howard Taft* (Lawrence, Kansas: University Press of Kansas, 1973), 183-201; Arthur S. Link, *Woodrow Wilson and the Progressive Era* (New York: Harper & Row, 1954), p. 93.

48. The legal aspects of this case are treated in William H. Harbaugh, *Lawyer's Lawyer: The Life of John W. Davis* (New York: Oxford University Press, 1973), 98-101.

49. Ibid., 109–113; Arthur S. Link, *Wilson: Campaigns for Progressivism and Peace* (Princeton, N.J.: Princeton University Press, 1965), pp. 89–92.

50. Skowronek, *American State*, generally.

Chapter 5: The Constitution of the Hoover and F. Roosevelt Presidency During the Depression Era

1. Alfred D. Chandler, Jr. and Louis Galambos, "The Development of Large-Scale Economic Organizations in Modern America," *Journal of Economic History* 30 (March 1970), 209–211.

2. I have discussed this stream of thought and action in "Herbert Hoover, the Commerce Secretariat, and the Vision of an Associative State," *Journal of American History* 61 (June 1974), 116–40; "Herbert Hoover and American Corporatism, 1929–1933," in Martin Fausold and George Mazuzan, eds., *The Hoover Presidency: A Reappraisal* (Albany, N.Y.: SUNY Press, 1974), 101–19; " 'Industrial Policy' in the 1920s and 1930s," in Claude Barfield and William A. Schambra, eds., *The Politics of Industrial Policy* (Washington: American Enterprise Institute, 1986), 63–81; and "The Corporate Ideal as Liberal Philosophy in the New Deal," in Wilbur J. Cohen, ed., *The Roosevelt New Deal* (Austin, Texas: LBJ School, 1986), 85–98. See also Robert F. Himmelberg, *The Origins of the National Recovery Administration* (New York: Fordham University Press, 1976); Guy Alchon, *The Invisible Hand of Planning* (Princeton, N.J.: Princeton University Press, 1985).

3. See William E. Leuchtenburg, "The New Deal and the Analogue of War," in John Braeman et al., eds., *Change and Continuity in Twentieth-Century America* (Columbus, Ohio: Ohio State University Press, 1964), 80–143; Gerald Nash, "Experiments in Industrial Mobilization, WIB and NRA," *Mid-America* 45 (July 1963), 157–74; Otis L. Graham, Jr., *Toward a Planned Society* (New York: Oxford University Press, 1976), 9–17, 23; James S. Olson, *Herbert Hoover and the Reconstruction Finance Corporation* (Ames, Iowa: Iowa State University Press, 1977), 44–46.

4. For efforts to apply this idea in the years from 1917 to 1935, see especially William J. Breen, *Uncle Sam at Home: Civilian Mobilization, Wartime Federalism, and the Council of National Defense, 1917–1919* (Westport, Conn.: Greenwood Press, 1984); Carolyn Grin, "The Unemployment Conference of 1921: An Experiment in National Cooperative Planning," *Mid-America* 55 (April 1973), 83–107; Albert U. Romasco, *The Poverty of Abundance* (New York: Oxford University Press, 1965), 143–72; and James T. Patterson, *The New Deal and the States* (Princeton, N.J.: Princeton University Press, 1969), 102–128.

5. The point is discussed in some detail in Barry D. Karl, "Executive Reorganization and Presidential Power," *Supreme Court Review* (1977), 1–37.

6. On the anticonstitutionalism of the period and its concern for men rather than rules, see Herman Belz, "The Realist Critique of Constitutionalism in the Era of Reform," *American Journal of Legal History* 15 (October 1971), 288–306, and "Changing Conceptions of Constitutionalism in the Era of World War II and the Cold War," *Journal of American History* 59 (December 1972), 640–69. See also Edward A. Purcell, Jr., "American Jurisprudence between the Wars," *American Historical Review*, 75 (December 1969), 424–46; Frederick F. Blachly and Miriam E. Oatman, *Administrative Legislation and Adjudication* (Washington, D.C.: Brookings Institution, 1934), 37–39.

7. See Belz, "Changing Conceptions of Constitutionalism," p. 645. The key sections were the general welfare, commerce, and necessary and proper clauses of Article I, Section 8, the executive power clause of Article II, Section 1, and the recommending of measures and "take care" clauses of Article II, Section 3.

8. Good accounts of the arguments and the new jurisprudence informing them can be found in Gary Jacobsohn, *Pragmatism, Statesmanship, and the Supreme Court* (Ithaca, N.Y.: Cornell University Press, 1977); John W. Johnson, *American Legal Culture, 1908–1940* (Westport, Conn.: Greenwood, 1981); and Wilfrid E. Rumble, Jr., *American Legal Realism* (Ithaca, N.Y.: Cornell University Press, 1968). See also Robert L. Stern, "That Commerce Which Concerns More States than One," *Harvard Law Review*, 48 (May 1934), 1335–66; F.D.G. Ribble, "The Current of Commerce," *Minnesota Law Review* 18 (February 1934), 296–318; Oliver P. Field, "The Constitutional Theory of the National Industrial Recovery Act," *Minnesota Law Review* 18 (February 1934), 269–96; Walton Hamilton and Douglass Adair, *The Power to Govern* (New York: Norton, 1937); Edward S. Corwin, "Some Probable Repercussions of 'Nira' on Our Constitutional System," *Annals of the American Academy of Political and Social Science*, 157 (March 1934), 139–144.

9. See, for example, W. E. Binkley, *The Powers of the President* (Garden City, N.Y.: Doubleday, Doran, 1937), 249–56; Harold J. Laski, *The American Presidency* (New York: Harper, 1940), 132–33; Emmet J. Hughes, *The Living Presidency* (New York: Coward, McCann & Geoghegan, 1973), 98–101; Louis W. Koenig, *The Chief Executive*, (New York: Harcourt, Brace & World, 1968 ed.), 366–68. On the generally accepted characteristics of "strong" and "weak" presidents, see Robert S. Hirschfield, in Hirschfield, ed., *The Power of the Presidency* (New York: Aldine, 1982 ed.), 9–11.

10. For a discussion of the revisionist work, see my "Herbert Hoover and Modern American History: Fifty Years After," in Mark O. Hatfield, comp., *Herbert Hoover Reassessed* (Washington, D.C.: Government Printing Office, 1981), 449–68, and the bibliographical essay in Martin L. Fausold, *The Presidency of Herbert C. Hoover* (Lawrence, Kan.: University Press of Kansas, 1985).

11. Herbert Hoover, *The Challenge to Liberty* (New York: Scribner's, 1934), especially 20–21, 76, 116.

12. See Fausold, *Presidency of Hoover*, 48–54; Romasco, *Poverty of Abundance*, 13–16, 229; David Burner, *Herbert Hoover: A Public Life* (New York: Knopf, 1979), 234–36; Ira H. Carmen, "The President, Politics, and the Power of Appointment," *Virginia Law Review* 55 (May 1969), 649–659.

13. Herbert Hoover, *The Memoirs of Herbert Hoover*, III: *The Great Depression, 1929–1941* (New York: Macmillan, 1952), p. 104.

14. See Romasco, *Poverty of Abundance*, 107–08, 214–15, 222–23; Jordan A. Schwarz, *The Interregnum of Despair* (Urbana, Ill.: University of Illinois Press, 1970), 7–9, 161–73; Lawrence H. Chamberlain, *The President, Congress, and Legislation* (New York: Columbia University Press, 1946), 131, 249.

15. Adam C. Breckinridge, *The Executive Privilege* (Lincoln, Neb.: University of Nebraska Press, 1974), 52–54; Harris G. Warren, *Herbert Hoover and the Great Depression* (New York: Oxford University Press, 1959), 74–75; Edward S. Corwin, *The President: Office and Powers (New York: New York University Press, 1957 ed.)*, 76#77; *Public Papers of the Presidents of the United States: Herbert Hoover* (Washington, D.C.: Government Printing Office, 1974–77), 1930: 291–92; 1931: 11–16, 34–39.

16. Gene Smith, *The Shattered Dream* (New York: Morrow, 1970), 98–99.

17. See Jordan A. Schwarz, "Hoover and Congress: Politics, Personality, and Perspective in the Presidency," in Fausold and Mazuzan, eds., *Hoover Presidency*, 87–100, Craig Lloyd, *Aggressive Introvert* (Columbus, Ohio: Ohio State University Press, 1972), 159–75.

18. In addition to Hawley, "Hoover and American Corporatism" and Alchon, *Invisible Hand of Planning*, see Joan Hoff Wilson, *Herbert Hoover: Forgotten Progressive* (Boston: Little, Brown, 1975) and William J. Barber, *From New Era to New Deal: Herbert Hoover, the Economists, and American Economic Policy, 1921–1933* (New York: Cambridge University Press, 1985).

19. Hawley, "Hoover and American Corporatism," 103–16; Barber, *From New Era to New Deal*, 41, 65–71, 80–82; *Public Papers: Hoover*, 1919: 384–85, 453–55, 472–74; 1930: 178–79, 511–13; 1931: 299–306; Rexford G. Tugwell, *The Enlargement of the Presidency* (Garden City, N.Y.: Doubleday, 1960), 385–90.

20. Specifically, the National Business Survey Conference, the National Building Survey Conference, the President's Emergency Committee for Employment (and its successors), and the Conference of Banking and Industrial Committees. See Romasco, *Poverty of Abundance*, 27–65, 198–99; Barber, *From New Era to New Deal*, 83–85, 99; Himmelberg, *Origins of NRA*, 169–73.

21. Specifically, through such agencies as the Federal Farm Board, the Railway Credit Corporation, the National Credit Association, the Federal Oil Conservation Board, and the Timber Conservation Board. See David E. Hamilton, "From New Day to New Deal: American Agriculture in the Hoover

Years, 1928-1933'' (Ph.D. Unpublished Dissertation, University of Iowa, 1985); Romasco, *Poverty of Abundance*, 87–96, 106–21; William G. Robbins, *Lumberjacks and Legislators* (College Station, Tex.: Texas A & M Press, 1982), 155–64; Himmelberg, *Origins of NRA*, 100–03; *Public Papers: Hoover*, 1931: 641–42.

22. Specifically, the Public Construction Division, the President's Emergency Committee for Employment (and its successors), the National Drought Committee, the White House Conference on Child Health and Protection, and the White House Conference on Home Building and Home Ownership. See Romasco, *Poverty of Abundance*, 52–55, 144–47, 162–64; Burner, *Hoover*, 221–23; David E. Hamilton, "Herbert Hoover and the Great Drought of 1930," *Journal of American History*, 68 (March 1982), 854–62.

23. *Public Papers: Hoover*, 1929: 472–74; 1930: p. 175; 1932: 173–78; Arthur Krock, "President Hoover's Two Years," *Current History*, (July 1931), p. 491; Corwin, *The President*, 71–72; Fausold, *Presidency of Hoover*, 59–62; William Goldsmith, *The Growth of Presidential Power*, 3 vols. (New York: Chelsea House, 1974), III, 1563–64.

24. Corwin, *The President*, 71–72; *Public Papers: Hoover*, 1929: 472–74; 1930: 305–06; Goldsmith, *Growth of Presidential Power*, III, 1563–64.

25. *Congressional Record*, 72 (1930), 4147, 6099–100, 12635, 12643; 75 (1932), 4247, 12485–86. Congressman Louis T. McFadden also saw Hoover's actions in regard to war debts, the Bonus Army, Federal Reserve Board appointments, and secret diplomatic conversations as being unconstitutional. Such charges were listed in a resolution of impeachment that McFadden offered in the House of Representatives in 1932. The resolution was tabled by a vote of 361 to 8. See *Congressional Record* 76 (1932), 399–402, and Impeachment File, in Hoover Presidential Papers (Subject Files, Box 174), Hoover Presidential Library.

26. *Congressional Record* LXXV (1932), p. 4247.

27. *Public Papers: Hoover*, 1932: 292–94; *Congressional Record*, LXXV (1932), 12485–86, 14929–30, 14575; Goldsmith, *Growth of Presidential Power*, III, 1689.

28. Himmelberg, *Origins of NRA*, 170–72; Romasco, *Poverty of Abundance*, 198–99; *Public Papers: Hoover*, 1932: 384–87, 390–96.

29. U.S. Senate, *Federal Commissions, Committees, and Boards* (Senate Doc. 74, 71 Cong., 2 Sess., 1930); Walter Newton to James Watson, June 14, 1930; Lists prepared for publication, 1930, 1931, 1932, all in Commissions File, Hoover Presidential Papers (Subject Files, Box 107); Himmelberg, *Origins of NRA*, 90–106.

30. Himmelberg, *Origins of NRA*, 157–64, 167–68; Hawley, "Hoover and American Corporatism," 110–17; Fausold, *Presidency of Hoover*, 117–18.

31. *Public Papers: Hoover*, 222–24, 256–58, 396, 469; Hawley, "Hoover and American Corporatism," 116–17; Olson, *Hoover and the RFC*, 44–46.

32. Romasco, *Poverty of Abundance*, 188–93, 221–23; Schwarz, *Interregnum of Despair*, 90–178; Chamberlain, *President, Congress, and Legislation*, 288–295; Peri E. Arnold, *Making the Managerial Presidency* (Princeton, N.J.: Princeton University Press, 1986), p. 82; *Public Papers: Hoover*, 1932: 55–61. The credit, economy, and revenue measures were grounded in the powers to borrow, tax, and spend. The executive reorganization provision of the Economy Act was less clearly constitutional since it involved use of a legislative veto. But there was no debate about the constitutionality of this at the time.

33. *Public Papers: Hoover*, 1929: p. 471.

34. Two leading examples were when he was told that the commerce power could not be used to regulate oil production and that the use of mobile units of the federal army to deal with local lynch mobs was probably unconstitutional. See E. S. Rochester to Hoover, April 3, 1929, Oil Matters File, and Attorney General William D. Mitchell, Memorandum for the President, January 6, 1932, Colored Question—Lynching File, Hoover Presidential Papers (Subject Files, Boxes 216, 107). Speaking to a lawyers' group in 1931, Mitchell credited Hoover with "exceptional qualities." Given the president's organizational and activist bent, he said, one might expect "a chafing under the legal restraints and limitations which define the executive power and slow up its action." But in practice Hoover had "shown the utmost care to keep himself well within constitutional and legal limits, and to refrain from infringing on the functions of legislative or judical departments, [while] at the same time, whenever challenged, maintaining a vigorous defense of the constitutional powers of the executive branch." Address by Mitchell, Minneapolis, April 15, 1933, Justice File, Hoover Presidential Papers (Cabinet Series, Box 22).

35. For some insightful comments concerning the Hoover Period and presidential expansion, see James T. Patterson, "The Rise of Presidential Power before World War II," *Law and Contemporary Problems* 40 (Spring 1976), p. 53.

36. Carmen, "President, Politics, and Power of Appointment," 658–59; Francis W. O'Brien, "Bicentennial Reflections on Herbert Hoover and the Supreme Court," *Iowa Law Review* 61 (December 1975), 397–419.

37. See Leuchtenburg, "New Deal and Analogue of War"; Hawley, "Corporate Ideal as Liberal Philosophy"; Peter H. Irons, *The New Deal Lawyers* (Princeton, N.J.: Princeton University Press, 1982), 17–34. Also relevant is my "The New Deal State and the Anti-Bureaucratic Tradition," in Robert Eden, ed., *The New Deal and its Legacy* (Westport, Conn.: Greenwood, 1989), 77–92.

38. Paul L. Murphy, *The Constitution in Crisis Times, 1918–1969* (New York: Harper & Row, 1972), 128–29; Goldsmith, *Growth of Presidential Power*, III, 1409–11; Edwin C. Hargrove, *The Power of the Modern Presidency* (Philadelphia: Temple University Press, 1974), 10, 53–54; Tugwell, *Enlargement of the Presidency*, p. 393. Speaking in 1930 as governor of New York, Roosevelt had complained about the theory of social regulation by "master minds" in Washington and

about the "steady process of building commissions and regulatory bodies and special legislation like huge inverted pyramids over every one of the simple constitutional provisions." After 1933, the speech would become ammunition in the hands of his critics. See, for example, Merlo J. Pusey, *The Supreme Court Crisis* (New York: Macmillan, 1937), p. 27.

39. Samuel I. Rosenman, comp., *The Public Papers and Addresses of Franklin D. Roosevelt*, 13 vols. (New York: Random House and Macmillan, 1938–50), II, 14–15.

40. Goldsmith, *Growth of Presidential Power*, III, p. 1551; Clinton L. Rossiter, "War, Depression, and the Presidency, 1933–1950," *Social Research* 17 (December 1980), 418–23; Patterson, "Rise of Presidential Power," 53–55; Clinton L. Rossiter, *Constitutional Dictatorship: Crisis Government in the Modern Democracies* (Princeton, N.J.: Princeton University Press, 1948), 256–64. The major statutory grants of power were under the National Industrial Recovery Act, Agricultural Adjustment Act, Emergency Banking Act, Emergency Railroad Transportation Act, and Home Owners Loan Act. These were all products of presidential legislative leadership. But as some scholars have noted, this leadership also built upon or responded to legislative initiatives and movements in Congress. The latter's contribution was not entirely that of "rubber stamping" laws prepared in the executive branch. See, for example, Chamberlain, *President, Congress, and Legislation*, 18–19, 453–54.

41. John A. Rohr, *To Run a Constitution* (Lawrence, Kan.: University Press of Kansas, 1986), 116–20; Murphy, *Constitution in Crisis Times*, 129–31; Irons, *New Deal Lawyers*, 23–36, 115–18; Stern, "That Commerce Which Concerns More States than One," 1338–48, 1362–63; Field, "Constitutional Theory of NIRA," 270–71; Corwin, "Probable Repercussions of Nira," 139–42.

42. Homer S. Cummings, "Modern Tendencies and the Law," *American Bar Association Journal* 19 (September 1933), 576–79. See also Arthur M. Schlesinger, Jr., *The Politics of Upheaval* (Boston: Houghton Mifflin, 1960), 449–52.

43. Roosevelt's Fireside Chat of May 7, 1933, quoted in Arthur B. Tourtellot, *The Presidents on the Presidency* (Garden City, N.Y.: Doubleday, 1964), p. 252.

44. S. Alexander Rippa, "Constitutionalism: Political Defense of the Business Community during the New Deal Period," *Social Studies* 56 (January 1965), 187–89; Murphy, *Constitution in Crisis Times*, p. 142; Raoul E. Desvernine, *Democratic Despotism* (New York: Dodd, Mead 1936); Michael Kammen, *A Machine That Would Go by Itself* (New York: Knopf, 1986), 220–26, 270; Patrick A. McCarran, "The Growth of Federal Executive Power," *American Bar Association Journal* 19 (September 1933), 591–92; Frederick M. Davenport, "The Growing Power of the Presidency," *Boston University Law Review* 14 (June 1934), 655–67; Goldsmith, *Growth of Presidential Power*, III, p. 1954.

45. Home Building and Loan Association v. Blaisdell, 290 U.S. 398; Nebbia v. New York, 291 U.S. 545; Schlesinger, *Politics of Upheaval*, 252–54; Murphy, *Constitution in Crisis Times*, 110–12. The cases were decided by five to four decisions, and it was hoped that the five justices in the majority (Charles Evans Hughes, Owen Roberts, Louis Brandeis, Benjamin Cardozo, and Harlan Stone) would be receptive to New Deal legal reasoning. There was no hope that the minority (George Sutherland, Pierce Butler, Willis Van Devanter, and James McReynolds) would be so.

46. Murphy, *Constitution in Crisis Times*, 133–35; Irons, *New Deal Lawyers*, 39–45, 71–74, 154–55, 185–89.

47. Panama Refining Co. v. Ryan, 293 U.S. 388; Irons, *New Deal Lawyers*, 72–73. The law authorized the president to stop interstate shipment of oil produced in violation of state proration laws.

48. Humphrey's Executor v. U.S., 295 U.S. 602; Louisville Joint Stock Land Bank v. Radford, 295 U.S. 555; Schechter Poultry Corp. v. U.S., 295 U.S. 495; Irons, *New Deal Lawyers*, 100–04.

49. Myers v. U.S., 272 U.S. 52; William E. Leuchtenburg, "The Case of the Contentious Commissioner: Humphrey's Executor v. U.S.," in Harold M. Hyman and Leonard W. Levy, *Freedom and Reform* (New York: Harper & Row, 1967), 295–99; William J. Donovan and Ralstone R. Irvine, "The President's Power to Remove Members of Administrative Agencies," *Cornell Law Quarterly* 21 (February 1936), 215–48.

50. Schechter Poultry Corporation vs. U.S., 295 U.S. 495; Irons, *New Deal Lawyers*, 101–03; Edward S. Corwin, "The Schechter Case—Landmark or What?" *New York University Law Quarterly Review* 13 (January 1936), 151–90.

51. Irons, *New Deal Lawyers*, 104–07; William E. Leuchtenburg, "The Origins of Franklin D. Roosevelt's 'Court-Packing' Plan," *Supreme Court Review* (1966), 356–358; Schlesinger, *Politics of Upheaval*, 284–90, 385–98; Murphy, *Constitution in Crisis Times*, 140–41.

52. The major laws were the National Labor Relations Act, Social Security Act, Banking Act of 1935, Public Utility Holding Company Act, Revenue Act of 1935, Guffey-Snyder Bituminous Coal Stabilization Act, and Motor Carrier Act.

53. Leuchtenburg, "Origins of Court Packing," 350–56; Murphy, *Constitution in Crisis Times*, p. 141.

54. Leuchtenburg, "Origins of Court Packing," 360–63; Schlesinger, *Politics of Upheaval*, 283–84, 453–54.

55. The major decisions were U.S. v. Butler, 297 U.S. 1, invalidating much of the AAA program; Jones v. S.E.C., 298 U.S. 28; and Carter v. Carter Coal

Co., 298 U.S. 269, invalidating the 1935 coal legislation. The Carter decision invoked the Schechter principles concerning the commerce power and delegation of lawmaking power to private groups. In addition, the act in question was said to violate the reserved rights of the states. The Jones decision invoked due process guarantees against the SEC's administrative methods. And the Butler decision, although accepting a broad construction of the "general welfare" clause, held that the power thus recognized was limited by the reserved rights of the states and could not be made the basis for a tax helping to establish federal control over agricultrual production. For a description of the decisions and the accompanying reactions in New Deal circles, see Schlesinger, *Politics of Upheaval*, 470–78. For what the Court was being urged to do, see *New Deal Lawyers*, 187–92, 250–51; Corwin, "Schechter Case—Landmark or What," 189–90; Thomas Reed Powell, "Commerce, Pensions, and Codes, II," *Harvard Law Review*, 49 (December 1935), 229–38.

56. Leuchtenburg, "Origins of Court Packing," 365–82; Murphy, *Constitution in Crisis Times*, 147–51; Morehead ex rel. New York v. Tipaldo, 298 U.S. 602.

57. Leuchtenburg, "Origins of Court Packing," 382–99; Irons, *New Deal Lawyers*, 272–76; *Congressional Record* 81 (1937), 877–81.

58. William E. Leuchtenburg, "Franklin D. Roosevelt's Supreme Court 'Packing' Plan," in Harold M. Hollingsworth and William F. Holmes, eds., *Essays on the New Deal* (Austin, Tex.: University of Texas Press, 1969), 74–76; *Public Papers of FDR*, VI, 123–24, 126–29, 133. In this same fireside chat (March 9, 1937), Roosevelt quoted the Constitution as empowerig Congress to "levy taxes. . .and provide for the common defense and general welfare of the United States." His use of the ellipsis contributed to the popular misimpression that there was in the Constitution an independent power to provide for the general welfare. See Rohr, *To Run a Constitution*, 121–22.

59. Leuchtenburg, "FDR's Court Packing Plan," 76–108; Murphy, *Constitution in Crisis Times*, 152–54; James M. Burns, *Roosevelt: The Lion and the Fox* (New York: Harcourt, Brace, Jovanovich, 1956), 297–313; West Coast Hotel v. Parrish, 300 U.S. 386; N.L.R.B. v. Jones & Laughlin Steel Co., 301 U.S. 1.

60. Irons, *New Deal Lawyers*, 277–95; C. Herman Pritchett, *The Roosevelt Court* (New York: Macmillan, 1948), 74–81, 168–69; Robert Scigliano, *The Supreme Court and the Presidency* (New York: Free Press, 1971), 153–54; Robert L. Stern, "The Commerce Clause and the National Economy," *Harvard Law Review* 59 (1946), 679–83, 886–947; Vincent M. Barnett, "The Supreme Court and the Capacity to Govern," *Political Science Quarterly* 63 (September 1948), 346–62; Paul L. Murphy, "The New Deal Agricultural Program and the Constitution," *Agricultural History* 29 (October 1955), 167–68; Paul R. Benson, Jr., *The Supreme Court and the Commerce Clause, 1937–1970* (New York: Dunellen, 1970), 75–93; Sotirios A. Barber, *The Constitution and the Delegation of Congressional Power* (Chicago: University of Chicago Press, 1975), p. 95; Robert L. Hale, *Freedom through Law: Public Control of Private Governing Power* (New York:

Columbia University Press, 1952), 361–62; Robert H. Jackson, "Back to the Constitution," *American Bar Association Journal* 25 (September 1939), 745–49; Rogers M. Smith, *Liberalism and American Constitutional Law* (Cambridge, Mass.: Harvard University Press, 1985), 154–56; Robert E. Cushman, *What's Happening to Our Constitution?* (New York: Public Affairs Committee, 1942), 3–9, 14, 10–26. The cases completing the "constitutional revolution" are generally regarded to be: (1) Steward Machine Co. v. Davis, 310 U.S. 548 (1937), and Helvering v. Davis, 301 U.S. 619 (1937), upholding the social security system as a valid exercise of the taxing power to provide for the "general welfare"; (2) Santa Cruz Fruit Packing Co. v. N.L.R.B., 303 U.S. 453 (1938); Electric Bond & Share Co. v. S.E.C., 303 U.S. 419 (1938); Sunshine Anthracite Co. v. Adkins, 310 U.S. 381 (1940); Mulford v. Smith, 307 U.S. 38 (1939); U.S. v. Darby Lumber Co., 312 U.S. 100 (1941); and Wickard v. Filburn, 317 U.S. 711 (1942), further expanding the commerce power and repudiating dual federalism; (3) Driscoll v. Edison Light and Power Co., 307 U.S. 104 (1939), and Olsen v. Nebraska, 313 U.S. 236 (1941), reinterpreting due process guarantees; and (4) Currin v. Wallace, 306 U.S. 11 (1938), and U.S. v. Rock Royal Co-operative, 307 U.S. 533 (1939), moving away from the Schechter delegation doctrine. The "restoration" idea has not gone unchallenged. Critics have argued that the broad interpretationists of the founding period were seeking to undercut local interference with property rights, not lay the basis for a national regulatory and social service system. See Murphy, *Constitution in Crisis Times*, 167–68.

61. Pritchett, *Roosevelt Court*, 9–14, 74–77. In the four years between 1937 and 1941, Roosevelt appointed seven new justices: Hugo L. Black in 1937; Stanley Reed in 1938; Felix Frankfurter and William O. Douglas in 1939; Frank Murphy in 1940; James F. Byrnes and Robert H. Jackson in 1941. Of the old Court, only Owen Roberts and Harlan Stone remained; and the latter had been elevated by Roosevelt to the chief justiceship when Hughes retired in 1941.

62. Burns, *Roosevelt*, p. 315; John W. Chambers, "The Big Switch: Justice Roberts and the Minimum Wage Case," *Labor History* 10 (Winter 1969), 44–73; Michael E. Parish, "The Hughes Court, the Great Depression, and the Historians," *The Historian* 40 (February 1978), 286–300; Erik M. Eriksson, *The Supreme Court and the New Deal* (Roesmead, Cal.: Roesmead Review Press, 1940), 201–04; Samuel Hendel, *Charles Evans Hughes and the Supreme Court* (New York: Columbia University Press, 1951), p. 279. Most students of the subject have been skeptical of Roberts' subsequent claim that he did not "switch," i.e., that his vote in Morehead would have been affirmative if New York had asked for the controlling precedent to be overrruled rather that distinguished. Some, however, have noted that the federal measures upheld in 1937 were much better framed and crafted, with greater attention to constitutional basing, than were those overthrown in 1935 and 1936, and have seen this difference in legal craftsmanship as an important factor in the Court's decisions.

63. For a contrary view, see C. Perry Patterson, *Presidential Government in the United States* (Chapel Hill, N.C.: University of North Carolina Press, 1947).

64. Paul L. Murphy, "The New Deal and Judicial Activism," in Cohen, ed., *Roosevelt New Deal*, 294–302; Leuchtenburg, "FDR's Court Packing Plan," 109–12; Arthur J. Goldberg, "The Constitutional Limitations of the President's Powers," *American University Law Review* 22 (Summer 1973), 677–82; Pritchett, *Roosevelt Court*, 284–86; Abe Fortas, "The Constitution and the Presidency," *Washington Law Review* 44 (August 1974), 990–94; Maeva Marcus, *Truman and the Steel Seizure Case: The Limits of Presidential Power* (New York: Columbia University Press, 1977), p. x; Stephen L. Wasby, "The Presidency before the Courts," *Capital University Law Review* 6 (1976), 41–43; Belz, "Changing Conceptions of Constitutionalism," 652–69; Tugwell, *Enlargement of the Presidency*, 421–28; Burns, *Roosevelt*, 305–15, 339–52; James T. Patterson, *Congressional Conservatism and the New Deal* (Lexington, Ken.: University of Kentucky Press, 1967), 117–27, 331–37.

65. U.S. v. Curtiss-Wright Export Corp., 299 U.S. 304 (1936); U.S. v. Belmont, 301 U.S. 324 (1937); Arthur M. Schlesinger, Jr., *The Imperial Presidency* (Boston: Houghton Mifflin, 1973), 95–104; Charles A. Lofgren, "United States v. Curtiss-Wright Export Corporation: An Historical Reassessment," *Yale Law Journal* 83 (November 1973), 1–32; Hale, *Freedom through Law*, p. 350; Rossiter, "War, Depression, and the Presidency," p. 429. Sutherland had long held this view of presidential power in the foreign policy sphere. He had advanced it in an article in 1909 and a book (*Constitutional Power and World Affairs*) in 1919.

66. Schlesinger, *Imperial Presidency*, 103–15; Corwin, *The President*, 237–46, 261; Rossiter, "War, Depression, and the Presidency," 423–32; Patterson, "Rise of Presidential Power," 56–57; Rossiter, *Constitutional Dictatorship*, 265–69; Edward H. Foley, Jr., "Some Aspects of the Constitutional Powers of the President," *American Bar Association Journal* 27 (August 1941), 485–90; Alfred H. Kelley and Winifred A. Harbison, *The American Constitution* (New York: Norton, 1970 ed.), 827–28; John L. Blackman, *Presidential Seizure in Labor Disputes* (Cambridge, Mass.: Harvard University Press, 1967), p. xv; Louis Fisher, *President and Congress* (New York: Free Press, 1972), p. 185; Paul L. Murphy, *The Constitution in the Twentieth Century* (Washington, D.C.: American Historical Association, 1986), 17–18.

67. Norton E. Long, "Bureaucracy and Constitutionalism," *American Political Science Review* X1VI, 46 (September 1952), 808–18; C. Perry Patterson, "The President as Chief Administrator," *Boston University Law Review* 22 (January 1942), 8–42; Vincent M. Barnett, "Modern Constitutional Development: A Challenge to Administration," *Public Administration Review* 4 (Spring 1944), 159–64; Peter Woll, *American Bureaucracy* (New York: Norton, 1963), 25, 177; Rohr, *To Run a Constitution*, 181–84; J. Roland Pennock, *Administration and the Rule of Law* (New York: Rinehart, 1941), ix–x, 213–21; Theodore J. Lowi, "The New Public Philosophy: Interest Group Liberalism," in Thomas Ferguson and Joel Rogers, eds., *The Political Economy* (Armonk, N.Y.: M. E. Sharpe, 1984), 56–65; Frederick F. Blachly and Miriam E. Oatman, *Federal Regulatory Action and Control* (Washington, D.C.: Brookings, 1940), 3–5.

68. Arnold, *Making the Managerial Presidency*, 83–84, 88–92; Karl, "Executive Reorganization and Presidential Power," 3–4; A. J. Wann, *The President as Chief Executive: A Study of Franklin D. Roosevelt* (Washington, D.C.: Public Affairs Press, 1968), 23–27, 32–33, 38, 68–74; Leuchtenburg, "Case of the Contentious Commissioner," p. 308.

69. Rohr, *To Run a Constitution*, 138–49; Wann, *President as Chief Administrator*, 75–98; Arnold, *Making of Managerial Presidency*, 87–88, 92–108; Richard Polenberg, *Reorganizing Roosevelt's Government* (Cambridge, Mass.: Harvard University Press, 1966), 11–30; Barry D. Karl, *Executive Reorganization and Reform in the New Deal* (Cambridge, Mass.: Harvard University Press, 1963), 29–30, 195–247.

70. Arnold, *Making the Managerial Presidency*, p. 98.

71. *Public Papers of FDR*, V, p. 673.

72. Rohr, *To Run a Constitution*, 136–37; Karl, "Executive Reorganization and Presidential Power," 21–28.

73. Polenberg, *Reorganizing Roosevelt's Government*, 33–51; 68–101, 142–67; Karl, *Executive Reorganization*, 249–57; Richard Polenberg, "Roosevelt, Carter, and Executive Reorganization," *Presidential Studies Quarterly* 9 (Winter 1979), 36–37; Polenberg, "The National Committee to Uphold Constitutional Government, 1937–1941," *Journal of American History* 52 (December 1965), 582–91; David L. Porter, *Congress and the Waning of the New Deal* (Port Washington, N.Y.: Kennikat Press, 1980), 89–90.

74. Polenberg, *Reorganizing Roosevelt's Government*, 181–88; Karl, *Executive Reorganization*, 99–112; Rossiter, "War, Depression, and the Presidency," p. 434; Porter, *Congress and Waning of New Deal*, 91–108; Barry D. Karl, "In Search of National Planning," Paper Presented at Meeting of Organization of American Historians, Cincinnati, Ohio, April 1983.

75. See Graham, *Toward a Planned Society*, 59–68; Karl, "In Search of National Planning"; Polenberg, "Roosevelt, Carter, and Executive Reorganization," 39–45; Karl, "Executive Reorganization and Presidential Power," 30–31; Rohr, *To Run a Constitution*, 149–55, 181–84; Don K. Price, *America's Unwritten Constitution* (Baton Rouge: Louisiana State University Press, 1983), 9, 53–54, 60; Hargrove, *Powers of Modern Presidency*, 79–83; Long, "Bureaucracy and Constitutionalism," 811–18; Henry J. Merry, *Constitutional Function of Presidential-Administrative Separation* (Washington, D.C.: University Press of America, 1978), 1, 47, 105–06; Hughes, *Living Presidency*, 186–88.

76. See the discussion in Scigliano, *Supreme Court and Presidency*, 51–54.

77. Jerold S. Auerbach, *Unequal Justice: Lawyers and Social Change in Modern America* (New York: Oxford University Press, 1976), 226–30; Auerbach, "Lawyers and Social Change in the Depression Decade," in John Braeman

et al., eds., *The New Deal,* I (Columbus, Ohio: Ohio State University Press, 1975), 163–65.

78. See, for example, Arthur S. Miller, *Democratic Dictatorship: The Emergency Constitution of Control* (Westport, Conn.: Greenwood, 1981), 93, 209; Herman Belz, "New Left Reverberations in the Academy: The Antipluralist Critique of Constitutionalism," *Review of Politics* 36 (April 1974), 265–83; Kenneth M. Dolbeare and Linda Medcalf, "The Dark Side of the Constitution," in Dolbeare and John Manley, eds., *The Case against the Constitution* (Armonk, N.Y.: M. E. Sharpe, 1987), 120–42; Arthur Shenfield, "The New Deal and the Supreme Court," in Robert Eden, *Legacy of the New Deal* 167–176; Lino Graglia, "A Theory of Power," *National Review* (July 17, 1987), 33–36.

Chapter 6: The Constitution of the Truman Presidency and the Post-World War II Era

1. See Edward S. Corwin, *The President: Office and Powers* (New York: New York University Press, 1957); Richard E. Neustadt, *Presidential Power* (New York: John Wiley and Sons, 1961); Clinton Rossiter, *The American Presidency*, Rev. Ed. (New York: Harcourt, Brace and Co., 1960); Athan G. Theoharis, ed., *The Truman Presidency: The Origins of the Imperial Presidency and the National Security State* (Stanfordville, N.Y.: Coleman Enterprises, 1979).

2. Emmet John Hughes, *The Living Presidency* (New York: Coward, McCann & Geoghegan, 1973), p. 32.

3. Jonathan Daniels, *The Man of Independence* (Philadelphia: J.B. Lippincott, 1950), p. 294.

4. *Public Papers of the Presidents of the United States: Harry S. Truman,* 8 vols. (Washington, D.C.: Government Printing Office, 1961-66), June 11, 1948, p. 330.

5. *Ibid.,* Nov. 11, 1946, p. 478.

6. *Ibid.,* Feb. 21, 1952, p. 169.

7. Robert H. Ferrell, ed., *Off the Record: The Private Papers of Harry S. Truman* (New York: Harper and Row, 1980), p. 239.

8. Hughes, *Living Presidency,* p. 137.

9. *Public Papers,* Oct. 19, 1948, 820–21.

10. *Memoirs by Harry S. Truman: Year of Decisions* (Garden City, N.Y.: Doubleday & Co., 1955), p. ix.

11. *Public Papers,* Sept. 13, 1946, p. 430.

12. *Ibid.,* Sept. 27, 1949, p. 489.

13. See Dorr v. United States, 195 U.S. 140 (1904), and Jacobson v. Massachusetts, 197 U.S. 22 (1905).

14. Truman, *Memoirs: Year of Decisions*, 325–26.

15. *Public Papers*, May 13, 1947, p. 238. See also *ibid.*, Feb. 15, 1950, p. 157; June 27, 1950, p. 493; Sept. 17, 1951, p. 521; June 26, 1945, p. 142.

16. *Ibid.*, Nov. 11, 1946, p. 478.

17. William F. Swindler, *Court and Constitution in the Twentieth Century: The New Legality* (Indianapolis: Bobbs-Merrill Co., 1970), p. 95; Henry J. Abraham, *Justices and Presidents: A Political History of Appointments to the Supreme Court* (New York: Oxford University Press, 1974), p. 54.

18. Ferrell, ed., *Off the Record*, p. 22.

19. Ronald G. Marquardt, "The Judicial Justice: Mr. Justice Burton and the Supreme Court" (Unpublished Ph. D. dissertation, University of Missouri-Columbia, 1974), p. 55.

20. Ferrell, ed., *Off the Record*, p. 46.

21. Frances Howell Rudko, *Truman's Court: A Study in Judicial Restraint* (Westport, Conn.: Greenwood Press, 1988), p. 30.

22. Ibid., 25–33; Abraham, *Justices and Presidents*, p. 63; Swindler, *Court and Constitution*, p. 182.

23. Rudko, *Truman's Court*, p. 32.

24. Glendon A. Schubert, Jr., *Constitutional Politics* (New York: Holt, Rinehart and Winston, 1960), passim.; Alfred H. Kelly and Winfred A. Harbison, *The American Constitution* (New York: W.W. Norton & Co., 1970), chaps. 31,32.

25. Glendon A. Schubert, Jr., *The Presidency in the Courts* (Minneapolis: University of Minnesota Press, 1957), p. 365.

26. *Ibid.*, p. 347.

27. For some of Truman's appointment problems, see Andrew J. Dunar, *The Truman Scandals and the Politics of Morality* (Columbia: University of Missouri Press, 1984).

28. The federal appellate judiciary voided only thirty-seven executive actions from George Washington through Truman. Schubert, *Presidency in the Courts*, 361–65.

29. See Robert J. Donavan, *The Presidency of Harry S. Truman*, 2 vols. (New York: W.W. Norton & Co., 1977, 1982); Harold F. Gosnell, *Truman's Crises* (Westport, Conn.: Greenwood Press, 1980); Donald R. McCoy, *The Presidency of Harry S. Truman* (Lawrence: University Press of Kansas, 1984).

30. Truman, *Memoirs: Year of Decisions*, p. 330.

31. *Public Papers*, May 15, 1948, p. 262.

32. *Ibid.*, May 15, 1951, p. 282.

33. *Ibid.*, Sept. 28, 1950, p. 661.

34. *Ibid.*, June 19, 1952, p. 434; Rossiter, *American Presidency*, 88, 121; Arthur M. Schlesinger, Jr., *The Imperial Presidency* (Boston: Houghton Mifflin Co., 1973), p. 236.

35. Schlesinger, *Imperial Presidency*, 153–54; Theoharis, ed., *Truman Presidency*, iv-v; Raoul Berger, *Executive Privilege: A Constitutional Myth* (Cambridge, Mass.: Harvard University Press, 1974), passim; Richard M. Fried, *Men Against McCarthy* (New York: Columbia University Press, 1976), 75–76; Donovan, *Presidency of Truman*, II, p. 174.

36. Walter Ehrlich, *Presidential Impeachment* (St. Charles, Mo.: Forum Press, 1974), p. 115.

37. *Public Papers*, Apr. 3, 1950, p. 241.

38. *Ibid.*, June 30, 1950, p. 510.

39. *Ibid.*, May 17, 1951, 289–91.

40. Rossiter, *American Presidency*, p. 157.

41. Larry Berman, *The Office of Management and Budget and the Presidency* (Princeton, N.J.: Princeton University Press, 1979), 30–47.

42. Dorothy B. James, *The Contemporary Presidency* (Indianapolis: Bobbs-Merrill Co., 1974), 309–10.

43. Donald R. McCoy and Richard T. Ruetten, *Quest and Response: Minority Rights and the Truman Administration* (Lawrence: University Press of Kansas, 1973), 48–53, 79–95, chap. 6.

44. *Ibid.*, passim.

45. *Public Papers*, Feb. 2, 1948, p. 122.

46. *Ibid.*, June 29, 1947, p. 311.

47. Peter H. Irons, "American Business and the Origins of McCarthyism," in Robert Griffith and Athan Theoharis, eds., *The Specter* (New York: New Viewpoints, 1974), 79–84; Theoharis, "The Escalation of the Loyalty Program," in Barton J. Bernstein, ed., *Politics and Policies of the Truman Administration* (Chicago: Quadrangle, 1970), 242–68.

48. Theoharis, "The Escalation of the Loyalty Program," p. 250.

49. McCoy, *Truman Presidency*, chap. 6; Robert Griffith, "American Politics and the Origins of 'McCarthyism'," in Griffith and Theoharis, eds., *Specter*, 15–16; Theoharis, "The Rhetoric of Politics," in Bernstein, ed., *Politics and Policies*, 196–241; Schlesinger, *Imperial Presidency*, p. 128; Kelly and Harbison, *American Constitution*, chap. 32. See also C. Herman Pritchett, *Civil Liberties and the Vinson Court* (Chicago: University of Chicago Press, 1954).

50. *Public Papers*, Aug. 19, 1948, p. 455.

51. *Ibid.*, Aug. 8, 1950, 571–76.

52. *Ibid.*, Sept. 22, 1950, 645–53.

53. *Ibid.*, June 25, 1952, 441–47; McCoy, *Truman Presidency*, 234–35; William R. Tanner and Robert Griffith, "Legislative Politics and 'McCarthyism'," in Griffith and Theoharis, eds., *Specter*, 174–89; Richard P. Lonaker, *The Presidency and Individual Liberties* (Ithaca, N.Y.: Cornell University Press, 1961), 56–57.

54. McCoy, *Truman Presidency*, p. 233.

55. Fried, *Men Against McCarthy*, p. 233.

56. McCoy, *Truman Presidency*, 274–75.

57. Kelly and Harbison, *American Constitution*, 991–92; Greene v. McElroy, 360 U.S. 474 (1959).

58. Berman, *Office of Management and Budget*, 30–47.

59. Senate Library, comp., *Presidential Vetoes, 1789–1976* (Washington, D.C.: Government Printing Office, 1978), p. ix, passim.

60. McCoy, *Truman Presidency*, passim.

61. Rossiter, *American Presidency*, p. 27. See also *Public Papers*, Oct. 18, 1948, p. 815.

62. See Thomas G. Paterson, *Soviet-American Confrontation* (Baltimore: Johns Hopkins University Press, 1973).

63. See Donovan, *Presidency of Truman*, vols. I and II; Gosnell, *Truman Crises*; McCoy, *Truman Presidency*; Bert Cochran, *Harry Truman and the Crisis Presidency* (New York: Funk & Wagnalls, 1973); Alonzo L. Hamby, *Beyond the New Deal* (New York: Columbia University Press, 1973); Daniel Yergin, *Shattered Peace* (Boston: Houghton Mifflin Co., 1977).

64. *Public Papers*, Jan. 4, 1951, p. 2.

65. *Ibid.*, Mar. 1, 1951, p. 176. See also Donovan, *Presidency of Truman*, II, chaps. 19, 20, 21; McCoy, *Truman Presidency*, chap. 10; Schlesinger, *Imperial Presidency*, 130–35.

66. Stephen E. Ambrose, *Eisenhower; The President* (New York: Simon & Schuster, 1984), 68–70, 154–55.

67. Ferrell, ed., *Off the Record*, p. 314.

68. Donovan, *Presidency of Truman*, II, 47–49; Schlesinger, *Imperial Presidency*, 135–40.

69. *Public Papers*, Jan. 11, 1951, p. 19.

70. Donovan, *Presidency of Truman*, II, 110–13, chap. 33.

71. In re Yamashita, 327 U.S. 1 (1946).

72. *Public Papers*, Feb. 17, 1949, 137–38.

73. Reid v. Covert, 354 U.S. 1 (1957); Kinsella v. Krueger, 354 U.S. 1 (1957); Kinsella v. United States, 361 U.S. 234 (1960); Grisham v. Hagan, 361 U.S. 278 (1960); McElroy v. United States, 361 U.S. 281 (1960).

74. Korematsu v. United States, 323 U.S. 214 (1944).

75. McCoy, *Truman Presidency*, 59–60; Rossiter, *American Presidency*, p. 120.

76. Woods v. Miller, 333 U.S. 138 (1948); Kelly and Harbison, *American Constitution*, p. 878.

77. Harold C. Relyea, "Reconsidering the National Emergencies Act," in R. Gordon Hoxie, ed., *The Presidency and National Security Policy* (New York: Center for the Study of the Presidency, 1984), 276, 298.

78. *Public Papers*, Feb. 3, 1949, p. 126.

79. *Ibid*, Oct. 27, 1949, p. 534.

80. Donovan, *Presidency of Truman*, II, chap. 36, p. 386 for quotation.

81. *Public Papers*, Feb. 19, 1952, 160–61; Apr. 7, 1952, 240–41.

82. *Ibid.*, Apr. 24, 1952, p. 290.

83. *Ibid.*, Apr. 27, 1952, p. 301.

84. McCoy, *Truman Presidency*, 291–92.

85. Maeva Marcus, *Truman and the Steel Seizure Case* (New York: Columbia University Press, 1977), passim.

86. *Public Papers*, May 22, 1952, 362–63.

87. Youngstown Sheet & Tube Co. v. Sawyer, 343 U.S. 579 (1952); Marcus, *Steel Seizure Case*, passim.

88. Youngstown v. Sawyer, passim.

89. Schlesinger, *Imperial Presidency*, 146–50.

90. Hughes, Living Presidency, p. 281 n. See also Schlesinger, *Imperial Presidency*, 157–58.

91. Theoharis, ed., *Truman Presidency*, p. vi.

92. *Public Papers*, Dec. 15, 1952, p. 1077.

93. Ibid., June 26, 1945, p. 139.

Chapter 7: The Constitutional Presidency in American Political Development

1. Theodore Lowi, *The Personal President* (Ithaca, N.Y.: Cornell University Press, 1985); see also Bruce Ackerman, "Neo-Federalism," in Jon Elster and Rune Slagstad, eds. *Constitutionalism and Democracy*, (Cambridge, Eng.: Cambridge University Press, 1988) 153–194; Fred I. Greenstein, "Change and Continuity in the Modern Presidency," in *The New American Political System*, Anthony King, ed. (Washington, D.C.: American Enterprise Institute, 1977).

2. This gist of this argument was first suggested to me by Herbert J. Storing. See especially his "The Problem of Big Government," in *A Nation of States*, Robert A. Goldwin, ed. (Chicago: Rand McNally, 1974), 67–90.

3. Gordon Wood, *The Creation of the American Republic 1776–1787*, (New York: W.W. Norton, 1969).

4. Gary J. Schmitt and Robert Webking, "Revolutionaries, Antifederalists and Federalists: Comments of Gordon Wood's Understanding of the American Founding," *Political Science Reviewer*, XX (Feb., 1979), 195–229. See also Herbert J. Storing, *What the Anti-Federalists Were For* (Chicago: The University of Chicago Press, 1981), p. 83, note 7.

5. *The Federalist*, No. 15.

6. One of the persistent difficulties of constitutional rule is to maintain a commitment to limited government once the need for unlimited power has been recognized. See Hamilton's various reflections on this theme in *The Federalist*, for example, "a power equal to *every possible contingency* must exist somewhere in the government" (*Federalist*, No. 26, my emphases).

7. See especially *Federalist*, No. 46 (and No. 45 in light of No. 46).

8. The finest statement of these problems and the benefits of decentralization is still Tocqueville's *Democracy in America*.

9. For a superb rendering of the different political cultures presupposed by commercial and agrarian commitments, see Anne Norton, *Alternative Americas: A Reading of Antebellum Political Culture* (Chicago: The University of Chicago Press, 1986).

10. *The Federalist*, No. 10.

11. Ibid., my emphasis. For a detailed and perceptive reading of *Federalist*, No. 10, see David Epstein, *The Political Theory of the Federalist* (Chicago: The University of Chicago Press, 1983).

12. See especially *Federalist*, No. 32.

13. Charles Thatch, *The Creation of the Presidency* (Baltimore: Johns Hopkins University Press, 1969, orig. publ. 1921).

14. *The Federalist*, No. 70: "There is an idea, which is not without its advocates, that a vigorous executive is inconsistent with the genius of Republican government. The enlightened well-wishers of this species of government must at least hope that the supposition is destitute of foundation; since they can never admit its truth, without at the same time admitting the condemnation of their own principles."

15. Richard Neustadt, *Presidential Power*, 3rd ed. (New York: John Wiley & Sons, 1980; orig. publ. 1960), p. 8.

16. See Joseph M. Bessette and Jeffrey Tulis, "The Constitution, Politics and the Presidency," in *The Presidency in the Constitutional Order*, Bessette and Tulis, eds. (Baton Rouge: Louisiana State University Press, 1981), 3–30.

17. Greenstein, "Change and Continuity"; Arthur Schlesinger, Jr., *The Imperial Presidency* (Boston: Houghton Mifflin Co., 1973); Richard Neustadt, "The Presidency at Mid-century," *Law and Contemporary Problems* (Autumn 1956), 610–11.

18. See Louis Fisher, *Constitutional Conflict between the Congress and President* (Princeton, N.J.: Princeton University Press, 1985).

19. I discuss these dilemmas in *The Rhetorical Presidency* (Princeton, N.J.: Princeton University Press, 1987).

20. William F. Harris II, "Bonding Word and Polity: The Logic of American Constitutionalism," *American Political Science Review* (March 1982), 34–45.

21. Sotirios A. Barber, *On What the Constitution Means* (Baltimore: Johns Hopkins University Press, 1984).

22. Ibid.

23. I focus upon chapters two and three: Lowi, *The Personal President*, 22–66.

24. *The Federalist*, No. 23.

25. Lowi, *Personal President*, p. 46, (my emphasis).

26. Ibid., p. 34.

Chapter 8: The Constitution and Presidential Budget Powers: The Modern Era

1. "Congressional Budget Process" (part 3), hearings before the House Committee on Rules, 98th Cong., 2d Sess. (1984), p. 161.

2. Louis Fisher, *The Politics of Shared Power* (Washington, D.C.: Congressional Quarterly Press, 1987), 40–41.

3. Louis Fisher, *Presidential Spending Power* (Princeton, N.J.: Princeton University Press, 1975), 17–18. For the efforts of other presidents and secretaries of the treasury, see other sections in this chapter.

4. Allen R. Richards, "The Heritage of the Eighteenth and Nineteenth Centuries," in James W. Fesler, ed., *The 50 States and Their Local Governments* (New York: Alfred A. Knopf, 1967), p. 59.

5. *Harper's Weekly*, August 12, 1882, p. 497.

6. Ibid., July 3, 1886, p. 421. For discussion of the Arthur and Cleveland vetoes, see Fisher, *Presidential Spending Power*, 25–27.

7. *The Need for a National Budget*, H. Doc. No. 854, 62d Cong., 2d Sess., 1912, p. 138. Emphasis in original.

8. 37 Stat. 415 (1912).

9. Frederick A. Cleveland, "The Federal Budget," *Proceedings of the Academy of Political Science* 3 (1912–13), 167–68. Emphasis in original.

10. William Howard Taft, *Our Chief Magistrate and His Powers* (New York: Columbia University Press, 1916), 64–65.

11. H. Rept. No. 362, 66th Cong., 1st Sess., 1919, 1–3.

12. H. Rept. No. 14, 67th Cong., 1st Sess., 1921, 4–5.

13. Ibid., 6–7.

14. For Fitzgerald, see "Budget Systems," *Municipal Research* 62 (June 1915), pp. 312, 322, 327, 340; see also William Franklin Willoughby, *The Problem of a National Budget* (New York: Appleton, 1918), 146–149. For Houston, see David Houston, *Eight Years with Wilson's Cabinet* (Garden City, N.Y.: Doubleday, Page, 1926), II, p. 88. Wilson's other secretaries of the treasury took the same position. See *Annual Report of the Secretary of the Treasury*, 1918–19, p. 121 (testimony of William McAdoo) and ibid., p. 117 (testimony of Carter Glass).

15. Charles Wallace Collins, "Constitutional Aspects of a National Budget System," *Yale Law Journal* 25 (1916), p. 376.

16. S. Rept. No. 524, 66th Cong., 2d Sess., 1920, p. 4.

17. 42 Stat. 20 (1921).

18. *Weekly Compilation of Presidential Documents* 8 (December 11, 1972), p. 1752.

19. Fisher, *Presidential Spending Power*, 175–201.

20. *Washington Post*, March 7, 1973, p. A4.

21. H. Rept. No. 147, 93rd Cong., 1st Sess., 1973, p. 39.

22. Paul E. Peterson, "The New Politics of Deficits," in John E. Chubb and Paul E. Peterson, eds., *The New Direction in American Politics* (Washington, D.C.: American Enterprise Institute, 1985), p. 375.

23. New Haven v. United States, 634 F.Supp. 1449, 1458 (D.D.C. 1986). This decision was affirmed in New Haven v. United States, 809 F.2d 900 (D.C. Cir. 1987).

24. H. Rept. No. 1152 (Part 1), 98th Cong., 2d Sess., 1984, p. 43. See also my charts reprinted in "Issue Presentations Before the Rules Committee Task Force on the Budget Process," prepared by the House Committee on Rules, 98th Cong., 2d Sess., 1984, pp. 81, 83.

25. Louis Fisher, "Ten Years of the Budget Act: Still Searching for Controls," *Public Budgeting & Finance* 5 (1985), 3–28.

26. 122 Cong. Rec. 13761 (1976) (Cong. Schneebeli); ibid., p. 10519 (Senator Packwood).

27. Trent Lott, "The Need to Improve the Budget Process: A Republican's View," in Allen Schick, *Crisis in the Budget Process* (Washington, D.C.: American Enterprise Institute, 1985), p. 72.

28. See the remarks of Rudolph Penner, CBO Director, in ibid., p. 69, and Allen Schick, "How the Budget Was Won and Lost," in Norman J. Ornstein, ed., *President and Congress: Assessing Reagan's First Year* (Washington, D.C.: American Enterprise Institute, 1982), p. 25.

29. David A. Stockman, *The Triumph of Politics* (New York: Harper & Row, 1986), p. 159.

30. Ibid., p. 91.

31. 129 Cong. Rec. 25417 (1983) (Cong. Wright).

32. 122 Cong. Rec. 17843 (1976) (Cong. Steed).

33. *Weekly Compilation of Presidential Documents* 21 (November 15, 1985), p. 1411.

34. "Congressional Budget Process," hearings before the House Committee on Rules, 97th Cong., 2d Sess. (1982), p. 239.

35. For the author's testimony on the unconstitutionality of Gramm-Rudman, see "The Balanced Budget and Emergency Deficit Control Act of 1985," hearings before the House Committee on Government Operations, 99th Cong., 1st Sess. (1985), 197–232.

36. Bowsher v. Synar, 106 S. Ct. 3181, 3186 (1986).

37. Ibid., pp. 3186, 3187, 3188, 3192.

38. *Weekly Compilation of Presidential Documents* 21 (July 14, 1984), p. 1040.

39. H. Rept. No. 916, 98th Cong., 2d Sess. (1984), p. 48.

40. For the text of the NASA letter and other legislative vetoes after *Chadha*, see Louis Fisher, "Judicial Misjudgments About the Lawmaking Process: the Legislative Veto Case," *Public Administration Review* 45 (Special Issue November 1985), 705–11. See also Louis Fisher, "The Administrative World of *Chadha* and *Bowsher*," *Public Administration Review* 47 (May/June 1987), 213–219.

41. *Washington Post*, August 13, 1987, p. A13.

42. 83 Cong. Rec. 355–356 (1938).

43. 130 Cong. Rec. S5312, S5323 (daily ed. May 3, 1984).

44. 131 Cong. Rec. S135–136 (daily ed. January 3, 1985); 131 Cong. Rec. S9947 (daily ed. July 24, 1985).

45. *Weekly Compilation of Presidential Documents* 22 (February 4, 1986), p. 136.

46. Louis Fisher and Neal Devins, "How Successfully Can the States' Item Veto be Transferred to the President?," *Georgetown Law Journal* 75 (October 1986), 159–97.

47. Executive Office of the President, *Executive Policy Study #12*, p. 59 (September 6, 1983).

48. State v. Holder, 76 Miss. 158, 181 (1898).

49. Fergus v. Russel, 270 Ill. 304, 348 (1915).

50. State ex rel. Kleczka v. Conta, 264 N.W.2d 539, 557 (Wis. 1978) (Hansen, J., concurring in part, dissenting in part).

51. Cascade Telephone Co. v. State Tax Commission, 176 Wash. 616 (1934); Tacoma v. State Tax Commission, 177 Wash. 604 (1934).

52. Cascade Telephone Co. v. State Tax Commission, 176 Wash. at 623 (Steinhart, J., dissenting). See also Washington Ass'n of Apt. Ass'ns v. Evans, 88 Wash. 2d 563 (1977).

53. Commonwealth v. Dodson, 176 Va. 281, 290 (1940).

54. Ibid., p. 302.

55. State ex rel. Kleczka v. Conta, 264 N.W.2d at 557 (Hansen, J. concurring in part, dissenting in part). See also Washington Federation of State Employees v. State, 682 P.2d 869 (Wash. 1984).

56. Anderson v. Lamm , 579 P.2d 620, 624 (Colo. 1978).

57. La. Const., art. III, § 16.

58. Ala. Const., art. VI, § 45.

59. H. Rept. No. 866, 98th Cong., 2d Sess., 1984, 19–22.

60. 130 Cong. Rec. S5307 (daily ed. May 3, 1984).

61. *Item Veto*, Hearings before the House Committee on the Judiciary, 85th Cong., 1st Sess., 1957, p. 94 (Budget Director Percival Brundage).

62. *Economic Report of the President*, February 1985, p. 96.

Chapter 9: The Modern Presidency and the Constitution: Foreign Policy

1. In Edward S. Corwin, *The President's Control of Foreign Relations* (Princeton, N.J.: Princeton University Press, 1917), pp. 28–29.

2. Edward S. Corwin, *The President: Office and Powers* (New York: New York University Press, 1941), p. 200.

3. James Hart, *The American Presidency in Action, 1789* (New York: Macmillan, 1948), pp. 78, 102.

4. Charles A. Lofgren, "War-Making Under the Constitution: The Original Understanding," *Yale Law Journal* 81 (January 1972), p. 672.

5. The Hamilton-Madison debate is discussed in Edward S. Corwin, *The President's Control of Foreign Relations* (Princeton, N.J.: Princeton University Press, 1917), 28–33.

6. In Corwin, *The President: Office and Powers*, 177-78.

7. Adam Clymer, "Senate Votes to Give up Canal," *New York Times*, April 19, 1978, A1, A16.

8. Myres S. McDougal and Asher Lans, "Treaties and Congressional Executive or Presidential Agreements: Interchangeable Instruments of National Policy," *Yale Law Journal* 54 (March 1945), p. 209.

9. For the text of the president's statement, *see New York Times*, December 16, 1978, p. 8.

10. *Congressional Quarterly Almanac, 1975,* p. 845.

11. Bernard Schwartz, *The Powers of Government, volume 2, The Powers of the President* (New York: Macmillan, 1963), p. 66.

12. McDougal and Lans, "Treaties and Congressional-Executive or Presidential Agreements," p. 209.

13. Ibid., p. 204.

14. Louis Henkin, *Foreign Affairs and the Constitution* (Mineola, N.Y.: Foundation Press, 1972), p. 46.

15. Lofgren, "War-Making Under the Constitution," 675–76.

16. Ibid., 693–94.

17. John Norton Moore, "The National Executive and the Use of the Armed Forces Abroad," in Richard A. Falk, ed., *The Vietnam War and International Law,* vol. 2 (Princeton, N.J.: Princeton University Press, 1969), p. 81.

18. Note: "Congress, the President, and the Power to Commit Forces to Combat," *Harvard Law Review* 81 (January 1968), p. 1771.

19. U.S. Department of State, "Authority of the President to Repel the Attack in Korea," *Department of State Bulletin* 23 (1950), p. 173.

20. 2 Bl. 635 (1863).

21. Clinton Rossiter and Richard P. Longaker, *The Supreme Court and the Commander in Chief* (Ithaca, N.Y.: Cornell University Press, 1951 and 1976), p. 76.

22. Ibid., p. 145.

23. Dwight D. Eisenhower, *Mandate for Change* (Garden City, N.Y.: Doubleday, 1963), 129–30, 271.

24. 77 L. Ed. 2nd 317.

25. R. Gordon Hoxie, *The President and National Security Policy* (New York: Center for the Study of the Presidency, 1984), 380–86.

26. *Congressional Quarterly Almanac, 1983,* 115–17.

27. Ibid., p. 111.

28. Laurence H. Tribe, "Reagan Ignites a Constitutional Crisis," *New York Times,* May 20, 1987, p. A31.

29. I.M. Destler, "National Security Management: What Presidents Have Wrought," *Political Science Quarterly* 95 (Winter 1980–81), p. 580.

30. Dom Bonafede, "Who's on First in the Foreign Policy Game?" *National Journal* (February 17, 1979), p. 271.

31. Michael R. Gordon, "At Foreign Policy Helm: Shultz vs. White House," *New York Times*, August 26, 1987, p. A1 and 8.

32. Corwin, *The President's Control of Foreign Relations*, p. 167.

33. Rossiter and Longaker, *The Supreme Court and the Commander in Chief*, p. 70.

34. 301 U.S. 324 (1937).

35. 418 U.S. 683 (1974).

36. 299 U.S. 304 (1936).

Chapter 10: Presidential War Powers, the War Powers Resolution, and the Persian Gulf

1. Bas v. Tingy, 4 U.S. 37 (1800).

2. Barry M. Blechman and Stephen S. Kaplan, eds., *Force Without War: U.S. Armed Forces as a Political Instrument* (Washington, D.C.: Brookings Institution, 1978).

3. For a general discussion of the constitutional issues see Robert Scigliano, "The War Powers Resolution and the War Powers," in Joseph M. Bessette and Jeffrey Tulis, eds., *The Presidency in the Constitutional Order* (Baton Rouge: Louisiana State University Press, 1981), 115–143.

4. W. Taylor Revely III, *War Powers of the President and Congress* (Charlottesville, Vir.: University Press of Virginia, 1981).

5. Jonathan Elliot, *Debates of the Several State Conventions on the Adoption of the Federal Constitution* (Philadelphia: J.B. Lippincott, 1896).

6. For the restrictive view, see David Gray Adler, "The Constitution and Presidential Warmaking: the Enduring Debate," *Political Science Quarterly* 103, 1, 1988, 1–36.

7. Max Farrand, *The Records of the Federal Convention of 1787*, II, (New Haven, Conn.: Yale University Press, 1911), p. 318; see also Arthur M. Schlesinger, Jr., *The Imperial Presidency* (Boston: Houghton Mifflin, 1973), 2–5.

8. U.S. v. Smith, 27 F. Cas. 1192 (1806).

9. Jules Lobel, "Covert War and Congressional Authority: Hidden War and Forgotten Power," *Pennsylvania Law Review* 34 (June 1986), p. 1035.

10. *The Congressional Globe*, 30th Cong., 1st Sess., June 3, 1848, p. 95.

11. Kirk H. Porter and Donald B. Johnson, *National Party Platforms, 1840–1960* (Urbana, Ill.: University of Illinois Press, 1961), p. 34.

12. Alexander Hamilton, "Pacificus" No. 1 [29 June 1793], Harold C. Syrett, ed., *The Papers of Alexander Hamilton*, XV (New York and London: Columbia University Press, 1969), 33–43.

13. James Madison, "Helvidius" Number 1 [24 August 1793], Thomas A. Mason *et al.*, eds., *The Papers of James Madison*, XV (Charlottesville, Va.: University Press of Virginia, 1985), 66–73.

14. Jeremy Stone, "Presidential First Use is Unlawful," *Foreign Policy* 6 (Fall 1984), 94–112.

15. Asa Clark IV and Richard M. Pious, "Waging War: Structural vs. Political Efficacy," *Armed Forces and Society* 14 (Fall 1987), 129–47.

16. 119 *Cong. Rec.* 36, p. 187 (1973).

17. P.L. 93–148, 93rd Cong., 1st sess., J. Res. 542, Nov. 7, 1973.

18. See Richard M. Nixon's October 23, 1973 veto of the War Powers Resolution, *Public Papers of the Presidents, 1973*, (Washington, D.C.: Government Printing Office, 1973), 893–95.

19. U.S. Department of State, "The War Powers Resolution and Anti-Terrorist Operations, *Current Policy* 832 (1986), p. 2.

20. Michael J. Glennon, "The War Powers Resolution Ten Years Later: More Politics than Law," *American Journal of International Law* 78 (July 1984) 571–81.

21. INS v. Chadha, 462 U.S. 919 (1983). Justice White observed in dissent that the majority opinion would "invalidate all legislative vetoes irrespective of form or substance." That may not be the case, but it is doubtful that the concurrent veto of the WPR would pass muster with the Rehnquist court.

22. Crockett v. Reagan, 558 F. Supp. 893 (1982), affirmed 720 F. 2d 1355 (D.C. Cir., 1983).

23. Robert Zutz, "The Recapture of the S.S. Mayaguez: Failure of the Consultation Clause of the War Powers Resolution," *New York University Journal of International Law and Politics* 8 (1976), p. 457.

24. Thomas Franck and Edward Weisband, *Foreign Policy by Congress* (New York: Oxford University Press, 1979), p. 72.

25. On the administration rationale for the invasion see *Department of State Bulletin*, Dec. 1983, 68–70; on the events see Michael Rubner, "The Reagan Administration, the 1973 War Powers Resolution, and the Invasion of Grenada," *Political Science Quarterly* 100 (Winter 1985–86), 627–47.

26. S.J. Res. 159, P.L. 98–119, reprinted in *The New York Times*, October 13, 1983.

27. *Weekly Compilation of Presidential Documents*, vol. 19, 1983–4, p. 1422.

28. On the Libyan incidents see Michael Rubner, "Antiterrorism and the Withering of the 1973 War Powers Resolution," *Political Science Quarterly* 102 (Summer 1987), 193–215.

29. Ibid., p. 206.

30. *Public Papers of the Presidents, Jimmy Carter, 1980*, I (Washington, D.C.: GPO, 1981), p. 197.

31. *Congressional Quarterly Weekly Reports*, April 23, 1988, p. 1058.

32. *The Congressional Record*, S4234, April 18, 1988.

33. *Congressional Quarterly Weekly Reports*, April 23, 1988, p. 1055.

34. NYT/CBS POLL, *The New York Times*, September 22, 1987.

35. *Washington Post National Weekly Edition*, Nov. 2, 1987.

36. William J. Fulbright, *The Crippled Giant* (New York: Vintage Books, 1972), p. 194.

Chapter 11: The Presidency and the Future of Constitutional Government

1. The quoted phrase is from James David Barber, "How Irangate Differs from Watergate," Op-ed in *New York Times*, August 9, 1987, p. E25.

2. "The Brighter Side," late July 1987. In an earlier piece, entitled "We Need an Election," Reston wrote that Reagan's capacity for leadership had been irreparably damaged by the scandals, but that the system provided for renewal here, too. Already the 1988 campaign had begun, he wrote, and within eighteen months (!) there would be a new president.

3. The quoted phrase is from R. W. Apple, Jr.'s, introduction to *The Tower Commission Report* (New York: Bantam Books and Times Books, 1987), p. xiii.

4. Ibid., pp. xvi, xviii.

5. 299 U.S. 304 (1936).

6. Quoted by Ralph Ketcham, *Presidents Above Party* (Chapel Hill, N.C.: University of North Carolina Press, 1984), p. 6, from an essay by Madison published in 1792. Madison's theory is surely closer to the original American understanding of Constitution-making than Sutherland's construction.

7. For a thorough and devastating analysis of Sutherland's opinion, see Charles A. Lofgren, *"Government from Reflection and Choice"* (New York: Oxford University Press, 1986), 167–205, a republication of Lofgren's essay from *The Yale Law Journal* 83, 1–32.

8. *Report*, p. 87.

9. Ibid., p. 94; cf. pp. 92 and 93.

10. Youngstown Sheet and Tube Company v. Sawyer, 343 U.S. 579, 634 (1952).

11. Marshall made this speech as a member of the House of Representatives on March 6, 1800. At stake here was the extradition of a British subject to England to face murder charges, pursuant to the Jay Treaty of 1795. Lofgren, *Government*, xxx–xxx, quoting 10 Annals of Congress 613–14 (March 6, 1800). Among those who misuse this quotation from Marshall is Justice Sutherland, in his opinion in the *Curtiss-Wright* case (at 319).

12. There is even some evidence that Hamilton, in his heart of hearts, hoped to rid the American system of parties altogether. At the New York ratifying convention of 1788, he is reported to have said that "we are attempting by this Constitution to abolish factions and to unite all parties for the general welfare." Quoted in Clinton Rossiter, *Alexander Hamilton and the Constitution* (New York: Harcourt, Brace & World, 1964), p. 149.

13. Hamilton, *Federalist Papers*, number 70, p. 427 of Rossiter edition.

14. Abraham D. Sofaer, *War, Foreign Affairs and Constitutional Power: The Origins* (Cambridge, Mass.: Ballinger, 1976), 167–228.

15. Donald L. Robinson, *Slavery in the Structure of American Politics, 1765–1820* (New York: Norton, 1981), p. 383.

16. See Hamilton, *Federalist Paper*, Number 69, p. 418 of Rossiter edition.

17. Donald L. Robinson, *"To the Best of My Ability"* (New York: Norton, 1987), 28–34; also Forrest McDonald, *Novus Ordo Seclorum* (Lawrence, Kan.: University of Kansas Press, 1985), 209–213, passim.

18. For further examples, see Robinson, *"To the Best of My Ability"* chapters 5 and 9; also Theodore Lowi, *The Personal President* (Ithaca, N.Y.: Cornell University Press, 1985), chapters two and three; and James L. Sundquist, *The Decline and Resurgence of Congress* (Washington, D.C.: Brookings Institute, 1981) 130–140, passim.

19. Richard Loss, ed., *Presidential Power and the Constitution: Essays by Edward S. Corwin* (Ithaca, N.Y.: Cornell University Press, 1976), p. 157.

20. Letter to Senators David Boren (D-Ok) and William Cohen (R-Me.), in *Weekly Compilation of Presidential Documents*, August 7, 1987, p. 910.

21. Tower Report, pp. 89, 92.

22. *"To the Best of My Ability"*, 270–71, 274–81.

23. In those days, presidential elections were apparently not perpetual.

Afterword: Presidential Power
and the Ideological Struggle
Over Its Interpretation

1. I am grateful to William F. Grover for providing the Brecht comment, in his excellent book, *The President as Prisoner* (Albany: State University of New York Press, 1989), p. xi.

2. James MacGregor Burns, *The Deadlock of Democracy* (Englewood Cliffs, N.J.: Prentice-Hall, 1963).

3. Richard E. Neustadt, *Presidential Power* (New York: John Wiley & Sons, 1980), p. v.

4. I stress neo-conservative because many conservatives who are believers in the War Model are former liberals conservatized by Cold War and their faith in the idea of the Evil Empire.

5. Quotes are from "The Talk of the Town," *The New Yorker*, July 23, 1990, pp. 21–22.

6. Korematsu v. United States, 323 U.S. 214 (1944).

SUBJECT INDEX

Administrative law, 93
Administrative Reorganization Act
  of 1939, 103
Administrative state
  incorporated into modern system,
    104–105
  as managerial solution to Great
    Depression, 85
  presidential control of, 101–104
  problems of, 101
  T. Roosevelt's design for, 73
Agricultural Marketing Act of 1929, 88
Ambassadors, 179–180
Anglo-American-Japanese Accord
  American recognition by, of
    Japan's suzerainty in Korea,
    78–79
  origin of, 78–79
Angola, U.S. support for, 186–187
Anthracite Strike, T. Roosevelt's
  plan to seize mines in
  constitutional grounds for, 66–67
  under war power, 66–67
Antitrust action
  allowed by beef trust case, 71
  under Hoover, 90
  under McKinley, 71
  under T. Roosevelt, 71
Articles of Confederation
  Constitution as amendments to, 146
  deficiencies in, 10–11
  states sovereign under, 136
Associative state, 85
  extragovernmental self-regulation
    in, 89
  Hoover's use of, 88–89
  Hoover's role in, 88–89

An Autobiography (T. Roosevelt), 75,
  81

Backdoor spending
  borrowing authority, 153
  contract authority, 153
  mandatory entitlements, 153
  restrictions on, 155
Bank War, 33, 229
Bowsher v. Synar, 161, 162, 222
Boxer Rebellion, 65
Bricker Amendment, 121
Budget
  centralization of, as bad for
    Congress, 158
  changes in system of
    after Civil War, 148
    after World War I, 151
  deficits, 156
  legislative aspects of, 152
  process
    effectiveness of old style, 168
    ineffectiveness of new style,
      168–169
    lack of coordination in, 153–154
    scorekeeping results under old
      system, 159
  requests, as original custom, 149
  resolutions, inaccuracy of, 160
  Select Committee on lack of
    accountability condemned by,
    151–152
Budget Act of 1974, 148, 153, 154
  defended, 157
  establishment of Congressional
    Budget Office by, 155

Budget Act of 1974 (*continued*)
impoundments under
deferral, 155
rescission, 155
process of, 157
proliferation of budgets under, 159–160
Reagan's exploitation of, 158
restrictions by, on backdoor spending, 155
results of, 156–157
side effects of, 157
decline in president's responsibility, 159–160
increase in president's power, 157–159
structure of, 154–155
White House control of Congress under, 158
Budget and Accounting Act of 1921, 148
creation of Bureau of the Budget by, 152–153
suggested reforms by, 152
Budget, Bureau of the, 152–153
Budgeting
necessity for citizens to understand, 148
presidential power of, 147
Bureau of Corporations, 75
Bureaucracy
as ''fourth branch'' of government, 101
growth of, 220
in New Deal, 95
not considered by framers, 220
as presidential structure, 101
F. Roosevelt's control of, 101–102
Byrd-Warner Resolution, 208

Cabinet officer
accountability of, 34
authority of president to remove, 34
Caribbean, U.S. intervention in, 80

Case Act of 1972, 179
Central Intelligence Agency, 190
Centralization
government regulation necessary because of, 72–73
as method of governing, 68
T. Roosevelt's support for, 68
Supreme Court rulings regarding, 71
as turn-of-century phenomenon, 66, 71
Chadha. See *Immigration and Naturalization Service v. Chadha*
Challenge to Liberty, The (Hoover), 87
Checks and balances
as controlling factor in executive policy, xix
examples of, xix, xx
reason for, xx
dependency of system on, 242
efforts to strengthen, 221–222
change in incentives as, 224
by statutory adjustment, 223
Jefferson's emphasis on, 11
and Madisonian model, xix
special elections as, 224–225
Cherokee Nation
refusal of, to submit to Georgia law, 39
removal of, to west of the Mississippi, 40
Cherokee Nation v. Georgia, 39
Chief legislator, president as, 118
Citizenship
Jefferson's concept of, 20, 26
quality of, necessary for good government, 7
improvement in, 26–27
Civil rights, Truman's support for, 115
Civil service, professionalization of, 74
Civil War, 199
Commander in chief. *See also* Executive; War power
clause in Constitution, 197
ambiguity of, 197
scope of, 197

emergency powers as, 123
executive as, 119
Truman's powers as, 122–123
Commission on Department
  Methods (Keep Commission), 75
Commission on Internal Security
  and Individual Rights, 117–118
Competency of electorate
  for Constitution framers, 10
  electoral college as assurance of,
    13–14
  to elect qualified president, 18
  for Hume, 8
  improvement of, 11, 17
  Jefferson's emphasis on, 7
  for Mason, 14–15
  nurturance of, 17
Competent powers, xviii
Confiscation Act, 57
Congress
  committee system of, restructured
    after Civil War, 149
  efficiency in executive agencies
    recommended by, 150
  fiscal power of
    to appropriate, 147
    to tax, 147
    source of, 148
  legislation by, to control suspen-
    sion of habeas corpus, 56
  as partner with president
    in domestic policy, xx
    in fiscal policy, 162, 163
    in foreign policy, xxi
    restoring balance between,
      242–243
    stalemate between, xviii, xxi
  power of, to terminate treaties, 176
  public perceptions of, 149
Conservatives, political, 235–236
  commitment of, to heroic
    presidency, 235
  Congress-bashing by, 235
  in Republican party, 235
Constitution
  as abandonment of classical
    republicanism, 135

as amendments to Articles of
  Confederation, 146
committed Americans to a large
  republic, 136
conservative interpretation of, 236
contrast between state and
  national governments in,
    144–145
debates regarding adoption of,
  134–135
federal government soverign
  under, 136
flexibility of, 108
  arguments for 86–87
implied powers in argued by
  Hamilton, 145
as instrument of change, 143, 144
Jefferson's response to, 18–19
laissez-faire interpretation of, 94
as organic entity, 70, 93, 105, 128
president's discretion implied in,
  52
president's share in legislative
  power delegated by, 56–57
as protector of individual rights, 135
F. Roosevelt's broad interpretation of, 93
states' rights in, 137
Truman's opinion of, 108–109, 110
uses of active government
  imbedded in, 27
writ of habeas corpus considered
  in, 50–51
  authorization of suspension of, 52
Constitution framers, 36
  bureaucracy not considered by, 220
  checks and balances by, 34, 216
  competence of electorate
    emphasized by, 10
  congressional power, problems
    of, 172
  distinction between domestic and
    foreign affairs not made by,
      218–219
  emphasis of, on quality of
    government, 9

Constitution framers (*continued*)
  and executive power, problems
    of, 11–12, 171–172
  focus of, on legislature, 10
  focus of, on treaties and war, 175
  influence of classical background
    on, 7–9
  influence of Enlightenment on, 8
  intentions of, 94, 98, 243–244
    commerce as business trans-
      actions, 93
    conservative interpretation of,
      236
    constitutional frame of mind
      not dependent on, 142–143
    to create a republic, 36
    election of executive, ix–x
    equilibrium between executive
      and legislature, xvii, 34
    government pursuit of the
      public interest, 7, 9–10
    incompatible with managerial
      government, 86
    influences on, 172
    limited role of courts in, 32
    mix of democratic, oligarchic, and
      monarchical government, 32
    in proposing electoral college, 18
    regarding executive power, 139,
      214–217
    United States as "empire for
      liberty," 23
    Washington's presidency as
      clue to, 173
  and Iran-Contra affair, 187
  and self-government, problems
    of, 11–12
  view of president as represen-
    tative of all the people, 34
  and war powers, concern for,
    180–181, 196, 197
Constitutional authority, xxiv–xxvi
Constitutional commitments, 134–135
  features of, 142
Constitutional "dictatorship,"
  Lincoln accused of, 47, 56

Constitutional frame of mind,
  142–143
Constitutional logic, 134
  features of, 142
Constitutional revolution
  legacy of, 99
  New Deal as, 98–99, 133–134, 140
  Roosevelt's role in, 98
  Supreme Court's role in, 98–99
Constitutionalism, radical
  as alternative to liberalism or con-
    servatism, 241–243
  definition of, 241
  test of, 241
Constitutionality
  delegated power as question of,
    93, 95, 100
  of Louisiana Purchase, Jefferson's
    scruples about, 21–22
  legislative veto as, 155
  of managerial state, 87
  of New Deal, Supreme Court
    decisions on, 94–95
  of undeclared war, 196
Continuing resolutions, proliferation and lengthening of, 156–157
Corporative state, 85
  definition of, 95
  in New Deal measures, 95
  rejection of, by Supreme Court, 95
  resisted by Hoover, 90
  Roosevelt's support for, 92, 101
Court reform plan, 97–98, 99, 105
  objections to, 97–98
Courts
  abuse of executive power sup-
    ported by, 127–128
  intentions of Constitution framers
    regarding, 32
  as interpreter of Constitution, 32
  limited role of, for Constitution
    framers, 32
  supportive of president's foreign
    affairs power, 190–191
Creation of the American Republic,
  The (Wood), 135

Crisis management, presidential
flexibility in, xix
Crockett v. Reagan, 202

De Laudibus Legum Angliae
(Fortescue), x
De Legibus et Consuetudinibus Angliae
(Bracton), x
Democracy, evolution of United
States into, 36
Depression, Great
Hoover's and Roosevelt's solutions compared, 104
as managerial problem, 84–85
managerial solutions to
administrative state, 85
associative or corporative state,
85, 90, 92, 95
emergency state, 85, 95
localistic state, 85
social machinery for, 85–86
Dollar diplomacy, 79, 80
Domestic Necessity Model, 236
as liberal model, 234, 235
Domestic policy
Congress and president as
partners in xx–xxi, 218
and foreign affairs, difference
between, 218–219
Hamiltonian model for, xx
ingredients for xx–xxi
lack of presidential flexibility in,
xix
limits to, xx
Dred Scott v. Sandford, 48

Electoral college
as assurance of competence of
electorate, 13–14
intention of Constitution framers
regarding, 18
Jackson's objection to, 37
proposed in Constitutional Convention, 13–14

Emancipation Proclamation, 57, 58
Embargo of 1807, 21
abandonment of, 25
alternatives to, 24
assessment of, 23–24
description of, 23
domestic effects of, 24, 25–26
enforcement of, 25
ineffectiveness of, 24
as least of evils, 23–24
as measure short of war in international relations, 23
opposition to, 25
Emergency powers, 123–124
executive's, as commander in
chief, 123
in *Youngstown Steel* case
decision in 125, 126
implications of, 126
Emergency state, 85
resisted by Hoover, 90
F. Roosevelt's support for, 92
Enlightenment, influence of, on
Constitution framers, 8, 27
Ex parte Merryman, 50, 51–52, 53
Supreme Court's repudiation of,
53–54
Ex parte Milligan, 54
Executive
advantages of, in foreign relations, 173
budgetary responsibilities of, 147,
149
as commander in chief, 119
construction of, in Constitutional
Convention, 12–14
delegation of power to Congress
by Lincoln, 46–47
by Taylor, 46
democratized, 140
legitimized by Wilson, 140–141
as direct representative of the people
Polk's assertion, 46
T. Roosevelt's assertion, 52, 66,
140
Wilson's assertion, 228

Executive (*continued*)
  distribution of patronage by, 47,
    48
  duty of, to decide what is
    constitutional, 31–32
  duty of, to execute laws, 199, 215
  election of, by the people, 12–13
    as radical idea, 13
  foreign affairs staff of, 187–190
  growth of, 232
  Hoover's influence on popular
    expectations concerning, 91
  independence of, 162
    lack of restraints on, 221
    not compatible with republican
      government, 221
  leadership, Jefferson's idea of, 26
  modern, 140
  obligation of, to defend Constitu-
    tion, for Lincoln, 48–49
  as partner with Congress
    in domestic policy, xx
    in fiscal policy, 162–163
    in foreign policy, xxi
    restoring balance between,
      242–243
  as party leader, 47
  precedents affecting, 80
  privilege
    not claimed by Lincoln, 56
    for Truman, 114
  as protector of the people, 13,
    17–18. *See also* Stewardship,
    presidential
    Jackson as, 31, 33, 34–35
    objection to idea of, 35
  role of
    in constitutional government,
      213
    Jefferson's theory of, 20
    Morris's theory of, 12–13
    questions concerning, xxv
    Wilson's theory of, 11–12, 13
  structural properties of, 139
  Truman as, 113

Executive agreement, 175–179
  categories of
    congressional-executive
      agreements, 178
    presidential agreements, 178
  definition of, 176
  early examples of, 177
  foreign policies made via, 177
  in 20th century, 177, 178–179
  increase in importance of, since
    World War II, 177–178, 179
  interchangeable with treaties, 178
  as threat to constitutional balance
    of powers, 179
Executive, heroic
  alternatives to, 233
  for conservatives, 235–236
  for liberals, 234
  war as supporting condition for,
    236–237
Executive, limited
  Bracton's delineation of, x
  Fortescue's delineation of, x
  inherent in idea of limited
    executive, x
Executive Office of the President, 103
Executive power
  abuse of, supported by courts or
    Congress, 127–128
  Article I as delegation of, 51
  Constitution framers' intentions,
    171–172
  to deploy troops in peacetime, 65
  derived from
    Congress, 112–113
    Constitution, 112
    predecessors, 112–113
  domestic, 100
  establishment of, 219–220
  expansion of, 219–222
    by Lincoln, 48–49, 52, 55
    by McKinley, 65
    by F. Roosevelt, 92
    by T. Roosevelt, 66
    Taft's and Wilson's concern for,
      80

fear of, by American Whigs, 46
federative power, 172
in foreign affairs, 100
as function of executive duty
for Lincoln, 53, 56, 59, 61
for Supreme Court, 53
for Grant, 59
alleged abuse of, 60
for Hayes, 60–61
for Hoover, 90–91
for Andrew Johnson, 59, 61
problems with, 243
questions concerning, xxiv–xxv
to remove cabinet officers, 34
F. Roosevelt's attempt to
consolidate, 102–104
for T. Roosevelt, 67
and the "Square Deal," 65–73
to terminate treaties, 176
for Truman, 109, 113
war power merged with, 100–101
war power not inherent in, 54
Washington's view of, 174
Wilson's ideas about, 11–12, 13, 61
Executive Reorganization Bill, 102
Executive staff
appointment of, 188
creation of, 187–188
Executive, strong
characteristics of, xviii
according to Hamilton, xviii
as good for the nation, 17
importance of, for Democrats, 47
as instrument of good, 17–18
Jackson as, 35, 41
opposition to, 35
Jefferson as, 19
Jefferson's support for, 19
Polk as, 47–48
as threat to constitutional government, 212

Faction
in *Federalist* Number 10, xx,
216–217

legislation as means of
regulating, 138
political economy as remedy to
problem of, 137–138
regulation of, as principal task of
legislation, 138
theory of
and executive, 217
in *Federalist* No. 10, xx, 216–217
Hamilton's, 217
Federal Convention, 11
Federal power
affirmed in *In re Debs*, 64
growth of, in late 19th century,
64–65
Federal system, Lincoln's
commitment to, 58
Federalism, doctrine of dual, 96
Federalist Papers, 23, 140, 142, 173, 191
constitutional commitments in, 134
foreign relations in, 219
Number 10 (Madison), xx, 137, 142
factions in, xx, 216–217
Number 47 (Madison), 162
Number 51 (Madison), xvii, xix
Number 69 (Hamilton), xxi, 197
regarding foreign policy, xxi
Number 70 (Hamilton), xviii, 217
political economy in, 137
taxation in, 138
Foreign afairs
after World War II, 119
checks and balances lacking in, 218
congressional and executive
cooperation in, 76
congressional power to conduct,
174–175
courts' support of president's
power in, 190–191
and domestic affairs, difference
between, 218–219
executive power to conduct,
188–119, 174–175, 213–214, 218
executive staff for, 187–190
T. Roosevelt fascinated by, 77
and separation of powers, 173

Foreign affairs (*continued*)
  stewardship theory and, 77
  and war power, questions con-
    cerning, xxv-xxvi
Foreign policy, 171-193
  concentration of, in persident's
    hands, 120
  executive and legislative clashes
    over, 100
  of Jackson, 41
  presidential flexibility in, xix
  presidential independence in, xxi
    examples of, xxi-xxii
    guaranteed by National
      Security Act, xxii
  presidential initiatives in, xxi
  president's staff for, 187-190
  recent abuses of
    Iran-Contra Affair, xxiii
    Vietnam War, xxii
    Watergate, xxii-xxiii
  of F. Roosevelt, 99-101
Forest Service, professionalization
  of, 74
Fort Sumter, 49
Frazier-Lemke Farm Bankruptcy
  Act, 95

Gibbons v. Ogden, 229
Government
  active pursuit of the public
    interest by, 7, 21
  defining features of, 136
  essential qualities of, 9
  inherent limits on, 243
  Jefferson's principles of, 6
  protection of individual liberty
    first object of, 138
  quality of citizenship necessary
    for good, 7
  shrinkage of federal, 230
  as umpire, for Truman, 110
Government, quality of
  Aristotelian view of, 8, 10
  emphasis on, by Constitution
    framers, 9

  as a function of integrity of the
    executive, 19
  importance of, in human affairs,
    19-20
  Lockean emphasis on, 10
  Pope's view of, 10
Government, strong
  Jefferson's ideas of, 6
  in capacity to act in public
    interest, 6
  in popular support for, 6
Gramm-Rudman-Hollings Act of
  1985, 148, 153, 155, 160-163
  comptroller general under, 161
  invalidated by Supreme Court
    in Bowsher, 161-162
  deferral authority
    abused by Reagan administra-
      tion, 155-156
    as item veto, 156
  description of, 160-161
  implications of, 160
  sequestration process under, 161
Grenada, U.S. invasion of, 203

Habeas corpus, writ of
  issued by Taney to Merryman, 50
  Lincoln's objection to, 51
  suspended by Lincoln, 49, 55
  suspension barred by Constitu-
    tion, 50
  suspension granted to Congress
    in emergency, 50
Hamiltonian model of strong
  presidency
  characteristics of, xviii
  and crisis management, xix
  examples of presidents in, xix
  in Federalist Number 70, xviii
  and foreign policy, xix
  independence of executive in, xxii
    recent events demanding, xxii
  liabilities of, xxii
  limits to domestic policy in, xx-xxi
  presidential preference for, xix

Helvering v. Davis, 232
History, Jackson's sense of, 30, 43
Home Building & Loan Association v. Blaisdell, 95
House Committee on Un-American Activities (HUAC) and Nixon, 114, 117
Truman's actions regarding, 114
Humphrey's Executor v. U.S., 162
Hundred Days of F. Roosevelt
crisis atmosphere of, 93
shortening of legislative process during, 92

Immigration and Naturalization Service v. Chadha, 155, 163, 185, 202, 222
Impeachment
ineffectiveness of, 211, 224
of A. Johnson, 59
proceedings against Nixon, 127
Imperial Presidency (Schlesinger), 65
Imperial presidency, xxii
of Jackson, 43
of F. Roosevelt, 104-105
In re Debs, 67, 71
federal power affirmed in, 64
In re Neagle, 64, 231
In re Yamashita, 122
Interest groups
definition of, xx
in *Federalist* No. 10, xx
Interstate Commerce Commission, 64
loss of power of, 72
reconstituted by T. Roosevelt, 72
Iran-Contra Affair, 112, 127, 212-213, 222
as abuse of foreign policy, xxiii
conclusions of Tower Board regarding, 213, 214, 223
and Constitution framers, 187
conclusion drawn by Tower Board, 213, 214
redeeming features of, 212-213
as subversion of War Powers Resolution, 187

Item veto, 163-168
budget ramifications of, 167
description of, 163-164
power relationships at stake in, 167-168
presidential deferral authority as, 156
problems with, 164
examples of, 165-166
state use vs. federal use, 164, 165-166
statute to give president authority proposed, 164
use of, in state government, 164, 165
variations in, 164

Joint Congressional Committee on the Conduct of the War, 56
Jones & Laughlin Steel case. *See National Labor Relations Board v. Jones & Laughlin Steel*

Keep Commission, 75
Knight Sugar Trust suit, 71
Korean War, U.S. intervention in, 120-121
Korematsu v. United States, 241, 244
Kuwaiti tankers
U.S. escort of, 206
U.S. reflagging of, 206

Lebanon, U.S. forces sent to, 204
Lebanon Resolution, 186, 204
Legislation, regulation of factions as principal task of, 138
Legislative veto
in Budget Act of 1974, 155
ruled unconstitutional, 155
Legislature
Constitution framers' focus on, 10
of 18th century states
deficiencies in, 10-11
improvements in, 11

Letters (T. Roosevelt), 69
Liberals, political
  assessment of president by, 234
  commitment of, to heroic
    presidency, 234
  domestic necessity Model of, 234
  need for presidential power for, 234
  presidency as developmental
    phenomenon for, 234
Libertarianism, radical, 240
Limited government, Madisonian
  model of, xvii–xviii
Line-item veto. *See* Item veto
Localistic state, 85
Louisiana Purchase, 21–23
  events leading to, 21
  Jefferson's scruples about the
    constitutionality of, 21–22
  public advantages of, 22
  public support for, 22

McCarran Internal Security Act, 117
  Truman's veto of, 117
McCarran-Walter Immigration Act
  of 1952, 117
McCulloch v. Maryland, 31, 229
Madisonian model of limited
  government
  advantages of, xvii
  checks and balances in, xix
  liabilities of, xviii, xx
Mails, freedom of, 38
Majority rule, 9
  Jackson's belief in, 36–37
  Jefferson's idea of, 7
  potential for abuse of, 12
Managerial state, 232
  constitutionality of, 87
  incompatible with Constitution
    framer's intentions, 86
  as solution to Great Depression, 85
  types of
    administrative state, 85
    associative of corporative state, 85
    emergency state, 85

  localistic state, 85
  social machinery for, 85–86
Mandatory entitlements, 153
Marshall Plan of 1948, 119
Mayaguez crisis, 202–203
Meat Inspection Amendment, 72
*Memoirs by Harry S. Truman: Year of
  Decisions* (Truman), 109–110, 113
Mexican-American War, 198, 218
  Lincoln's condemnation of, 198
Midwest Oil case, 81
Military
  action, 197
  trials of civilians, 54
Mississippi v. Johnson, 54–55
"Modern presidency," incorpor-
  ated into modern system, 104–105
Monroe Doctrine, 78
Morehead v. Tipaldo, 96
Mutual Defense Assistance Act of
  1949, 120
Myers v. U.S., 95

National Emergencies Act of 1976,
  124
*National Labor Relations Board v.
  Jones & Laughlin Steel*, 98, 232
National security assistant, role of,
  in making foreign policy, 189
National Security Council Act, 223
National welfare, questions
  concerning, xxv
Nebbia v. New York, 95
New Deal
  as constitutional revolution,
    98–99, 133–134, 140
  as natural outcome of Constitu-
    tion, 134
  Supreme Court decisions on
    constitutionality of, 94–95
New Deal, Second, 96
Nixon v. United States, 191
North Atlantic Treaty, 119, 175
  controversy over, 121–122
Nunn-Warner Resolution, 208

Operation El Dorado Canyon, 205
Operation Prairie Fire, 204–205

Panama Canal treaties, 176
Party government, 47
Patronage system, 59
  as key element in relations
    between president and
    Congress, 48
Permissive legislation, 113–114
Persian Gulf, U.S. interests in,
  205–206
Personal President, The (Lowi),
  144–146
Plebicitary presidency, 134
Pocket veto, 56
Political economy, 137–139
  as means toward eliminating
    tyranny, 141
  as remedy to problem of faction,
    137–138
Politics (Aristotle), 7
Politics of Justice, The (Hall), 38
Popular leadership, 139–140
President. *See* Executive
Presidential Power (Neustadt), 139
Presidential stewardship. *See*
  Stewardship, presidential
President's Committee on
  Administrative Management, 232
President's Committee on Civil
  Rights, 115
Prize Cases, 53, 184
Pullman Strike of 1894, 64
Pure Food and Drug bill, 72

Reagan tax plan, ineptitude of,
  158–159
Reconstruction, Lincoln's
  maneuvering for, 57
Regulation, government
  of big business, 71
  business support for, 73
  centralization requiring, 72–73

executive efforts stifled, 72
measures to execute, 72
Relief and Construction Act of
  1932, 88
Religion, freedom of, T. Roosevelt's
  view of, 69
Report on Administrative Procedure, 104
Republican government, 135–136
Republican party, conservatives vs.
  libertarians in, 235
Republicanism vs. Grantism
  (Sumner), 60
Rio Pact, 119
Rise and Growth of American Politics
  (Ford), 61

Santo Domingo, United States
  seizure of customs office of, 78
Schechter Poultry Corporation v. U.S.,
  95, 96, 98
Second National Bank
  Biddle's request for recharter of, 31
  Jackson's veto of recharter bill
    for, 31
Secretary of State
  extent of role of, 188
Sedition Act of 1918, 69
Self-rule, people's capacity for, 38
Separation of powers
  advantages of, xvii
  dependency of system on, 242
  in *Federalist* No. 51, xvii
  liabilities of, xviii, xx
  questions concerning, xxv
  Taft's and Wilson's concern for, 80
Sherman Anti-Trust Law, 66, 71, 89
  T. Roosevelt's effort to revise, 73
  T. Roosevelt's alleged violation
    of, 75
Slavery, abolition of, 57–58
Special agents, 179–180
  appointed solely by president, 180
  definition of, 179
  examples of, 179
  problems with, 180
  use of, implied in Constitution, 180

Speech, freedom of, T. Roosevelt's
  view of, 68–69
Statecraft as Soulcraft (Will), 240
States' rights
  T. Roosevelt's view of, 68
Statesmanship, encouraged by
  Constitution, 140
Steel dispute of 1952
  controversy over, 125
  resolution of, 126–127
  Supreme Court decision in, 125, 126
  Truman's refusal to use Taft-
    Hartley Act in, 124
  Truman's seizure of steel mills,
    124, 125
Steward Machine Co. v. Davis, 232
Stewardship, presidential, 52
  affirmed by Supreme Court, 74
  foreign affairs and, 77
  and T. Roosevelt's character, 67
  T. Roosevelt's theory of, 66
  Taft's attack on, 80
Subversion, Truman's concerns
  with, 116
Suffrage, 17
  and attachment to polity, 14–15
  Franklin's ideas regarding
    qualifications for, 15–17
  restrictions on, 14–15
Suppression of domestic violence,
  law for, of 1795 and 1807, 49, 52,
  53, 54
Supreme Court
  abuse of executive power and, 53
  change in composition of New
    Deal by, 96
  decision in steel dispute of 1952,
    125, 126
  decisions of, as attempt to
    discover Constitution's
    meaning, 143
  decisions of, on constitutionality
    of New Deal, 94–97
  as interpreter of constitution, 32, 38
  invalidation of Gramm-Rudman
    in *Bowsher*, 161–162

as policy-making institution, 70
  presidential stewardship affirmed
    by, 74
  rejection of corporative state by, 95
  repudiation by, of *Ex parte
    Merryman*, 53–54
  role of, in constitutional
    revolution, 98–99
  rulings regarding centralization, 71
  Truman's approach to, 111–112
  Truman's nominees to, 111

Taft-Hartley Labor Relations Act,
  114, 124, 126
Tariff Act of 1930, 88
Taiwan Relations Act, 176
Taxation
  in *Federalist Papers*, 139
  necessity and propriety of, in
    federal government, 139
Temporary Joint Committee on
  Deficit Reduction, 161
Tower Board, conclusions of,
  regarding Iran-Contra affair, 213,
  214, 223
Treaties, 175
  consultation between president
    and Senate in, 175
  interchangeable with executive
    agreements, 178
  Panama Canal, 176
  power to terminate, 176
  Taiwan, 218
  two-thirds vote needed to make, 176
Truman Doctrine of 1947, 120
Two-track system, ix, x, 191–193
  components of, 192
  first track (fast track)
    description of, 238–239
    examples of, 191–192
    necessary in War Model, 239
  inherent in idea of limited
    executive, x
  necessity of, in a popular
    government, x

second track (slow track)
  description of, 239
  examples of, 192

Uniform Code of Military Justice
  Act of 1950, 123
Union, 136–137
  perpetuity of, 42–43
United Nations, 119, 175
United States v. Belmont, 100, 190–191
*United States v. Curtiss-Wright Export
  Corporation*, 100, 191, 213, 214

Veto, 47
  Jackson's interpretation of
    to expand the role of the
      president, 33
    to participate in legislative
      process, 32–33
  unconstitutionality as only
    ground for, 32
  Webster's opposition to, 33
Vietnam War, 127, 185

Wade-David Reconstruction Act,
  56, 58
War, declaration of, 198
  loss of congressional power for, 121
  not requested for Korean War,
    120–121
  rare, 181
War model
  Congress as enemy in, 238
  conservative need lodged in, 236
  fast track necessary under, 239
  In re Neagle as contribution to, 231
  Lincoln presidency as example of,
    230
  morality and patriotism in, 237–238
  as response to threat to national
    security
    Cold War as, 237
    War on Drugs as, 238

T. Roosevelt presidency as
  example of, 231
War power, 180–187
  and balance between branches,
    183, 199
  erosion of, 183–184
  concentration of, in president's
    hands, 120
  concern for, by framers, 180–181,
    196, 197
  Congress's, 197, 198, 207–208
    erosion of, 183
    involvement in, 187
    questions concerning, 198
    stop-go quality of, 199–200
  efforts to modernize, 184–187
    Congress's version of, 185
    Eisenhower's formula for, 185
  expansion of president's
    in Civil War, 182
    events and environment, 182–183
    involvements in minor
      hostilities, 182
    lack of judicial intervention in, 184
  and foreign relations
    questions concerning, xxv–xxvi
    as used by McKinley, 65
  for Lincoln, 182
  not conferred by inherent
    executive power, 53–54
  in the Persian Gulf, 205–209
  president's, 197–198
    assumption of, 181–182
    continuity of, 200
  recent presidential appropriation
    of, xxiii–xxiv
  scope of, 199
  sudden attack and, 181–182
War Powers Act of 1973, 124
War Powers Resolution, xxiii–xxiv
  American public opinion and, 209
  compliance with, 208–209
  description of, 175
  and Kuwaiti tankers, lack of
    application to, 206–207
  limited impact of, 201

War Powers Resolution (*continued*)
  presidential disregard for, 186
    alienation of Congress by, 209
  president's arguments against, 201
  president's lack of incentive to
    cooperate with, 202
  purpose of, 200
  requirements of, 200
    reporting, 201–202
  test of, 186
War, undeclared
  constitutionality of, 196
  examples of, 181, 195–196

reasons for, 181
types of, 197–198, 199
Watergate scandal, 185
West Coast Hotel v. Parrish, 98, 99
Worcester v. Georgia, 39
  Jackson's reaction to, 39–40
Workmen's Compensation Law
  (New York), 71

*Youngstown Sheet & Tube Co. v.
  Sawyer*, 125

NAME INDEX

Acheson, Dean, 117
Adams, Henry, 20
Adams, John, 195
Adams, John Quincy, 37, 229
Albert, Carl, 154
Aquino, Corazon, 179
Arias, Oscar, 222
Aristotle
 view of, of quality of govern-
  ment, 8, 10, 26, 27
 influence of, on Constitution
  framers, 7, 26
Arthur, Chester A., 149
Auerbach, Jerold, 105

Bacon, Francis, 8
Baker, Howard, 207
Baker, James, 207
Barber, Sotirior A., 143
Bates, Edward, 51, 53, 54
Beard, Charles, 105
Beggs, James M., 163
Belz, Herman, 32
Bennett, William, 238
Biddle, Nicholas, 31
Black, Hugo, 126
Blackstone, William, 172, 220
Blum, John, 68
Boland, Edward, 187
Bolingbroke (Henry IV of England), 8
Bracton, Henry, x
Brandeis, Louis, 99
Brewer, David J., 64
Bricker, John W., 121
Brownlow, Louis, 102
Brutus, 145

Bryce, James, 61
Brzezinski, Zbigniew, 189
Buchanan, James, 48, 49
Bundy, McGeorge, 189
Burns, James MacGregor, xxi, 234
Burton, Harold, 111
Bush, George, 182, 192, 201,
 239–240
Butler, Banjamin F., 58
Butler, Elizur, 39, 40
Butler, Pierce, 196
Byrd, Robert, 207, 208
Byrns, Joseph W., 90

Calhoun, John C., 30, 34, 43
Cardozo, Benjamin N., 91, 99
Carlucci, Frank, 189, 206
Carter, Jimmy, xix, 160
 and Panama Canal treaties, 176
 and Taiwan treaty, 218
 use of national security assistant
  by, 189
 use of war power by, 186, 203, 205
Cato (English), 8, 9
Chandler, Alfred, 84
Chase, Salmon P., 58
Cheney, Richard, 212
Cicero, influence of, on Constitu-
 tion framers, 7, 8–9
Clark, Dick, 187
Clark, Tom, 110, 111, 124, 126
Clay, Henry, 30, 36, 43
 and electoral college, 37
 objection to idea of president as
  people's representative, 35
 theory of executive veto, 32

Cleveland, Grover, 61, 63, 80
  and Pullman strike of 1864, 64
  veto used by, to control budget, 150
Coehlo, Tony, 209
Coffee, John, 40
Cohen, William, 212
Collins, Charles Wallace, 152
Condon, Edward U., 114, 117
Connally, Tom, 175
Cooley, Thomas McIntyre, 61
Corwin, Edward S., 55, 173, 190,
  221, 222, 242
Cranston, Alan, 209
Cummings, Homer S., 93, 94, 97
Cushing, Caleb, 38

Dana, Richard Henry, 184
Daniels, Jonathan, 109
DeConcini, Dennis, 176
Denfield, Louis, 122
Dickinson, John, 14, 15
Dodd, Chris, 222
Dole, Robert, 208, 209
Douglas, Stephen A., 48
Douglas, William O., 123, 126
Duane, William, 33
Dulles, John Foster, 188

Edwards, Mickey, 163
Eisenhower, Dwight D., 109, 115
  efforts to modernize war power
    by, 184-185
  as strong president, 233

Ferenbacher, Don, 332
Fitzgerald, John J., 152
Foley, Tom, 212
Ford, Gerald, 186, 201, 202-203
Ford, Henry Jones, 61
Fortescue, John, x
Franklin, Benjamin, 31
  ideas of, regarding qualification
    for suffrage, 15-17
Fulbright, William J., 210

Galambos, Louis, 84
Garfield, James, 61, 75
Gerry, Elbridge, 14, 180
Gorbachev, Mikhail, 237
Grant, Ulysses, 60
  presidential power of, 59, 61
Gulick, Luther, 102

Habib, Philip, 179
Hakim, Albert, xxiii
Hall, Kermit, 38
Hamilton, Alexander, xviii, xx, 140,
  218, 229
  argument for implied powers in
    Constitution, 145
  argument for strong presidency,
    xviii, 19, 139, 174, 197, 221
  and factions, theory of, 217
  in Federalist No. 70, xviii
  and foreign relations, 172
  involvement of, in budget
    process, 148-149
  political economy for, 138
  support of, for central govern-
    ment, 68, 136
Hamilton, Lee, 212
Harriman, W. Averell, 114
Harris, William F., 142
Hatfield, Mark, 167
Hayes, Rutherford B., 60-61
Helms, Jesse, 208
Hobbes, Thomas, 8
Hodges, Albert G., 52
Homer, 8
Hoover, Herbert, 83-105
  associative managerial solution to
    Depression used by, 88
  extragovernmental self-
    regulation, 89
  president's role in, 88-89
  business collaboration to sustain
    spending under, 89-90
  as businessman, 88
  compared with strong presidents,
    88

influence of, on popular expectations concerning the
  presidency, 91
libertarian thinking of, 87
presidential commissions under, 89
  Congressional objections to, 89–90
separation of powers under, 87–88
and states' rights, 96
use of veto by, 88
as weak president, 87
Hopkins, Harry, 179
House, Edward, 179
Houston, David, 152
Hughes, Charles Evans, 91, 98
Hughes, Emmet, 108, 127
Hume, David, 8, 220
Humphrey, William E., 95

Inouye, Daniel, 212

Jackson, Andrew, xix, 29–43, 46, 109
  cabinet officer under president's
    authority, 34
  case by, for perpetuity of Union, 42
  censured by Senate, 35
  collection of foreign debts by, 42
  contradictory nature of, 30–31
  contributions of, 229
  dismissal of Duane by, in Bank
    War, 33
    constitutionality of, 33–34
  election of judges advocated by, 37
  expansion of powers of president
    by, 36
  foreign policy of, 41
  "imperial" presidency of, 43
  interpretation of veto by
    to expand the role of the presi-
      dent, 33
    to participate in legislative
      process, 32–33
  as liberal paradigm, 234
  majority rule, 36–37
  opposition of, to electoral college, 37

popularity of, with electorate, 31
proposal by, to alter president's
  term, 37
as protector of the people, 31, 33,
  34–35, 41, 52
reaction of, to *Worcester v.
  Georgia*, 39–40
respect of, for Congress, 41–42, 239
right of all branches to determine
  constitutionality argued by, 38
and Second National Bank, veto
  of, 31
sense of the past, 30, 43
sense of responsibility of, 41
strong presidency of, 35, 41
  opposition to, 35
view of checks and balances, 34
Jackson, Robert, 123, 126, 214, 241
James, Dorothy B., 114–115
Jay, John, 218
Jefferson, Thomas, x, xix, 5–27, 31, 128
  concept of citizenship of, 20, 26–27
  emphasis of, on checks and
    balances, 11
  emphasis of, on competence of
    electorate, 7
  first inaugural address, 5–7
    majority rule in, 7
    principles of government in, 6
  idea of government in the public
    interest, 26
  idea of president as friend of the
    people, 18, 228
  presidency of
    Embargo in, 21, 23–25, 239
    federalist actions as, 20–21
    as government in the public
      interest, 21
    Louisiana Purchase in, 21–23,
      218, 239
    republican actions in, 20–21
    as strong executive, 19
    style of, 20, 228
  support for strong executive by, 19
  views of, of presidency, 20
  war power of, 183

Johnson, Andrew, 54, 109
  impeachment of, 59
  Supreme Court under, 55
Johnson, Lyndon, xix, xx, xxi, xxii
  and declaration of war, 121, 183
  and war power, 185

Katsura, Taro, 78–79
Kennedy, John, xix, 115, 188
Khadaffi, Muammar, 204, 205
Khomeini, Ruhollah (Ayatollah), xxiii
Kissinger, Henry, 188–189
Knox, Philander, 67
Kohl, Helmut, 237

Leigh, Benjamin W., 35
Lincoln, Abraham, xix, 45–61, 65, 79
  and abolition of slavery, 57
  accused of creating a constitutional
    dictatorship, 47, 56
  actions in Civil War condemned, 199
  case by, for perpetuity of Union,
    42–43
  condemnation by, of Mexican-
    American War, 198
  and congressional power, 56, 57
  defiance by, of Taney, 55
  delegation of power to Congress
    by, 46–47
  establishment of broad presidential
    powers by, 48
  support for, 48–49, 52
  executive privilege not claimed
    by, 56
  expansion of power by, 55, 61
  and federal system, 58
  maneuvering by, to secure
    Reconstruction plan, 57
  obligation to defend Constitution
    argued by, 48–49
  power to suspend habeas corpus
    asserted by, 50–51, 52
  president's emergency powers in
    time of crisis asserted by, 51, 127

  presidency of, as example of War
    Model, 230, 239
  promise by, to enforce national
    law in the South, 49
  expansion of army and navy,
    49–50, 182
  invocation of law for the
    supression of violence (1795
    and 1807), 49
  suspension of writ of habeas
    corpus, 49, 182
  war power of, 182, 183
Link, Arthur S., 80
Livingston, Edward, 43
Livingston, Robert, 179
Livy, 8, 9
Locke, John
  federative power, 172
  influence of, on Constitution
    framers, 7, 8, 9, 172
  view of, of quality of govern-
    ment, 10
Lodge, Henry Cabot, 78
Lott, Trent, 157
Lowi, Theodore, 144–146

MacArthur, Douglas, 122
McCarthy, Joseph, 238
McDonald, Forrest, 240
McKinley, William, 63, 80
  antitrust proceedings in, 71
  and Boxer Rebellion, 65
  executive power expanded by, 65
McLean, John, 40
McReynolds, James, 97, 100
Madison, James, xvii, xix, xx, 31,
  174, 214, 229
  constitutional analysis of
    American character by, 142
  executive and legislative power, 162
  and factions, theory of, 216–217
  object of government for, 138
  and right of suffrage, 15
  and war power, 180, 196
Marcos, Ferdinand, 179

Marshall, John, 68, 70, 174, 215
Marshall, Thurgood, 225
Mason, George
  competence of electorate in, 14–15
  and qualification for suffrage, 17
Mattingly, Mack, 164
Meese, Edwin, 207
Merriam, Charles E., 102
Merryman, John, 50, 51
Miller, James C., 163
Minton, Sherman, 111
Mitchell, George, 212
Monroe, James, 229
Montesquieu, 8, 162, 172
Moore, Barrington, 230
Morris, Gouverneur, 68, 219
  and role of executive, 12–13, 18
  as Washington's private
    diplomatic agent, 173, 179
Muskie, Edmund, 213

Nast, Thomas, 149, 150
Neustadt, Richard, 234
Nixon, Richard, xxii–xxiii, 235
  and "Battle of the Budget," 154
  and executive agreements, 177, 178
  and HUAC, 114, 117
  impeachment proceedings
    against, 127
Noriega, Manuel, 182, 201
North, Oliver, xxiii
Nunn, Sam, 207, 212

Obey, David, 160, 163

Paterson, William, 198
Phillips, Wendell, 48
Pike, Sumner T., 117
Pinchot, Gifford, 74–75, 81
Pinckney, Charles
  view of popular elections, 14
  and war powers, 180
Pine, David, 125
Plutarch, 8

Poindexter, John, 205
Polk, James K.
  claim of, that president is direct
    representative of the people, 46
  and Mexican-American War, 198,
    218
  qualifications of, for budgeting, 149
  strong presidency of, 47–48, 55
Pope, Alexander, 10
Publius, 145

Randall, James G.
Randolph, John, 20
Reagan, Ronald, xix, xx, xxi, xxiii,
  177, 188, 192
  budget practices of, 155, 156, 160,
    162
  as conservative, 235, 239
  "New Federalism" of, 137
  use of special agents by, 179
  use of war power by, 183, 186,
    203, 218
  and War Powers Resolution, 209
Reston, James, 213
Roberts, Owen J., 91, 98, 99, 111
Roosevelt, Franklin D., xvii, xix,
  xxii, 83–105, 108, 113, 120, 188
  bureaucracy under, 91–92, 228
  court reform plan of, 97–98
    objections to, 97–98
  Hundred Days of, 92
  legislative process initially
    shortened by, 92
  as modern president, 140
  president as instrument of
    Congress for, 94
  use of emergency powers by,
    123, 124
  use of executive power by, 92
Roosevelt, Theodore, xix, 63, 65,
  89, 177, 188, 231
  administrative state designed by, 73
  antitrust proceedings in, 71
  appeal by, for recall of judicial
    decisions, 70–71

Roosevelt, Theodore (*continued*)
　attempt of, to inhibit court
　　power, 73
　attitde of, toward Japan, 77–78
　conception by, of national
　　interest, 77
　conflicts of, with Congress regarding
　　forest reserves, 74–75
　　Keep Commission, 75
　　United States Steel, 75–76
　courts as lawmakers for, 70
　and effective government, 79
　fascination of, with war, 77
　and foreign affairs, 77, 99–101
　freedom of speech, view of, 68
　national policies of, 70
　as pragmatist, 67
　presidency of, view of, 79, 239
　and presidential power, 67, 68, 230
　presidential stewardship theory
　　of, 52, 66, 140
　professionalization of civil service
　　by, 74
　and states' rights, 68
　support of, for centralized
　　government, 68
Root, Elihu, 65, 67, 79
Rossiter, Clinton, 56
Rudman, Warren, 212

Schlesinger, Jr., Arthur, xxii, 65,
　78, 234
Schubert, Glendon, 112
Secord, Richard, xxiii
Shultz, George, 154, 188, 206, 212
Sidney, Sir Philip, 7
Smith, Adam, 8
Sofaer, Abraham, 205
Stevens, Thaddeus, 52, 99
Stevenson, Adlai, 117
Stockman, David, 155, 158
Stokes, Louis, 212
Stone, Harlan F., 91
Sutherland, George, 100, 191, 214
Swope, Gerard, 90

Taft, William Howard, 63, 64, 69, 78
　authority to withdraw lands, 80–81
　dollar diplomacy of, 79
　growth of executive under, 80
　recommendation to reform
　　budget process, 150–151
Takahira, Kogoro, 79
Taney, Roger, 51, 53, 70
　Lincoln's defiance of, 55
　writ of habeas corpus issued to
　　Merryman by, 50
Taylor, Zachary, 46
Thach, Charles, 220
Theoharis, Athan, 127
Thieu, Nguyen Van, 178
Tower, John, 212
Treveleyan, George Otto, 79
Truman, Harry, xix, 107–128
　actions of, regarding HUAC, 114
　advisory process developed by, 114
　approach of, to Supreme Court,
　　111–112
　belief of, that president must be
　　assertive, 109
　as chief legislator, 118
　committees used by, 115
　concerns of, with subversion, 116
　cooperation desired by, 110–111
　and emergency power, 124
　executive power of, 112
　government as umpire for, 110
　legacy of, 232–233
　nominees of, to Supreme Court, 111
　original impression of, 108
　primacy of Bill of Rights for, 110
　responsibility of, for welfare of
　　people, 109, 110
　seizure of steel mills by, 124, 125,
　　184, 214
　as strong president, 191–192, 233
　support of, for civil rights cases, 115
　treaty negotiations and, 175
　use of veto by, 118
　use of war power by, 183
Tully, influence of, on Constitution
　framers, 7

Vallandigham, Clement L., 54
Van Devanter, Willis, 98
Vance, Cyrus, 203
Vandenberg, Arthur, 175
Vinson, Fred, 111, 124
Virgil, 7, 8

Walsh, Lawrence, 212
Washington, George, 31, 79
  as commander in chief, 55
  consultation between Senate and
    executive for, 175
  creation by, of executive offices, 220
  presidency as analogous to
    European monarchy for, 173
  presidency of, 173–175
  use of special agents by, 179
  view of executive power, 68, 174
Webster, Daniel, 30, 43
  opposition of, to veto power of
    president, 33
Weinberger, Caspar, 206, 212
Whiting, William, 56, 57

Will, George, 240
Wilson, Charles, 125
Wilson, James
  ideas of, on executive power,
    11–12, 13, 68
  and qualification for suffrage, 17
  support of, for strong executive,
    17–18, 219
  and war power, 196, 197
Wilson, Woodrow, 63, 92, 97, 108,
  224–225
  cooperation of, with Congress, 81
  growth of executive under, 80
  ideas of, about executive power,
    11–12, 13, 61
  president as representative of all
    the people, 228
  request of, for fiscal restraint, 152
  theory by, of congressional
    supremacy, 65, 221
Wirt, William, 40
Worcester, Samuel A., 39, 40
Wright, Benjamin, 220